Developing a Teaching Style

Methods for Elementary School Teachers

ROBERT D. LOUISELL
St. Cloud State University

JORGE DESCAMPS
The University of Texas at El Paso

 HarperCollins*Publishers*

Executive Editor: Christopher Jennison
Full-Service Manager: Michael Weinstein
Production Coordinator: Cindy Funkhouser
Project Coordinator, and Cover Design: Caliber/Phoenix Color Corp.
Cover Illustration/Photo: ©Don & Pat Valenti/Tony Stone Worldwide
Production Manager: Priscilla Taguer
Compositor: Caliber/Phoenix Color Corp.
Printer and Binder: R.R. Donnelley & Sons Company
Cover Printer: The Lehigh Press, Inc.

pp. 122–124: Reproduced with permission of Macmillan/McGraw-Hill School Publishing Company from *Merrill Science*, Teacher's Edition, Grade 4, by J. K. Hackett; R. H. Meyer; and D. K. Adams. Copyright © 1989 by Merrill Publishing Co..

DEVELOPING A TEACHING STYLE: Methods for Elementary School Teachers

Library of Congress Cataloging-in-Publication Data

Louisell, Robert.
    Developing a teaching style / Robert Louisell, Jorge Descamps.
        p. cm.
    Includes bibliographical references and index.

    ISBN 0-06-044109-7

    1. Teaching.   2. Education, Elementary—United States.
  I. Descamps, Jorge. II. Title.
  LB1025.3.L69   1992
  372.11'02—dc20   91-40294
                                                CIP

95 94 93 92 9 8 7 6 5 4 3 2 1

DEDICATION

To all those who teach children.

Contents

Preface   xiii
Acknowledgments   xv

CHAPTER 1
Children in Schools   1

The Child's World   1
    Children's Ideas   2
    Egocentric Thought   4
    Developmental Stages in Children's Thinking   9
    The Child's World Summed Up   16
What Society Expects of Schools   17
What Children Learn in Schools   19
Teachers' Assumptions About Teaching and Learning   21
Glossary   25

CHAPTER 2
Instructional Settings   26

Traditional, Self-Contained, Graded Settings   26
Issues Underlying the Differences Between Traditional and
    More Individualized Approaches to Instruction   29

Team-Taught, Nongraded, Individualized Settings   33
    The Organization of a Team   37
    The Organization of One Team Member's Classroom   42
Informal, Self-Contained, Family-Grouped Settings   44
Alternative, Team-Taught, Multi-Aged Settings   51
    The Organization of a Team at Alternative Heights   52
    The Organization of Peter's Classroom   53
The Clusters Approach   56
Outcomes-Based Education   57
A Framework for Interpreting Instructional Settings   58
Summary   59
Glossary   60

CHAPTER 3
Teaching Techniques   62

Types of Instruction, Bloom's Taxonomy, and Gagne's Hierarchy   63
Using the Types of Instruction, Bloom's Taxonomy, and Gagne's Hierarchy   68
Questioning Techniques: How to Ask Questions   69
    Purposes of Questions   69
    Types of Questions   70
    Steps Within a Question   72
    Series of Questions   74
    Student-Initiated Questions   74
Techniques to Check for Understanding: How to Conduct a Recitation   75
Discussion Techniques: How to Conduct a Class Discussion   75
Input Techniques: How to Present Facts, Concepts, and Skills   77
Establishing Set Techniques: How to Open a Lesson   77
    Personalizing and Warming-Up the Climate   78
    Using an Attention Getter   78
    Relating the Lesson to the World of the Students   78
    Reviewing Past Work   79
    Advance Organizers   79
Closure Techniques: How to Close a Lesson   79
    Summary Reviews   79
    Eliciting Generalizations and Abstractions   79
    Feedback on Group Accomplishments   80
    Previewing the Next Lesson   80
Demonstration Techniques: How to Demonstrate a Concept or Skill   80
Role Playing Techniques: How to Facilitate Student Role Plays   81
    Role Plays as Tools to Develop Social Interaction and Problem-Solving   82
    Role Plays as Tools to Dramatize the Curriculum   83
Tutoring Techniques: How to Implement Tutoring Activities   83
    Reciprocal Tutoring   84
    Peer Tutoring   84

Cross-Age Tutoring   85
Feedback Techniques: How to Supervise and Critique Student Work   86
Glossary   87

CHAPTER 4
Teaching Methods   88

Presentation-Recitation-Discussion   89
How to Implement Presentation-Recitation-Discussion   90
Purpose of the Presentation-Recitation-Discussion Method   91
Role of the Teacher   91
Role of the Student   91
Instructional Materials   92
Evaluation Procedures   92
Mastery Teaching   92
How to Implement Mastery Teaching   93
Purpose of Mastery Teaching   95
Role of the Teacher   95
Role of the Student   95
Instructional Materials   95
Evaluation Procedures   95
Cooperative Learning   96
How to Implement Cooperative Learning   97
Purpose of Cooperative Learning   98
Role of the Teacher   98
Role of the Student   99
Instructional Materials   99
Evaluation Procedures   99
Mastery Learning   100
How to Implement Mastery Learning   100
Purpose of Mastery Learning   101
Role of the Teacher   101
Role of the Student   101
Instructional Materials   101
Evaluation Procedures   102
Teaching Thinking   102
Concept Attainment   105
Inductive Teaching   107
Teacher-Student Interaction for Teaching Thinking   109
Activities for Teaching Thinking   112
Teaching Thinking Summed Up   113
Topic Work   114
Teaching To Learning Styles   119
Glossary   120

CHAPTER 5
Planning for Teaching   121

Determining Which Skills Are Essential   121
Planning For Instruction   126
    Using and Writing Objectives for One's Students   126
    Making Lesson Plans   131
Self-Instructional Lessons   139
    Modules and Units   143
Nonacademic Aims and Goals of Today's Schools   157
Glossary   159

CHAPTER 6
Assessing Student Learning   160

Purposes of Assessment   161
    To Place Students in Instructional Activities   161
    To Evaluate a Student's Progress in Learning   161
    To Identify Special Difficulties in Learning   162
    To Assess Learning After Instruction Has Been Provided   162
Reporting Student Progress   162
    Marking and Reporting in Graded Settings   162
    Reporting Student Progress in Nongraded Settings   168
    Reporting Student Progress in Informal Settings   171
    Reporting Student Progress at Alternative Heights   173
Testing   173
    Teacher-Made Tests   176
    Standardized Tests   183
Glossary   189

CHAPTER 7
Classroom Management: Establishing the Socio-Emotional Environment   191

Human Relations   193
    Communication Skills   193
    Conflict Resolution Skills   197
    Establishing a Positive Classroom Climate   199
    Fostering a Sense of Individual Importance: Love and Acceptance   201
    Fostering a Sense of Belonging   202
    Team Work Skills   203
Class Rewards   204
    Effects of Competitive Learning Environments   204

Effects of Cooperative Learning Environments   205
Effects of Individualistic Learning Environments   205
Types of Rewards and Their Effects   206
Types of Consequences and Their Effects   207
Self-Concept and Teacher Expectations   208
Values   212
Glossary   214

CHAPTER 8
Classroom Management: Considering the Teaching-Learning Environment   216

The Teaching-Learning Environment   216
How Teaching and Management Are Related   216
How Teaching-Learning Environments Are Kept Going   217
The Teacher's Management of Time   220
The Socialization Process   221
The Importance of Routines   222
Managing the Physical Environment   224
Managing Records   226
Supervising Paraprofessionals   227

CHAPTER 9
Classroom Management: Managing Student Behavior   228

The 20-Step System of Discipline   231
How to Establish Standards of Behavior   232
How to Match Teacher Actions with Student Behaviors   234
Prevention Steps   235
Redirection Steps   241
Consequence Steps   246
Team Support Steps   249
Conditions Necessary for the 20-Step System of Discipline to Work   252
The Goals and Values of the School Program   252
The Role of the Teacher   252
The Role of the Student   253
A School Discipline Approach Must Be Aimed at Helping Students
Grow into More Advanced Ways of Behaving   253
Summary   253
Glossary   258

CHAPTER 10
Promoting Student Involvement in Classrooms   259

Motivation: How To Promote Student Interest, Effort, and Good Performance   259
 Making the Learning Task Challenging   260
 Deemphasizing Testing and Grades   261
 Providing Assistance Without Being Overprotective   261
 Shifting from Extrinsic to Intrinsic Rewards   261
 Using Praise Appropriately   262
 Having High Expectations for Each Student   262
 Providing Knowledge of Results   263
 Promoting Success for All Class Members   263
 Increasing Student Perceptions of Control   264
 Changing the Classroom Goal-Reward Structure   264
Group Process Skills: How to Organize, Facilitate, and Monitor
 Small Group Work   264
 Advantages of Small Groups   265
 Role of the Teacher   265
 Forming Groups   266
 Group Decision Making Methods   266
 Areas of Group Work   268
 Organizing Small Groups   268
 Prerequisite Skills for Group Interaction   271
 Six Types of Small Groups   272
Glossary   275

CHAPTER 11
Developing a Teaching Style   276

Instructional Settings   278
The Organization, Selection, and Presentation of Subject Matter   279
 Methods of Instruction   280
 Approaches to Planning   283
 Approaches to Evaluation   285
 The Type of Classroom Climate Established   287
 Approaches to Motivation and Control   289
 Approaches to Behavior Management   291
 How to Interpret Teaching Style Preferences   294
Glossary   299

References   300

Appendix
Sample Topic Unit   306

Index   315

Preface

Beginning teachers need to be prepared for the comprehensive scope of teaching today. They must develop a philosophy of teaching that will help them choose among the many alternatives available to them for instruction and classroom management. At times, the variety of choices may overwhelm them. This text is intended to help teachers—especially beginning teachers—to cope successfully with the choices that they face.

Each chapter in this text presents the reader with choices which elementary teachers must typically make as they practice their craft. The final chapter helps beginning teachers to reflect on these choices and how they relate to their personalities and to the backgrounds of their students. This coverage will help novice elementary teachers decide what kinds of instructional settings are most compatible with their own professional orientation. It should also help teachers during their first few years of teaching to gain insights into the many instructional alternatives available to them.

Our text is intended for preservice courses on elementary curriculum, classroom management, and general elementary methods of teaching. It should also be useful in graduate and undergraduate courses required for alternative certification of elementary teachers.

Chapter 1 discusses the nature of children, especially their intellectual development. It remains faithful to the authentic Piagetian perspective while supplying examples of things children say and do. It also discusses society's expectations for schools, children's experiences in schools, and teachers' assumptions about teaching and learning.

Chapter 2 examines the range of instructional settings found in schools today. Graded settings are contrasted to nongraded, team-taught settings to self-contained, informal settings to graded and nongraded settings alike, and so on. The details of each of these approaches to instruction are explained.

Chapters 3 and 4 focus on those teaching strategies, techniques, and methods most recognized today. Mastery teaching, mastery learning, cooperative learning, and teaching for thinking are all explained. Individual techniques used to apply these methods—for example, establishing set, closure, and role-playing—are also discussed while using Bloom's taxonomy and the Types of Instruction as a frame of reference.

Chapter 5 thoroughly outlines instructional planning for the beginner. The scope and sequence of a curriculum, the development of objectives, lesson planning, self-instructional lessons, modules, and topic units are all explained. Examples of each are provided in the form of charts and appendices.

Chapter 6 discusses evaluation of student learning. Assessment and reporting in a variety of school settings are explained. Evaluation for placement and for formative and summative purposes is also discussed. Portfolios, teacher-made tests, and other forms of classroom assessment and reporting are described. The administration and interpretation of standardized tests are also discussed.

Chapter 7 is intended to help teachers develop a nurturing social-emotional climate for their students. It explains basic skills related to communication, conflict-resolution, providing rewards and consequences, and the development of the student's self-esteem.

Chapter 8 considers the relationship between instruction and management concerns. It explains the basic dynamics of managing groups and individuals in a classroom setting. It also deals with the teacher's management of physical space, record-keeping, and classroom support personnel.

Chapter 9 integrates the most popular approaches to school discipline into a simple, but practical 20-step system that deals with the prevention and redirection of misbehavior and provides team support strategies when prevention and redirection have failed.

Chapter 10 focuses on the important problem of how to motivate and empower elementary school students. It also explains the group process skills every elementary teacher needs in order to be a successful motivator.

Chapter 11, the final chapter, helps beginning teachers to choose from the variety of approaches articulated throughout the text.

An instructor's guide, complete with suggested lectures, activities, role-plays, and test bank, is available with this text at no charge when instructors adopt it for use in their courses.

One further note. We made every possible attempt to omit sexist language in the writing of this text. Nevertheless, because of the nature of discussions about the teaching process (which involve interactions between teacher and child as well as interactions between a teacher and *groups* of children), it was sometimes necessary to specify opposite genders in order to make referents clear to the reader. In these cases, we adopted the procedure of alternating chapters. Thus, in Chapter 1, the teacher is referred to by using a female pronoun while the child is a male. In Chapter 2, the teacher is a male while the child is a female. And so on.

Robert Louisell
Jorge Descamps

Acknowledgments

We would each like to thank our families—our spouses and children—for the many sacrifices which they made so that we could write this book. We hope to reap the rewards of our sacrifices.

We would also like to thank those of our students who read and responded to the ideas presented in this book. The knowledge which they demonstrated in class sessions and exams motivated us to continue our work.

The editorial staff at HarperCollins gave us essential advice and assistance and carried this project through to its completion. We especially appreciate the help given by Christopher Jennison, Lee Wood, and Alan McClare. Thanks are also due to David Banner, of Caliber, for his careful attention to the manuscript.

Robert Louisell would also like to thank Jack Easley and Bill and Betty Swyers for the teaching and friendship which they gave during the formative stages of his career. Their ideas have influenced his writing in many sections of this book.

Jim Raths also provided a helpful critique of the outline for Chapter 6.

Finally, Robert Louisell extends his gratitude to the parents of the children whom he taught during his first years as an elementary classroom teacher. By trying out his ideas about teaching with these children, he was able to develop his own teaching style.

Chapter
1

Children in Schools

THE CHILD'S WORLD

While supervising education majors in a local school, I made the following entry in my diary:

> I'm watching a first-grade child as he cuts out a pattern which has been given to him by his teacher. He puts his tongue in his cheek and rolls it through his cheek as he cuts. Another child, working at the same table as the first child, uses her lips. She moves them in certain directions as she cuts out the pattern. When the first child has to turn his scissors in order to continue cutting, he tilts his head sideways and rolls his tongue in the direction that he will have to cut. Piaget was right. The actions and thoughts of children at this stage are not yet completely distinct. The body language of these children is just another example of so-called "motor thought."[1]

The children whom I observed as noted in the diary entry were normal children, and they used "body language" to help them think through the activity which they were supposed to complete. We all use body language now and then—during a game of tennis or golf, when our car has just broken down, etc. But, when it comes to body language, children and adults differ in one basic way. Adults don't really believe in body language. To them, it's a sort of superstition which they entertain when it is convenient. Young children, on the other hand, at least until age 7 or 8, have never had the occasion to question it. They haven't really noticed that they use it. It's something that they do unconsciously and naturally. It goes with their actions.

This is what Piaget meant when he said that the actions and thoughts of children were not yet distinct in children (Piaget, 1929). To a child, an action and a thought are

Figure 1.1 Schools should be places that foster happiness and self-respect.

pretty much the same. Ask a 4 1/2 year old about his dreams and he will tell you that the dream occurs in his room, outside his head (Piaget, 1929). At breakfast one morning, a mother asked her child if he had experienced pleasant dreams during the previous night. The child responded by saying, "Well, you should know! You were in them." Such is the reasoning of children during this state.

Children's Ideas

When asked to explain everyday events, most young children will eventually resort to magic. Take, for example, this entry which came from the diary of one of my graduate students.

> Tonight I was dusting the furniture and Adam (almost 5 years old) was observing me. I asked him where he thought all the dust came from. At first he said he wasn't sure, but after watching me some more he said he had figured it out.
>
> "Mommy, there are dust fairies!" He figured they carry it around and, when they land, they shake it off. I asked why we can't see them and he said that he **had** seen them. He said that when the sun came through the window, he had seen them in the air.[2]

Many young children will claim that they are responsible for the movement of the moon or the wind. Consider the following excerpt which we have adapted from one of Piaget's books (Piaget, 1929, p. 215):

> ADULT: Does the sun move?
>
> JAC (a child, 6 years old): Yes, when you walk, it follows you. When you turn around, it turns around too. Doesn't it ever follow you too?
>
> ADULT: Why does it move?
>
> JAC: Because when you walk, it goes too!
>
> ADULT: Why does it go?
>
> JAC: To hear what we say.
>
> ADULT: Is it alive?
>
> JAC: Of course! Otherwise, it couldn't follow us. It couldn't shine!
>
> ADULT: Does the moon move?
>
> JAC: Yes, when you walk, it walks too, more than the sun, because if you run, the moon goes as fast as you can run but, when you run with the sun, it only goes as fast as you can walk. The moon is stronger than the sun, and so it goes faster. The sun can't ever catch up to the moon.

Actions and the appearances of things strongly influence the ideas of young children. If something moves, they reason, it is alive. If it is not alive, then perhaps some being (e.g., a dust fairy) is responsible for making it move. Consider one more diary entry about a child's ideas of mountains. In this entry, Julie, a parent, is asking her son, Seth, some questions about how mountains came to be. Seth is 5 years old.

> JULIE: What are mountains?
>
> SETH: Big piles of rocks.
>
> JULIE: How do the rocks get there?
>
> SETH: Men dug rocks and piled them up and stuck them together.
>
> JULIE: How did the men stick the rocks together?
>
> SETH: They piled them one by one so they wouldn't fall.
>
> JULIE: How long did it take the men to make the mountain?
>
> SETH: A couple of years.[3]

In this example above, someone is responsible for the way things are. If there are mountains, then someone made them. Seth can only guess how long it might take people to make these mountains, what process they might have used to do so (i.e., piling rocks on top of each other), and so on. Much of the child's life has been organized by adults. Why not assume that everything has been organized by them?

When they are asked, "Where does the wind come from?", children between the ages of 5–7 often respond by attributing it to some man-made machine, or "God." For example, one 7 year old child whom I interviewed answered by telling me that "God coughs." Children of the ages 7–9 frequently respond to the question by naming the trees, the dust, the clouds, etc. In sum, anything which they have seen moving with the wind is responsible for it (Piaget, 1929, p. 36).

> ADULT: How is the wind made?
>
> CHILD: By God?
>
> ADULT: How?

CHILD: He bends?

ADULT: What does he bend?

CHILD: He bends the trees.

ADULT: And then?

CHILD: That makes them move and then, when there's a lot of wind, it makes them fall down.

ADULT: Does the wind make the tree move or do the trees make the wind?

CHILD: The trees make the wind.

A child may believe that things are alive when they are not alive (for example, he may believe that the moon and the stars are alive and "follow" him). A child may believe that some things cause other things to happen when they do not (He may believe, for example, that the trees make the wind). And a child may believe that things are organized according to a grand plan which revolves around him and the other humans in this world. (For example, he may believe that the sun and moon shine to give us light, that the rain falls so we can have water and the grass will grow, that mountains have been placed on earth so that mountain goats can climb on them[4], and so on.)

But none of these things has been organized for the sole good of the child and the rest of humanity. The moon, the stars, the sun, the wind, and the trees are not alive. God does not make the wind by coughing, nor do the trees make the wind. We could say that the child's ideas are imaginative. We could say that they are different from adults. Or we could say that the child has not yet developed, in his own mind, a clear distinction between actions and ideas. We could say all of these things.

Egocentric Thought

The word which Piaget used to describe the way in which young children (ages 4–7) think is "**egocentric**." It does **not** mean that children at this stage are "self-centered." It means that children who are in this stage of thinking have a tendency to "center" their thinking on one perspective. They have difficulty considering multiple perspectives simultaneously. For example, consider the following experiment which Piaget did with many children in this age range (Piaget, 1964; Duckworth, 1979).

First, the child is given two balls of clay of exactly the same size and is asked whether each ball has the same amount of clay in it. If the child answers "Yes, each ball has just as much as the other," then the adult resumes the experiment. If the child responds by saying that one ball has more clay in it, however, the child is told to "fix them so that neither one of the two balls has more clay than the other." After the child has moved bits of clay back and forth from one piece of clay to the other and has decided that each ball has the same amount of clay in it, then the experiment is resumed (See Figure 1.2).

The child is instructed to take the second ball of clay and to "roll it into the shape of a sausage." As the clay achieves its more elongated, sausage-like, form (See Figure 1.3), the child is asked, "Now look at that other ball of clay that we haven't touched. Does that ball have just as much clay as the clay you have in your hands? Or, is there more clay one place or the other?" Children in the egocentric stage say that the amounts of clay are different.

"It's longer (pointing to the sausage-shaped clay) so there's more!" is a typical response for a child in this stage.

Figure 1.2

Figure 1.3

In the experiment just described, Piaget says that the child focuses on only one perspective; for example, the length of the clay. The child "centers" on that one perspective—its increase in length. He ignores the decrease in thickness of clay which has resulted from the same action which made the clay longer. In Piaget's terms, the child does not "decenter" and consider both of these perspectives at the same time. It has, after all, increased in length while, at the same time, it has decreased in thickness. It is the child's inability to decenter that Piaget has called "egocentrism."

Let's examine one more experiment, Piaget's famous "conservation of number" experiment.

First, the interviewer sets out two rows of identical objects such as bottle-caps, checkers, or unifix cubes. Each row has the same number of objects in it. Seven in each row is usually a good amount with which to start. It is not a good idea to use more objects than the child can count. I prefer to use colored cubes or checkers because that enables me to put the objects in two rows which are identical in every way except color.

The objects are arranged so that the objects for the two rows are in one-to-one alignment (See Figure 1.4).

At this point, the child is told that one of the rows of objects is for the inter-viewer and the other row of objects is for the child. The child is then asked, "Does one of us have more or do we both have the same number of cubes?" The child may count the objects in either row if he wishes to do so. Whether they do or don't count the objects, most children decide that there are equal numbers of objects in each row.

Next, the interviewer rearranges one of the rows (e.g., the top row) by spreading out the objects so that they occupy about twice as much space as they did at first (See Figure 1.5). The child is then asked the same question, "Does one of us have more cubes, or do we both have just as many?" At this point, children from the egocentric state of thought respond that one person has more objects than the other.

"You have more and I have less!" is a typical response which is given by children at this stage of thought.

In this experiment, as in the previous one, the child "centers" on one perspective (e.g., how much more space is filled by the row of cubes which has been spread out) and ignores other perspectives (e.g., how much less empty space exists between objects in the row which has not been changed). Children who answer the interview questions in this way are said to be **non-conservers** for number. That is, the child does not appear to realize that the amount of objects is the same no matter how they have been arranged.

The child concentrates on one point of view while ignoring another one. He is not "self-centered," but he has a tendency to look at things from one perspective at a time. He does not "decenter" and consider two perspectives simultaneously. This is why Piaget has called the child's thinking during this stage "egocentric."

In contrast, a child who **conserves** number is able to decenter his thinking and examine the problem from multiple points of view. For example, here are some examples of how children who conserve number answer the interviewer's questions.

We both have the same amount. I know because all you did was change where they are. See, you spread them out. But, watch, I can put them back where they were and they are still the same [as they were before the interviewer spread them out].

It's still the same. Your row is longer, but they [the objects] are closer together in my row. That [the objects being close together in one row] makes up for it [the objects being spread out in the other row].

In the first response, the child does not center his thinking in one direction. A more egocentric thinker might say, "Before they were the same, but now your row has more!" This child would have watched an action as it was completed (the objects being spread out) and would have thought only about that action. A more decentered thinker looks at the *completed action and the state of the objects before the action occurred.* Since the child realizes that one action can "cancel" the other, the conclusion is that the amounts are equal.

Figure 1.4

In the second response, the child does not center his thinking on one dimension. He first examines the row which has been "spread out" and observes that it takes up more space than it did before. Next, he examines the row which has not been changed. Comparing each row with the other, he observes that the row which has been spread out takes up more space but he also observes that the row which has not been changed has less "empty" space between the objects. This child's thinking is **decentered** because the child focuses on two dimensions. In contrast, a more egocentric child might conclude that one row had more objects than the other because it occupied more space.

Figure 1.5

Many other researchers have replicated these experiments (Ginsburg and Opper, 1988; Flavell, 1963; Kamii, 1985) with similar results.

Developmental Stages in Children's Thinking

Children do not stay in the egocentric stage forever, of course. They develop more objective patterns of thinking. Piaget divided the development of thought from infancy to adolescence into four general periods: the **sensorimotor** period, the **preoperational** period, the period of **concrete operations**, and the period of **formal operations**. Although it is difficult to summarize Piaget's periods in a few pages, we offer a brief synopsis of these periods below.

The Sensorimotor Period (birth to about 2 years). When infants are first born, they don't show many signs of being intelligent. They do have reflexes, however, and these reflexes are used by infants as they interact with their environment. For example, they suck their mothers' nipples so that they can get milk. Sucking is a reflex which infants make use of to survive. This may surprise you, but infants are actually able to develop their intelligence by making use of the reflexes with which they are born.

They begin their intellectual development by **assimilating** objects to these reflexes. At this stage, assimilation is the process by which an action is performed on an object in order to accomplish something. When a child sucks the nipple, for example, sucking is the action which the child performs, the nipple is the object which is being assimilated, and getting milk is what the infant is accomplishing.

As objects are assimilated to reflexes, these reflexes **accommodate** to the characteristics of the objects, for example, their shape, their location in space, etc. With each assimilation and accommodation, a reflex becomes more capable of being applied to a wide variety of objects. Soon it can no longer be described as simply a reflex; rather, it has become a "pattern of action." Piaget calls these patterns of action **schemes.** Eventually, infants assimilate more than just objects to their schemes; they also assimilate schemes to each other.

For example, when infants are born, they have a **grasping** reflex. They cannot yet pick up objects, however. A few months after birth, they develop a scheme for visually **tracking** the movement of objects. By this time, they have also developed a scheme for **reaching** (at birth, their arms only "flail around" aimlessly). In order for an infant to pick up an object, its grasping scheme must assimilate a tracking scheme (so the child can locate the object visually) and a reaching scheme (so the child can bring his or her hand within grasping distance of the object). As the infant makes use of each of these schemes, he makes several adjustments (accommodations) to his external world. His eyes move, his arm reaches, and his hand grasps.

As he coordinates these schemes, he becomes aware that they are not all the same. He makes use of each of these schemes (e.g., his tracking, reaching, and grasping schemes) to achieve a goal (i.e., picking up an object). Through this process of "reciprocal assimilations" (i.e., the assimilation of schemes to each other), infants begin to distinguish between means and ends. As the infant becomes more aware of the distinction between means and ends, his or her actions reflect more purpose. During the final stage of infancy, the infant's ability to distinguish between means and ends has resulted in what Piaget considers to be "true intelligence." At this point, a child's schemes (patterns of action) can be carried out mentally. Piaget refers to this phenomenon as "internalized actions." In other words, the child now can employ schemes of thoughts as well as actions. Two milestones which the child has achieved by this final stage are: 1) A knowledge of object permanence; 2) The ability to represent absent objects and events. This ability to represent things is then employed by the child in the development of his or her language.

The Preoperational Period   (roughly, age 2–7). Although the sensorimotor period is one in which infants are tied to their immediate fields of action (i.e., they cannot know anything beyond their immediate present), with the development of representation, children acquire the ability to reflect upon their actions and to think beyond their actions and the objects in their environment. Using symbols to represent objects and events, children construct language. Words can be used to recall a distant person or event. But thought is still closely tied to the child's world. Piaget's own child did not recognize her baby sister when she had changed from normal clothes to a swimsuit and bathing cap! (Flavell, p. 160) She had apparently concluded that an entirely new person had arrived on the scene.

It is during the latter half of the preoperational period (roughly, age 4–7) that the child develops "egocentric" schemes of thought (this type of thought was explained in a previous section of this chapter). The child has difficulty considering matters from another's point of view. He finds it difficult to draw what an object looks like from a different angle or perspective than his own. Children in this stage make little or no effort to justify their reasoning or to look for contradictions in it. During experiments which are conducted to discover whether they conserve number or substance, they attend to "states" instead of transformations. Thinking is "irreversible."

Take as an example the conservation of substance experiment, which we described in a previous section of this chapter, in which the child manipulates a ball of clay into the shape of a sausage. After the child has reshaped the ball of clay into a sausage-like shape, he concludes that he now has more clay than he did before he reshaped the clay. He focuses on the **states** of the clay—before and after—but he forgets about the **transformation**—the process by which he changes the shape from that of a ball to that of a sausage. If he thought more about the transformation, he might understand that he still has the same amount of clay! But he doesn't focus on transformations at this stage. It's one of the limitations of his thinking. If he could **reverse** his thinking, he might imagine what would happen if the sausage-like shape were manipulated back into the shape of a ball. By imagining this action, he might come to realize that the amount of clay does not change with its shape. But his thinking is not reversible at this stage, and he doesn't imagine what would happen if the actions which he performs were reversed.

The Period of Concrete Operations   (roughly, ages 7–11). In this period, children develop a **system** for explaining their world. Now they understand that the greater length of the clay (when it has taken on the shape of a sausage) is compensated for by its increased thinness (when compared to the ball of clay). They can mentally **reverse** the action of shaping the clay into the shape of a sausage, and they can realize that, if the clay were manipulated back into its original, ball-like shape, the clay would look the same as before. They can reason that the identity of the clay is the same ("It's still the same clay!") regardless of what shape it takes on.

Understanding "compensations" (e.g., length is compensated by thinness), imagining "reversals" of actions, and reasoning about identities are schemes which have been acquired by the child during the transition from the preoperational period to the period of concrete operations. The ability to establish exclusive classes—for example, the ability to distinguish between dogs and non-dogs—is also acquired at this time. Along with the development of **classification** schemes, the child acquires the ability to form a variety of **relations**. For example, when a preoperational child who happens to have a brother is asked, "Do you have any brothers?", that child is able to respond, "Yes, one, his name is Peter and he is 9 years old." However, when the child is asked whether "Peter" has any brothers, he responds with "No." Why? Piaget believes it is because the child does not have a complete grasp of relations. The child is able to comprehend that he has a brother, but he is not able to decenter and consider matters from another's perspective (i.e., Peter's) and to realize that Peter must also have a brother (him).

The child who is functioning at the concrete operations period, however, can comprehend the relation from both perspectives—that is, his own, and that of his brother. He has a more organized, systematized, understanding of this relation (hence the term "operation"). Not only has the concrete operations child developed an understanding of this type of relation—that is, relations among brothers or sisters—but he has also constructed several other types of relations. For example, he knows that there is a relation which exists among classes; that is, that mammals are a class which includes classes such as dogs and "non-dogs," that dogs are a class which includes German Shepherds and "non-German Shepherds," etc. This relation is called **class inclusion**. Any child who has developed this particular relation is able to move up and down a hierarchy of classes (see Figure 1.6). For example, he is able to comprehend that dogs are included in the class of mammals but alligators cannot be included in the mammal class (because they are reptiles, which is a class which is excluded from the mammal class, or because they do not have the characteristics which are associated with mammals, etc.).

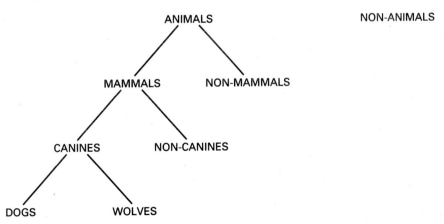

Figure 1.6

In fact, children at the preoperational level appear to have much difficulty handling **part-whole** relations, whereas children at the concrete operations level appear to handle this type of thinking very readily.

For example, there is the experiment which Piaget conducted using wooden beads. Most of the beads (e.g., 14) were painted brown, but the rest of the beads (e.g., 3) were painted white. Piaget would begin the experiment by asking the child, "How many wooden beads are there altogether?", and the child would answer correctly (e.g., 17). Next, Piaget would ask the child, "How many brown beads are there?", and the child would again answer correctly (e.g., 14). Next, Piaget would ask the child, "How many white beads are there?", and the child would again answer correctly (e.g., 3). Finally, Piaget would ask the child, "Are there more brown beads or wooden beads?", and the preoperational child would answer, incorrectly, that there were more brown beads.

At this point in the interview, Piaget would review the facts with the child.
"How many beads are there altogether?"
"Seventeen."
"And how many brown beads are there?"
"Fourteen."
"And how many white beads?"
"Three."
"So, there are seventeen wooden beads altogether and there are fourteen brown beads and there are three white beads, right?"
"Right."
"Are there more brown beads or are there more wooden beads altogether?"
"More brown beads."[5]

According to Piaget, children in the preoperational period fail with the above task because they cannot move up and down a class inclusion hierarchy. In other words, they cannot think about **parts** (e.g., brown beads or white beads) and **whole** (e.g., all of the beads) at the same time (see Figure 1.7). Once the child has developed concrete operations, however, he is able to move easily between parts and whole and can succeed at the task of comparing a part to the whole.

In sum, there are many mental schemes which the child develops as he enters the period of concrete operations, and these schemes are not evidenced in the child's thinking during the preoperational period. These schemes include, but are not limited to, classification and seriation schemes, conservations (e.g., of number and substance), reversible thought, class inclusion, and an understanding of part-whole relations. Piaget calls these schemes **cognitive structures** because they are schemes which are organized, or given direction, by the child's thinking. These cognitive structures are more independent of the child's actions than any of the preoperational child's schemes were. Piaget uses the term **operations** to denote the more systematic thought

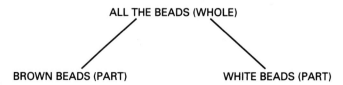

Figure 1.7

demonstrated by children in this period. To denote that the child's thinking at this level deals primarily with the real, Piaget uses the term **concrete**. One should not misinterpret this to mean that children at this age cannot think about anything which isn't the real or concrete, however. Nothing could be further form the truth. Rather, the child at this stage is "beginning to extend his thought...from the actual to the potential" (Flavell, 1963, p 203).

The Period of Formal Operations   (roughly, age 11 and on). While the child's thinking in the period of concrete operations is far more systematic than it is during the preoperational period, it does not yet demonstrate the integrated network of thought which is present during the period of formal operations. The concrete operations child has mastered various individual operations (e.g., reversibility of thought, class inclusion, seriation, etc.) but he is not yet able to use them in combination with each other in order to solve more complex problems. In fact, Piaget was especially surprised to discover that **children acquire their conservations** (i.e., of number, of substance, volume, etc.) **one at a time**!

One could expect that children who had arrived at the conclusion that the substance doesn't change when the clay's shape is altered would also realize that the number of objects doesn't change when the cubes are spread out. But the concrete operations child doesn't apply his newly developed logic to everything in his experience. The adolescent (or pre-adolescent) who has entered the period of formal operations, on the other hand, realizes that logic can be applied to all of his experiences and he proceeds to do so.

As an example, let's examine the interviews which Piaget conducted with children to find out their answer to the questions, "Why do some objects float and not others?"

During the **preoperational period,** children gave contradictory answers and made no effort to eliminate these contradictions. For example, one child was asked to predict whether a wooden plank would sink or float in the container of water which was supplied for the interview. The child predicted that it would sink. It floated. When asked why it floated, the child replied, "Because it's bigger [than other objects being tested in the water during the interview]." Next, the child was asked why a ball floated. "Because it's smaller [than other objects being tested in the water]" was the reply which this child gave. Thus, one object floats because it is big, and another object floats because it is small. For other children, some things floated because they were "heavy" while others floated because they were "light."

At the **concrete operations** level, however, the child made an effort to eliminate these contradictions. Instead of vacillating between contradictory explanations (this one floats because it is light, and this other one sinks because it is light), the child attempted to compare the weight of an object to the weight of the water in which it was being placed. But, when making this comparison, the child did not realize the importance of structuring his comparisons so that each variable was equal. He compared the weight of his object to the weight of the entire tub of water which was being used for the experiment. Consequently, his conclusions were often incorrect. When they were correct, they were correct through luck; not logic.

At the **formal operations** level, however, the child compared the **weight of an object** to the **weight of an equal volume of water**. Here, the child has made a valid comparison because he has **held all things equal**.

One thing which has contributed to the child's ability to do this is the concrete operation of **class inclusion**. The child has become aware that not all large objects are heavy and not all small objects are light (see Figure 1.8).

In other words, he has realized that heavy objects are made up of two general weights—that is, heavy and light—according to the materials which comprise them. Once the child realizes this, he can no longer settle for an absolute explanation (e.g., these sink because they are heavy); instead, he must compare them to the weight of the water on which they will float or sink. (Summarized from Piaget, 1958, Chapter 2)

According to Flavell, there are three characteristics which distinguish formal from concrete operations (Flavell, 1963, p. 204-206). First, one considers all the possibilities which could be true for the given data and tries to determine, through experimenting and applying logic to the problem at hand, which of these possibilities is actually true. Second, one makes use of concrete operations by taking the results of these operations and casting them as propositions ("If ... then"). Third, one systematically isolates all variables and combinations of variables so one can determine their effects on the outcome of the experiment.

Let's consider another interview. This one deals with the question of what causes a pendulum to swing faster or slower (speed is here defined as so many swings per specified time interval).

> The **preoperational** child approaches the task without any plan. He randomly tries various combinations. He may test a long pendulum which has a light weight attached. Next, he may test a short pendulum with a heavy weight attached. Last, he may hypothesize that the force of the "push off" makes the difference. After testing this idea out, he may conclude, incorrectly, that the "push off" does in fact make a difference. Perhaps the child is still at the stage where "thinking makes it so." If the child had more carefully observed his results (for example, if he had counted the number of swings which occurred in a minute), he would not have concluded as he did.
>
> The **concrete operations** child is more systematic and he observes his results carefully. However, he does not control for all variables (He does not hold all things equal). For example, he may try a longer string and conclude, correctly, that the length makes a difference. Next, he may try a heavy weight **on a long string** and a light weight **on a short string** and conclude, incorrectly, that weight makes a difference.

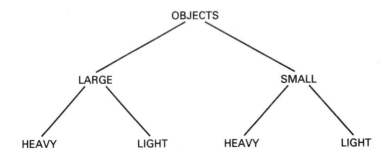

Figure 1.8

The **formal operations** child will hold things constant and test for one variable at a time. In the case of the pendulum, if he is testing for length, he will hold all other variables (e.g., weight, "push off," etc.) constant. In other words, he will make sure that all other variables remain unchanged as he alters the length of the string. (Summarized from Ginsburg and Opper, chapter 5.)

In the above experiment, the **formal operations** child **considers all possibilities;** for example, length, weight, "push off," height of drop, etc. Whether or not he articulates them, he uses a series of **"If ... then" propositions**. If the length of the string makes a difference, he hypothesizes, then a change in the length of the string will bring a change in the number of swings. If the length of the string does not make a difference, then a change in the length of the string will not change the number of swings. And so on. Finally, he **isolates each variable and holds the others constant**. He changes the length of the string while keeping the weight, drop, and "push off" the same. Next, he varies the weight while keeping the length, drop, and "push off" the same. And so on.

In sum, the adolescent or child who has reached the period of formal operations is one who is capable of using concrete operations to test out hypotheses in a systematic and logical fashion, one who exhaustively considers each possibility and tests to determine whether it in fact holds true, and one who realizes that "all other things must be equal" (other variables must be held constant) when a hypothesis is tested.

Implications of These Stages for Curriculum   Not every educator and psychologist agrees with Piaget's stages. In recent years, some Piagetians have moved away from interpreting children's thinking according to stages. Some authors claim to have found examples of very sophisticated thinking in early periods—even infancy![6] Piaget himself moved away from his theory of stages in his last works.

Those who do believe these stages apply to children's thinking disagree about how they ought to be used when planning curriculum. Some (see, for example, Copeland, 1974) believe that children should not be taught anything about number until they can conserve number. Others, including Piaget (Duckworth, 1973), believe that the child should be exposed to work with number but that teachers should not make the mistake of assuming that the children are learning what the teachers intend them to learn from the experience. In other words, teachers should provide experiences which involve children with number, but they should not develop specific expectations about what the children will learn from these experiences.

Of course, for Piaget, stages "come and go." As educated adults, we can be reasonably certain that we have achieved the stage of formal operations. But we don't always use these formal operations in our everyday lives. We overlook possibilities routinely. Sometimes the consequences are severe and sometimes they are insignificant. Piaget classified children into particular intellectual levels when they became **capable** of functioning at that level. He was aware that they would not always make use of this capability.

There are some recommendations which we can make about teaching, however, on the basis of our understanding of Piaget's periods of development. For example, the average child in the primary grades (grades 1-3) should not be expected to conduct experiments which test hypotheses and control variables. Some elementary school science fairs do, in fact, require primary students to do just that (conduct experiments which require that one control variables). Obviously, the typical primary child has not yet reached the period of formal operations. Some may not have reached the concrete operations period. It would be very unreasonable for a teacher, a principal, or a curriculum director to expect that students perform at an intellectual level far beyond their capabilities!

Also, most textbooks which are published for use in elementary schools are arranged according to grade levels. So long as they continue to be arranged in this way, it would make sense to eliminate certain content from the primary grades. For example, if a typical 6 year old child believes that the moon follows him, perhaps the study of a model of the solar system should wait until the intermediate grades (grades 4–6). If he believes that the wind is created by a giant fan, or because "God coughs," then the study of prevailing wind patterns and their effects on the weather will probably be too great an intellectual challenge for that child. Yet, many primary science textbooks do require the study of prevailing wind patterns.

Kamii (1985) believes that because the typical first-grade child has not yet mastered the concrete operation of class inclusion, place-value (tens and ones) should not be taught during first grade. Yet, we are unaware of any first-grade math text which does not include place-value in its curriculum. There are dozens of such instructional "matches" or "mis-matches" which we could identify as implications of Piaget's periods of intellectual development. We also believe that primary children should learn science and math through "hands-on" experiences which involve them in performing actions. Our reason for recommending this is that, according to Piaget, a child's actions and thoughts are very closely related at this stage of development (see the first section of this chapter).

We could make many recommendations about teaching and curricula because of Piaget's stages. However, we would rather that each of you, as future teachers, made your own decisions about these matters. The important thing, from our perspective, is that you need to become sensitive to how children think during the elementary grades, that you need to be aware that they may think differently than adults and that children in one stage (e.g., preoperational) may think differently than children in another stage (e.g., concrete operations or formal operations). If you are sensitive to the thinking of children, and aware of the differences between children's thinking and the thinking of adults, then you will be able to be more responsive to children as you go about teaching them.

The Child's World Summed Up

The child's world is different from the adult's world in several respects. His actions and thoughts are closely related. Thinking is less objective. He frequently expresses egocentric beliefs during the early years (up to about age 7 or 8). Natural phenomena are explained by magic. Appearances sway the child's beliefs about reality; for example, when he does not conserve number after the row of cubes has been spread out.

Piaget has classified the intellectual development of children into four periods: sensorimotor, preoperational, concrete operations, and formal operations.

During the **sensorimotor** period, the child develops intelligent thought by using reflexes and action-schemes to act upon his world. With this intelligence comes the ability to represent absent objects and events. The child makes use of this ability to acquire the language of his parents.

During the **preoperational** period, the child's thinking shows a tendency to center on one perspective. It appears to be unsystematic. He has not yet reached an understanding of conservation of number or substance.

Beginning with the period of **concrete operations,** the child's thinking is better organized and reversible. He understands conservation. He has mentally constructed a system of class inclusion. His thinking is primarily focused on the real, but he is beginning to extend his thinking to possibilities.

Finally, in the **formal operations** period, the adolescent (or pre-adolescent) has acquired a systematized network of logical thought which can be applied to any problems involving the real or the possible. In solving these problems, the adolescent makes use of his concrete operations as he isolates variables and tests hypotheses. At this point, the child has reached the highest stage of intellectual development which Piaget identified.

Not everyone agrees that intellectual development occurs in stages. Those who do interpret children's thinking according to stages, however, believe that teachers should become familiar with the characteristics of each stage of children's thinking. By doing so, they believe, teachers will be able to be more sensitive to, and responsive to, the ideas of their students. We endorse this belief.

WHAT SOCIETY EXPECTS OF SCHOOLS

Although you are reading this book because you plan to become a teacher, you have probably not asked yourself the question, "What are schools for?" Why not? Probably, the answer is obvious to you. You are probably thinking, "Schools are for learning, aren't they?" Ask yourself why you want to be a teacher, however, and your answer will include several reasons that have nothing to do with **teaching** children. For example, you may say that you like children or "have a way with them." You may say that you "have a lot to offer." These statements may be true, but they do not have much to do with the idea that schools are for learning.

Why do so many things occur to us when we think about being a teacher of children, which have nothing to do with transmitting knowledge to children? Part of the answer to this question must be that **society has many expectations of its schools**. Society does expect our schools to teach its children. It expects that we, as teachers, will teach children literacy, math skills, the important content from each of the major academic subject areas, and the social skill of "getting along." But society expects many other things from schools, also.

For example, society expects that schools will provide a **custodial role** for its children. Many parents work during the time that their children are in school. These parents depend upon the schools to take care of their children while they are away at work. While other parents do not work during the school day, they still rely on the school for its "babysitting" function.

Through the parents of the children who go to school, society also expects schools to provide for the **safety** of its children. Parents expect that you, the teacher, will take care of their children as well as they would if they were at home with them. They expect their children to return, at the end of the day, alive, happy, and secure. This expectation (that schools provide for the safety and well being of the child) can be considered an extension of the school's custodial role.

Although the people of our society do not always articulate this expectation, society also expects its schools to **socialize** its children. Here, we are not talking about providing children with opportunities to "socialize" (Although this is something which schools should also do, it relates more to the goals of "getting along" which we have already mentioned). As we are using the term here, **socialize** refers to the transmission of cultural values. In other words, schools are expected to teach children about "how things are done" in our culture. If we, as adults, line up to wait for our turn when we go to a movie or a restaurant, our children must learn to line up to wait for their turn for something. If we must fulfill responsibilities in order to receive rewards (e.g., salary, vacations, etc.), then our children must learn to complete responsibilities, also. And so on.

We have said that society does expect schools to teach literacy, math skills, academic content, etc. What we have not said is that one of the chief reasons that society expects schools to do this is that society expects schools to train children to become **competent to survive in our culture**. Competence, in this instance, could include skills in literacy and mathematics, academic content knowledge, the skill of "getting along," socialized behavior (demonstration of the values of our culture), and anything else which relates to the successful adjustment of children to their culture as they enter adulthood and become full-fledged citizens.

Society also expects schools to act as a **center for correcting social ills**. Our society is one with a growing number of problems which seem to be out of control. Segregation and drug abuse are two societal problems with which schools have recently dealt. Society expects schools to correct these problems. It remains to be seen whether schools are capable of accomplishing these kinds of tasks.

But, of all those things which society expects schools to do for children, perhaps the greatest expectation which society holds is to **educate children so that they can become free**. (Spodek, 1976) For more than a century, many people within our society have expected schools to enable children to function independently. Of course, the competence to successfully adapt, which was discussed earlier, relates to this goal but functioning independently involves much more than this. If adults in our society are really to function independently, they must make their own judgments and decisions. To do so, they must trust themselves.

The expectation that teachers enable children to make their own judgments and decisions sometimes conflicts with the expectation that teachers impart knowledge. For example, some teachers may encourage their students to question the information which is presented to them. These same students may do just what they have been encouraged to do—that is, question authority—when other teachers (or even the very same teachers!) are **not** encouraging them to question. In this situation, societal expectations have come into conflict with one another and the perceptive student learns a valuable lesson about schools and how much they practice what they preach.

The teacher's role as a person who is responsible for the lives and education of children during the school day is an important one. The child looks to the teacher as a substitute parent and caretaker, arbiter of disagreements, and source of information and knowledge. But, if the teacher always interacts with children as an expert and director of their schoolday lives, when will children develop the skill of making their own decisions and judgments? If someone is always taking care of them, when will children learn to take care of themselves?

Let's examine an example of a teacher acting as an "expert" (Spodek, 1976):

> Imagine a classic experiment in school science. A teacher in a class of young children sets out a candle, a jar, and a match. While the children watch, she lights the candle, waits a while, and then covers the candle with the jar. She asks the children "What happened?" They respond that the flame went out. She then asks "Why did it happen?" If there is no response, she explains to the children that the flame consumed the oxygen in the air that was trapped in the jar. Since oxygen is needed to support combustion, the flame was extinguished when there was no more oxygen available.
>
> What have the children learned? Can they see the oxygen in the jar? Can they test for its absence or presence? Can they determine whether or not combustion can take place in a variety of media? What the teacher has taught the children is that the source of scientific knowledge is authority—in this case, the teacher—who can never be proven wrong. She has mystified science.
>
> From a value point of view, this activity has oppressed rather than liberated children because they are not able to independently validate knowledge provided by the teacher.

Schools exist for multiple purposes. On the one hand, we want children to be protected from the overwhelming task of surviving in our adult society.[7] On the other hand, we want children to learn to be independent and to think for themselves. On the one hand, we want children to acquire those skills which we think are essential for survival in our society. Because of this, we specify what things they should be taught. On the other hand, we want children to acquire the skill of finding answers to their own questions. Because of this, we provide our students with opportunities to express themselves and to pursue knowledge about topics which are of interest to them. Throughout this text, you will be presented with examples of school settings, teaching techniques, and teaching methods which will be better at achieving one of these goals than another. You will have to make your own decision, as a future teacher, about which of these goals is most important to you. Our job is to help you make an informed choice.

WHAT CHILDREN LEARN IN SCHOOLS

We believe that all those things which society expects of schools are actually being taught by schools to some degree. In addition to those things which society expects schools to teach its students, children may be inadvertently learning some other things which no one in society is expecting them to learn. Unfortunately, some of the things which they are learning are undesirable.

For example, you might assume that children learn to be curious and reflective while pursuing the concepts and skills to which they are exposed during school. However, some educators believe the opposite. They think that the longer children are in school, the less curiosity they display (Wasserman and Ivany, 1988; and Trumbull, in

Duckworth, et al., 1990). Teaching which consistently puts the teacher in the role of expert can have a negative effect on a child's curiosity over the long term. As Trumbull puts it (in the introduction for Duckworth et al.):

> Most approaches to instruction assume that children should be passive learners or, if active, should have freedom to act only to meet the goals set by others. As a result, pupils do not learn how to direct their own learning activities or to set their own goals for learning.

Children may inadvertently learn that knowledge comes from experts, and by implication, **that it cannot be acquired on one's own**.

Children may also learn that schools are not very democratic. One of the most important values of American society has to do with the rights of citizens—especially those rights guaranteed by our constitution in its first 10 amendments (the Bill of Rights). Let's examine another example of a classroom situation.

> This fifth-grade teacher was in the final day of a unit on the Bill of Rights. For three weeks, her students had studied the history and meaning of this document, memorized important passages, dramatized situations to which these important rights applied, and so on. Now, this teacher was conducting a recitation during which she reviewed the importance of each of the amendments with her students. Calling on one student, she said, "John, what right does the fourth amendment guarantee?" John looked down at his desk. He did not remember what right was guaranteed by the Fourth Amendment to our great constitution. The teacher repeated her question, and this time she added, "You are supposed to know this, John! You will be graded on your knowledge of each amendment. Do you know the answer?" John's reply was prompt and to the point.
>
> "I refuse to answer that question because the information which it requires may tend to incriminate me." [John pleads the Fifth Amendment]
>
> "Oh, really?" said the teacher. "Perhaps we should take a little trip to the principal's office and place a call to your parents."[8]

John has learned a valuable lesson from this little scene. He has discovered that the Bill of Rights does not apply to him. It appears not to apply to any children—at least not in school. Perhaps schools are not democratic. Or, perhaps schools are not democratic where children are concerned. In any case, **children may learn,** as John did, **that what they learn in school does not apply to their everyday lives**—not even their everyday school lives! Children may learn this in a variety of ways. They may read about science concepts which seem to contradict their personal experiences. When they bring up these experiences in class, their teachers frequently discourage them from exploring these contradictions further. (Duckworth et al.) Or, they may learn that mathematics, or reading, is something which is only done during school hours.

Once, while an education professor was interviewing a group of children about their ideas on mathematics, he asked, "Is there any time when you use math outside of school?" At first all of the children responded that there was never a time when they used mathematics **outside** of school. But, finally, one child volunteered, "Yes, there is a time when we use math outside of school." Ecstatic that someone had realized that this was true, the professor followed with the question, "When do you use math outside of school?" and the student replied, "Sometimes, we take our math books home and **then** we use math outside of school."[9] From the child's perspective, so many things (the Bill of Rights, science information, mathematics) appear to be learned solely for school.

Finally, **children may learn that schools are not good places for being truthful.** Let me give another example, this one a multicultural one.

> Many hispanic children are raised to be always truthful—especially with adults or persons with authority. During math class one day, a little boy named Roberto was called upon by his teacher to solve a math problem.
>
> "Roberto, would you like to go up to the board and solve this problem in front of the class?" his teacher asked. But Roberto did not like working in front of the entire class, and he had been raised to be always truthful, so he replied "No."
>
> "Oh!" said the teacher, "Then, would you like to stay in from recess and write your name on the board 1000 times?"
>
> Roberto did not like to write anything 1000 times. It was embarrassing to have his name all over the board like that and he had been raised to be truthful, so again he responded "No."
>
> "Oh!" said his teacher, a bit angrier this time, "Then, maybe you would like to stay after school for a week and do some extra schoolwork! Is that right?"
>
> Once again, Roberto responded with a simple "No." [10]

Is Roberto a slow learner? If not, why can't he master the obvious lesson that schools are not places where you are supposed to tell the truth?

We would all hope that none of us will ever turn off a child's curiosity, or refuse to allow children to apply what they learn in school to their daily lives, or discourage our students from telling the truth. But, our actions often betray us—even when we have the best of intentions. Hopefully, a greater awareness of our goals and attitudes, coupled with a greater sensitivity to the attitudes of our students, will help us to interact with our students in ways which foster the most positive of qualities.

TEACHERS' ASSUMPTIONS ABOUT TEACHING AND LEARNING

Teachers carry different assumptions with them into their classrooms. The assumptions which teachers make about how children learn, what they should be taught, and how they should be taught can dramatically affect the type of teaching which goes on in their classrooms. What are your assumptions about how children learn? Do you know how they will affect your own teaching? How would you respond to the following two questions? Read the instructions and use the rating scale provided.

Instructions Using the rating system below, rate the following assumptions about learning according to your personal opinions. [11]

Rating scale:

1 = I very much *dis*agree.

2 = I disagree.

3 = I am unsure about this.

4 = I agree.

5 = I strongly *agree*.

1. _____ Children are innately curious and will explore their environments without adult interventions.

2. _____ Children are naturally curious except when they are threatened.

Discuss your response to these questions with other students of education. Perhaps your professor will conduct a class discussion of these questions and the others which follow. If you believe that children are innately curious, how will that affect your teaching? Suppose you believe that adult interventions are frequently necessary to motivate children to explore their worlds. What kind of teaching interaction would this imply? If children are naturally curious, doesn't that mean that the teacher's job is more or less to foster this curiosity and get out of their way? If children need adult interventions, teachers will be more involved in telling children what to do. Now try these next four questions.

3. _____ Active exploration in a rich environment, which offers a wide array of manipulative materials, will facilitate learning.

4. _____ Children will be likely to learn if they are given considerable choice in the selection of materials they wish to work with and in the choice of questions they wish to pursue with respect to those materials.

5. _____ To young children, there is no difference between play and work when it comes to learning something new.

6. _____ If a child is fully involved in, and having fun with, an activity, learning is taking place.

Do you believe that children should "actively explore" in schools? Should schools provide a wide array of manipulative materials? If you believe this, then what kind of a classroom will yours be? What kinds of teacher-student interactions will take place? If you do not agree with question number 3, what kinds of student activities do you envision taking place in the classroom?

Do you agree or disagree with question number 4? Should children be allowed to choose the materials with which they will work? Should they pursue those questions which occur to them when they are involved with these materials? If they should be allowed to do so, then what does that imply about the type of teacher-student interaction which should occur in the classroom?

Is it true, as question number 5 states, that young children do not distinguish between work and play when they go about their learning? If so, what does this imply about how you will make classroom "assignments"? Do you agree with question number 6's claim that learning is taking place whenever the child is having fun with an activity. Why or why not? Now examine these next questions.

7. _____ When a child learns something which is important to him or her, he or she will wish to share it with others.

8. _____ Knowledge is organized uniquely by each person and therefore cannot be separated neatly into categories or "disciplines."

9. _____ Evidence of a child's learning is best assessed intuitively, by direct observation.

10. _____ The best measure of a child's work is his or her work.

If question number 7 is correct, then what does this imply about the attitude which a teacher should display about children talking during classroom instruction periods? If question number 8 is correct, then why do we teach according to separate subjects (e.g., reading, math, science, social studies, etc.) in our elementary schools? If the statements for questions 9 and 10 are correct, then why do we test children so often in our elementary schools?

If you agree with the statements made in questions number 3–10, then you may prefer to teach in an "informal" school setting. This setting is described in Chapter 2 of this text.

The following three questions relate to each other in some ways. See if you can figure out how they are related.

11. _____ Confidence in oneself is highly related to capacity for learning and to making important choices which affect one's learning.

12. _____ Children learn and develop intellectually at their own rate and in their own style.

13. _____ Objective measures of performance may have a negative effect upon learning.

If confidence in oneself is related to one's capacity for learning, what does that imply about the teacher's role in helping children to learn? If children really do develop at their own rate, then what does this imply about graded schools in which children work on the same concepts all together? If objective measures can have a negative effect upon learning, then what is the best way to assess whether students have learned? If you agree with each of these questions, you would probably prefer not to teach in a graded school setting. More than likely, you would be attracted to the nongraded approach, which individualizes for rate of learning and uses a variety of means of assessment. Chapter 2 will introduce you to this type of school setting.

Now examine questions 14–18. Again, we have grouped these questions together because we believe they have some ideas in common.

14. _____ Children have both the competence and the right to make significant decisions concerning their own learning.

15. _____ Little or no knowledge exists which is essential for everyone to acquire.

16. _____ Those qualities of a person's learning which can be carefully measured are not necessarily the most important.

17. _____ "Being" is more important than "knowing." Knowledge is a means of education; not its end. The final test of an education is what a person is and not what he knows.

18. _____ It is possible, even likely, that an individual may learn and possess knowledge of a phenomenon and yet be unable to display this knowledge publicly. Knowledge resides in the knower, not in its public expression.

Do children have the right to make significant decisions about what they are to learn? Are they competent to make these decisions? Is being more important than knowing ? Is there much knowledge which is essential for everyone to acquire? If not, what does that imply for schooling? If so, what knowledge is essential? How should it be taught to students? Is it true that the most important learning can not be measured? Is it also true that children may know something but not know how to express it? If you agree with these statements (numbers 14–18), you may prefer a school setting such as the one at "Alternative Heights." This setting is described, in detail, in Chapter 2 of this text.

Now let's examine three relatively unrelated statements.

19. _____ Errors are necessarily a part of the learning process. They are to be expected and even desired because they contain information which is essential for further learning.

20. _____ Verbal abstractions should follow direct experience with objects and ideas, not precede them or substitute for them.

21. _____ The best way of evaluating the effect of the school experience on the child is to observe the child over a long period of time.

If you believe that errors are a necessary aspect of learning, how will that affect your approach to teaching and grading? What types of teacher-student interactions might result in classroom discussions?

If you agree that direct experience should be provided prior to experience with verbal abstractions, what would this imply about our reliance on lectures, textbooks, and worksheets in elementary schools today? Whether you agree or disagree with question 20, you will want to give careful study to our *Types of Instruction* chart which is introduced in Chapter 3. It helps teachers to decide when to provide direct experience in their teaching. For each of the above 21 questions, there are no right or wrong answers. However, the assumptions which you make about teaching and learning will radically affect your classroom teaching. You should reflect upon these questions frequently to determine where you stand on each of them. Throughout this book, you will be given the opportunity to make decisions about how you want to teach. If your teaching is not consistent with your beliefs about teaching and learning, then you will not be happy with your work. Unintentionally, you will also be setting a dishonest example for your students.

Our chief purpose in this book is to inform you about your options. We want you, a future teacher, to understand the options which are available to you and the consequences which they imply. By examining your assumptions about teaching and learning, you will be better prepared to make rational choices which reflect your true philosophy. Good luck!

NOTES

1. Personal diary, February 8, 1990.
2. Debbie Koopmeiners, diary for course on children's thinking.
3. Julie Lembeck, diary for course on children's thinking.
4. From two separate diary entries, one from Julie Lembeck and another from Debbie Koopmeiners.
5. Adapted from Kamii (1985), Chapter 1.
6. Personal conversation with Jack Easley, Professor Emeritus, University of Illinois at Urbana-Champaign, June, 1990.

7. Classroom conversation with Bernard Spodek, Professor, University of Illinois at Urbana-Champaign, Spring, 1977.
8. Thanks for this example goes to John McGill (deceased), Professor, University of Illinois at Urbana-Champaign, classroom presentation, Fall, 1976.
9. Personal conversation with Jack Easley, 1980-81.
10. Thanks to my good friend, Rogelio Chavira, for this example (personal conversation, 1986-89).
11. Adapted from Roland Barth, "Open Education: Assumptions About Children's Learning," in Rathbone (1971).

GLOSSARY

assimilation Incorporating a new object (or idea) to an already existing scheme.

accommodation The resistance of an object (or idea) to assimilation. This resistance is a result of the difference between the object (or idea) and the scheme which is being applied to it.

class inclusion A cognitive structure which establishes a system of classifications such that a class can include several subclasses.

cognitive structures An organized pattern of thought which can be applied to experiences in one's world.

conservers Children who understand that the arrangement of a phenomenon (e.g., a row of objects, a piece of clay, etc.) does not effect its identity or measured quantity.

egocentric Tendency to look at one's world from one perspective only; the opposite of "decentering."

non-conservers Children who do not understand that the arrangement of a phenomenon (e.g., a row of objects, a piece of clay, etc.) does not effect its identity or measured quantity.

operations Cognitive structures which are systematized and reflect reversible thought.

part-whole relations The understanding of class inclusion; the knowledge that parts can be contained in a whole.

reversible thought The understanding that an action or idea can be reversed; that is, that an opposite action can be performed which would bring about the state which existed before the initial action was performed; the understanding that an idea can be mentally negated.

schemes Patterns of behavior, either physical or mental.

Chapter
2

Instructional Settings

Not all schools and classrooms are the same. This may seem obvious, but I am frequently surprised by the comments of parents, and even some teachers, who talk as if every school, and every classroom, were alike. For the last ten years, there has been a growing trend among urban school districts to allow parents to choose the type of school or classroom organization that they want their children to attend (Clinchy and Cody, 1978; ASCD, 1990; and *Educational Leadership*, 1990/1). As a result, teachers are frequently required to receive training in ways of organizing schools with which they are not familiar (so they can prepare to teach in them). Although there is great diversity among ways of organizing schools and classrooms, we believe most of these approaches can be classified into one of five patterns to which we have given the following names: 1) Graded, 2) Nongraded, 3) Informal, 4) Alternative Heights, and 5) Clustered. The graded pattern is still the most frequently used of these patterns, and each of the other four patterns developed as a reaction to its faults. In order to understand each of the other patterns, one must have a grasp of the graded approach, and so we begin by discussing it.

TRADITIONAL, SELF-CONTAINED, GRADED SETTINGS

Traditional schools are organized by age-grades. Students who enter school having reached (or about to reach) the age of 6 are assigned to Grade 1. Grade 2 is made up of 7 year olds, and so on. Students are assigned to specific teachers within their grades.

The teacher who a child is assigned to is responsible for that child's education for the school year, and that child will receive most instruction from that teacher. In fact, some children in self-contained, graded classrooms get **all** their instruction from their assigned teacher. In most graded settings, however, the child will receive instructions from two other sources: 1) Specialists who are responsible for teaching the children art, music, or physical education, computers, etc.; and 2) Special education personnel who are responsible for teaching children who have special academic or social needs such as learning disabilities or emotional disturbances. Of course, these specialists are provided in each of the classroom settings which we will describe—not just in the graded settings.

In addition to the age-related feature of graded schools, graded schools are known for two other salient characteristics. First, the content of the curriculum is organized according to grades. That is, certain content is designated for study in Grade 1, certain other content for study in Grade 2, etc. Second, graded schools are known for giving evaluative marks, or "grades" (i.e., A, B, C, D, F), to communicate student progress to parents and school personnel. Since a grade of F connotes failure, some students enter Grade 1 at age 6 but repeat Grade 1 at age 7. These letter grades, or marks, may be based upon comparisons of a student's progress to that of other students of the same age-grade, or they may be based upon an average percentage of scores earned by an individual student on his or her work and tests. (For more on letter grades, see the section in Chapter 6 dealing with evaluation in graded settings.)

One disadvantage of traditional classrooms is that teachers in these settings must prepare to teach their students in all subject areas (except for those areas taught by specialists). Students in any graded classroom may be of the same age, but they usually represent a wide divergence of academic abilities. Preparing for instruction in seven different academic areas can be difficult enough without having to cope with a wide range of abilities and needs! Traditional schools sometimes employ one or more of the following approaches to partially solve this problem.

First, some school principals in traditional settings still try to create homogeneously grouped classrooms. A **homogeneous** classroom is one which the students have been assigned to because of their similar abilities. Thus one Grade 4 teacher may get a class of students who have been assigned to him because they are all considered to be above average in their abilities or achievement. Another Grade 4 teacher may be assigned a class of students who are considered to be average. Still another Grade 4 teacher may be assigned to teach students who are considered to be below average. This manner of assigning students to teachers for a particular grade level is obviously unequal and results in frequent complaints on the part of teachers (they do not want to be assigned classes with low abilities). That may be the reason that not very many schools still employ this approach. Most principals in traditional school settings seem to opt, instead, for **heterogeneously** grouped classrooms. This approach is supported by the arguments of many educators who claim that children who are placed in groups which have a wide range of academic abilities receive a more intellectually enriching and stimulating educational experience than children who are grouped homogeneously.

Second, teachers within a grade level may decide to team-teach for their reading/language arts or mathematics program. For example, a typical elementary school may contain three Grade 2 level classes. In an effort to respond to the range of individual needs within their classrooms, each of these teachers, working in isolation, may create three different basic reader groups, according to reading achievement. However, if they pool their total forces, they may have only a total of three to five basic reader levels within their entire grade. In that case, students can be assigned to appropriate basic reader groups and each teacher can take responsibility for one group. (Or if there are five groups for the entire grade, two teachers will have to teach two groups.) Obviously, this situation is preferred by many teachers since preparing to teach one or two reading groups will take much less time than preparing to teach three. A similar arrangement is frequently made for mathematics.

Third, some teachers in traditional, graded schools opt to teach only particular subjects. For example, one teacher may choose to teach only social studies and reading while another may teach science and mathematics. Thus if a particular grade level in a school has only two classes, these classes will each be assigned to a particular teacher for a homeroom period, but all students will go to one teacher for social studies and reading and another teacher for mathematics and science. Students from Class A may go to the reading/social studies teacher during the morning while students in Class B attend science and math. Then, in the afternoon, students in Class A will attend science and math while Class B attends reading and social studies. This arrangement is usually referred to as **departmentalizing.**

Of course, one of the main approaches which teachers in graded settings make use of to cope with a wide range of individual differences is to behave as if all students in their classroom have the same abilities. Thus, for social studies, science, health, etc. (and in some traditional classrooms, even for reading and/or mathematics), the traditional teacher frequently teaches the entire class as one group. All students are to read the same page together with their teacher, complete the same workbook page when the class is working on that workbook page, etc. Teachers conduct class discussions of material, and they give lessons on particular concepts or skills as they encounter these concepts or skills during the course of the standard curriculum. In this type of setting, the teacher takes the entire class, page-by-page, through the curriculum for each subject area for that grade, for example, first reading, then language arts, then math, etc. (See the sample schedule for traditional settings which is included in the next section of this chapter.)

The traditional, self-contained graded setting is still the most frequently used approach to organizing instruction, but it has many inherent problems. Its goals are typically fixed. They come from the adopted text or curriculum for the school district. That text or curriculum is strongly emphasized. Personal interests of the students may be pursued only if time allows. The adopted curriculum must be covered first. Time is scheduled according to subject areas. (A typical announcement in such a classroom would be, "It's time to quit math and take out your speller.") Repetition and "drill" are usually important means of teaching in such settings. Evaluation is usually competitive; that is, students' grades are frequently based upon comparisons of their work to the work of other students in their grade or class. This can take the form of direct comparisons ("John performed better than Susan on this test and thus deserves a better grade") or indirect comparisons ("This was designed so that those who score 90% correct on it will be awarded a grade of A, 80% will get a B, etc.").

Such an approach may help to prepare children for participation in adult society by stressing such behaviors as following instructions and waiting one's turn for attention. Its chief advantage is that it offers children a predictable environment. They know what to expect in such a setting and they know what is expected of them. And some classes today may not be able to be controlled in any other way. However, its chief disadvantage is that it seems to do an extremely poor job of adjusting to the individual needs of students.

We have said that the traditional, graded pattern of organizing classrooms and schools is the most frequently used pattern. We have also said that the other patterns which we will discuss are a reaction to the faults of this pattern. Before we describe the other four patterns, we must first discuss the issues which have resulted in the development of alternative patterns. While discussing these issues, we will give some contextual examples from each of the five patterns. These should help you to understand some of the basic differences that exist between traditional and more individualized patterns.

ISSUES UNDERLYING THE DIFFERENCES BETWEEN TRADITIONAL AND MORE INDIVIDUALIZED APPROACHES TO INSTRUCTION

We have already mentioned that the traditional method of organizing an elementary school is to classify students into grades, by age, and to assign students of the same grade to a particular teacher in a specific classroom. A student typically spends most of his or her day in that classroom with that teacher. For this reason, such classrooms are usually described as "self-contained." Within a self-contained classroom, the teacher normally schedules instruction according to traditional curriculum divisions. A sample schedule is included here.

S	8:00	General meeting and routine tasks.
C	8:20	Reading and language arts.
H	9:20	Recess.
E	9:35	Reading and language arts (continued).
D	10:05	Math.
U	10:55	Physical Education.
L	11:25	Lunch.
E	12:00	Science and Health (alternating by semesters).
	12:30	Social Studies.
	1:00	Art and Music.
	1:30	Story-time or independent reading.
	1:45	End-of-day routines.
	1:55	Dismissal.

Of course, a teacher in a self-contained classroom usually has the option of deviating from his schedule according to his wishes since the only people affected by such a decision are himself and his students (except during lunch, which is scheduled for several classes simultaneously, or during art, music, or physical education when specialists provide instruction in these areas during scheduled periods).

Self-contained, graded, classrooms are normally confined to the "graded" curriculum. Teachers are sometimes prevented from dealing with instructional content which might interest their students because that content is reserved for use in a different grade. It is assumed that students will be taught specific concepts and skills during particular years. For example, simple addition will be taught in Grade 1, addition with carrying will be taught in Grades 2 and 3, etc. Students are paced together; that is, they are taught as a whole class, one topic or skill at a time. This situation is often referred to as "the lockstep" (Hillson, 1971, pp. 3–13).

The advantage of the lockstep approach, for teachers, is that they know what each student is supposed to be doing at any time—that is, the group task of that moment. The disadvantage of this approach, for students, is that many students are locked into a pace that is either too easy or too difficult. While exceptionally bright students are frequently bored as they wait for other students to catch on to what they have already mastered, slower students are often frustrated because they are being expected to learn things which are either beyond their capabilities or based upon prerequisite skills which they have not yet acquired.

In contrast to the traditional approach just described, an individualized approach to instruction attempts to teach each student at a level which is challenging enough to be of interest without being so difficult that it is frustrating. The philosophy which underlies individualized approaches has radically different assumptions from those of traditional instruction. Where traditional instruction assumes that all children should achieve particular knowledge during particular grades, individualized approaches assume that children should learn according to their individual abilities and at their own respective paces. Where traditional instruction assumes that children must be motivated to learn via grades (i.e., "marks"), individualized approaches prefer to compare children to their own capabilities. And while traditional instruction assumes that students who experience failure will be motivated to try harder next time, individualized approaches assume that all children need to experience success at learning if they are to be motivated to continue their efforts to learn.

During the late 1960s and early 1970s, some teachers and curriculum authors interpreted "individualized" to mean that each student should be provided with a different packet of instructional materials or computer software so that each student could work alone. With this approach, it was very uncommon for any two students to be studying the same content at the same time. This approach to individualizing has now been rejected by most educators.

Another interpretation, one which has survived the 1960s and 1970s and is still widely accepted (Hodgkinson, 1988; Houston, 1989, pp. 34–38), is that small instructional groups should be formed, within the classroom or team, on the basis of each student's current learning needs. For example, a student who has been placed in a group which has been working on simple addition is not kept in that group after learning to add. Once a student has mastered a particular skill, that student is moved to a different instructional group which is working on another concept. Traditional, self-contained, graded classrooms usually teach the whole class of students as one group. However, as we have mentioned in the previous section, for the teaching of reading or mathematics, these classrooms sometimes divide the students into two or three groups (e.g., based on high and low achievement, or high, medium, and low achievement). Frequently, students in the high group for reading also participate in the high group for math, regardless of their skill in math. This type of grouping is actually based on achievement in only one subject area, since students may have been placed in the high group based on reading ability (even though they will also study mathematics with the same group). This form of grouping is very different from the more specific **skills groups** which are common to nongraded, individualized settings.

For example, a student in the high math group in a traditional classroom works on mathematics whenever she participates in the math group, but, over the duration of the year, the particular math concepts which she studies will change. The instructional groups in individualized settings, however, are usually task specific. A student may be in a math group to learn two-digit addition with "carrying" during one instructional period, then move to a reading **achievement group** which may include none of the students from her math group (other than herself). When this student masters two-digit addition with "carrying," she will move on to another mathematics group (for example, a group which is learning about two-digit subtraction with "borrowing") which may or may not include any of the students from her former math group. Children are grouped according to their specific learning needs, that is, students work on those concepts or skills which they are ready to learn, and they usually do this as members of a group of students who have similar needs at that point in time. Groups change frequently—every two to three weeks. Instructional packets and computer software can be used by individual students or small groups of students whenever they assist students in the achievement of instructional goals.

Because there is a great difference between the approaches of traditional classroom settings and those approaches used in more individualized settings, many urban school districts offer parents the opportunity to choose from among a variety of instructional settings for their children. These settings range from the very traditional to the extremely innovative. Individual schools sometimes offer options within their building. For example, one school in a midwestern school district offers three options—one per building wing—traditional, informal, and "middle-of-the-road."

Many school districts also attempt to comply with federal desegregation laws by offering parents the option to send their children to "magnet" schools. These schools are usually located in low-income neighborhoods and have unique programs (for example, a special emphasis on fine arts, or on science, technology, and mathematics) which are designed to be attractive to parents in middle-class and high-income neighborhoods. The term "magnet" is used because, if a school's program can "attract" students from non-minority neighborhoods, then desegregation will be achieved voluntarily. Whether school districts offer alternative instructional settings because of educational philosophy or to comply with desegregation guidelines (many districts offer options for both of these reasons), they frequently distribute brochures so parents can make informed choices (see Figure 2.1, Minneapolis Public School District's *Guide to K-12 programs*). "Word of mouth," however, is still one of the main ways that information about school programs is communicated.

While most of the options provided to parents are usually comprehensively planned by school administrators and school board members, some of these options

Elementary Programs

ALTERNATIVES INCLUDE:

Fundamentals

Burroughs (K-6) .... p. 23
Lincoln (K-6) .... p. 47
Wilder (K-7, will expand to K-8) .... p. 76

Contemporary

Andersen (4-6) .... p. 12
Armatage (K-3) .... p. 15
Cooper (K-3) .... p. 24
Fulton (K-6) .... p. 29
Hamilton (K-4, will expand to K-6) ...... p. 33
Hiawatha (K-3) .... p. 34
Howe (K-3) .... p. 36
Keewaydin (K-3) .... p. 40
Kenny (K-3) .... p. 42
Kenwood (K-6) .... p. 46
Loring (K-3) .... p. 49
Lyndale (4-6) .... p. 50
Morris Park (K-3) .... p. 53
North Star (K-3) .... p. 57
Olson (K-6) .... p. 59
Putnam (3-6) .... p. 62
Sheridan (4-6) .... p. 66
Tuttle (K-6) .... p. 69
Waite Park (4-6) .... p. 70
Wenonah (K-3) .... p. 73
Wilder (4-6) .... p. 74

Continuous Progress

AT&T Site (formerly Seward) (K-7, will expand to K-8) ... p. 17
Bancroft (3-6) .... p. 18
Bethune (K-3) .... p. 21
Ericsson (K-2) .... p. 27
Field (4-6) .... p. 28
Hale (K-3) .... p. 30
Holland (4-6) .... p. 35
Jefferson (K-6) p.37

Open

Andersen (K-8) .... p. 14
Barton (K-8) .... p. 19
Marcy (K-6) .... p. 52
Webster (K-8) .... p. 72
Windom (K-8) .... p. 80

Montessori

Hall (K-6) .... p. 30
Seward (K-6) .... p. 65

MAGNETS INCLUDE:

American Indian Program within Andersen Schools (K-8, 4-6) .... p. 12-14
American Indian and French Immersion at Mt. Sinai Site (K-8) .... p. 55
International/Fine Arts at Ramsey (K-8) .... p. 63
Math/Science/Technology at Sheridan (K-3, expanding to K-8) .... p. 67
Math/Science/Technology at Pillsbury Site (K-6) .... p. 61
Math/Science/Technology at Wilder (K-5, expanding to K-8) .... p. 77
Math/Science/Technology at Willard (K-6) .... p. 79
Public School Academy at Bethune (K-6) .... p. 22
Spanish Immersion at Jefferson (K-8) .... p. 39
Urban Environmental at Dowling (K-6) .... p. 26
Urban Environmental at Northrop (K-6) .... p. 67
Urban Environmental at Shingle Creek (K-4, expanding to K-6) .... p. 68

MIDDLE SCHOOLS:

Anthony (6-8) .... p. 81
Anwatin (6-8) .... p. 83
Chiron (5-8) .... p. 84
Folwell (6-8) .... p. 86
Franklin (6-8) .... p. 87
Northeast (6-8) .... p. 88
Sanford (6-8) .... p. 90

Also see elementary programs with 6-8 grades listed in index above.

Figure 2.1 1991 Guide to Early Education, Kindergarten, Elementary, and Middle School Programs, Minneapolis Public Schools (Used with Permission).

simply develop as a result of the initiative of individual teachers, groups of teachers of like minds, or the leadership of a school principal.

Options in instructional settings have become a fact of life in the urban school district. Although some rural school districts still offer only the traditional school program, features of more innovative instructional settings are usually incorporated into these traditional programs. There is a growing trend among school districts in the nation to experiment with various approaches to organizing for instruction. Teachers must be prepared to function in any type of setting in which they may be required to work. Our purpose in this text is to inform those who are preparing to teach about the types of school organizations which exist. We classified the total variety of instructional settings into five "patterns" to simplify the extensive variety which exists among school and classroom settings. While some approaches may not fit neatly into any one pattern, we believe that all settings combine features taken from two or more of the patterns which we are describing. We have already described the traditional, graded setting. Let us turn, now, to each of the remaining approaches.

TEAM-TAUGHT, NONGRADED, INDIVIDUALIZED SETTINGS

Trust Elementary School is a nongraded school. When it comes to the organization of the school, this means two things. First, the school is divided into teams, comprised of children and teachers, which follow a cooperative teaching arrangement. For example, Susie's team contains 87 children for which three teachers, including Susie, are responsible. Second, the organization of instruction in these teams is nongraded.

Nongraded programs have two basic features. First, students are not confined to instructional content which is intended for a specific grade level. There is no "ceiling" or "floor" to their learning. In a nongraded school, any student who is capable of working on mathematics material reserved for Grade 5 may do so. A student may study Grade 5 mathematics content at the age of 7 (although, at this age, the student in question would be in Grade level 2 if she were attending a graded school) just as 11 year old children who are not capable of learning this material may be assigned to less advanced tasks. In other words, the lockstep of the grade is eliminated and grade levels do not determine what instructional content is assigned to students. Personnel in nongraded schools firmly believe that age is not an appropriate criterion for determining what content the students should learn. Rather, they believe that students should be assigned learning tasks according to their existing capabilities and knowledge.

Second, marks (i.e., "grades" such as "A," "B," "C," etc.) are **not** part of the nongraded school's evaluation process. Student progress is not evaluated by comparison to other students. Instead, students are evaluated in terms of progress toward goals which they can achieve. These goals come from the school's curriculum; that is, the school has one set of goals and each student is expected to achieve only those goals which she is capable of achieving. Personnel in nongraded schools assume that some students will achieve all school goals and even many of the goals for the middle school and high school curriculum. They also assume that some other students may not master all the elementary school's goals in the time that they spend there. Thus, a student who attends elementary school for a specified number of years (e.g., six) and then leaves elementary school to begin middle school will be assessed at the receiving middle school where her education is to be continued.

In other words, expectations for students depend upon their capabilities and existing knowledge. The student is her own baseline, and she is evaluated according to progress made towards her own goals—goals which have been assigned by the teacher based on his assessment of the students' knowledge and ability (Hillson and Bongo, 1971, p. 8).

In nongraded settings, children are assigned to multi-aged classrooms. While a traditional, graded, classroom may have 30 children who are each 7 years of age, a multi-aged classroom may have 30 children who vary in ages from 6–8 years. In a team-taught, nongraded, setting, children are not assigned to one classroom alone. Rather, they are assigned to a team of several classrooms and teachers.

At Trust School, teams are limited to a maximum age difference of three years. Primary teams, which are made up of children aged 5–7, or 6–8, are located in particular wings of the school building. Each primary team is situated adjacent to an intermediate team which is made up of children aged 8–10 or 9–12. A cooperative teaching arrangement, in which all teachers on the team are responsible for the education of that team's students, enables teachers to group students according to the individual needs of their students. Groups are disbanded and new groups are formed according to the instructional needs of the students. This contrasts with the typical grouping in traditional, self-contained, classrooms. These usually have two to three homogeneous groups which, once established, never disband until the end of the school year. In team-taught settings, an hour is usually set aside in the teacher's daily schedule for collaborative or individual planning. This planning period may occur in the morning before students arrive, in the afternoon after the students have left, or during the day while specialists (e.g., art, music, and physical education teachers) teach the team's students.

Trust School's decision-making is structured to maximize teacher input while minimizing the amount of teacher time that must be spent on schoolwide matters. Each team has a team leader who represents it at weekly meetings which are attended by the principal, the team leaders, and any other interested staff. At these meetings, decisions are made which affect curriculum and school procedures. Frequently, solutions to particular problems are discussed at these meetings and then presented by the team leaders to the other team members during the meetings of the individual teams. At a subsequent weekly meeting, the team leader votes for the position which holds a consensus among his team's members. Meetings of the entire faculty occur regularly, but these meetings do not deal with curriculum since this is taken care of during the weekly meetings of the principal and team leaders. Consequently, meetings of the entire faculty are short, fun, and to the point.

The organization of the curriculum at Trust School reflects a strong emphasis on the use of instructional objectives. **Instructional objectives** state what the students need to know, do, or become in order to be successful in work, school, and society. An example of an instructional objective for an elementary mathematics curriculum would be:

"The student will solve two-digit addition problems with **regrouping (carrying)**."

Trust School makes use of lists of instructional objectives which have been developed by teachers, commercial publishers of curricula which have been adopted by the school district, or a research and development center for education (Board of Regents, University of Wisconsin, 1972). These objectives have been sequenced according to difficulty or, sometimes, according to the list-writer's ideas about the most logical order in which students should learn the objectives. After administering a written assessment to each student to determine which objectives a student has already mastered, each student is placed in an instructional group or in an independent program. This kind of assessment-placement procedure is followed for each student in the areas of mathematics and in the reading-related areas of word attack, comprehension, and study skills. The intention of such a placement is to give each student a learning task which is neither so advanced that it causes failure for the student, nor so unchallenging that it bores the student (because the material has already been mastered). Usually, these lists of objectives are organized according to levels (several objectives are listed for any one level). In abbreviated form, these objectives are listed on individual cards, one card per student, so that teachers can easily keep track of which objectives each student has mastered (see Figure 2.2).

An alternative to using cards to manage a curriculum which is organized according to objectives would be to keep track of each students' progress by using a micro-computer and a software program designed for this purpose.

The assignment of specific instructional goals to students is based on a belief that, by working on concepts which they are capable of mastering, the student will experience success. According to this line of reasoning, consistent experiences with success at learning should, ultimately, foster success at learning in general. ("Success breeds success.") (Frazier, 1980). Another assumption of this approach is that it is unfair to expect students to learn things when they do not have the prerequisite knowledge which is necessary for learning these things. It would be unfair, for example, to expect a student in mathematics to learn to carry before she had learned to add.

An assumption which underlies the objectives-based approach to instruction is that any particular concept can be broken down into smaller steps which, when achieved, make the understanding of that concept easy. To be able to understand the arithmetic process of "carrying," for example, one must first understand simple addition, place-value, and regrouping. Lists of specific objectives in curricula are an attempt to itemize the small steps which are necessary to achieve more general instructional goals.

Organizing a team's efforts at instruction according to objectives enables teachers to meet the individual needs of students in several ways. First, as we have already pointed out, the student is able to work on something which she is capable of achieving rather than being obliged to take pot luck on her ability to master a particular concept or skill. In a traditional classroom, tasks are often assigned to the entire class regardless of variations in the achievement of individuals. Second, the **pace** of the instruction can be varied according to the aptitudes of individual students. It may take a very gifted student two weeks to master "carrying," while a more typical student could spend several months mastering this skill. In a team arrangement such as the one at Trust School, students can usually proceed at their own pace. Instructional groups can be established for students who experience the same needs simultaneously and these groups can then be disbanded when they no longer serve a useful purpose.

WISCONSIN DESIGN FOR READING SKILL DEVELOPMENT

© 1972-The Board of Regents of the University of Wisconsin System   V36037X   LITTON ABS

LEVEL A:

- 1 Rhyming words
- 2 Rhyming phrases
- 3 Shapes
- 4 Letters, numbers
- 5 Words, phrases
- 6 i — Colors
- 7 Initial consonants

All A skills

WORD ATTACK

NOTE: Skills marked **i** are assessed by a performance test or teacher observation.

LEVEL C:

- 1 i — Sight vocabulary
- 2 Consonant variants
- 3 Consonant blends
- 4 Long vowels
- 5 Vowel + <u>r</u>, <u>a</u>+<u>l</u>, <u>a</u>+<u>w</u>
- 6 Diphthongs
- 7 Long & short <u>oo</u>
- 8 Middle vowel
- 9 Two vowels separated
- 10 Two vowels together
- 11 Final vowel
- 12 Consonant digraphs
- 13 Base words
- 14 Plurals
- 15 Homonyms
- 16 Synonyms, antonyms
- 17 i — Independent application
- 18 Multiple meanings

All C skills

WISCONSIN DESIGN FOR READING SKILL DEVELOPMENT

PUPIL NAME _____ DATE _____

UNIT ____ GRADE ____ SPECIAL CODE ____ LEVEL ____

SKILL	RS	M	%C

LEVEL D:

- 1 i — Sight vocabulary
- 2 Consonant blends
- 3 Silent letters
- 4 Syllabication
- 5 Accent
- 6 Unaccented schwa
- 7 Possessives

All D skills

LEVEL B:

- 1 i — Sight vocabulary
- 2 i — Left-right sequence
- 3 Beginning consonants
- 4 Ending consonants
- 5 Consonant blends
- 6 Rhyming elements
- 7 Short vowels
- 8 Consonant digraphs
- 9 Compound words
- 10 Contractions
- 11 Base words
- 12 Plurals
- 13 Possessives

All B skills

DATE	NO. OF SKILLS	GROWTH
____	____	____
____	____	____
____	____	____
____	____	____
____	____	____
____	____	____

Figure 2.2 Keysort Card from Wisconsin Design for Reading Skill Development: Word Attack, published by The University of Wisconsin, Madison (Used with Permission).

Another advantage of organizing curriculum according to objectives is that some objectives may be attainable for some students while other students may be incapable of ever reaching them. In a curriculum based on objectives, the delivery of the curriculum is individualized and students are not held accountable for the achievement of goals which they are not capable of achieving.

When instruction is organized according to objectives, a variety of instructional materials can be collected to help in the teaching of any particular objective. These instructional materials can be stored in a central location within a school building. Usually, activities for teaching a particular objective, as well as any materials necessary for carrying out these activities, are stored in a packet labeled according to objective. Teachers can then make use of these packets whenever they find the need to form an instructional group to focus on an objective. Sometimes a particular activity intended for teaching an objective meets with failure for a particular group of students. When this happens, a teacher can try one of the many other activities which is described in the school's packet for that objective. In this way, students with similar instructional needs who have different learning styles can be assisted with instructional materials most suited to their individual learning styles.

There are also times when a particular student may be the only one who needs to work on a particular objective at that point in the academic year. When this occurs, self-instructional materials (such as the self-teaching activities described in Chapter 5) can be provided to students so that they can proceed with learning what they most need to learn.

If you have gotten the impression, from what you have read thus far, that teachers in nongraded settings do not hold their students to high expectations, you have jumped to an incorrect conclusion. Teachers in nongraded settings do hold their students to high expectations, but they apply these expectations on an individual basis. Graded settings, on the other hand, apply the same expectations to each of their students; those who can easily attain these expectations and those who can attain these expectations only with great difficulty are all evaluated according to the same criteria. Now let's take a look at how a team organizes for instruction in a nongraded setting.

The Organization of a Team

When the academic year began at Trust Elementary School, Ted's team consisted of three teachers and 87 students, ages 6–8. (These students would have been placed in Grades 1 and 2 in a traditional school.) Students were randomly grouped into three heterogeneous homerooms. These three teachers met during workshop week to plan their instructional program and to decide the extent to which they would team-teach as they began their year. Because these teachers were new to each other and their students, they opted for a team structure which allowed for a modest degree of collaboration at the beginning with the opportunity to increase the degree to which they collaborated as they progressed through the academic year. They agreed to consider "all students in common" and to meet regularly to discuss the progress of their 87 students. They set up a common schedule.

S	8:00	Teacher planning, individual or as a team.
C	8:55	"Homeroom" period. Teachers meet with students assigned
H		to their respective homerooms. Attendance and lunch count
E		is taken. Students are "settled in." Daily schedule is reviewed.
D		Personal concerns are discussed.
U	9:15	Communications period for the team. Students move to the teacher
L		and room which they have been assigned to for this period.
E		Reading and language arts are taught during this period.
	10:15	Team recess.
	10:30	Communications (continued).
	11:15	Word Attack skills (team).
	11:45	Lunch.
	12:50	Students return. Homeroom period.
	1:05	Math (team groups).
	1:45	Music or Art.
	2:15	Physical education.
	2:45	Social studies/science/health.
	3:15	Homerooms.
	3:40	Dismissal.

The teachers on this team agreed to collaborate at first in two instructional areas: mathematics and word attack skills for reading. They decided to teach the students in their own homerooms during all other periods, but they also agreed to extend their collaboration, throughout the year, as opportunities arose.

They decided to write their own instructional objectives for mathematics by determining which of the objectives listed in the adopted math program were essential for the advancement of their students in this area. One of the teachers developed a pretest which assessed each student's knowledge for each objective. This test was administered to the students during the first few school days; the results were recorded on individual student cards, and students were then placed in instructional groups according to their needs in the area of mathematics. Each teacher on the team took responsibility for two to five math groups. These groups were regarded as temporary. When a particular student was thought to have mastered an objective, she was placed in another group which dealt with another of that student's instructional needs. Groups were disbanded and formed as student needs changed. The teacher in charge of a student's instructional group made the judgment about whether she had mastered that objective. This judgment was based on that teacher's personal observation of the child's work, samples of the student's written work, or the results of a written posttest.

For instruction in word attack skills for reading, students were administered a pretest which had been developed by an educational research and development center. This test assessed student mastery of each instructional objective in the word attack curriculum. The results of these tests were entered on individual keysort cards such as the one displayed in Figure 2.2 of this chapter. Any objective which the student has passed is "punched out" on that student's keysort card (see Figure 2.3).

Figure 2.3 Sample Keysort Card

Thus, when the teachers for this team wanted to create instructional groups, they simply aligned all the keysort cards for students on their team (e.g., with Level A of each card on the left, Level B of each card on the bottom etc.), inserted a pin through the hole next to any particular objective (A-5, for example), and shook the pin from side to side. This caused all the cards which had been punched out to fall to the table below. The cards remaining on the pin were the cards belonging to those students who had not yet mastered that specific objective. Those which had fallen to the table belonged to students who had been determined, by the test, to have mastered that objective.

By this simple pin-sorting procedure, the teachers were able to form several instructional groups, and divide up responsibility for these groups, once every two weeks during their teacher-planning periods. The groups were continued for two to three weeks until the teachers on the team were of the opinion that a majority of the students had either mastered their objectives or had received as much instruction in them as could be beneficial for them at that time. Then a posttest was administered, the results were recorded on the student cards, and new instructional groups were formed. Similar cards, with a similar pin-sorting procedure, were used to manage the mathematics program.

I need to point out that many teachers in team-taught settings prefer to form instructional groups in a manner very different from that which I have just described. **Achievement-grouping** allows teachers to cut down on the differences in academic range which would be present among students in a normal, heterogeneously grouped, homeroom. By grouping students according to basic reader levels for reading instruction, or according to general achievement in mathematics (e.g., how much content of a math text the students have covered), teachers in team-taught settings can create groups which are more homogeneous than the groups they would be able to form if they were in a traditional, self-contained setting.

The range of academic achievement among students in an achievement group is probably less than the range of academic achievement for a skill group which has been formed for instruction in a specific objective (e.g., as those described for Trust School's team were). The achievement-grouping approach has advantages and disadvantages when compared to skills groups. By forming achievement groups, teachers are able to minimize planning (they can simply follow the page-by-page instructions given in the Teacher's Manual) and provide extended continuity for the group. (Groups usually last for the entire school year.)

However, grouping according to specific objectives offers another kind of homogeneity: similarity of specific instructional needs. Every student in a particular skills group needs instruction in that specific skill which is being taught to the group. In contrast, when a student in an achievement group has a specific skill need, the teacher must choose between providing some type of individual assistance (e.g., tutoring) or instructing an entire group in a skill which is giving difficulty to only one of the group's students.

Aside from the grouping arrangement for word-attack skills, the "communication" period of Trust School's team began the year in much the same way as the self-contained classrooms would have begun. Each teacher was in charge of his or her homeroom students for instruction in reading and language arts. It did not take long for more collaboration to develop, however. Two of the team members, Susie and Nancy, preferred to form achievement groups for instruction with the basic readers. After they had assessed their students and placed them in basic reader levels, they divided their responsibilities according to instructional levels, that is, one teacher took the lower levels of basic reader groups while the other teacher took the higher ones. This arrangement cut in half the total number of groups that each teacher would have needed to form if they had been teaching in self-contained, traditional settings.

Next, another arrangement—this one affecting the entire team—was made. Although the third teacher, Ted, did not make use of basic reader groups for his communications program, all three of the teachers on the team agreed that Ted's program would best benefit those students who were most capable of independent work. Students were subsequently moved, in individual cases, into or out of Ted's classroom based on the teacher's judgments about the child's learning style. This process of exchanging students began about six weeks into the school year and continued throughout the school year.

Soon after this last team arrangement was made, Nancy, who was teaching the high achievement groups for reading, became interested in a program which Ted was using during the communications period (Wachs, 1974). The program consisted of sets of games which were intended to help students to develop certain skills which are seldom given much attention in elementary classrooms. Nancy and Ted decided to prepare only specific kinds of games; for example, Ted prepared the gross motor games while Nancy prepared the discriminative movement games. They exchanged their students on alternate days so that each student received experience with each type of game.

As the respective reading programs of these three teachers gained momentum, it became clear to them that their team had many struggling readers at each age level. These students needed an instructional program that was different from anything that these three teachers were presently offering. In response to this need, Susie, who had been teaching the lower achievement groups, volunteered to pilot a new program, LEIR II (Allen & Allen, 1970), and so the team regrouped its students to facilitate instruction for those students who had been identified for participation in this pilot program. This decision was made in December.

Another collaborative decision was made prior to the conclusion of the school year. In April, Nancy and Ted decided to schedule certain groups of students into each other's respective programs on alternate days during part of the communications period. This was done so that Ted's more independent learners could take advantage of Nancy's creative dramatics program and so that Nancy's students could take advantage of Ted's phonics and creative writing program. By this time, the team had completed its word attack grouping for the year, but Ted was continuing his phonics/writing program (Spalding & Spalding, 1969).[1]

Collaboration for social studies instruction developed shortly after the math and word attack programs had been established. Teachers took turns taking charge of the general planning for a social studies unit to be used with the entire team. All three teachers on the team taught groups of children for these units and each teacher made his or her own lesson plans. Science instruction was taught during the same period as social studies (see schedule on page 38), but in alternate academic quarters. For science, a selection of three or more units were offered (one unit per teacher, and more than three units were offered when either the principal or the district science specialist was available to teach one). Students chose to participate in one of the units being offered. Usually, these were Elementary Science Study (ESS) units.[2] When too many students chose a particular unit, some of those students were assigned to the unit which they had designated as their "second choice."

Physical education was the combined responsibility of the physical education specialist and the teaching team. The specialist instructed one-half of the team's students each day and the team members took turns teaching the remaining students. Art and music education were taught by specialists.

Of course, there were more minor collaborations developed by the team, but these were for brief periods of time (three weeks or less) and were too numerous to mention. The "activity choices" in the next section are an example of this type of co-planning.

The Organization of One Team Member's Classroom

Now that we have discussed collaboration among team members, we will explain how one teacher functions in this type of setting. Because every teacher is unique, different teachers will display many variations in the way they function on a team. First, because he is a member of a teaching team and his students are instructed by different teachers during different periods of the day, Ted's day is scheduled more carefully than it would need to be if he were teaching in a self-contained classroom. In addition to the team schedule which was agreed to by the members of the team (see page 38), whenever Ted teamed with another teacher for any part of the school day, additional scheduling arrangements had to be made. Ted's individual schedule changed during the course of the year, but, in mid-November, it looked like this:

S	8:00	Team or individual planning.
C	8:55	Students arrive. Homeroom period. Teacher-pupil
H		planning. "Share-time."
E	9:15	Communications.
D	10:15	Recess.
U	10:30	Communications (continued).
L	11:15	Wisconsin Design for Reading: Word Attack Skills.
E	11:45	Lunch dismissal.
	12:50	Students return. Homeroom period.
	1:05	Math.
	1:45	Music or Art (Prep time).
	2:15	Physical education (Prep time, two of three days).
	2:45	Social studies/Science/Health.
	3:15	Activity choices.
	3:45	Dismissal.

Each teacher on the team provided one of the "Activity choices"—for example, papier-mâché, weaving, building structures—among which the students chose for the period which began at 3:15. Ted's schedule **within** the communications period, and a brief description of the activities which took place, is included in Box 2-1.

Box 2-1 **Ted's Schedule for Communications**

9:15 *Storytime.* Read story aloud to children. Read samples of children's writing from the previous day.

9:30 *Independent writing:*
Proficient readers write stories independently, seeking assistance for ideas and spelling as needed.

Phonograms:
Beginning readers receive instruction in printing and sound-letter relations.[3]

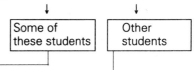

| Some of these students | Other students |

Individualized reading[4]:
Students read independently from trade books and basic readers. Teacher briefly listens to each student reading, asks questions, and makes notations about reading strategies.

Language experience[5]:
Children ask teacher for "key words." Teacher writes key words on *Language Master* cards. Children tie cards together to make story-sentences. Each child reads own story-sentence to the group. Story-sentences are displayed daily.

Work cards: Activities in comprehension assigned to students in individualized reading program.

Spelling: Teacher meets with these students to give practice in using phonograms in the writing of regularly spelled words.

10:15   RECESS   RECESS   RECESS   RECESS

10:30: *Spelling:*

Teacher meets with groups which have been formed due to patterns of errors discovered in the writings of these students.

Activity centers and learning centers[6]:

During this period, these students are encouraged to play or work at any of these centers or to work on any other activity of their choice.

10:45 *Activity centers,
        learning centers, and games:*

During this period, these students are encouraged to work or play at any of the centers or to develop a project or to work on any other instructional activity of their own choosing.

Games[7]: These games were designed to help primary-aged children develop those kinds of "thinking" skills which are not commonly taught in schools but which are important for success in school-related tasks. (e.g., large and small-motor thought, logical, social thought, etc.).

At 9:15 ("storytime") all students are together as a group. At 9:30 students are divided into one of two groups ("independent writing" and "phonograms") according to their needs and capabilities. These activities last about 20-25 minutes. Then, as students from "independent writing" finish their compositions, they begin "individualized reading." Meanwhile, students in "phonograms" are divided into two groups—those who are capable of participating in "individualized reading" and those who need instruction via language experience. About 15 minutes later, most students who are involved with "individualized reading" begin to complete "work cards." The students who were receiving instruction via language experience are then given instruction in spelling. Recess occurs at 10:15 and students resume work at 10:30. Ted gives spelling instruction to those students who were involved with individualized reading and work cards before recess. Meanwhile, those students who had been instructed with language experience and spelling (before recess) are independently pursuing their own interests in the activity and learning centers. Finally, at 10:45 students from the left-hand column choose to participate in one of many activity centers, learning centers, or games while Ted supervises the games (in which all students from the right-hand column participate).

In sum, in the team-taught, nongraded setting, students work on tasks which they are capable of achieving, at their own pace, with materials appropriate to their learning styles, and they are not expected to achieve goals which are unattainable for them. Organization of instruction in such a school is truly individualized. However, this approach has a set of assumptions about how knowledge is acquired which, when rigidly adhered to, can complicate the process of instruction. By oversimplifying the process by which the student acquires new knowledge, it can interfere with a teacher's good sense and hinder his ability to approach learning as the holistic matter that it often is. Ted's team seems to have avoided many of the potential hazards of this setting by varying the purposes for which they group their students.

INFORMAL, SELF-CONTAINED, FAMILY-GROUPED SETTINGS
(This section was written by Peter Frost and Robert Louisell)

While nongraded schools differ from graded schools in their elimination of the lockstep and in their focus on teaching objectives rather than "covering the text," informal schools differ from both graded and nongraded settings because they provide students with choices about what to learn. These choices occur within the context of what British educators like to call "topic work." **Topic work** is virtually synonymous with **unit work,** a term developed by progressive American educators who were trying to apply John Dewey's beliefs about education to practices in schools during the first half of this century.

In topic work, teachers and children pool together their resources to plan a program of activities which will integrate skills across the entire curriculum. A **theme** is selected (for example, "Ourselves") and teachers and children brainstorm to identify topics which relate to the theme and will interest the students. When teachers use this approach, they must consciously strive to provide a balance of skills which cross the entire curriculum in the long run. For example, a teacher may select a theme which

CORE PREDICTION

MATHS	SCIENCE	ENGLISH

Figure 2.4 Skills Chart

emphasizes science concepts during the beginning of the year; however, the next theme selected might stress social studies knowledge. When planning themes for the year, teachers may make use of a chart such as Figure 2.4. These can be used to keep track of which skills will be emphasized before the conclusion of the school year.

Resources which will be used in the teaching of the theme (i.e., topic) are then collected and made. The teacher decides how the topic will be organized and how it will be introduced. Next, the teacher develops a long-term plan which projects how the topic will develop, stage by stage, while the students are involved with it. He also describes each activity which he plans to provide in order to teach the topic, and he lists the skills which he intends to teach through these activities. These skills are often chosen on the basis of the needs of the majority of the members of the class. Of course, this long-term plan is only a projection which is used for planning, and the teacher does not stick religiously to his plan when the students come up with questions to pursue which he has not anticipated. However, if a teacher has given careful thought to his long-term plan, he will be better prepared to make judgments about when to depart from this plan. Evaluation of students progress during topic work is done in a variety of ways which include "before and after" records of individual students, skill checklists, and written records of teacher observations. (See Chapter 6, *Assessing Student Learning*, for further information about evaluation in this setting.)

Informal classrooms are frequently **family-grouped.** This means that a range of ages will be found among the children in such classrooms. Usually, the range of ages does not exceed three (for example, ages 6–8). Just as nongraded and graded settings demonstrate philosophical differences related to how children should be grouped (i.e., by age, in graded schools, or by instructional needs, in nongraded settings), so do various informal settings disagree about whether to group vertically or horizontally. **Vertical grouping** refers to "mixed age" grouping (a synonym for "family grouping"). It is a form of multi-aged grouping. **Horizontal grouping,** on the other hand, groups children according to common ages (as in graded settings).

The arguments for vertical grouping go something like this. Young children (ages 4–7 in England, or 5–7 in America) need the security of a classroom system which is consistent from day to day and year to year. In a vertically grouped classroom, older children will have been members of the classroom for one or two years already. They will be very familiar with the routines and expectations of their teacher and will therefore be able to help younger children to "settle in" to their classroom. They will also be able to assist younger children in simple academic tasks (e.g., checking their addition work) and non-academic routines (e.g., tying a young student's shoe, or helping a young child with her coat and mittens). As the young children become more familiar with class routines, they, in turn, help other younger children with their adjustment to the classroom. The responsibility which children demonstrate in such a setting relieves the teacher of some mundane tasks and enables him to move between groups better and to function more as a teacher. Furthermore, within this type of structure, the teacher can form groups based on age, or homogeneous groups (based on achievement), whenever his purposes require this. Since a student remains with one teacher for a period of three years in vertical grouping arrangements, the teacher is in an ideal position to get to know the child, and her instructional needs well. This will help to insure that appropriate skill and concept development is provided for each child.

The arguments for horizontal grouping can be summarized in the following manner. It is important that teachers work with a manageable range of achievement among their students. Horizontal grouping reduces the range of achievement with which a teacher will have to deal. This enables teachers to teach the whole class at once for most of their activities. Also, horizontal grouping avoids one of the dangers of vertical grouping; that is, that a child might form a negative relationship with her teacher and be locked into that negative relationship for a period of three years.[8]

Occasionally, American classrooms will set up informal classrooms within schools which follow the traditional, graded, structure. Some schools will even designate one wing of a building for informal teaching, leaving other wings for more traditional approaches, and offer parents a choice as to which type of education they prefer for their own children.[9] Many British primary schools follow the informal pattern, and some informal settings in America are attempting to "import" the best aspects of these British schools to the United States.

Time in informal classroom settings is dealt with in an entirely different manner than it is for either graded or nongraded settings. It would be misleading to assume that children are roaming around with complete freedom to do whatever they wish. However, it would be equally misleading to assume that children follow a rigid schedule, moving from one learning center to the next at the sound of a bell. In truth, most teachers make use of a "group system" for about two-thirds of the school day. In such a system, about five groups of students are involved in five different activities which have been carefully arranged. For some of these group activities, children undertake individual tasks within the context of their groups. For other group activities, children may cooperate and share tasks. For example, a problem may have been posed which should be solved by the group. Or roles may have been arranged within the group so that students could complete some group task.

In some cases, each subgroup within the class rotates among each of the activities (e.g., the five group activities referred to above). This must be done flexibly because different groups will have students of varying capabilities and the activities must adjust to the students. In other classrooms, class subgroups do not rotate among the different activities. However, at the end of the day, teachers in these classrooms will have a sharing time in which children discuss the tasks which they pursued, and the things which they learned, while participating in the activities for their respective groups.

Generally, when teachers employ this group approach to managing their learning centers, they specify which centers and activities are required for each group. One group may complete the work at each of the centers except one. Another group may complete only the first four of these centers. Still another group may complete the first four of the learning centers plus one additional center which has been developed specifically for them.

Sometimes, groups are rotated among centers by days rather than within one day. For example, group #1 may be at learning center #5 on Monday. On Tuesday this same group could then work at learning center #1; on Wednesday, at learning center #2; etc. Or at the beginning of each week, the children of each group may be given a suggested "cycle" of centers which they are to complete by the end of the week, as a group, in any order that they prefer. Certain free activities then become available to the student in each group as they complete their required cycle.

Other teachers prefer to schedule whole class sessions or small group sessions throughout the week and to allow students to complete their learning center assign-ments during their unscheduled time. With either approach to grouping, teachers in informal settings discuss assignments at the start and end of each day, and while assisting individuals and small groups throughout the day. This helps to insure that children understand their tasks clearly and are pursuing them correctly.

The term "integrated day" has been used to describe the approach to time which informal classrooms usually employ. The most important aspect of this approach, as far as the use of time goes, is that while graded and nongraded classrooms schedule specific times by subjects (e.g., math, social studies, reading and language arts, art, etc.), informal classrooms normally have several of these subjects integrated into the learning tasks for any group activity which they have provided at any one of their learning stations. This makes it extremely important that the teacher plan her learning centers in such a way as to vary her obligations to assist; that is, some learning centers should involve a little amount of teacher time while the students are working at them. This will free the teacher to spend more time assisting students at other centers. It also makes it possible for the teacher to spend some time roving among centers, checking on student progress and identifying which students will need help.

The teacher's work in this type of setting is more that of a "facilitator" than it is that of a whole-class instructor. He listens to his students and guides them in directions which he believes will be productive for them as learners. He teaches individuals, small groups, and the entire class as he is needed. He checks on the progress of individuals and groups.

Since groups play a key role in the organization of the classroom, the teacher must be sure to bring the entire class together for periods of sharing. This prevents students from becoming too isolated from their other class members and provides students with an opportunity to communicate what they have learned. In addition to these periods of sharing, the teacher will usually have a teacher-student discussion period during the first part of the morning. During this discussion period, students and teacher will discuss the tasks of the day and raise any questions or related problems which they have identified. Also, students will use this period to share stories or to show things which they have brought to school for the other students and the teacher to see.

These discussions normally occur on a carpeted area of the classroom; one which has no chairs on it but which is large enough to provide space for all the students and the teacher.

Of course, any informal teacher will provide some whole class experiences during the week. These may include writing practice, discussions, oral work in mathematics, discussions of findings and problems which have come up through the ongoing topic work, and story reading during which the teacher reads to the entire class. There will also be whole class experiences which take place outside of the classroom; for example, physical education, school assemblies, etc.

The use of space in informal classrooms is very different from the use of space in most graded classrooms. The most traditional use of space in a graded classroom is one with desks in rows and the teacher's desk somewhere in the front of the classroom. In informal classrooms, room must be set aside for learning centers (where most of the topic work is done) and large areas for whole class discussions. Informal settings can be self-contained or can involve some team-teaching.

In self-contained, informal classrooms, a variety of areas are required. There is usually a carpeted area, mentioned already, at which students and teacher can meet to introduce activities at the beginning of the day, to discuss findings at the conclusion of a day, and to carry out group activities during any time which they may be needed throughout the day. Ideally, this area should be somehow "separate" from the rest of the room so that a sense of privacy and calm is created. There should also be a "wet" area, usually tiled and near a sink, at which messy activities (e.g., art and science activities) can take place. Sand and water tables, if they are included in primary classrooms, are placed in this area. Some teachers arrange each of the parts of their classrooms according to the activities which will take place there. Thus, resources which will be needed for these types of activities can be sorted in cabinets and storage trays which provide ready access for the students.

When teachers from neighboring classrooms team-teach, space can be better economized. There are two large areas, one in each room, which are set aside in order to provide each class with a "home base." Between these two home bases, and in any other space not reserved for this use, space is subdivided into "shared areas" which allows children from two classes to share materials and space. A wet area will be provided. A "quiet area" will also be provided. A diagram of a typical arrangement between two classes is provided in Figure 2.5. Some American teachers even share classroom space by designating one room a "noisy" activities area and the other room a "quiet" room.

The philosophy of informal classrooms includes the idea that the classroom environment should interest the students in learning. Classroom displays, educational bulletin boards, and the like, can be found in every available space in the best examples of these classrooms (see the photographs, Figure 2.6, on the following pages). Artifacts

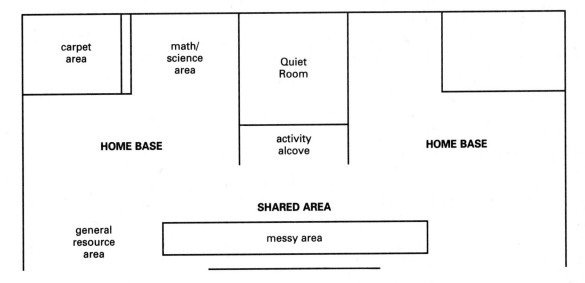

Figure 2.5 Diagram of a Two-Class Unit

Figure 2.6 Scenes from an Informal Classroom

and materials which can be handled and used by the students are set out throughout the classroom. Student work is mounted and displayed. When one walks into a typical informal classroom, one can tell, from the materials displayed, exactly what topics are presently being studied.

The informal setting demands a tremendous amount of planning on the part of the teacher. We will describe the details of this planning process in the last section of Chapter 5 of this text.

Teachers in this setting spend much more of their time interacting with individual students than they do in graded or nongraded settings. The teacher appears to be more "busy" in this type of setting. Sometimes, long lines of students may be waiting to get assistance from the teacher. Obviously, teacher aides and parent volunteers can provide important assistance in this type of setting. The student, also, must be given more trust, freedom, and responsibility in this type of setting in order for it to succeed. There is an underlying philosophy at work here that students will be better motivated to learn if they have had some say in what they are learning. As one famous British primary teacher puts it (Schiller, 1979):

> What makes sense to children is what is happening to them here and now. Our conversation with them makes most sense when it is about what is actually being experienced … The basis of true learning … is direct experience perceived and responded to with interest and feeling. It is for us to make the experiences available and with us lies the great responsibility of providing the means by which children may come to terms with them.

ALTERNATIVE, TEAM-TAUGHT, MULTI-AGED SETTINGS

Alternative Heights School can be characterized by its relaxed, informal atmosphere. It is a K-12 school, but, for most purposes, the children are divided into elementary and secondary levels within the school building. In the elementary level, three teams, consisting of two or three teachers per team, teach children the basic skills of reading, language arts, and mathematics, during the mornings. Each team has its own approach to teaching these skills. Each student chooses her "advisor" and, by so doing, chooses which team of advisors she will be instructed by. In the afternoons, students choose from a variety of classes which are offered.

A typical elementary student's day at Alternative Heights went something like this. For the first half-hour of the day, she visited or played with friends in the building, usually confining herself to the team area at which she would spend the remainder of her time that morning. The age range of children on her team was 6–11. For the remainder of the morning, she attended the "learning activities period" at her team's area. This was the period during which basic skills were taught. It was interrupted by a 20–30 minute recess, and, after this recess, it continued until lunch. After lunch, this student attended three classes which she had selected from a variety of choices, and which she had committed herself to for the entire quarter, then returned to her team area until dismissal. At team area, she visited with friends or, sometimes, participated in "advisory" meetings which were intended to help students build lasting friendships and discuss personal, social, or academic problems. The schedule for the entire elementary level of Alternative Heights thus looked like this:

S	8:00	Students and teachers visit within teams.
C	8:30	Learning Activities Period.
H	10:00	Recess or special classes.
E	10:30	Learning Activities Period.
D	11:30	Lunch.
U	12:00	Outdoor and indoor activities (e.g., soccer, board games, etc.).
L	12:30	First elective class.
E	1:30	Second elective class.
	2:00	Third elective class.
	2:30	Advisory groups.
	2:55	Dismissal.

For the learning activities period, students frequently worked independently or together in small groups, seeking assistance from teachers and fellow students as they felt the need for it. Instruction (i.e., directed interaction between teacher and students for the purpose of helping students to learn a particular concept or skill) was less common in this setting but it did occur. Students were encouraged to initiate their own activities and explore their own interests during this period.

For example, one student was working on a novel for children called "The Underground Path." She had already completed over 50 pages, complete with illustrations. A small group of students was organizing a play which they planned to present to their class in the following week. A few students were reading about science experiments and gathering together the materials which they would need to conduct these experiments. Two students were planning to cook something, and were examining recipes to see which ones they could most easily get materials for. Other students simply read books of their choosing, worked in their math books, participated in math games or various activities at centers.

At the recess, some students elected to participate in special classes such as "Great Books" or instruction in musical instruments. For the afternoon program, courses offered ranged from model-building and gym to wildlife and creative writing. These classes seemed to interest the students far more than the typical fare in traditional classrooms and they were, for the most part, a real success.

Progress of individual students in the basic skills, and progress in the afternoon classes, was evaluated without comparison to other students. Folders containing samples of each student's work, and narrative reports of each student's progress, were shared with parents at conferences three times per year or, when requested, more frequently. Narrative reports included teacher **and student** comments. (For samples of Alternative Heights reports, see Chapter 6.)

The Organization of a Team at Alternative Heights

Peter and Rod were full-time teachers on this team. Vaughn, who taught half-days on the secondary level of Alternative Heights, joined this team during the first half of the learning activities period and the morning recess. The first decision which Peter and Rod were faced with was how to organize for the basic skills instruction of over 60 children when the ages of these children ranged from 6–11. To be certain that all areas were dealt with fully, they separated the basic skills into two general categories: reading/language arts and mathematics.

For reading and language arts, these teachers listed the elements which they believed belonged in any comprehensive reading and language arts program, that is, basic reader groups for those who were learning to read or developing basic reading skills, regular experiences reading from trade books, creative writing, creative dramatics, puppetry, listening and speaking activities, etc. They then divided their students into three levels, according to the kinds of experiences which they would need: 1) Beginning readers, who needed daily instruction with language experience, basic readers, storytelling, puppetry, etc. 2) Developing readers, who needed instruction in strategies for identifying words, daily experiences reading from trade books, creative writing, creative dramatics, etc. 3) Proficient readers, who needed instruction in critical reading, the varieties of fiction and nonfiction, study skills, etc. Each teacher (Rod, Peter, and Vaughn) took responsibility for the instruction of one of these levels, and Vaughn agreed to offer creative dramatics to all interested students from any of the three levels during the morning, one-half-hour recess period.

For mathematics, they grouped students into either Rod's or Peter's classroom. Students who needed to work on the primary mathematics curriculum went to Peter's classroom. Those students who needed to learn intermediate level mathematics went to Rod's classroom. Within their respective classrooms, each teacher used a combination of group and individual activities to assist students in learning the concepts.

Their schedule for the morning looked like this:

S	8:00	Students and teachers meet, socialize, within teams.
C	8:30	Learning Activities Period (Literacy emphasis).
H	10:00	Recess or special classes.
E	10:30	Learning Activities Period (Math emphasis).
D	11:30	Lunch.
U		
L		
E		

The Organization of Peter's Classroom

Peter took responsibility for the beginning readers. His schedule for the learning activities period, early during the year, looked like this:

S	8:30	Meet with all students to read story to them, suggest topics or
C		creative writing for those who are capable of writing independently,
H		and introduce new centers.
E	8:45	Conduct language experience lesson with students who cannot
D		yet write independently on Tuesday and Thursday. Conduct basic
U		reader lessons with same group on Monday, Wednesday, and Friday.
L	9:05	Meet with students who need assistance with strategies for
E		identifying words on Tuesdays and Thursdays. Listen to
		independent readers on Monday, Wednesday, and Friday.

9:30	Conduct basic reader lesson with students who can write but cannot read independently, Monday, Wednesday, and Friday. Assist students at learning centers and activity centers, Tuesday and Thursday.
10:00	Recess. Lead soccer activity or supervise on playground.
10:30	Math. Students work with groups, math games, or math workbooks according to their individual contracts. Contracts are based on teacher's assessment of child's progress (see sample contract, Figure 2.7).
11:30	Lunch.

Students in Peter's classroom worked at a variety of activity and learning centers during the entire learning activities period, but they also met with particular groups and completed assigned activities (e.g., creative writing) and contracts. Occasionally, Peter and Rod teamed to provide particular group lessons in mathematics. For example, Peter might teach simple multiplication to students from Rod's and Peter's room. Shortly afterwards, Rod might teach a group lesson on beginning division. More frequently, Peter formed math groups according to needs within his own classroom. As he noticed that three or four students needed group instruction in place-value, Peter formed an instructional group for this concept. As more children became in need of such a group, they joined it. When students no longer needed the group instruction, Peter advised them to stop attending it. (Usually, the students who no longer needed this help asked to stop attending so they could get their contracted work completed more quickly.)

Meantime, two students may have been introduced to simple subtraction problems via their math workbooks. Not understanding how to do this work, they will come to Peter for assistance. He will either give them an introductory, manipulatives-based lesson right then or schedule it for the following day.

To summarize this pattern, we can say that Alternative Heights has a pleasant absence of pressure to accomplish things, a pressure which is very common in most elementary schools. Learning is perceived to be fun by its students, and children participate with pleasure in a great many of the educational activities which are provided by its teachers. One reason that learning is perceived as fun is that teachers at Alternative Heights hold a philosophy that schools **should be** fun and responsive to the interests of their students. One way to respond to students' interests is to offer a variety of choices in terms of instructional activities. Teachers at Alternative Heights work very hard to offer as many choices of activities as is possible in their afternoon electives and during the learning activities period in the morning. Perhaps unwittingly, efforts to carry out instruction seem to get less emphasis in such a setting. Students there seem to have acquired the idea that they don't have to do anything which does not capture their immediate interests. Such an attitude is obviously at ends with some of the academic and social goals of the school.

Because of its relaxed environment, students at Alternative Heights seem to enjoy learning and they demonstrate more initiative at developing their personal interests than do students in most traditional schools. However, this same relaxed environment conveys a disturbing lack of clarity, on the part of its staff, about what the essential goals for students in this school ought to be, that is, which concepts and skills must be learned. The relaxed school atmosphere also affected the social behavior of its students.

MATH CONTRACT

This week I will try to learn more about:

___ addition	___ measurement
___ subtraction	___ fractions
___ multiplication	___ geometry and shapes
___ division	___ graphing
___ something else (_____)	

To learn, I will do these things:

___ math pages, _____

___ lessons from Ted on _____

___ math cards or sheets _____

___ math games _____

END OF WEEK REPORT

This is what I did:

1. _____

2. _____

3. _____

4. _____

5. _____

Figure 2.7 Example of a Student Contract

Academic and social responsibilities seemed less important to students in this setting than they were to students in some other settings. While one of the school's major philosophical goals was to provide students with experiences making decisions for themselves, we have the impression that many of the students at Alternative Heights are not yet ready to fully benefit from a freedom with such wide parameters. More guidance of the students by the teachers, in the form of academic assignments and social responsibilities, would probably improve this setting.

THE CLUSTERS APPROACH

Before we begin our description of this pattern, we need to point out that, so far as we know, this approach has not yet been tried at the elementary level. At present, it is an idea which we have developed to solve certain problems which are inherent in all the other patterns which we have discussed to this point.

The **clusters** approach[10] combines strengths from the nongraded and informal patterns in order to deal with the problem that departmentalized teaching addresses in traditional schools. Departmentalized teaching was developed in some traditional schools because teachers in traditional settings must teach all content areas. An advantage to this arrangement is that the teacher in a traditional setting gets to know his students extremely well. A disadvantage to this arrangement is that no one teacher can possibly be extremely knowledgeable in so many different content areas.

Departmentalized teaching allows teachers to "specialize". In a traditional setting which has departmentalized, a teacher may be responsible for only one to three content areas (rather than six to eight). The teacher in such a setting may teach as many as three or more classes in a particular content area (e.g., science), but he will only need to prepare lessons in one to three content areas. The rationale behind this arrangement is that students will receive better instruction, provided by more knowledgeable and happier teachers, than the type of instruction they would receive in a setting which is not departmentalized.

The advantage to the clusters arrangement is that it can combine strengths from other settings while accomplishing a degree of specialization similar to that which is achieved through departmentalized teaching. In a clusters arrangement, areas of a school building (for example, the wing of a building) are set aside for teams of teachers who specialize in particular clusters of knowledge. We recommend four clusters: 1) Communications (dealing with reading, writing, storytelling, creative dramatics, word-processing, and similar skills); 2) Math-Science; 3) Fine arts; and 4) Human relations (dealing with social studies, personal social relations, etc.). Teachers who taught in the human relations cluster would also provide academic and personal counseling, a "home" room for a group of students, etc. Teachers could be assigned to more than one of the four clusters since personnel demands might require that teachers not be limited to one content area. However, teachers would be specializing in two or less content areas, and they would be able to develop strengths in those content areas for which they were responsible.

Departmentalized settings do not necessarily provide for individual differences among students any better than a normal traditional setting. Nongraded settings, on the other hand, are able to better provide for individual differences. Nongraded settings, however, have the disadvantage of requiring much more organizational effort on the part of the teacher; for example, keeping track of which students have mastered which objectives. Teachers in nongraded settings who are responsible for all content areas are at a disadvantage since, in addition to the many preparations which they must make (similar to the preparations of teachers in traditional settings), they must also organize the records of student progress according to objectives in each content area. A nongraded approach would be easier for teachers to use in combination with a clusters approach since they would only need to keep track of student progress towards objectives in one or two content areas.

Informal settings provide for a variety of choices on the part of the student. This helps to assure student motivation and it fosters creativity and initiative on the part of the student. Traditional settings do not typically provide for this and nongraded settings do not necessarily provide for it, either. In a school which is organized according to clusters, however, teachers should have more time to develop learning centers and offer mini-courses or units from which students can choose since such centers or mini-courses would always relate to a particular knowledge cluster. Further, the fact that a nongraded approach (which keeps track of student progress towards objectives within content areas) can be combined with an informal approach (which provides for student initiative and creativity in the development of units, or topics, of study) helps insure that the lack of instructional goals found in Alternative Heights would be avoided. In sum, although this approach has not been tried nor have the details been worked out in practice, we are very optimistic about the potential of this approach for organizing schools and teams for instruction.

OUTCOMES-BASED EDUCATION

In the past several years, a national trend towards **outcomes-based education** has been developing. While not an instructional setting, the philosophy of outcomes-based education can influence instructional settings profoundly when it is taken seriously. We believe that the nongraded instructional setting is consistent with the philosophy of outcomes-based education, but almost any instructional setting can be adapted to an outcomes-based approach if adaptations are taken seriously.

What is outcomes-based education? First, it is a philosophy of education which posits that each learner can, and should, be successful. Schools are charged with bringing about this success among learners. This involves a rethinking of how schools operate and includes, among other things, changes in how children are grouped for instruction, when they make transitions from one level to another (e.g., when they graduate), and changes towards a more personalized approach to instruction.[11]

Outcomes-based education is partly derived from research on mastery learning, which is discussed in Chapter 4 of this text. Essentially, this involves a minimum competency approach to instruction. In other words, essential learner outcomes (objectives) are listed and students are instructed and assessed for mastery of these outcomes. However, for many students, simply mastering these outcomes is not enough since they have the potential to achieve beyond this minimum competency. For these students, extension and enrichment are also an essential ingredient of outcomes-based

Low Teacher Control **High Student Control**	**High Teacher Control** **Low Student Control**
Low Teacher Control **Low Student Control**	**High Teacher Control** **High Student Control**

Figure 2.8

education. In outcomes-based education, assessment and instruction must agree with outcomes. (Students will be tested and taught the essential learner outcomes of the school program.) (A Minnesota Vision for OBE, 1990).

A FRAMEWORK FOR INTERPRETING INSTRUCTIONAL SETTINGS

One way to interpret instructional settings is in terms of the simple diagram in Figure 2.8. In the right, upper box, we have located the traditional, graded setting. In this instructional setting, the teacher has a high degree of control over the teacher-student interaction in the classroom. On the other hand, the students in a traditional setting have very limited influence over this interaction.

In the lower right-hand box of this diagram, teacher and students alike have a high degree of control over the interaction which occurs in the classroom. Many informal settings could be represented here because the teachers and students have many opportunities to pursue topics of interest to themselves.

In the upper left box, students have a high degree of control over the events which take place in the classroom, but teachers do not have much influence at all. In essence, the teacher abdicates a good deal of authority in exchange for the opportunity to give students maximum freedom in deciding what to do. We would not place any of the settings which we have described in this box. However, settings such as Alternative Heights seem to vacillate between the upper left box and the lower right box of this diagram.

Finally, in the lower left box, students and teachers alike have little influence over what occurs in the classroom. The best description of this type of situation would be an instructional program which reduces the students to completing individualized packets throughout their school days, leaving little time for interaction with other students or their teacher. Teachers in this setting are reduced to correcting tests and offering assistance to students who are experiencing difficulty with their learning. None of the instructional settings described in this chapter should be classified in this box. However, many of the so-called "individualized instruction" programs of the 1970s might be classified here. Many graded, nongraded, and informal settings made use of these programs during the 1970s.

SUMMARY

There are many approaches which can be employed in the organization of schools, teams or grades, and classrooms. All over the country, school districts are experimenting with new settings. It is important that every person who is planning to teach at the elementary level become familiar with a variety of approaches to teaching. We have classified the extensive variety of approaches into five patterns. The first pattern, the traditional, graded, setting, is still the most commonly used one but its faults are so salient as to have inspired a wide variety of alternative approaches. The graded setting has two serious faults. First, it uses a lockstep approach which frustrates slow learners and holds fast learners back. Second, it compares students to each other via a competitive marking system. In addition to these faults, the graded approach relies heavily on the textbook.

The nongraded approach eliminates the lockstep and uses a marking system which judges the student according to her individual potential. No slow learners are penalized for not keeping up with the class, nor are fast learners bored by unchallenging activities which are aimed at teaching concepts they they have already mastered. The nongraded approach also emphasizes learning objectives rather than coverage of the text.

Despite their differences, however, the graded and nongraded approach share one common feature. In both the graded and nongraded settings, the teachers and school administrators decide what the students will learn. Accommodation of student interests is not guaranteed with either approach.

The informal approach, on the other hand, provides for student input into the selection of learning goals by including the child in the process of topic selection and the choice of study tasks related to these topics. Within the confines of teacher expectations related to basic skills and concepts, children have some say about what they will be learning. The Alternative Heights approach expands this adjustment to student interests by having the students choose to take those afternoon courses which most interest them.

Each of these four approaches has strengths and weaknesses. The clusters approach attempts to combine the best features of the nongraded, informal, and Alternative Heights settings. The clusters approach is especially concerned with solving a problem which can pervade each of the other four settings, that is, the problem of expecting teachers to teach several subjects well. The clusters approach creates teaching specializations so that children will get excellent teaching in each of the subject and skill areas. It does this without sacrificing the interdisciplinary approach of the informal setting.

We have described the main features of the traditional, graded, approach at the school-wide level, grade-level (or team level), and at the level of the individual classroom teacher. We have done the same for the four alternatives to the graded approach. In our final chapter, we provide you with some self-assessments which can be used to determine which patterns of organization best match your personal preferences and philosophy.

NOTES

1. We do not fully endorse this program since it recommends daily instruction in sound-letter relations in isolation from words.
2. Elementary Science Study (ESS), available from Delta Education, Inc.
3. Spalding and Spalding, 1969.
4. See Veatch, 1959.
5. Louisell, "The Key Word," January, 1983.
6. *Activity centers* provide children with opportunities to work with some of the basic tools of humankind, for example, at the clay center, the water-table, or a writing area. The child's activity in such centers is analagous to that of a craftsman. Thoroughness is emphasized. Play and work are indistinct to children as they make use of such centers.

   Learning centers are environments which have been carefully structured so that children will learn about particular topics or master specific skills. The content of these centers can range from general themes (e.g., Africa, Space, etc.) to specific skills (e.g., how to write in cursive script). Students make use of learning centers with little or no assistance from their teachers.
7. Furth and Wachs, 1974.
8. See Boydell, 1978, for further details of this debate.
9. Credit to Yankee Ridge Elementary School in Urbana, Illinois, for this idea.
10. The faculty of The Center for Teaching and Learning at The University of North Dakota, Grand Forks, developed the idea of organizing curriculum according to knowledge "clusters" and they used this form of organization for their undergraduate teacher-education program. We have adapted this idea for the improvement of elementary school instruction.
11. Many of the ideas in this section are presented in an unpublished paper by Ken Kelsey, St. Cloud State University, entitled, "What Outcomes-Based Education Should Be."

GLOSSARY

achievement grouping The placement of students in instructional groups according to the academic level which they have achieved, usually for reading or mathematics instruction (sometimes called "ability grouping").

basic reader group A group of elementary students who study from the same basic reader, meeting on a regular basis with their teacher for instruction, and proceeding one story at a time together, with accompanying workbook activities.

clusters An arrangement by which academic knowledge is classified according to broad categories and delivered by teachers who specialize in these categories. The delivery of instruction is non-graded and incorporates informal methods.

departmentalized instruction An arrangement whereby instruction is organized according to content areas so that teachers can specialize in particular content areas rather than be required to teach all subjects.

family grouping Randomly grouping children according to a mix of ages. Similar to multi-age grouping.

heterogeneous grouping Grouping students in such a way that their range of academic diversity is preserved within the groups.

homogeneous grouping Grouping students according to similarities in academic achievement; for example, most able students in one group, average students in another group, and least able students in another group.

horizontal grouping Grouping students according to age. Similar to graded grouping.

multi-aged grouping The placement of students of different ages in the same classroom, for example, placing 6, 7, and 8 year olds in the same classroom. Multi-aged grouping is the opposite of graded placement, an arrangement for which students are assigned to their classrooms according to age; for example, in graded arrangements, 6 year olds are placed in grade level 1.

outcomes-based education A philosophy of education, based on learner outcomes, which posits that all learners can, and should, be successful. Schools are charged with the responsibility for bringing about this success among learners.

self-contained classroom In self-contained classrooms, the teacher is responsible for the education of his or her students. No team-teaching is involved and decisions about the education of his or her students are made by the teacher responsible.

skills grouping Grouping students for the purpose of instruction in a particular skill; instructing a group of students for one objective until they have either mastered it or demonstrated that they are not yet ready to master it.

team-teaching In team-taught settings, teachers share the responsibility for their students and they make many of the decisions about the education of their students as a group.

topic work The study of a particular topic (e.g., "outer space") by a particular group of students. Topics are usually broken down into themes.

theme A subtopic. Stars, pulsars, and black holes would each be examples of a theme when the topic is "outer space."

vertical grouping Randomly grouping children by mix of ages. Synonymous with "family grouping."

Chapter
3

Teaching Techniques

*F*or anything which one might want to teach, ther are a variety of ways to go about teaching it. The topic of study for Chapters 3 and 4 of this book is the variety of ways which one can use to teach anything. We call these ways of going about teaching "techniques" and "methods." There are certain **techniques** which all teachers must master in order to perform professionally in the classroom. The average person would not know enough about teaching to make use of them. Trained teachers, on the other hand, can be expected to demonstrate these techniques when they teach. They are the foundation—the "building blocks"—of the teaching methods which have been developed and implemented in elementary classrooms throughout the years. Teaching techniques may be applied to many different teaching and learning situations. They are not restricted to particular instructional subjects. We have identified some basic teaching techniques which we will present in Chapter 3.

In Chapter 4, **methods** of teaching are described. These methods employ several of the teaching techniques which we will discuss in Chapter 3. Teaching methods can be combined in a variety of ways. Using one method does not prohibit a teacher from using another. In some cases, teachers may use more than one method during the same instructional period. Teachers often alternate between methods during the course of the day.

We hope that persons preparing to be teachers will learn these techniques and methods well, so that they will be able to choose intelligently among them for each of the teaching activities which they select throughout their teaching careers. But there are important factors which teachers must consider when making such choices, since all teaching methods are not equally effective for all purposes. To help teachers to "match" their techniques and methods with their objectives, we now present three important theoretical frames of reference: *Types of Instruction*, Bloom's *Taxonomy of Educational Objectives*, and Gagne's *Hierarchy of Knowledge*.

TYPES OF INSTRUCTION, BLOOM'S TAXONOMY, AND GAGNE'S HIERARCHY

Types of Instruction is a classification of instructional activities which organizes classroom experiences into six different types. We have developed this classification scheme from a variety of sources on the topic (Bruner, 1966; Dale, 1969; and Swyers, 1972). It applies the assumption that "experience is the best teacher" to learning situations in schools. In Figure 3.1, pure experience is represented in level 6 (at the bottom of the chart). The chart implies that "the real life operational situation" is the most effective and concrete learning situation which can be provided for any student. Very often it is also the most difficult type of learning experience for a teacher to prepare and this difficulty can be thought of in terms of expense when we consider the time, money, and effort which might go into providing this effective type of learning situation for one's students. Field trips might be included in Level 6. Most elementary teachers value field trips very much, and they frequently complain that their school districts will not fund more than one or two field trips per classroom during the course of a year. School districts may have very good reasons for this funding policy, and their main reason is probably that field trips are extremely expensive!

Financial expense forces teachers to consider learning situations at the upper levels (e.g., Levels 1 and 2) on our *Types of Instruction* chart. Difficulty of preparation is also a consideration for teachers when they select learning activities. Even if school districts could afford to let teachers take field trips on a daily basis, a good teacher would have to expend a great deal of time and effort in arranging these trips and preparing to make the most of them. This "expense" in terms of a teacher's effort would probably be prohibitive. Levels 1 and 2, on the other hand, involve lecture and the reading of books or other printed matter, and these types of learning activities are neither difficult to prepare nor are they financially expensive. Consequently, they are widely used.

In sum, the most abstract types of instruction—lectures and readings—are at the top of our chart (Levels 1 and 2). Instructional activities which are experienced through audiovisual media—pictures, audiotapes, films, and videotapes—are found in the middle of the chart (Levels 3 and 4). At the bottom of the chart are the most concrete types of instructional activities—simulations, games, and real-life situations (Levels 5 and 6).

The *Types of Instruction* chart provides teachers with a tool which they can use to analyze the degree to which their classroom activities are likely to engage the students and foster learning. Teachers who find themselves constantly utilizing Levels 1 and 2

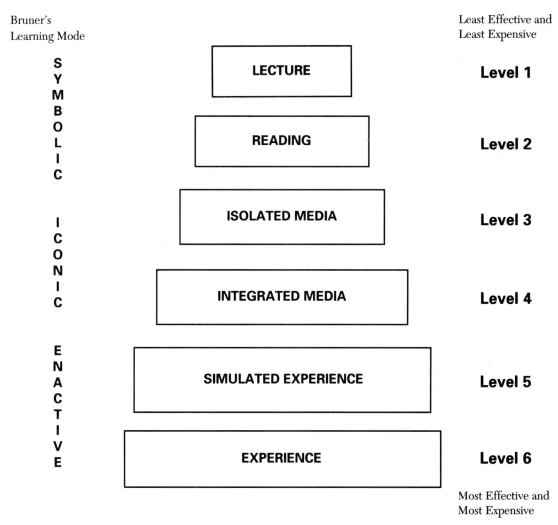

Figure 3.1

for instructional activities need to think about their selection of activities and consider enriching their offerings with activities from the middle and bottom levels of the chart. Books and storytelling may be effective when your goal is to acquaint your students with folk tales, but if you are trying to teach your students how to drive a car, how to swim, or how to ride a bike or skateboard, you will have to provide your students with some real experience and, perhaps, some training simulations. These types of activities will come from Levels 5 and 6.

The *Types of Instruction* classification resembles Jerome Bruner's (1966) modes of learning. Levels 5 and 6 correspond to Bruner's **enactive** learning mode; Levels 3 and 4 correspond to the **iconic** learning mode; and Levels 1 and 2 correspond to

symbolic learning. Enactive learning engages the students in doing and directly experiencing what is to be learned. In iconic learning, the material is experienced through visual or sensorial representations. In symbolic learning, the material is conveyed through symbols such as words, numbers and formulae.

Bloom's *Taxonomy of Educational Objectives* (Bloom, 1956) provides a framework for classifying educational objectives according to hierarchical categories. It also has six levels (see Figure 3.2): 1) Knowledge, 2) Comprehension, 3) Application, 4) Analysis, 5) Synthesis, and 6) Evaluation.

Level 6:	Evaluation
Level 5:	Synthesis
Level 4:	Analysis
Level 3:	Application
Level 2:	Comprehension
Level 1:	Knowledge

Figure 3.2

The lowest level, **knowledge,** is defined in a far more narrow sense than our everyday usage of the term. For Bloom's taxonomy, "knowledge" means information which one remembers. More specifically, its definition is "the remembering, either by recognition or recall, of ideas, material, or phenomena" (p.62). For example, fifth-grade teachers may expect their students to remember that George Washington was the first president of the United States. Although this type of knowledge is low in Bloom's hierarchy, many educational objectives in use in today's schools would be classified within this level.

Bloom's knowledge level within his taxonomy is not restricted to facts only, however. For example, knowledge of the levels, and their order, in Bloom's taxonomy is an objective which we have for you, the reader, as we write this section of our book. Knowledge of these things involves information—not just a simple recalling of facts.

Level 2 in Bloom's taxonomy, **comprehension,** deals with the understanding of the literal message which has been communicated in either written or verbal form (p. 89). Bloom believes that comprehension represents the largest class of intellectual skills which are emphasized in schools (p. 89). Comprehension involves several subskills; for example, the ability to "translate" a lengthy message into its essential points.

Teachers sometimes express the belief that "If a student really comprehends the subject matter under study, then she can apply it." But, this is not necessarily correct. One study which Bloom cites found that students who had mastered basic knowledge of adolescent development had nevertheless failed in the task of applying this knowledge. **Level 3, application,** deals with the ability to apply one's understanding in appropriate situations even when the manner of solving the problem has not been given. It differs from comprehension because in comprehension one can apply a principle which one has learned as long as the application of this principle has been specified beforehand (p. 120).

During the 1960s in England, a school decided to devote their entire sixth grade mathematics curriculum to the building of a pond for the school (to be used in wildlife education, etc.) (Nuffield, 1968). They had evidently decided that it is one thing to know and comprehend the basic principles of arithmetic, but it is another thing to be able to use them in relevant situations. The year-long effort at building the pond was intended to give them, among other things, experience applying their basic arithmetic skills.

Level 4 of the taxonomy, **analysis,** involves breaking something down into the parts which make it up and detecting the relationships which exist among these parts (Bloom, 1956, p.144). A typical elementary school science activity can serve as an example. Each student is given a closed, opaque wooden box which contains three everyday objects which the student cannot see. Perhaps one student's box contains a marble, a metal washer, and a wooden cube. The student's task is to try to figure out what is inside the box. The student can act on the box in any way he chooses to (e.g., shake it, turn it upside down, rotate it, etc.) but the box cannot be opened (see Figure 3.3). As the student performs his actions on the box, he is testing certain ideas which have occurred to him about what is in the box. Perhaps he believes that something flat is in the box. The behavior of the marble as it rolls will cause the student to question this belief. Perhaps the student will develop a belief that the objects inside are round. The behavior of the cube will probably cause the student to question this belief.

As the student tests his ideas by acting on the objects, he is engaged in analysis. Each idea which is tested has a hypothesis (e.g., that the objects are round) and data to support (e.g., one of the objects rolls) or negate (e.g., one of the objects doesn't roll) this hypothesis. The hypothesis is being analyzed into its constituent parts, or statements. If it is round, it will roll. If it does not roll, it is not round. Etc.

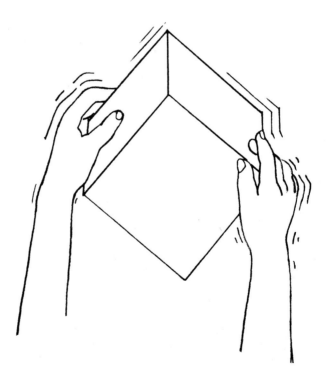

Figure 3.3

Level 5 of the taxonomy, **synthesis,** involves the putting together of parts to make something which is clearly more than the materials which were there when the project began (p.185). The terms "parts" and "materials" may refer to objects or ideas. Ideas can be synthesized in a unique way—as they are in a song or a poem, for example.

Another example of synthesis can be demonstrated by describing the work of three sixth grade students who were working together on a project for an elementary school science fair. They wanted to make a working model of a submarine. After reading and learning much about how submarines work, they went about trying to build their working model. The first model failed to work. The second model failed. So did the third. With each failure, they developed new ideas about what was wrong with their model and why it did not work. They tested each of their ideas out by introducing a change in the model. Finally, they succeeded. As they thought about the various factors which could have been responsible for the failure of their model, these students were engaging in analysis (Level 4 on Bloom's taxonomy). When they finally solved their problem and developed their own working model of a submarine, they engaged in synthesis.

Level 6 in Bloom's taxonomy, **evaluation,** involves using standards or criteria to make judgments about the value of something (p. 185). Its everyday usage includes "snap judgments" and opinions, but Bloom's category of evaluation does not include this type of thinking. He says that, "only those evaluations which…can be made with distinct criteria in mind are included in his sixth level" (p. 186). One example of evaluation would be the case of a fifth grade child who has just pointed out to a friend that his last statement contradicts a previous one. By identifying this "faulty logic," he has engaged in evaluation. Another example could be provided by the child who is asked, in a moral education simulation, to decide whether a mother should steal food when she and her children are starving. When a child considers the merits of opposing courses of action (stealing and saving one's children, not stealing and letting one's children perish), he engages in evaluation.

Bloom notes that he placed evaluation at the highest level in his taxonomy because it makes use of each of the other types of thinking included in his taxonomy. He is careful to point out, however, that it "is not necessarily the last step in thinking or problem solving" (p. 185). In fact, he says that evaluation may sometimes trigger an effect to acquire low-level knowledge, comprehension, application, analysis, or synthesis (p.185).

Gagne's *Hierarchy of Knowledge* classifies subject matter into 4 types of hierarchical categories: 1) Facts, 2) Concepts, 3) Generalizations, and 4) Principles.

Facts are specific events or representations of reality. They are the most simple form of information or knowledge. Sometimes, they have no meaning by themselves and they can be overwhelming in number. Events, such as dates and happenings, can be facts. Characteristics of organisms or machines are also facts. For example, "On July 14, 1789, the French Revolution began" is a fact. Facts are best learned when they are clustered or interrelated to form one or more ideas.

Concepts are mental images which result from grouping together related facts. Concepts constitute the second level in Gagne's hierarchy of knowledge. A class, or group, of facts forms a concept. Concepts are the most simple form of abstraction because they consist of facts which can be meaningfully grouped. Concepts have characteristics that distinguish them and make them unique, differentiating them from other concepts. For example, the concept "table" is unique and different from other concepts such as "chair."

Concepts may be concrete or abstract events and may vary in their level of difficulty. "Table " is a concrete concept. It is easy for students to visualize and understand. "Justice," on the other hand, is an abstract concept, more difficult for children to grasp. Concrete concepts may be communicated through pictures or objects. Abstract concepts can only be communicated through language. "Revolution" is an example of an abstract concept. It must be explained through the use of words and not by pointing at an object or a pictorial representation.

Generalizations are statements of relationship between two or more concepts. Generalizations are the third level in Gagne's hierarchy. Just as concepts result from the combination of facts, so generalizations result from combining concepts. Generalizations are always abstractions and vary in their degree of difficulty. An example of a generalization is "tools improve man's efficiency."

Like generalizations, **Principles** also state relationships between two or more concepts, but they explain phenomena with more specificity than generalizations. Principles have predictive characteristics. They constitute the fourth and highest level in Gagne's hierarchy of knowledge. Examples of principles include "Water freezes at 0 degrees Centigrade" and "the perimeter of a square is the sum of the length of its sides."

All the subject matter that is taught and learned can be classified as being either fact, concept, generalization or principle. By being familiar with Gagne's *Hierarchy of Knowledge,* teachers are able to organize subject matter so their students learn the main concepts, generalizations, and principles of a discipline rather than unrelated facts and ideas.

USING THE TYPES OF INSTRUCTION, BLOOM'S TAXONOMY, AND GAGNE'S HIERARCHY

We have presented three theoretical frameworks: the *Types of Instruction,* Bloom's *Taxonomy* and Gagne's *Hierarchy.* Each of these frameworks should help teachers to reflect upon their choices of instructional techniques and methods.

The *Types of Instruction* should help teachers to analyze the types of teaching activities which they choose for their students. Every instructional technique or method has its strengths and weaknesses. Some are very effective but very expensive. Others are less effective, but inexpensive. If they will do the job for less expense (whether that "expense" is stated in terms of dollars or a teacher's time), perhaps they should be preferred to more ideal strategies.

Blooms' *Taxonomy of Behavioral Objectives* provides teachers with a classification scheme which they can use to better understand the levels at which their students are working. Are they working at the knowledge level? Some techniques and methods are ideal for use when the teacher's objectives fall in the lowest two levels of Bloom's taxonomy. These same techniques and method may be almost useless when the teacher's objectives fall in the higher levels of the taxonomy, however. Are the students engaged in higher level thinking? Some techniques and methods are perfect when the teacher's objectives fall in the higher levels of the taxonomy. However, these techniques and methods may be ineffective for teaching factual knowledge. Some techniques and methods seem to be effective at more levels than others. Bloom's taxonomy helps teachers find out if the level of learning and thinking taking place in their classrooms corresponds to their objectives.

Gagne's hierarchy should help teachers to reflect upon the content which they are about to teach. It should assist teachers in organizing the content into meaningful units so that students will truly understand, rather than simply memorize, the content of their lessons.

We believe that it is very important that beginning teachers acquire knowledge about how to make use of each of the methods and techniques which are discussed in this textbook. We also believe that it is important for teachers to learn the relative advantages and disadvantages of each technique and method. Knowledge of the pros and cons of each technique and method will help teachers with the task of choosing teaching styles. With that in mind, we can now begin our study of teaching techniques.

QUESTIONING TECHNIQUES: HOW TO ASK QUESTIONS

Questioning may be the most commonly used teaching technique in teaching. Whatever method a teacher implements in the classroom, it usually requires the teacher to know how to ask questions. Without an understanding of questioning techniques, it is difficult to learn other teaching methods. This is why we begin this section of the chapter with questioning.

Purposes of Questions

There are three major reasons for teachers to ask questions in the classroom: to promote student thinking, to verify student understanding, and to foster student participation. Questions should not be asked to embarrass students whose behavior needs to be changed. Questions are academic tools, not discipline instruments.

By asking questions, teachers can affect the levels at which students think. If most questions asked by a teacher are of the memory type, the student's level of thinking will be restricted to remembering. However, if a significant number of questions asked are of the analysis type, the student's level will be expanded to critical and creative thinking.

While a teacher presents information in the classroom, many students nonverbally assent with their heads to indicate that they understand what is being taught. A novice teacher would be surprised to see how few of those students are able to answer questions about the material which they are nonverbally indicating that they understand. By asking frequent questions, a teacher is able to check for understanding on the part of the student. The feedback obtained in this way will enable the teacher to determine whether to proceed with the presentation or to explain the concept further.

It is difficult for children to pay attention to a presentation when they are not actively involved. After a while, their minds tend to wander. By asking frequent questions, a teacher is able to keep the students involved. When students are involved and participating, they become more interested in the subject.

Finally, questions should not be asked to embarrass students whose behavior is undesirable. In those situations, the teacher will use discipline strategies rather than questions to redirect student behavior. Questions should not be used to make students feel badly about themselves.

Types of Questions

There are several ways of classifying the different types of questions that teachers and students ask in the classroom. Teacher questions can match any of the levels in Bloom's taxonomy (See Table 3.1).

Knowledge questions are used to verify the student's recollection of facts which are essential for the understanding of concepts or the application of rules. Knowledge questions have only one correct answer and refer to information presented to the students through the lesson or reading materials. They may also be used to review material which has been previously learned or to warm-up class members and give them a sense of accomplishment before moving on to a new learning task. Examples include:

"Who was the president of the Union during the Civil War?"

"What is the formula to calculate the area of a square?"

"Where is Canada?"

"When did the American Civil War begin?"

Table 3.1   QUESTIONS

TYPE	Level 1 KNOWLEDGE	Level 2 COMPREHENSION	Level 3 APPLICATION	Level 4 ANALYSIS	Level 5 SYNTHESIS	Level 6 EVALUATION
FUNCTION	remember information	organize information	apply principles and rules, demonstrate	think critically	think creatively	assess value
KEY WORDS	who? what? where? when?	explain concept	how? which? how much? an example	why? meaning inferences	what if? what would? can you?	should? would you?
* FREQUENCY suggested	30%	10%	20%	20%	10%	10%
* WAIT-TIME suggested	3 sec	5 sec	5 sec	10 sec	15 sec	15 sec

*We have no research evidence to support these suggestions. With wait-time, however, we do know that higher level questions require greater response time.

Comprehension questions are designed to verify understanding of the ideas, concepts, and generalizations presented in class or through reading materials. When answering comprehension questions, the students should use their own words, rather than memorized definitions to demonstrate that they understand the concepts taught and are able to explain them. Comprehension questions require students to organize the information received. They are used by the teacher to check how much the students are grasping before moving on to a new idea or concept. Understanding is a more demanding intellectual task than recalling. Since the students are expected to explain something already presented to them, there is only one answer to the question, but it may be answered with various degrees of accuracy and detail. Unlike recall questions, there is an opportunity, in comprehension questions, for incomplete answers. For example:

"Can anyone explain what gravity is?"

"What is freedom of speech?"

"What is the difference between fact and opinion?"

Application questions require students to apply a rule or principle. Through application questions, the students are asked to find examples of abstract concepts or the use of rules. These exercises help elementary students to understand concepts as they relate to their worlds. It is through many application exercises that students come to master concepts and abstractions. Some examples would include:

"How can we find the phonetic pronunciation of 'fable'?"

"At what latitude and longitude is Boston located?"

"Which of the following words is an adjective?"

"How many centimeters wide is your desk?"

"Can you give an example of freedom of speech?"

Analysis questions require the student to find reasons, relationships, motives, meanings, or characteristics that have not been discussed in the lesson. They stimulate critical thinking in the learners and foster consideration of alternative points of view. By these questions, students are led to analyze information, draw conclusions, and form generalizations. Because there are many possible answers to analysis questions rather than a single correct one, teachers are able to establish a supportive environment when using them. Students do not have to fear being wrong. For example:

"Why do you think Johnny joined the circus?"

"What is it meant by 'America is the land of opportunity'?"

Synthesis questions encourage students to find solutions. They stimulate creative thinking and problem solving abilities. Given a situation, students make predictions, invent new ways to resolve a conflict, describe how a character could have acted, hypothesize relationships, come up with new names, and devise new rules. Synthesis questions do not have one correct answer. For example:

"What would be another ending to the story?"

"What would happen if we added more salt to the solution?"

"Can you come up with another way to move the piano?"

Evaluation questions require that students give educated opinions and judge the merits of events or actions. They stimulate critical thinking in a complex manner. While analysis questions focus on rather specific situations, evaluation questions address the larger picture and add the dimension of the value or desirability of a practice. Students are asked to support their judgments and opinions in a rational manner. There are certainly many ways to judge the same event. Evaluation questions are judged not by the position taken on the issue, but by the thoroughness of the justification. For example:

"Would you support the use of nuclear power to generate electricity?"

"Is it correct for Americans to consume such a high proportion of the earth's resources?"

"Should schools have dances for sixth graders?"

Steps Within a Question

There is more to the process of asking a question than mentally constructing it. Teachers follow five major steps when asking a question:

1. Selecting the type of question and its level of difficulty.
2. Phrasing the question and delivering it.
3. Allowing time for students to think (wait-time).
4. Choosing a student to answer the question.
5. Listening to the student response and providing feedback.

Selecting the Type of Question and Its Level of Difficulty   The selection of what type of question to ask depends on the objectives of the lesson, the progress made, and the learning needs of the students. The teacher decides whether to ask a recall, comprehension, application, analysis or evaluation question. The level of difficulty should be adapted to the academic ability of the members of the class in such a manner that approximately 75% of the questions asked are answered correctly (Brophy and Good, 1986).

Phrasing the Question and Delivering It   The wording of questions needs to be adapted to the language ability of the members of the class, keeping a style which is understood by as many students as possible. The question should be brief and concise, delivered with clear enunciation, and in a tone of voice which can be clearly heard at the back of the room. The eyes of the teacher should scan the room and nonverbally communicate that the question is for the whole group to think about, not for a pre-chosen student.

Allowing Time for Students to Think: Wait-Time   Many studies point out that teachers do not allow for sufficient wait-time before and after recognizing a student to answer a question. It is difficult for teachers, who are used to presenting at a fast tempo without allowing for long pauses and moments of silence, to shift gears and go into a kind of "slow motion" activity. The more energetic and enthusiastic the presentation, the more difficult it is to shift and become a quiet observer and listener. Different types of questions require different amounts of wait-time. Recall questions may not require more than three seconds, while analysis and synthesis questions may require as long as 15 seconds in order for students to be able to prepare an answer.

Choosing a Student to Answer a Question   Questions should be well distributed among members of the class so no student feels left out or exempted from the intellectual challenge presented by a question. Recognizing a variety of students—not only those who are raising their hands—assures broad participation. There are times, however, when the teacher may call on volunteers only to provide for a more relaxed learning atmosphere. In order to assure that the majority of the students respond correctly to the questions asked, the teacher mentally matches the difficulty of the question with the ability of each student, and generally does not direct the most challenging questions to those members of the class who are having academic difficulties.

As discussed earlier, the teacher asks questions not only to verify academic progress and mastery of the material, but also to actively involve as many students as possible. When asking questions, the teacher must have in mind the cognitive objectives of the lesson as well as the affective needs of the learners.

Listening to the Student Response and Providing Feedback   Once a student is recognized, more wait-time may be needed before the student responds. During this period, it is important for the teacher to communicate that the student who has been recognized "owns" the question, making sure no other student brings pressure into the situation by calling "teacher, teacher" or nervously waving his hand. The teacher must not convey a sense of hurry. The recognized student must feel it is his question and that the teacher and the rest of the group will wait patiently, in a supportive manner, until an answer is given.

The student may respond to the question in four major ways: 1) correctly, 2) incompletely, 3) incorrectly, or 4) by not responding at all.

When the response is **correct,** or acceptable, the teacher may give praise, elaborate on the response, probe, or move on to another question. To choose among these responses, a teacher must consider the lesson objectives and the characteristics of each particular student. Some learners need abundant reinforcement, and some are ready to be challenged so they develop a stronger sense of competence. At times, questions are asked in a rapid firing style, without feedback, to quickly review material and warm-up the class before the lesson. It is commonly assumed, in this case, that if the teacher does not comment, the answer is correct.

When the student response is **incomplete,** the teacher may help the student arrive at a correct or acceptable answer, or the teacher may add to the statement to make it correct. It is not helpful to have another student answer.

When the student response is **incorrect,** the teacher must decide whether the student is able, with some teacher help, to come up with an acceptable answer, or if it is best to respond by giving the correct answer (for example: "John, the answer to 2 x 2 is 4") and move on to the next question. Again, it is not helpful to have another student answer.

When students frequently do not respond at all to questions, it is time for teachers to evaluate their questioning procedures, particularly the amount of time allowed for response, and to decide whether to place priority on student thinking or quickness of response. Other matters to evaluate are the level of trust and spirit of cooperation existing among students and the teacher. Perhaps competition among class members is creating a negative atmosphere. Also, the percentage of questions which are not answered successfully can alert teachers to the possibility that their questions are too difficult.

Series of Questions

Asking questions in random order does not promote student thinking and the development of ideas. As a matter of fact, it may confuse students and make it more difficult for them to master the objectives of the lesson. Series of questions require a logical direction so that a cumulative effect occurs, and the students will follow the idea of the lesson from its atomistic and more simplistic levels to the more holistic and complex ones.

At times teachers initiate series of questions at the lower levels of Bloom's Taxonomy and progress toward higher level thinking. At other times, teachers begin their questions at the analysis level and remain at that level by asking several inter-related analysis questions. Or the teacher may ask an evaluation question to interest the students, and then move the topic through the various taxonomy levels until evaluation is reached again and the students are able to respond to the initial question. Depending on the lesson objectives, the teacher may also ask a series of questions which remain within the knowledge, comprehension and application levels. If the teacher asks a series of knowledge questions without progressing to comprehension or application, it may be inferred that the lesson objective is solely to memorize. The questions that teachers ask must have a logical direction and must address the objective of the lesson.

Student-Initiated Questions

The kinds of questions that students ask suggest to the teacher the level of academic and personal maturity of the group. Students who constantly ask procedural questions ("May I sharpen my pencil") may be telling the teacher that she needs to develop responsibility and self-direction in her students. (This topic will be discussed in Chapter 7). When students ask very few academic questions, it may be concluded that the group is working in a passive or "receiving" mode, at the lower levels of Bloom's Taxonomy. Such a teacher has not been able to get them involved in problem solving and higher order thinking.

Since student-initiated questions are a strong indicator of cognitive activity in the classroom, teachers may want to give emphasis to facilitating these questions. The teacher may ask students to work in small groups, and to compose several higher order thinking questions about the lesson; then she may have them present these questions to the other members of the class. Or, the teacher may call on students and ask them to come up with a "what if" or "what do you think?" type of question. Until students ask a variety of academic questions during lessons, the teacher cannot assume that a truly active, higher level intellectual functioning has been achieved by the students.

TECHNIQUES TO CHECK FOR UNDERSTANDING: HOW TO CONDUCT A RECITATION

We have just reviewed different types of questions and how they affect the levels at which children may be required to think. Lower order questions (questions from the lowest two levels of Bloom's Taxonomy) foster "reproductive" thinking and are used by teachers to verify that students have learned the material which has been presented in the lesson. Instructional activities in which students engage in lower order thinking, as they respond to recall, and comprehension questions, are called "recitations." One use of the recitation is to check for understanding.

Once students have been exposed to information about a new topic or skill, the teacher must verify that the students understand the material well enough to apply it or to move on to another topic or skill. A teacher may choose from several approaches to verifying understanding. Students may be given a written exercise or asked to come to the board. A very practical and simple way to check on student progress is to ask lower order questions about the material which has been covered. These questions are directed to the student in order that the teacher may find out how well the students remember (knowledge), understand (comprehension), and are able to demonstrate (application) the concept or skill in question. This technique is called "the recitation" because the students are required to reproduce the information or skills presented to them. The teacher should involve many students in the recitation.

An example of checking for understanding during a third grade social studies lesson on traffic signs would be to ask the following questions:

What kinds of signs were presented in the lesson? (Knowledge)

What shape and color is the stop sign? (Knowledge)

What does the arrow in the "One Way" sign mean? (Comprehension)

What is the speed limit on your own street where you live ? (Application)

DISCUSSION TECHNIQUES: HOW TO CONDUCT A CLASS DISCUSSION

Guided discussions are instructional activities in which students engage in higher order thinking as they respond to analysis, synthesis, and evaluation questions which have been presented by the teacher. Higher order questions (questions from the highest three levels of Bloom's Taxonomy) foster "productive," or critical-creative, thinking on the part of the students. Guided discussions may emphasize convergent or divergent thinking. Some guided discussions emphasize both convergent and divergent thinking.

When questions require mainly analysis, the students are guided through these questions until they discover new meanings and relationships. This type of teaching emphasizes convergent thinking. In it, the teacher carefully guides the students through analysis questions until they arrive at a specific knowledge or understanding.

When teacher questions require mainly synthesis or evaluation, the discussion becomes more open-ended. There is no specific knowledge or understanding which the teacher has in mind. This type of teaching emphasizes divergent thinking. In it the teacher fosters reflection on the part of the students without leading their thinking down any particular path.

Students can discriminate between discussions which emphasize convergent thinking and those which emphasize divergent thinking. In convergent thinking, the teacher knows the answer and the students must discover it. In divergent thinking, teacher and students search together for answers which would help to solve the problem in question. Some guided discussions emphasize both convergent and divergent thinking. In this case, the teacher asks analysis questions first, and then moves on to synthesis and evaluation questions.

Most elementary texts, as well as standardized tests at both the state and national levels, emphasize lower order thinking. As a result of this concern with basic content and skills, teachers feel forced to cover content through recitations rather than through approaches which foster critical-creative thinking.

If guided discussions are to promote productive thinking (rather than reproductive thinking), the following conditions must exist:

1. The teacher's questions must move beyond recall, comprehension, and application into the analysis, synthesis, and evaluation levels of the taxonomy.
2. Students must believe that their ideas will be respected.
3. Adequate time must be allowed for the discussion to unfold.
4. Broad student participation must be encouraged, but students must not be forced to give answers.
5. The teacher must adopt a role of facilitator, guiding the discussion while at the same time allowing the students to be active and involved.

In a guided discussion on traffic signs, the teacher might ask questions about the consequences of not having traffic signs. These questions would fall under the categories of questions which require analysis, synthesis, or evaluation. For example, the teacher might ask the following questions:

What would traffic be like if there were no speed limits? (Analysis)

How would this affect people's personalities? (Analysis)

Why are traffic lights important to drivers? (Application, Analysis)

If you lived in a country without traffic laws, which new laws would you make? (Synthesis)

If you lived in a country without traffic signs, which new signs would you make? (Synthesis)

Would you change any of our traffic laws? Why? (Evaluation)

Would you change any of our traffic signs? Why? (Evaluation)

Not all class discussions are guided by teachers. Some class discussions occur among small groups of students. In this case, the teacher provides a written list of higher order questions for students to discuss. Or the teacher may require the students to construct the questions themselves and then discuss them. Small group discussions require more skill and maturity on the part of the student. They also require careful preparation of materials by the teacher. Chapter 10 deals with this topic in the chapter section which deals with group process skills.

INPUT TECHNIQUES: HOW TO PRESENT FACTS, CONCEPTS, AND SKILLS

The presentation of new material to the student can be called "input." Input may be provided by the teacher, the printed word, audiovisual equipment, or the students themselves. Students spend a significant amount of time in classrooms receiving input about facts, concepts, and skills. **Facts** are the most simple units of knowledge and should always be taught in relation to concepts. **Concepts** are ideas which result from grouping together interrelated facts. When concepts are interrelated with each other, they form a body of knowledge or subject matter. Skills are knowledge about how to do things or how to apply subject matter to specific situations.

How are facts, concepts, and skills presented to children in the elementary classroom? They may be presented through teacher explanations or demonstrations. They may be communicated via films or recordings. The students may acquire them by reading a textbook or a library book. They may also acquire them through tutorial experiences or role plays. Several of the techniques for presenting and acquiring information will be described in the following sections of this chapter.

When providing input, the teacher must keep in mind the different levels of activities which are depicted in our *Types of Instruction* chart. According to it, input may be conveyed via various types: Levels 1–2 (Symbolic), levels 3–4 (iconic), and Levels 5–6 (Enactive).

ESTABLISHING SET TECHNIQUES: HOW TO OPEN A LESSON

The first minutes of a lesson are extremely important because it is in these minutes that the teacher gains the interest, attention, and cooperation of the students. When learners perceive the lesson as something that is interesting and valuable, they are more likely to straighten up in their seats and be prepared to work. When the beginning to a lesson does not make clear what will be learned and the topic appears to be of little consequence to the students' lives, students are likely to sink deeper into their desks with that glassy-eyed look that is so discouraging to teachers.

The beginning of the lesson sets the tone for the lesson and is commonly called "establishing set." Teachers may begin a lesson by using five brief, easy to implement, techniques:

1. Personalizing and warming-up the climate.
2. Using an attention getter.
3. Relating the lesson to the world of the students.
4. Reviewing past work.
5. Using advance organizers.

Personalizing and Warming-Up the Climate

For this technique, the teacher, in a cheerful manner, shares positive feelings about events, work of the students, or a personal high point (e.g., "Isn't it wonderful that Spring is here?", "I am very proud of the performance of our class in the school fair, and particularly of all the work that Diana and Adrian did to make it happen!", "I am especially happy today. My daughter scored very high in the S.A.T.") As a result of these comments, the socioemotional climate of the class becomes more positive and up-beat.

Using an Attention Getter

This technique makes use of an attention getter; for example, dressing-up or bringing in objects that are related to the lesson and are novel to the students such as old coins, rocks, plants, clothing, and tools. It tends to arouse the class interest and willingness to actively participate. Pictures, posters, brief slide presentations, and audiotapes of music, if related to the lesson, are other types of attention getters.

Relating the Lesson to the World of the Students

This is another way to enhance student interest. It is difficult for most learners to identify with events which occurred years ago, or in different regions, or to members of a different social class. To begin a lesson on a topic which the students have little background information about is likely to produce confusion, frustration, and alienation. For example, to present a lesson about the desert to students from the Pacific Northwest, or to talk about a trip to Russia to children who have not gone more than 10 miles away from their homes in all their lives, or to talk about grammar to children whose parents barely "grunt" across the dinner table, is not likely to help, unless the teacher establishes some linkages between the new concept and the students' prior experiences.

Teachers must establish linkages between the experimental world of the students and the topics to be introduced if learning is going to take place. Before starting an explanation on "construction workers," the teacher may ask the students how many of them know a carpenter, an electrician, a plumber, etc. and let them briefly talk about it. Or the teacher, when comparing "grass eater and meat eater species" may ask about students' pets and the foods they eat. Or when talking about a trip to a new country with children from low socioeconomic environments, the teacher may ask how many of them have visited the other side of town, or the nearest town, and how did it feel to go to a new place.

Reviewing Past Work

This is a very efficient way of establishing set and introducing a lesson. The teacher asks as many students as possible to bring back recollection, understanding, and critical thoughts about facts, concepts, and skills learned in the past few lessons. These answers provide the intellectual context or framework for the new lesson to be introduced, not as an isolated piece, but as part of a larger unit of learning.

Advance Organizers

These are statements which will help the learners process, in a meaningful manner, the information about to be introduced. They help students organize the facts, concepts, and generalizations presented in a lesson. They are more abstract than the information which is presented during the lesson. One example of an advance organizer might be a city map when used to indicate that streets run east to west and avenues run north to south. When studying birds and their survival, an advance organizer would be to point out to students that birds with bright colored feathers usually encounter territorial battles with other birds while dull colored birds do not encounter as much territorial competition. Or when studying communities, the teacher might tell the students to try to find out, during the lesson, "What is the importance of cooperation in a community?" That would also be an example of an advance organizer.

CLOSURE TECHNIQUES: HOW TO CLOSE A LESSON

As the lesson comes to its final few minutes, an opportunity exists to extend learning through a closure activity. At this time, the teacher seeks to intensify the attention of the learners so they can reach conclusions and insights about what has been studied. It is a time for bringing apparently disconnected pieces into a meaningful whole. There are four major ways to close a lesson:

1. Have a summary review.
2. Elicit generalizations and abstractions.
3. Provide feedback on group accomplishments.
4. Preview the next lesson.

Summary Reviews

These may be carried out by asking many recall, comprehension, and application questions about the material just covered, or by inviting students to summarize what has been learned. Or the teacher may summarize the lesson, but this is a less desirable approach than one which involves the students.

Eliciting Generalizations and Abstractions

By asking higher order questions, the teacher can foster critical and creative thinking and extend student thinking at the end of a lesson. Questions such as, "What do you think…?", "What if…?", and "Should…" help the students to bring information together in the form of generalizations and principles.

Feedback on Group Accomplishments

Through feedback on group accomplishments, teachers can provide effective academic messages about student progress. The teacher can tell a group of students how well they have mastered the objective of the lesson, how impressed she is by their rapid advancement, and how proud she is of their efforts and participation. This closure technique is especially important when groups are insecure and need reassurance.

Previewing the Next Lesson

This is done after the teacher has briefly summarized the material which has been covered. With this technique, the teacher introduces some of the elements that will be covered in the next lesson and alerts the students to begin to prepare for it.

DEMONSTRATION TECHNIQUES: HOW TO DEMONSTRATE A CONCEPT OR SKILL

Teacher demonstrations are a form of input which relies on social learning theory, or "modeling." Students seem to learn new behaviors best through demonstrations in which information, practice, and feedback are provided (Bandura, 1977). Sometimes concepts and skills can be presented more effectively to students through teacher demonstrations than through a teacher's verbal explanation.

Demonstrations include showing and explaining (on the part of the teacher) and observing and replicating (on the part of the student). Demonstrations make a topic more concrete and real for students, allowing them to witness the actual event or skill while they attend to an explanation. Students who are exposed to demonstrations of concepts and skills achieve significantly higher than students who have been taught without modeling (Zimmerman & Kleefeld, 1985). Demonstrations are mainly utilized to teach procedural knowledge; that is, basic academic skills and psychomotor skills like how to add or how to jump rope.

The demonstration part of a lesson seldom lasts the full period since it is necessary that the students apply the concept or skill which has been demonstrated and since the teacher must also verify mastery and provide feedback. Demonstrations are carried out in five steps (Joyce and Weil, 1986):

1. Establish set.
2. Present prerequisite knowledge or a rationale.
3. Model the correct performance. This step usually requires that teachers do three things:
   a. develop, themselves, a thorough mastery of the concept or skill to be presented
   b. break down the concept or skill into smaller components and arrange them in an appropriate learning sequence

    c. follow a step-by-step written outline during the demonstration. This should include details about the use of materials.
4. Have students practice under controlled conditions.
5. Provide opportunities for transfer to more complex situations.

    Demonstrations are frequently used to teach basic academic skills, social behaviors, psychomotor skills, and laboratory processes. An example of a demonstration in a science lesson would be for the teacher to demonstrate how rain is made. The teacher would pour a cup of hot water into a jar and place a pie tin, with three ice cubes in it, on top of the jar. The students would then be told to observe what happens. The hot water would heat the air inside the jar and add moisture to it. The moist, hot air would rise, touch the cold pie tin, and then turn cool and condense. Eventually, water droplets would form and fall. This demonstration could lead to an inquiry lesson during which the teacher would pose analysis questions to the students until they were able to explain what had happened in this experiment.

    Another science demonstration might show how light travels in a straight line. The teacher would line up cards which are perforated in the center, space them about 15 centimeters apart, and have a student hold a flashlight so that it shines through the holes. Then, the teacher would arrange the cards so that their center holes did not coincide. Because of this, the light would not be seen by those students who were facing the last card. The teacher would then ask the students to replicate this experiment by positioning the cards at various distances when their center holes were either aligned or not aligned. The students would then describe their results.

    Teachers may set up *student* demonstrations to model the use of academic, social, or psychomotor skills. For example, when teaching communication skills, the teacher may present, with the help of students, vignettes which demonstrate the use of listening skills. Or after having explained the steps involved in resolving a conflict, the teacher may ask two students to present a demonstration. Student demonstrations are very effective since they prove to other students that the tasks can be mastered. Student demonstrations are sometimes called role playing.

ROLE PLAYING TECHNIQUES: HOW TO FACILITATE STUDENT ROLE PLAYS

Role plays are a form of student practice in which students "learn by doing" rather than by reading or listening. They are also a form of play. Role plays are very motivating instructional activities which engage the attention and emotions of students. Role plays can be classified in Level 5 of our *Types of Instruction* chart. The learners are physically involved with these activities through contrived or dramatized experiences.

    In role plays, students enact present, past or fictional situations and explore actions, values, and feelings. There are two major purposes for classroom role plays: 1) The development of social interaction and problem-solving skills, and 2) The "acting out" of the curriculum.

    Role plays may vary in their degrees of structure. In the case of younger children, the roles may be specified in detail. With older or more experienced students, the roles may be open-ended allowing for individual interpretations. Role plays foster student expression, problem-solving, and creativity.

During role play activities, the teacher has to plan, structure, facilitate, and discuss the enactment with her students. The major steps for the teacher to follow in order to effectively implement a role play are:

1. Explain the task.
2. Describe the roles to be played and identify the players.
3. Allow time for the players to prepare their interpretation and assist them as needed.
4. Have students enact the role play.
5. Facilitate a discussion of the activity, exploring its implications.

In order for students to actively participate in role playing activities, a climate of freedom of expression, trust, and cooperation must be established. If students are worried about making mistakes and being ridiculed, or about not being able to freely express their views and feelings, they will not be creative and participate actively in the role plays. Once the teacher has established a climate of acceptance, where risk taking is rewarded and learning is fun, role plays are easy to implement. Teachers who fail to provide this supportive climate should not be surprised when students refuse to role play or do it without enthusiasm.

Individual teachers, depending on the age of the students and the subject matter being taught, may choose to utilize role plays for the purpose of fostering the development of social interaction and problem-solving or to act out the curriculum.

Role Plays as Tools to Develop Social Interactions and Problem-Solving

Role plays can be especially useful when a teacher is working with young children who need to learn the following: how to communicate with another person (verbally and nonverbally) in different social and cultural contexts; how to listen to another person; how to disagree and present one's point of view in an acceptable manner; how to explore alternative solutions to a conflict; how to elicit, from another person, disclosure of views and feelings; how to express feelings of anger and frustration; how to accept someone else's feelings; and how to turn conflicts into opportunities to find more satisfactory solutions.

For example, after explaining the classroom rules to the children at the beginning of the year, a first grade teacher sets up role playing situations in which the students enact examples in which each rule is either followed or not followed. The teacher has the students discuss what happened after each role playing exercise. Through these role plays, the students practice the appropriate classroom behaviors and learn to recognize behaviors which either comply or do not comply with the rules of the classroom. Or when some children are having difficulty in sharing materials, the teacher might ask the class to role play positive and negative approaches to sharing materials.

Many students lack mastery of social interaction and conflict resolution skills. In fact, some children exhibit disruptive, bullying, selfish, intransigent behaviors. Primary classrooms are laboratories of life where children learn not only academic skills, but are gradually socialized into the ways of the culture. Teachers may address these skills systematically during social studies lessons as part of the prescribed curriculum, or they may address them when situations spontaneously arise in the classroom. Social interaction skills are best learned through modeling and practice. Students must actually enact contrived situations in order to practice and refine their mastery of these skills.

Role Plays as Tools to Dramatize the Curriculum

Role plays may be used to enact historical or fictional events, thereby bringing subject matter closer to the experiential world of the learner. Many students have a limited experiential background and lack exposure to many concepts. Textbook readings or traditional presentations seem remote and removed from reality to these students. They have difficulty identifying with the concepts which are presented through oral or written words. It is easier for these students, given their past experiences, to learn from modeling and from enacting approaches which are concrete and expressive.

For example, an intermediate grade class which is studying the Declaration of Independence may be assigned to do research in small groups on several of the key historical figures. Once students have gathered information about the founding fathers, the teacher may ask each group to prepare a role play of the signing of the document and invite them to present the role play to the rest of the class.

The Declaration of Independence is "an old thing" for students until they are put in a situation where they have to confront a problem that the American colonists faced and role play their world. Then they suddenly realize that history is not "an old thing," but it is a collection of very human conflicts similar to those experienced by people today. The stage and costumes may have changed, but the human drama remains, and the students identify with it, understand it, and learn.

When assigned to prepare a role play, students are likely to work hard at preparing the enactment. They do this because the work is fun and because they want to perform well in front of their teacher and their peers. Role play assignments provide a problem-solving context which require the students to use higher order thinking skills. Role plays bring segments of the curriculum closer to the students, and actualize and dramatize historical, contemporary or fictional situations. Through role playing, students gain insight and personal meaning, and explore feelings and values. As students discuss the actions of different individuals and their dilemmas, they engage in moral education and value development. Teachers may use role plays in language arts, social studies, science, mathematics, health, etc. Role plays provide an opportunity for students to vicariously experience many events which are not directly accessible to them. Role play is more than observing events through a film or video. It is an experience in which students enact their interpretation of reality.

TUTORING TECHNIQUES: HOW TO IMPLEMENT TUTORING ACTIVITIES

Tutoring is another technique which teachers utilize to get students to practice new skills or to learn new material. It is an instructional activity in which students teach students. There are three types of tutoring activities: 1) Reciprocal tutoring, 2) Peer tutoring, and 3) Cross-age tutoring. Most tutoring activities occur during the practice component of a lesson. Tutoring may also take place on a voluntary or paid basis after school.

Teachers use tutoring activities to provide greater opportunities for practice and feedback, to individualize instruction, to boost student responsibility and motivation, to maximize the use of human resources in the classroom, and to foster a sense of caring and mutual cooperation among students.

Tutoring activities may be utilized in any subject for which concepts and skills are being taught, particularly if the task can be broken down into clear steps for which there are correct or incorrect ways of performing. Tutoring activities are more difficult to structure, and less advisable for primary classrooms, when the task is complex, not sequential, or when it allows for a variety of possible answers.

Reciprocal Tutoring

The easiest type of tutoring activity to implement in the classroom is **reciprocal** tutoring. It occurs during the application, or guided practice, period of a lesson (see Chapter 4 for more on this), and it does not require the training of tutors. Students of comparable abilities are divided into pairs and asked to help each other practice the task the teacher has just presented or demonstrated. The students proceed to work on problems or materials provided by the teacher, who in turn supervises the progress made by each pair or group. For example, in a language arts lesson, the teacher might introduce the use of pronouns. She would then pair off students and assign them to do an exercise on a handout for which they are expected to underline the pronouns and then substitute nouns for these pronouns. The students must help each other to correctly answer the exercises while the teacher supervises them in their work. After enough time has passed, the teacher asks each pair or group to share its work.

Peer Tutoring

Peer tutoring is when two students of similar age but differing abilities are paired. One student is the **tutor** and the other is the **tutee**. Peer tutoring requires greater structure and preparation on the part of the teacher than reciprocal tutoring. Peer tutoring may also be implemented during the application, or practice, segment of a lesson, but it is different because high achieving students are paired with low achieving students. The teacher, after finding out the needs and degree of proficiency of the tutees, must:

1. Match the students to each other.
2. Develop easy to follow instructions and worksheets.
3. Prepare the tutors for their task.
4. Evaluate progress in order to continue with the next tutoring cycle.

A good way to prepare the tutors for their tasks is for the teacher to model the steps to be followed just before the tutoring activities begin. During the presentation segment of the lesson, the teacher demonstrates the steps involved in the learning task and leads the students as they practice these steps. Then, the teacher divides the class into tutoring groups and asks the tutors to help the tutees by following the steps modeled by the teacher and specified in the worksheets.

Peer tutors, in order to be effective, need to develop skills in explaining the objective, adjusting the teaching pace to the tutee's learning rate, giving praise for effort and accomplishments, and providing frequent feedback so the tutees are aware of their progress. Tutoring skills do not necessarily need to be developed during special training sessions. When teachers model effective teaching skills, daily, in their lessons, students readily learn them and imitate them.

For example, after a review on how to add fractions of like denominators, the teacher may pair students who have mastered the concept with students who are experiencing difficulty. The teacher gives each pair a worksheet with problems to be solved. The first problems are simple, so that the tutees will be motivated to attend to them and ask their tutors for further explanation. Next, the complexity of the problems is increased and the tutors proceed to help their peers to solve the problems. If the *tutor* needs help, the teacher steps in and provides assistance. When the tutoring session is over, the teacher collects the samples of the students' work and evaluates their progress in order to make plans for the next tutoring session.

Cross-Age Tutoring

Cross-age tutoring is when older students work with younger students. This form of tutoring, logistically more difficult to arrange in traditional elementary school settings, works very well in nongraded and multi-aged student groupings. Some after-school tutoring programs utilize cross-age tutoring. In this case, special training sessions for tutors should be offered, and an abundance of support materials should be available. In after-school cross-age tutoring programs, the tutors come to the situation without the benefit of the teacher demonstration and the learning task does not necessarily relate to content that was recently covered in class. Under these conditions, student tutors need more assistance and supervision, since they will work independently from the classroom context, and will not have the benefit of a teacher presentation and demonstration before the tutorial session.

For example, during after-school hours, students from the intermediate grades who are proficient in reading may tutor students from the primary grades who are having difficulty with reading. These tutors will need assistance in developing tutoring techniques since they are required to present a lesson to an individual student very much in the same manner that a teacher presents to the class (i.e., state the objective, explain, practice, evaluate, and make decisions for reteaching and further practice). Many schools which have after-school tutorial programs have a teacher in charge of the program who trains and assists the tutors. If a classroom teacher sets up an after-school volunteer tutoring program, the tutors should be given similar training and assistance to the one offered in formalized after-school tutorial programs.

FEEDBACK TECHNIQUES: HOW TO SUPERVISE
AND CRITIQUE STUDENT WORK

Whenever students are learning new knowledge or skills, they need information about how well they are doing. When teachers provide information to students about their progress and achievement, they provide **feedback**. Without feedback or knowledge of results, practice may become frustrating and of little value. For example, a primary student who is asked to complete ten math problems on a worksheet needs to know which of his answers are correct and which are incorrect. Unless a student is given prompt feedback, he may become discouraged. The student needs to know the answer to the question, "Am I doing okay?".

Bloom (1976) has identified feedback as the teacher behavior most consistently related to student achievement. Students need to have information about their progress, what they have learned, what is left to learn, and what corrections need to be made in order to improve their performance. In order to provide this information, teachers move around the room while students work to constantly check on their progress. Or, sometimes, the teacher reviews student work and comments on it as soon as it has been completed. In giving feedback, teachers follow five steps:

1. State clearly what is to be achieved (the performance task).
2. Break down the task into subtasks as much as possible.
3. Describe the degree of student progress toward meeting each subtask.
4. Make corrections and give suggestions for improving performance.
5. Verify student mastery of the task.

Teachers must communicate clearly to students what is expected of them before students engage in the learning activities. These expectations must be made explicit by providing a list of performance criteria for the desirable performance or by giving an example of the desired behavior.

In order to be able to describe the degree of student progress toward the attainment of the objective, the teacher must break down the task into subtasks as much as possible. The students will then be aware of the series of intermediate tasks they must master in order to achieve the objective, and the teacher will be able to give more detailed information about each of the subtasks. Once students begin to perform the tasks, the teacher gives information about their progress and makes suggestions for improvement.

For example, in the case of intermediate grade students who are learning to write an informal letter, the teacher would communicate the task and establish criteria on how to include the inside address, greeting, the body of a letter, and a closing. The teacher would then display a sample of an informal letter for all the students, making sure they understood what was expected of them and explaining each part of an informal letter. Then, the students would be asked to write a letter to a friend describing their plans for the coming holidays. As the students began to work on their letters, the teacher would circulate around the room and give feedback to her students, informing them, individually or as a class, as to which parts of the letter they were handling correctly or incorrectly.

Feedback can be provided verbally, in writing, or by playback of a videotape or audiotape. The teacher may be the source of feedback or other students may provide it. Some aspects to consider when giving effective feedback are:

1. Give feedback immediately after, or as close as possible to, the actual time of performance.
2. Use descriptive language rather than judgmental language.
3. Focus on the present performance rather than on past ones.
4. If possible, suggest alternatives rather than a single solution.
5. Tell the students only what they are able to manage at a given time rather than all that has happened.
6. Focus feedback on modifiable areas rather than on areas over which students have little control.
7. Emphasize achievements instead of shortcomings and maintain an optimistic and supportive class atmosphere (Hyman, 1974).

A teacher should not be the only source of feedback in the classroom. Students can be taught to evaluate their own performance as well as the work of their peers. Through the use of self-evaluation and peer evaluation, students can decide whether they are ready to proceed, whether they need to seek help, etc. When students learn to evaluate each other's progress, the teacher has more time to work with individual students who require special assistance.

GLOSSARY

convergent thinking Thinking for which the teacher guides the student until the material is learned; reproductive thinking.

divergent thinking Thinking in which the students go beyond the ideas presented in class and produce their own ideas; productive thinking.

enactive learning Learning which is characterized by students participating actively in hands-on activities.

iconic learning Learning in which the student is exposed to representational materials such as pictorial aids or audiovisuals.

mastery Successful performance of an objective.

methods Approaches to teaching which a teacher employs when carrying out instruction. Methods make use of techniques.

positive reinforcement Teacher behavior which follows a desirable student behavior and increases the likelihood that the behavior will be repeated; for example, teacher praise.

problem-solving context An approach to learning in which students are confronted with problematic situations which need to be solved.

productive thinking Thinking which requires the student to go beyond the ideas presented in class; thinking on the higher levels of Bloom's taxonomy.

reproductive thinking Thinking which requires the student to recall information or ideas; thinking on the lowest levels of Bloom's taxonomy.

simulation An educational experience during which a real-life situation is imitated so that peo-ple can learn about this situation without having to directly experience it..

social learning (also called modeling) A theory of learning which endorses the belief that humans learn by observing and imitating the behavior of other humans.

symbolic learning Learning in which the student is exposed to books or printed materials.

techniques Skills which a teacher employs when carrying out instruction.

Chapter
4

Teaching Methods

*I*n Chapter 3, we presented teaching techniques which all teachers must master in order to perform professionally in the classroom. These techniques were originally identified through a task analysis of the act of teaching and could be found in most professional lists of teacher competencies. These teaching techniques are the foundation or "building blocks" of specific teaching methods which have been developed throughout the years.

Theoretically, all teaching methods should be the result of different combinations of teaching techniques. For example, the Mastery Teaching method is very different from the Cooperative Learning method; yet, both methods employ many of the same teaching techniques (e.g., establishing set, questioning, and feedback techniques).

In this chapter, the most promising and commonly used teaching methods are described. The emphasis is on how these methods are implemented.

Some teaching methods are primarily teacher-directed (e.g., presentation and mastery teaching); some are more student-centered (e.g., topic work and cooperative learning); and, still others are mediated by materials (e.g., mastery learning and learning centers). In teacher-directed methods, the students learn by interacting with the teacher. The teacher is the center of attention and focus of the instructional activities most of the time. The students listen to the teacher, observe the teacher demonstrate, follow directions given by the teacher, answer questions asked by the teacher, and practice exercises monitored by the teacher.

In student-centered methods, the students learn primarily through interacting with each other. The interaction among students is the focus of the instructional activities most of the time. The students plan work together, tutor each other or gather materials for a group project, present a role play, or conduct a group discussion.

In the materials-centered methods, the interaction that occurs between the student and the instructional materials is the center of attention, or focus, most of the time. The students conduct experiments, carry out activities at a learning center, practice math exercises on the computer, or review a specific topic by reading articles in the library. We will begin by explaining two teacher-directed methods, the presentation and the mastery teaching methods.

PRESENTATION-RECITATION-DISCUSSION

All teachers in elementary school present a significant amount of information to students. While teachers in high school or college may engage in elaborate and lengthy presentations, called lectures, elementary teachers engage in presentations for briefer periods, and follow them with two types of activities: 1) recitation-discussion and 2) recitation-practice. Presentations followed by recitation and student practice are called "Mastery Teaching" and will be explained after the Presentation-Recitation-Discussion method is explained.

Presentation-Recitation-Discussion is a direct teaching strategy. It is used when the teacher is covering **declarative knowledge** and wishes for the students to recall, comprehend, and think critically about information (Gagne, 1985). Declarative knowledge includes the facts, concepts, generalizations, and principles of a discipline; it is concerned with the "what and why" of subject matter. Declarative knowledge can also be taught through methods other than presentation, for example, through guided inquiry, group open inquiry, cooperative learning, or independent study. A second type of knowledge, **procedural knowledge,** deals with skills and rules, the "how to do it" of subject matter. Procedural knowledge may be taught through several techniques and methods such as demonstration, role play, direct teaching, and mastery learning (Gagne, 1985).

The presentation-recitation-discussion method consists of three phases in which the teacher: 1) presents information (presentation), 2) asks the students questions to verify comprehension (recitation), and 3) asks higher order questions to relate new knowledge to previous knowledge and foster critical-creative thinking (discussion).

Kauchak and Eggen (1989) recommend that the presentation-recitation-discussion method be broken down into several short cycles. In each of these consecutive cycles, the teacher disseminates information, checks for understanding, and asks higher order questions to integrate knowledge. The content is broken down into smaller units, or mini-lessons, which constitute the cycles. Each cycle lasts only for a brief period of time. This multi-cycle approach is less demanding on the attention span of children, and avoids the passivity inherent in listening to a long presentation by quickly introducing questions and discussion.

There is an obvious difference between recitation and discussion. Recitation elicits lower-order learning, that is, what students recall and understand about the material just presented. Discussion fosters higher order discourse through analysis, synthesis and evaluation questions, that is, what students think about the material just covered. Many times teachers remain at the recitation phase without progressing to discussion. Their lessons become then a presentation-recitation approach which has the danger of emphasizing memorization instead of understanding and critical thinking. This tends to inhibit student involvement and expression.

While presentation and recitation are highly structured phases with the teacher clearly in control and directing the learning as planned, discussion is a phase which allows for more flexibility, depending on the answers which the students provide. In the discussion phase, the teacher is guiding the students toward the attainment of predetermined higher order ideas and conclusions.

How to Implement Presentation-Recitation-Discussion

The steps a teacher follows in this method are:

1. Establish set and state objectives.
2. Present information.
3. Check for understanding: conduct a recitation.
4. Guided discussion.
5. Closure.

The presentation-recitation-discussion cycle may be repeated several times during the lesson, depending on the age of the students. For example, when teaching the concept "family" in first grade, the teacher may break down the topic into three subtopics: one-parent family, nuclear family, and extended family. Each of the subtopics could constitute a cycle for which the teacher would explain, verify understanding, and lead a discussion. At the end of each cycle, during the discussion, the teacher would ask students to compare and contrast the characteristics of the last two subtopics presented. The lesson closure would seek to summarize all the ideas presented into an organized whole. This lesson, then, could be diagrammed as follows:

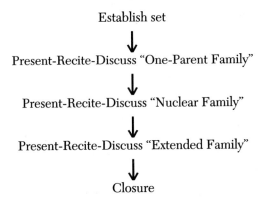

Establish set

↓

Present-Recite-Discuss "One-Parent Family"

↓

Present-Recite-Discuss "Nuclear Family"

↓

Present-Recite-Discuss "Extended Family"

↓

Closure

Let's consider an example of the first cycle. The teacher would **establish set** by "relating the lesson to the world of the student" (asking the students questions about their families). The **presentation** of the concept would follow. The teacher would define the concept "one-parent family," describe its critical characteristics, and present a few examples and nonexamples of one-parent families. These examples would be conveyed through verbal descriptions and visual representations (Levels 2 and 3 on our *Types of Instruction* chart).

In the **recitation**, the teacher would present a variety of new pictures and ask the students to identify which ones are examples and nonexamples of one-parent families. The teacher would also ask recall and comprehension questions about the concept to make sure the students understand and are able to verbalize the critical characteristics of the concept.

During the **discussion**, the teacher would ask higher order questions so the students could identify, on their own, some of the characteristics of the critical and noncritical attributes of one-parent families. For example, the students would discover that "age," "gender," and "blood kinship" are noncritical attributes, and explain why.

Next the teacher goes through a second presentation-recitation-discussion cycle on the nuclear family, and finally, the third cycle on the extended family. For the lesson's *closure*, the teacher might "elicit generalizations and abstractions" in order to extend student thinking. Analysis questions which require the student to compare and contrast the characteristics of the three different types of families would engage the students in critical thinking and assure that the knowledge presented, through the three cycles, is integrated in a meaningful manner to the knowledge which the students already possess.

In order to implement this method, teachers must be competent in the use of establishing set, presentation, questioning, and closure all covered in Chapter 3. By bringing together these four teaching techniques, you will be able to plan and teach lessons which use the presentation-recitation-discussion method.

Purpose of the Presentation-Recitation-Discussion Method

The major purpose of the presentation-recitation-discussion method is to transmit declarative knowledge to the learners and to foster higher order thinking about this knowledge.

Role of the Teacher

The main role of the teacher who uses this method is to conduct the learning activities. The teacher is the source of the information presented. The teacher checks for student understanding. The teacher guides the discussion and promotes higher order thinking.

Role of the Student

The role of the student being taught via this method is to acquire the declarative knowledge presented by the teacher and be able to think critically and creatively about it. Although the student participates actively in the discussion, the decision about what to learn and how to learn it is made by the teacher. The student is guided by the teacher throughout the lesson. This method is not designed to foster initiative and decision-making skills on the part of the students.

Instructional Materials

The instructional materials utilized in lessons conducted according to this method rely heavily on Bruner's *symbolic* and *iconic* stimuli (the top and middle levels of the *Types of Instruction*) rather than on direct or manipulative experiences. An abundance of printed materials, charts, and audiovisual materials are needed in order for the teaching approach to be carried out successfully.

Evaluation Procedure

Tests, whether teacher-made or developed by publishers, are the traditional evaluation procedures utilized to assess the extent to which the learning objectives of the lessons have been met. They measure declarative knowledge as well as anything can do so. Another more informal assessment procedure might be to observe individual students in tutorial situations and verify their degree of knowledge of the material covered.

MASTERY TEACHING

Mastery Teaching is a deductive instructional strategy that is taught in a step-by-step fashion. It can be used to teach procedural knowledge and, sometimes, declarative knowledge (Gagne, 1985). "Procedural knowledge" deals with basic academic skills, learning and thinking skills, and the skill components of the disciplines. Computation skills, reading and writing skills, library research skills, note taking skills, and analysis and evaluation skills are some examples of "procedural knowledge."

These skills vary in their degree of complexity. Some may be acquired through mere imitation, while others require the use of sophisticated mental processes. But all skills are useful tools which, once mastered, can be utilized spontaneously by the learners without conscious effort, and in diverse situations. For example, skills in addition (or writing, or analyzing information) may be used at school as well as at the store or home. Some disciplines like mathematics or music, have a very large amount of "procedural knowledge" to be mastered. Other disciplines, like the social sciences, have more declarative knowledge (which deals with the content of each discipline) and cannot be learned without the mastery of basic learning and thinking skills. Skill learning is a top priority in the elementary school since it is the foundation, and prerequisite, for the acquisition of declarative knowledge in middle school and high school.

Skill instruction has several names in the research literature: "direct instruction" (Good, 1979), "mastery teaching" (Hunter, 1982), "explicit skill instruction" (Pearson & Dole, 1985),"training model" (Joyce and Weil, 1986). Although the names vary, the authors agree on the characteristics of the method. In it, the teacher presents and demonstrates procedural knowledge, the students are asked questions to verify understanding, and the students practice the skill under guided and independent conditions until the skill is mastered. We have chosen the name "mastery teaching" (Hunter, 1982) because of the emphasis it makes on student performance.

There is a danger that instructors teach skills by "talking" about them and discussing their value and use without showing the students how to perform the skill and without having the students practice the skill. Skills cannot be taught through the presentation-recitation-discussion method. Skill learning requires that the students practice repeatedly after having observed the teacher demonstrate and explain the skill. For example, in order to learn listening skills, the students must witness modeling behaviors on the part of the teacher, or peers, and have ample opportunity to practice these behaviors. A lecture on listening skills will not lead to the development of the skills in the learners, even if the students are able to write a detailed essay about it. Unfortunately, it is not uncommon to find teachers who use a presentation-recitation approach to teach skills. Is it surprising, in those cases, that the students are unable to perform the skill? Teachers need to reflect on their purposes. When the purpose is instruction in a skill, the mastery teaching method is appropriate.

Some skills follow academically established rules, and lead to convergent outcomes; for example, grammar rules, multiplication operations, and map reading. There is only one correct manner of applying the skill. The learners have no choice. They must follow the rules as prescribed. Other skills, called "thinking skills," allow for a variety of approaches and interpretations, for example, comparing, classifying, and generalizing. There is not a correct product for these skills. Thinking skills lead to divergent outcomes. It is up to the learners to decide on how the skill will be applied.

How to Implement Mastery Teaching

The steps a teacher follows in the Mastery Teaching method (Hunter, 1982) are:

1. Establish set and state objectives.
2. Present information about the skill.
3. Demonstrate or model the skill.
4. Check for student understanding: conduct a recitation.
5. Provide guided practice.
6. Provide independence practice.
7. Use closure.

When presenting information about the skill, the teacher: a) defines the skill, b) explains how the skill works, and c) explains the uses, or application, of the skill. The demonstration of the skill must be accompanied by a verbalization of the various steps involved in its performance. Neglecting to verbalize may lead to imitation without understanding on the part of the learner. In this case students are able to perform the skill, but cannot explain what they are doing, or why. Guided practice consists of exercises in which the students practice the new knowledge under the direct supervision of the teacher and receive feedback. Guided practice continues until students perform most exercises without serious errors. Independent practice is assigned only after the teacher is convinced that the students are able to work on their own with little teacher intervention. At this point, some variations of the method may take place. For example, the teacher may continue guided practice with a few students while others work independently or in tutoring pairs. Or the teacher may work with the advanced students while the rest of the students do exercises in small groups.

Let's consider an example of a Mastery Teaching lesson on learning how to find latitude and longitude points on a globe. The teacher will first **establish set** by showing a playing board of the game "Battleship." The teacher would ask the students how many of them have played the game, what is the object of the game (to sink enemy ships by locating them through the use of coordinates), etc. Next, the teacher would state the objective of the lesson (to learn how to find points on the globe through the use of two coordinates called latitude and longitude). The **presentation** of information about the use of latitude and longitude would include an explanation of each term, how it is used, and how it applies to the game in question. The explanation of the concepts would follow these steps commonly recommended for teaching concepts: 1) the teacher would define the concept latitude, 2) describe its critical characteristics, and 3) present a few examples and nonexamples of latitude. These examples should be conveyed through verbal descriptions and the use of a large globe and several small globes around the room (using Level 5 of the *Types of Instruction*). A similar procedure is followed to present the concept longitude. Then, the teacher explains how latitude and longitude measures intersect at a point which is unique and different from all other points on the globe.

The teacher proceeds with a **demonstration** of how to find different latitude-longitude points on the globe while students follow the teacher's actions by manipulating their globes in small groups. The teacher asks questions (**recitation**) to make sure that students understand and can explain the concepts. In **guided practice**, the students are asked to find the names of places on their globes when they are given the latitude and longitude measures. Next, the students are given the names of places and asked to find their latitude and longitude measures. These exercises are conducted first with the whole group. As students begin to perform the skill correctly, without any major misconceptions or errors, the teacher passes out a worksheet with exercises for each individual student to complete. The teacher asks students to raise their hands if they have any doubts about how to complete the exercises. The teacher moves around the desks encouraging students, clarifying, giving feedback.

Now, time is running out! The teacher will not be able to complete the final activity (**independent practice**), a treasure hunt game using the globe, where teams of students are allowed to ask 20 questions about latitude and longitude measures to find the spot where the treasure is hidden. The teacher announces that the game will be played the next day, and assigns practice exercises for homework. Quickly, the teacher moves into **closure** by "providing feed-back on group accomplishments." The teacher tells the students how much they have learned today since latitude and longitude are challenging concepts to understand and learn how to use.

The next day the teacher will **establish set** by reviewing past work. After reviewing the concepts learned the day before, if the students are ready to proceed into **independent practice**, the teacher will distribute the rules for playing the treasure hunt game and begin the game. If there are several students having difficulty in mastering the skill, the teacher may have tutorial groups for a short activity before the game. If after the tutorial session there are still a few students having problems, the teacher may play the game with these students while the other members of the class play it on their own. Toward the end of the period, the teacher must assess how many students have mastered the skill. The children may have had great fun playing the game, but the teacher will still need to verify each individual's mastery of the concepts involved. A quiz should be given in which students are asked to explain the concepts and their uses, and to solve several problems of varying difficulty.

Purpose of Mastery Teaching

The major purpose of a Mastery Teaching method is to teach basic academic skills, learning skills, and thinking skills in a manner that leads to transfer. The students should be able to use the skills in different situations. The strategy is mostly used for the acquisition of cognitive skills, but it is particularly suitable for the teaching of psychomotor skills such as handwriting, physical education, art and music skills. As a matter of fact, most "life" skills that we learned as young children were taught to us through a homemade version of Mastery Teaching, for example, table manners, tying shoe laces, riding bike, etc.

Role of the Teacher

The teacher has a triple role in Mastery Teaching. At the beginning of the lesson, the teacher is the *focus of attention*. The teacher explains and demonstrates, asks questions to verify understanding, and directs students. As the lesson progresses, the teacher begins to take on a *coaching* role and the students become the center of attention. The students are asked to verbalize, to show, and to practice, while the teacher helps and encourages. Toward the end of the lesson, the teacher is more removed, observing the students work and *assessing* their progress and degree of mastery. At this point, the teacher gathers data which will determine what should be taught in the next lesson.

Role of the Student

The student is expected to be very attentive during the presentation and demonstration of the skill and to ask for clarification on how the skill is performed, since, by the end of the lesson, the student will have to demonstrate mastery of the skill. During guided practice, the student is expected to work through the sample exercises and to quickly point out to the teacher any difficulties encountered. During independent practice, the student is responsible for acquiring mastery of the skill.

Instructional Materials

The instructional materials utilized in Mastery Teaching lessons rely heavily on Bruner's *symbolic, iconic,* and *enactive* learning modes (all the levels of the *Types of Instruction*) to teach cognitive and basic academic skills. When teaching psychomotor skills, however, there is less need for printed materials and greater need for films, videos, models, simulations, and actual experiences.

Evaluation Procedures

The best way to determine if a student has acquired a basic or cognitive skill is to ask the student to submit a tangible product which demonstrates that the skill has been mastered. Exercises, compositions, research lists, classifications, essays, etc., are examples of such tangible products. To determine if a student has mastered a psychomotor skill, the teacher must observe the student performing the skill. Such skills include handwriting, drawing, singing, dancing, dribbling, etc. Next, we turn to a student-centered teaching method.

COOPERATIVE LEARNING

In the recent past, competitive reward structures have dominated the American classroom. Academic success has frequently been attained by students at the expense of the success of other students. Individualistic, noncompetitive activities, such as independent studies, collaborative activities, and group work, have been provided to a very small degree in elementary classrooms.

Cooperative learning is a teaching strategy used to: a) increase academic achievement through group collaboration, b) improve relations among students of diverse ethnic backgrounds and abilities, c) develop group problem-solving skills, and d) foster democratic processes in the classroom.

The students must cooperate in order to complete the learning task and be rewarded. Cooperative learning activities are set up in such a manner that students who prefer to work on their own, or compete with other students, have to make adjustments. They must shift to a more collaborative approach. Cooperative learning activities balance the experiences of students. The classroom should afford individualistic activities, competitive activities, and collaborative activities. All three types of learning experiences must be provided to students.

Cooperative learning work results in greater satisfaction for learning, increased motivation, and more positive attitudes toward school and peers (Sharan, 1980). Cooperative learning programs are being implemented throughout the nation, and their positive results have been documented (Stallings & Stipek, 1986). The most known approaches to cooperative learning are: STAD, Jigsaw, and Group Investigation.

Student Teams Achievement Division (STAD) was developed by Robert Slavin (1983). In this strategy, the teacher presents information first; next, students practice within their team until every member is ready to score perfectly on a quiz which will be given during the final phase of the lesson. Team achievement and improvement scores are then computed and publicly recognized. STAD is a deductive teaching strategy which lends itself to teaching lower order, convergent information. STAD could be diagrammed as follows:

Presentation→Team Tutoring→Evaluation→Recognition

JIGSAW, developed by Elliot Aronson (1978), is a strategy designed for students to learn, through team effort, higher order, divergent information. Each student on a team is assigned to a subtopic for a team topic and is responsible for finding information about this subtopic and for teaching this information to the other members of the team. Students from different teams who have the same subtopic form temporary groups called "expert groups." Each expert group meets to assist its members in mastering the subtopics. Then, "experts" go back to their original teams and teach the material to their team members. Students are tested individually on all the subtopics or they are evaluated as a group. Some teachers incorporate the Slavin approach by evaluating through a point system and recognizing team scores.

Expert Group Inquiry→Team Tutoring→Evaluation→Recognition

Group Investigation, developed by Shlomo Sharan (1984), is another form of cooperative learning designed for students to foster, through team effort, problem solving and research skills. Each team is given the responsibility to select a topic of interest to that team, divide assignments, and decide how to proceed in researching the subtopics. They must also integrate the material to form a group report. As a result of these in-depth investigations, reports are prepared and presented to the class.

How to Implement Cooperative Learning

The steps followed in cooperative learning lessons vary, depending on which version is used. Most teacher use STAD or JIGSAW. The main difference between these two approaches is the form in which information is initially conveyed. In STAD, the teacher presents the information. In JIGSAW, the students find the information. Once the information has been identified through a teacher presentation or student inquiry, the remaining steps of the lesson, which involve the team collaboration, are alike. The five steps followed in a Cooperative Learning lesson are:

1. Establish set and state objectives.
2. Present information (STAD)

    or

    Have students gather information (JIGSAW).
3. Have team members help each other master the lesson task.
4. Evaluate student progress.
5. Recognize team accomplishments.

Let's consider an example of a cooperative learning lesson using STAD to learn how to add two sets of fractions of different denominators. The teacher would **establish set** by reviewing past work. The teacher would explain the objective of the lesson, and explain how to add fractions of different denominators (**presentation**), defining the concepts and providing examples and nonexamples. The teacher would continue demonstrating, on the board, the solutions to several exercises. The teacher would then explain to the students what was expected during the team tutoring sessions that would follow and how they would take a quiz to assess their progress at the end of the lesson. The teacher would provide each team of five students with two sets of worksheets and answer keys so students would have to share the worksheets. The worksheets would include exercises on adding fractions of increasing difficulty. The first two problems would be explained step by step, and questions would be asked on the worksheet to verify student comprehension of the operation. The students would begin to work on the exercises (**team tutoring**), helping each other and testing each other to make sure that all team members know how to answer each exercise and could explain each step. The teacher would move around the room, giving assistance and support. Toward the end of the period, students would be asked to answer a quiz individually (**evaluation**). Scores would be calculated for each team, and **recognition** would be given by comparing a team's performance with its past scores or with the performance of other teams.

An example of a cooperative learning lesson using Jigsaw to learn the geography and natural resources of five Latin American countries would start with **establishing**

set by relating the lesson to the world of the learner. The teacher would ask students to tell how many of them had seen movies about Latin American countries, or knew people from those countries, or had visited those countries. Then the teacher would share the objective for the lesson and give detailed instructions about how to proceed in the learning teams. Obviously, the lesson would take more than one day, and the students would have to decide later how to structure the activities. Each student within a team would be assigned a different country: Mexico, Panama, Venezuela, Brazil, and Peru.

Materials with information about each country would be placed in front of the teacher's desk; for example, books, pamphlets, and maps. Information would also be available in the classroom's encyclopedia set. Two types of group meetings would take place. First, all students assigned the same country would step out from their teams and meet together **(expert group inquiry)** to gather information about their country. The students grouped by country would help each other until all had acquired the knowledge that they thought was necessary to teach the topic. Then students would return to their teams. At this point, each team of five students would have an expert for each of the five Latin American countries. They would begin **(team tutoring)** to teach each other the material. It would then become obvious that the material is very broad and requires more than one lesson to master it. The students would tell the teacher, "This is not possible," as they tangle with maps and lists of natural resources.

The Expert Group Inquiry session will have taken most of the period. The teacher will have known all along that this would happen but he wants the student to make decisions about how to structure their work time. The students will probably decide that in order to do a fair job it will require three more days to cover each country and learn the information which they will need to successfully complete a test. Some time will be spent deciding on time lines and homework assignments. Some students will go to the public library to find more information. For the next three lessons, the learning teams will immerse themselves in the geography and natural resources of Mexico, Panama, Venezuela, Brazil, and Peru.

On the third day, each student will take a test **(evaluation)** and the scores of each team will be calculated **(recognition)**. Another approach to evaluation would be for students to prepare an individual written report about three of the countries. This would require an extra day of individual writing, with some assistance from fellow team members.

Purpose of Cooperative Learning

The main purpose of cooperative learning is to increase academic achievement, improve relations among students of diverse ethnic backgrounds and abilities, and develop group problem-solving and group process skills. The strategy provides an unusual combination of academic, affective, and social learning outcomes. Few teaching strategies are so right in the manner in which they impact the cognitive, affective, and psychomotor domains of learning.

Role of the Teacher

The teacher has a particularly demanding role in cooperative learning lessons as an organizer of subject matter, students, and materials. The subject matter selected must be interesting and appropriate for the group level. Since the students are expected to exert a significant amount of self-direction and leadership, the material must be appealing and suitable to their level of development. The teacher has to explain the task (what students are expected to accomplish in the learning teams) and the grading procedures clearly. The teacher has to be very careful also in the formation of the learning teams in order to achieve a representative sample of the classroom within each team (abilities, gender, and ethnicity should be proportionally represented). It is also important for students to be satisfied with their assignment. The working instructions must be communicated in writing to avoid confusion. Finally, the teacher must communicate the value of collaboration and teamwork in order to overcome the reluctance of students who have been conditioned to work by themselves, in competition with others rather than through collaboration with others.

Role of the Student

Students, within the team structure, become both teachers and learners. They are responsible for the success of their team, and, as such, for the attainment of the lesson objectives. Students are expected to be active, accountable, cooperative, and caring. Assessment of progress toward team goals and reflection are important group skills for students to practice. Peer feedback and self-evaluation skills are another set of skills very necessary for successful group work.

Instructional Materials

An abundance of instructional materials, at the appropriate reading level and appealing to the students, is needed to implement cooperative learning lessons. The materials become the most important resource. The teacher stops presenting, and the students are left with the materials from which they may learn and teach other members of the team. The library becomes a very important support system. Besides books, there is a great need for workbooks and worksheets with an abundance of practice exercises and answer keys. These worksheets should have a wide range in levels of difficulty.

Evaluation Procedures

The students need immediate feedback in order to reinforce their newly acquired learning habits, which may run counter to what they have been taught about how one should work in a classroom. They have put forth effort, compromised, and demonstrated caring and patience with other members of the team. Now they deserve to have the satisfaction of feeling competent, having mastered a task, and completed a mission. Evaluation follows the team tutoring session in the form of a quiz, in the case of STAD and Jigsaw. This gives the student feedback about the results of their efforts. Some teachers emphasize competition among teams. Other teachers focus on team self-improvement. In this case, each team competes with itself to improve its past marks and achieve greater team scores. In some instances of Jigsaw and Group Investigation, the evaluation is based on a group report. Next, we will discuss a method of instruction which is materials-dominated.

MASTERY LEARNING

Mastery Learning is an individualized instruction approach in which the learners progress at their own pace through a structured curriculum divided into small learning modules. Mastery Learning, like Mastery Teaching, is a performance based teaching strategy. It defines very specifically, in behavioral terms, what the learner will be able to do at the end of the lesson. But while the interaction between teacher and student is the focus of the lesson in Mastery Teaching, the interaction between the student and the self-paced learning materials constitutes the core of the lesson in Mastery Learning.

Mastery Learning was originally developed by Benjamin Bloom (1971), based on the ideas of John B. Carroll (1971) about flexible individual learning time. Carroll believes that all students can master a set of objectives if sufficient time is provided along with appropriate materials and quality of instruction. According to Carroll, for any given task, the degree of student learning will be a function of the time allowed for learning, the motivation of the student, the quality of instruction, and the ability of the student to understand instruction. It is the intention of this method to increase the learning of all students in the classroom and to diminish the achievement differences among learners. Mastery Learning programs are used in many large urban districts to improve the learning of basic skills.

An important feature of Mastery Learning is the amount of responsibility and control given to the learners. The student decides how fast to move through the learning tasks and assume responsibility for mastering the objective. In this method, student achievement is closely related to effort and perseverance. Another very important factor in Mastery Learning is the quality of the instructional materials, which must be clear and appealing to the students. The success of the method also depends on the effort that students put forth when working with those materials.

How to Implement Mastery Learning

The steps a teacher follows in implementing Mastery Learning may vary according to the approach used. Some programs are very individualized and the students work at their own pace with structured learning materials. In other programs, the teacher presents the subject to be learned, before moving into self-paced work. Cooperative learning groups may also be used in conjunction with a Mastery Learning program. Regardless of the variations utilized, there are certain steps which are followed in any Mastery Learning program:

1. The subject matter of each learning unit is broken down into smaller components which can be evaluated on each incremental step.
2. Learning materials are prepared and an instructional strategy is selected.
3. Each learning component is accompanies by diagnostic tests to measure student progress and identify learning difficulties.
4. Results on diagnostic tests are used to decide when to provide supplementary instruction for students having difficulties, and when to provide enrichment instruction for those students who have mastered the objective.
5. A management system, to monitor individual progress and adjust prescriptions, is implemented.

Several versions of Mastery Learning programs have been developed for reading, mathematics, and science. These programs come prepared with learning modules, support materials, and diagnostic tests. The teacher will need to make only small adjustments to these programs, and is expected to act as a facilitator and support the interaction between learners and materials.

In some classrooms, teachers use a combination of Mastery Teaching and Mastery Learning. They begin the lesson by presenting information to the whole class, and then have students work with individualized materials at their own pace.

In order for a totally self-paced program to work, the materials must be very "student friendly" (the self-instructional activities presented in Chapter 5 were written with this goal in mind). The students must be also very motivated. It is difficult for young learners to spend hours of their time learning by themselves without interacting with the teacher or their peers.

Purpose of Mastery Learning

The main purpose of Mastery Learning is to increase the learning of all students in the classroom, and to diminish the achievement differences among learners. Instead of placing great emphasis on the diversity of student ability, the method relies on individual student effort, allowing for learning time to be used in a flexible manner, depending on the needs of different students.

Role of the Teacher

Mastery Learning places great demands on the teacher, who is no longer working with groups of students but facilitating and monitoring individual achievement. The teacher constantly diagnoses student progress, makes prescriptions for learning, prepares appropriate learning materials, maintains records on the progress of each student, provides frequent feedback, and interacts with students to increase motivation and effort.

Role of the Student

The student's attitude toward learning is the key element in Mastery Learning. Students must assume responsibility for their achievement. They make commitments to master the objectives and decide how much time to spend on each learning task. Students may need to work, on their own time, to complete a task. Mastery Learning puts the students in control of their academic progress.

Instructional Materials

The instructional materials are the core of the program. They must be hierarchically organized and allow for an abundance of remediation and enrichment activities at each level. The materials must be self-explanatory, easy to use, appealing to the students, and provide frequent opportunities for assessment and feedback. They frequently make use of the ingredients of self-instructional activities, which are detailed in Chapter 5.

Evaluation Procedures

Since the students are responsible for attaining mastery, it is essential that they be provided with information about their progress. Self-scoring quizzes are taken frequently to provide the needed feedback and to make decisions about further practice, remediation work, enrichment work, or proceeding to the next task. Comprehensive tests may be given at certain periods in order to assign grades, if this is required by the school. It is preferable that the report card describe progress along the hierarchy of tasks to be mastered rather than according to letter grades. Mastery Learning works best in a non-graded school.

Now we turn to a topic which is so broad that we hesitate to call it a method. It's more of an approach. It can be teacher-dominated, student-dominated, or materials-dominated. It is called by many names, but we call it "teaching thinking."

TEACHING THINKING

Bloom's taxonomy, which we presented in Chapter 3, includes six levels. The lowest three of these levels (knowledge, comprehension, and application), especially the lowest two levels (knowledge and comprehension), are usually referred to as **lower order learning** levels. The highest three levels on Bloom's taxonomy (analysis, synthesis, and evaluation), on the other hand, are usually called **higher order thinking** skills. Note that lower level skills are considered to be *learning* skills while higher level skills are referred to as *thinking* skills.

In education, "thinking" wears many hats. It is sometimes called "problem-solving," "reasoning," "higher order thinking," "critical thinking," cognitive strategy," "metacognition" (thinking about thinking), "study skills," or, simply, "thinking." What does it mean? It includes the following characteristics:

- Higher order thinking is **nonalgorithmic.** That is, the path of action is not fully specified in advance.
- Higher order thinking tends to be **complex.** The total path of thinking is not clear from any single vantage point.
- Higher order thinking involves **multiple solutions.**
- Higher order thinking involves **nuanced judgment** and interpretation.
- Higher order thinking often involves **uncertainty.** Not everything that bears on the task at hand is known.
- Higher order thinking involves **self-regulation** of the thinking process. We do not recognize higher order thinking in an individual when someone else "calls the plays" at every step (Resnick, 1987, p. 3).

Many teachers assume that students must master lower level knowledge before they can proceed to the higher, thinking, levels. But "higher-order" does not imply that lower-order learning must be acquired before higher-order thinking can occur. Children do not need constant drill in lower order skills before they are capable of independent thought. In fact, failure to develop higher order skills may be responsible for some of the major learning difficulties which occur in our schools—even at the elementary level! (Resnick, p. 8)

When teachers stress lower level, factual, knowledge, they reflect a philosophy of curriculum which emphasizes the "content" of a subject area. However, when subjects are taught as a collection of facts and lower levels concepts, much of the knowledge which is taught in this way becomes obsolete before it can be used (Taba, 1966, p. 33). Many educators believe teachers should, instead, emphasize the thinking processes which are employed by the experts in each of the subject areas. Scientists, for example, make use of many thinking processes to make discoveries and to verify their discoveries. Although scientific facts and concepts may become obsolete very rapidly, these thinking processes have been used for centuries and will be used in the near and distant future.

Raths and his coauthors described several processes which are used during thinking. They include comparing, summarizing, observing, classifying, interpreting, looking for assumptions, imagining, collecting and organizing data, hypothesizing, applying facts and principles to new situations, designing projects or investigations, and coding (Raths et al., 1967, pp. 6–23). Some of these processes (e.g., looking for assumptions, hypothesizing, designing projects or investigations) are only appropriate for students in the intermediate or middle grades. Raths and his collaborators believed that schools tend to overemphasize "bookishness" and underemphasize thinking processes such as observing. They also believed that an excellent way to develop the thinking process of collecting and organizing data was to give students opportunities to independently pursue topics of interest. The informal school settings described in Chapter 2 provide myriads of such opportunities! The final section of Chapter 5 deals with how to plan to provide these types of opportunities to your students. One of the following sections in this chapter which you are now reading ("Topic Work") deals with how to carry out this form of instruction.

Over the past 20 years, employers in the United States have increasingly complained about the lack of abilities among their employees to communicate clearly through speech and in writing, to read complex material, to make or evaluate arguments, and to use quantitative skills. These abilities involve some training, but they especially demand **thinking**. In fact, many business leaders today prefer to hire people with thinking skills rather than people who have mastered chiefly lower order knowledge. One business leader described his feelings this way:

> Business will always prefer people who have broad-based skills—people who can think critically, who can adapt well to new situations, and who can teach themselves. A person who is taught today's skills may have obsolete skills by the time he or she reaches the workforce. But a person who is taught to **think** well will always be able to adapt (Ruggiero, 1988, pp. 7–8).

Yet, a look at most elementary schools today will show anyone that teaching efforts are still directed at lower-order objectives. Why?

Some teachers may be afraid to stray from lower level learning objectives because lower level objectives offer "familiar territory"; that is, they know the answers to the questions which are asked at these lower levels. There is probably some "fear of uncertainty" which they associate with teaching thinking. When they teach thinking, students may ask questions which teachers cannot answer. Teachers may be stumped about how to solve problems which students have posed. Teachers may have to adjust their teacher-student interaction away from the typical recitation approach discussed in our previous section on presentation and they may be uncomfortable about trying out new methods of interaction.

Testing, also, may require more thought when one is teaching for higher level thinking rather than lower level knowledge. When a teacher emphasizes lower level knowledge, it is relatively easy to develop a test intended to assess how much of this knowledge has been learned. But when a teacher chooses to emphasize thinking, how will he determine whether his students have learned to do this?

The American public is holding teachers more accountable for their work in classrooms. When teachers want to prove that they are doing their jobs well, they look for something specific. Lower level knowledge can be identified in observable "bits." After testing for student achievement of lower level objectives, a teacher will be able to itemize which objectives her students have mastered. So, in a sense, elementary teachers of the 1990s are caught in a "Catch 22." The business community which awaits their graduates desires employees who can think and solve problems. But, the society which pays teacher salaries and sends children to school (that is, school board members, parents, tax-payers) wants proof that teachers are accomplishing their objectives. And the objectives which are most easy to measure happen to be those which are least valued by the business world.

Adopted curricula usually take the form of textbooks, with Teacher's Guides to accompany them, and most teachers rely heavily on these texts to plan lesson content, teaching procedures, and evaluation. Texts tend to emphasize lower level knowledge because the open-endedness of thinking and problem-solving usually requires a more complex learning process than can be provided by reading a textbook.

For all of these reasons, most teachers hesitate to abandon their emphasis on lower level knowledge. To most teachers, teaching lower level knowledge looks easier and less overwhelming than teaching thinking. But there are some very important reasons why teachers should **not** hesitate to teach thinking.

First, even at the lower two levels of Blooms's taxonomy (knowledge and comprehension), there is considerable variety. It is one thing to be able to recite information, but it is quite another thing to be able to **understand** a concept. (Reciting information is a knowledge level task, but understanding concepts requires one to perform at the comprehension level.) Concepts are increasingly important in our technologically complex society. They are helpful in the early stages of problem-solving, for example, in the identification of the problem. If students are going to be expected to solve problems, they will need to understand concepts. Yet some research is already telling us that students are not learning concepts well or, at least, that they are grossly distorting those concepts to which they are exposed (Easley, 1989; Erlwanger, 1975, pp. 7–26).

In fact, there is a growing body of research by psychologists and educators who study cognition in children which demonstrates that efforts to teach concepts—in math, science, and the social studies—are going badly. Some of these researchers are compiling information about the misconceptions which children have developed after having been "taught" concepts. Apparently, when students are taught concepts, they develop their own, unique, concepts. These unique concepts often differ radically from the concepts which the teachers are trying to teach their students. Students often distort concepts so much, as they construct their own version of them, that teachers don't recognize them as the concepts which they had originally attempted to teach (Easley, 1989; Erlwanger, 1975)!

Further, when teachers focus only on information, the students frequently get the information wrong. Since the students are not understanding the concepts in the way the teachers intend, and since they are not "regurgitating" information correctly, it actually is easier to teach thinking than to teach lower level knowledge. When one teaches thinking, the students must reason through their problems rather than simply regurgitate information. In this situation, the responsibility, as well as much of the credit, goes to the student. When you teach information, the blame goes to the teacher. (If the students haven't learned the information, so the argument goes, then the teacher hasn't taught it very well.)

In fact, children *prefer* to think. For example, as teachers, we may have planned a lesson which requires only that the students memorize information. Suppose, for example, that a child is involved in a lesson on spelling rules which is making use of the presentation method. Let's say the spelling rule which is the topic of this lesson is the famous "i before e" principle. A bright student, one who is at once interested in spelling and knowledgeable about its patterns, may be puzzled by this "i before e" generalization. She may be asking herself (or, she may ask her teacher), "What about the words 'receipt', 'receive', and 'weight'? They don't place i before e."

According to Dewey's model of thinking (Dewey, 1933 and Dewey, 1938), thinking begins with a troubled situation in which puzzlement stimulates exploration and mental reflection. In the example just given, the dullest of spelling lessons provides such stimulation to one student who is attending to the lesson. The teacher did not plan for such thinking to occur in his students. He may or may not have welcomed it when it occurred. Despite the teacher's plans to teach at the lower level, the student rose to a higher level of thought. Children seem to prefer to think at higher levels. Perhaps we all do.

The greatest wrong which results from too great an emphasis on lower level learning may be that students learn to accept information without question. When this occurs, students cease to seek meaning in the information which is given them. At times teachers even pass on information which they do not understand themselves. When teachers pass on information without understanding it, they send a message to their students; that is, "Don't worry about whether you understand the information—the important thing is that you be able to remember it." But, as Robert Gagne and others have shown us, even the smallest bits of information are better understood in relationship to other facts (Gagne, 1977).

Another reason to teach thinking is that it is a lasting skill, one which ought to be emphasized much more than lower level knowledge because it is used throughout one's lifetime, especially in our rapidly changing world. This rapidly changing world has made our business world more aware of the need for employees who can think and solve problems. Yet, they look to the schools to teach children to think since they expect graduates of schools to be skilled problem-solvers at the time when they become employed. If schools do not provide students with opportunities to think and solve problems, who will?

Having argued for the teaching of thinking, it is now time to explain some of the methods which can be used to accomplish the task. The following subsections do just that.

Concept Attainment

Joyce and Weil (1986, pp. 25–39) have summarized an approach to teaching thinking which was developed by Jerome Bruner, a noted American psychologist (Bruner et al.,

1956). It makes use of three general phases to develop concepts and teach thinking. In the first phase, the teacher presents information and the students attempt to deduce what concept is being discussed.

For example, you might be familiar with the old radio game "Twenty Questions." In such a game, a leader (the teacher, when the game is first introduced) writes down the name of a person, place, thing, or concept. The group (students, if this game is played in the classroom) then can ask up to twenty questions as they attempt to identify what the leader has written down. There is only one "catch" to this game, a rule. The leader may only answer those questions which can be answered with a "Yes" or a "No." No other questions may be answered. An old television game which uses the same principle was called "What's my line?" A newer version of this television game is called "Third Degree."

The first phase of concept attainment teaching is similar to "Twenty Questions" except that, in concept attainment teaching, the students are given examples which are labeled as either "yes" or "no." For example, a teacher may begin her lesson by saying that El Paso, Texas is an example of a "yes." Next, she presents an example (Duluth, Minnesota) which she labels as a "no." She follows by giving several pairs of examples (Miami, Florida; New Orleans, Louisiana; San Diego, California) and non-examples (Portland, Maine; Seattle, Washington; Palo Alto, California). Each example (a "yes") is always followed by a non-example (a "no").

Students may interrupt this sequence to ask questions or to discuss possibilities among themselves. Next, students hazard guesses (hypotheses) about what concept is being described by the examples and non-examples. Students must then examine the examples and non-examples to determine whether their hypotheses match the examples provided. Finally, when students have identified the concept, they attempt to make up a definition for this concept in their own words. We call this first phase the "Identification of Concept" phase.

In the second phase of teaching for concept attainment, students test out their concept to see how well they have deduced it. First, the teacher presents additional examples and non-examples, but this time she doesn't label them. Instead, she asks the students to tell her whether they should be classified as "yes" or "no." Next, if the students have consistently labeled the examples and non-examples correctly, the teacher confirms for the students that their hypothesis was correct, supplies the name for the concept (if the students have not already guessed this), and supplies the students with a definition of the concept. Finally, the students generate further example and non-examples on their own. The second phase is called "Testing Attainment of the Concept."

In phase three of teaching for concept attainment, the students discuss the thinking processes which led them to their conclusions. The teacher asks individual students to describe the ideas which they considered as they became involved in the group process of identifying and confirming the concept. The effect of particular examples and non-examples on the students' thought processes is also discussed. The teacher may even have the class list each idea which the students considered or classify these ideas into categories. This third phase of concept attainment is called "Analysis of Thinking Strategies."

Of course, a teacher must establish set rules before beginning a concept attainment lesson so that the students will know how to proceed.

In sum, there are four general steps which should be followed when using the concept attainment approach:

1. Establish set (explain the rules of the game and its purpose).
2. Present labeled examples and have students identify the concept (Phase 1).
3. Have students identify unlabeled examples in order to confirm their hypothesis. Name the concept for your students and supply a definition. Have students generate further examples (Phase 2).
4. Lead a discussion in which the students describe the thought processes which led them to the concept. Have them list the various ideas which they considered and explain why they thought these ideas might be the concept which they were attempting to identify (Phase 3).

Concept attainment is an approach which can be used for a variety of purposes such as: 1) Introducing a concept, 2) Assessing student understanding of a concept or reinforcing a concept, and 3) Extending unit study or project work (Joyce and Weil, 1986, p. 38).

Inductive Teaching

Hilda Taba (1967) has articulated another approach to teaching thinking which in some ways resembles Bruner's concept attainment approach. It is based on the assumption that thinking processes are more valuable to students than individual content. As Taba puts it:

> [Teaching which emphasizes lower level knowledge] stresses factual coverage and burdens the memory with unorganized and therefore perishable information. Within the teaching of the social sciences, this assumption is manifested, first, in overdescriptiveness; second, in dealing with highly obsolescent facts and concepts; in burdening the students' memory with aggregates of information for which they have no organizing conceptual schemata (1966, p. 33).

Taba believed that a curriculum should focus on "main ideas" rather than "all the facts" about a given topic. To do this, the teacher (or one who develops long-term plans for the teacher) must select samples of contrasting data which will lead the students to an understanding of the main ideas without requiring them to be familiar with all the facts related to the topic of study. This approach allows one to deal with the main ideas in greater detail while ignoring some of the specific facts.

For example, the traditional approach to studying geographic facts was to study the facts about each country, one country at a time. In studying Latin America, twenty-one countries might be studied. For each country, the students would learn sets of specifics which answered certain questions (e.g., populations of each of the countries and their capitals, imports and exports for each country, etc.). In Taba's approach, the students would study a limited number of countries, say, two or three, and these countries would be selected for study because they provided students with many opportunities to compare and contrast their factual details. Such comparisons allow students to perceive relationships and develop main ideas (Taba, 1967, pp. 19–23).

The philosophy behind this approach is that more can be learned by studying a main idea than by studying all the details related to a topic. In studying the original thirteen colonies of the United States, for example, one could study all thirteen colonies. However, one could learn much more by studying only two colonies and answering the following questions: Who came to the colony and what did they bring with them? Was the environment at which they arrived one hospitable for settling? Students must be familiar with related facts about each colony to answer such questions. If the teacher has selected two radically different colonies to study (e.g., Massachusetts and Virginia), the students will acquire much more respect for factual knowledge than if they are required to memorize such information in isolation from the relevant concepts (Taba, 1967, p. 21).

To make use of this approach, teachers must first choose which concepts and main ideas they plan to teach, then select specific content and facts which relate to these main ideas and concepts. But the teaching process works in the opposite direction. That is, the students begin by studying the specific content and then the teacher leads them through an inductive thinking process by which they finally arrive at the main ideas and concepts.

As with Bruner's concept attainment approach to teaching thinking, Taba's inductive teaching approach has three phases. In the first phase, called "concept formation," students list facts and details, group them according to common properties, and then apply category labels to these groups. In the second phase of this approach, which is called "interpretation of data," students identify critical relationships, explore these relationships, and make inferences. In the third phase, "application of principles," students are required to apply what they have learned to new situations by predicting consequences, explaining and supporting their predictions, and by logically testing these predictions.

As an example of the inductive approach, let's use the teaching of a unit on rocks to a group of students in the intermediate grades. A traditional approach might list 25 rocks and expect the students to memorize the many important facts about each of these respective rocks. Another approach might begin with just five rocks which are in one way similar. Perhaps each of them is whitish in color (Elementary Science Study, 1967). The teacher could distribute samples of each of these rocks to her students in groups of five to six.

Working in groups, these students are likely to notice the similarity of color and to group all of the rocks together. However, the teacher wants the students to list several characteristics; he does not want them to attend to only one feature. He asks them "See if you can figure out how to tell each of these rocks apart?" Now the students must examine their rock samples more carefully. They must notice details, and, as they discuss them, they will group some of these rocks into one category (e.g., "layered"), other rocks into another (e.g., "sparkly"), etc. At this point, the students have completed phase one, concept formation.

Students will complete phase two, interpretation of data, by pursuing the answer to the question which the teacher has already posed for them (How can you distinguish the rocks from each other?). In the previous phase, they will have formed concepts. For example, they may have noticed that certain rocks had a "glassy" finish to them. This "glassy" feature may be singled out by a group of students ("identify critical relationships among the categories") and students may ask themselves why these particular rocks resemble glass ("explore relationships"). Next, someone may hypothesize that the rock was formed by a process of melting which was followed by rapid cooling (as is the case with the volcanic rock, obsidian, for example). This hypothesis is an example of "making inferences."

For the third phase, "application of principles," the teacher might pose the following question to his students: What might the rock look like if it had cooled slowly? This question requires students to apply their knowledge to a new situation by predicting the results of a different set of circumstances ("predicting consequences"). As they give reasons for their predictions, students will be involved in "explaining and supporting their predictions." Finally, the teacher might ask his students if any of them have noticed a rock which resembles the rock which has just been predicted. This question would require the students to find a rock (e.g., pumice?) which verifies their prediction.

We believe that this approach should not be used with young children (Grade 2 or lower) because it requires a type of thinking which involves the generation and testing of hypotheses—thinking processes which young children are unable to perform (Piaget, 1928).

In sum, the inductive approach to teaching has three phases which include three steps within each respective phase. Of course, it is best to establish set before beginning the experience. These steps comprise a total of 10 steps.

   1. Establish set (Explain the activity).

   Phase 1: Concept Formation
   2. Have students notice and list specifics.
   3. Have students group specifics according to common properties.
   4. Have students apply category labels to these groups.

   Phase 2: Interpretation of Data
   5. Have students identify critical relationships.
   6. Have students explore these relationships.
   7. Have students make inferences, based on the facts and relationships which they have discovered.

   Phase 3: Application of Principles
   8. Have students predict consequences of a change in situation.
   9. Have students explain and support their predictions.
   10. Have students verify their predictions in some way.

Teacher-Student Interaction for Teaching Thinking

The pattern of interactions between teacher and student can dramatically affect the degree to which thinking is practiced by the students. If a teacher stresses "correct answers" during lessons or activities, the students will focus on lower levels of knowledge. On the other hand, if a teacher asks children to develop an hypothesis (Why it took an overnight express package two days to get from New York to Minnesota, for example), then higher level thinking will be fostered.

Those types of interaction which can inhibit pupil thinking include any instance in which the teacher brings closure to the student's ongoing thinking. We have recommended closure in a previous chapter (Chapter 3), but we recommended it for use in a different teaching approach, that is, one which emphasizes lower level learning. When one's aim is to help students to develop higher level thinking, closure is usually inappropriate. Examples of inadvertent closure can include: 1) Instances in which the teacher expresses agreement or disagreement with a student response, 2) When the teacher shows or tells the student what to do in order to solve a problem, 3) When the teacher cuts students off before they have an opportunity to clearly formulate a response to a question, and 4) When the teacher undermines the students' confidence in their own ideas (Wasserman and Ivany, 1988, p. 92).

Other types of interactions may reduce a student's opportunity to think. Examples of this can include: 1) Looking for a single correct answer or procedure, 2) Giving "clues" to lead the student to the correct answer or line of thought, and 3) In values discussions, leading students around to the teacher's point of view (Wasserman and Ivany, 1988, p. 93). Finally, although the presentation (recitation) approach to teaching may be effective for teaching lower level knowledge, many educators believe that it prevents the development of thinking in one's students. Rugguiero says:

> Perhaps the greatest impediment to thinking instruction has been misplaced faith in the efficacy of the lecture (or lecture/recitation) method. That faith rests on several unwarranted assumptions
>
> **1.** That learning a subject means being able to recall a large body of information. Recall is one kind of learning; another, arguably more important, kind is the ability to apply principles and concepts in solving problems and evaluating issues.
> **2.** That being able to use the vocabulary of a discipline, say, sociology… means being able to think like a sociologist. This assumption ignores the distinction between parroting words and speaking thoughtfully.
> **3.** That having right answers is important, but having control over the process by which they are reached is unimportant … (Rugguiero, 1988, p. 95).

On the other hand, some teacher interactions require students to think more deeply about their own ideas. These types of interactions foster the development of thinking. However, changing your style of interaction from a presentation approach to an approach which fosters the teaching of thinking is a bit like changing your role from that of a lecturer to that of a "coach."

> To appreciate the necessity of this change, consider how successful a basketball coach would be if he did nothing more than lecture his athletes on the requisite skills of the sport. On Monday, let us say, he lectured on dribbling; on Tuesday, on foul shooting; on Wednesday, on defense. However dramatic his anecdotes of exciting moments in the history of the game and however eloquent his urging to excel, his team's lack of opportunities for skill development would surely lead to their undoing in actual competition (Rugguiero, 1988. p. 97).

Teachers who desire to teach thinking must first establish an educational climate in which thinking can freely develop. Teachers must welcome student questions and encourage active involvement of students in classroom activities. Teachers should somehow orient their students towards this rather different way of proceeding since many students will be used to a more traditional, lecture approach. If, for example, a teacher wants her students to practice the thinking skill of observing, then she might demonstrate this skill herself before requiring her students to do so (Raths et al., 1967, p. 110).

Once a positive climate has been established, the following types of interactions will each help to facilitate the development of thinking among one's students. Teachers should extend their "wait time" (see Chapter 3) when they desire in depth thought on the part of their students (Rugguiero, 1988, p. 101). One can certainly not expect students to think deeply if the teacher allows only a few seconds before expecting a response. Calling attention to the reflective comments of one's students helps to create an interest in the ideas expressed by such comments (Wasserman and Ivany, 1986, pp. 94–96).

Asking one's students to share their ideas, points of view, and opinions will also help foster more thoughtful behavior.

Requiring students to analyze their own ideas is another strategy which fosters the development of thinking. This can be done by (Wasserman and Ivany, 1988, pp. 94–96):

1. Asking for examples. ("Elizabeth, you say that the greenhouse effect is ruining our environment. Can you give us an example?")
2. Asking students to relate how they acquired their ideas.
3. Asking students to summarize their ideas.
4. Asking students about inconsistencies in their reasoning.
5. Asking students to suggest alternatives. ("You say that coal emissions contribute to the greenhouse effect. Can you think of an alternative form of energy which could meet society's needs?")
6. Asking students to make comparisons. (For example, a teacher may ask his third grade students to think of ways in which airplanes and birds are alike. Then, he would ask them to think of ways in which they are different.) (Raths et al., 1967, p. 59)
7. Asking the students to supply information which supports their statements. ("You say that vegetarianism supports our environment. What information supports that statement?")

While requiring students to analyze their ideas fosters the development of thinking, some types of interactions actually challenge students to extend their thinking further. Examples of these include (Wasserman and Ivany, 1988, p. 96):

1. Asking the student to generate hypotheses. ("Why do you suppose this magnet picks up that rock?")
2. Asking the student to interpret data. ("The plants which were heavily watered died. Why would that be?")
3. Asking students to make judgements and to provide criteria for them. ("Do you think our president was right when he sent our air force in to bomb Iraq? What factors would you have considered if you had been president at the time?")
4. Asking students to apply principles to new situations.
5. Asking students to formulate a way to test a theory or an hypothesis. Because of their intellectual development, children in primary grades should not be expected to test hypotheses. However, they can be expected to provide "guesses" or predictions ("Do you think this clay will sink or float?") and to discuss the results of their activity ("I thought it would sink but it floated!").
6. Asking students to make predictions.
7. Raising a new idea or asking a question that opens a new line of inquiry.
8. Asking the students to examine their opinions with regard to values issues.

These types of challenging questions should be used sparingly because an overuse of them could threaten students and make them fearful of this type of interaction. These types of questions demand that students extend their thinking into new and unexplored territory. They require that students take intellectual risks, since the answers have not been discussed in class. They should be asked when the teacher believes that a student has reflected on an idea in depth and is now capable of making an intellectual leap beyond it (Wasserman and Ivany, 1988, p. 96).

In addition to the previous types of interactions it is very important that teachers who desire to teach thinking allow students to discover their own mistakes. In fact, it is probably correct to say that teachers can never really *teach* thinking. Rather, teachers can behave in a manner which facilitates children teaching themselves how to think. If a teacher interrupts a child's incorrect thought processes to explain the right answer or line of thought, how will the student discover this mistake on her own? Instead of correcting a student's idea, the teacher should listen to it and help the child determine how to explore it. Only then will the child refine her own ideas and develop a line of thinking which she truly owns.[1]

Activities for Teaching Thinking

Many of the types of interactions discussed in the previous section of this chapter suggest activities which might be used to teach thinking. Other types of activities which foster the development of thinking follow.

At the primary level, activities which require children to classify should be provided on a regular basis. "People Pieces" from the ESS *A-Blocks* kit (ESS, 1967) can be classified according to color, gender, adult or child, fat or thin, etc. Objects can be classified according to a variety of categories, including those which children invent themselves. At the intermediate level, students can continue to make use of their classification skills as they use categories in the sciences (e.g., herbivores and carnivores) and social sciences (e.g., transportation services and food services). Student will make use of this skill when they participate in the concept attainment and inductive teaching activities which have been discussed in previous sections of this chapter.

Second, experiences observing should be provided at both the primary and intermediate levels. At the primary level, a child may carefully observe the way food coloring creates "smoke swirls" when dropped in a container of water. Or perhaps the same student will observe a snail crawling up the side of an aquarium. Perhaps she will see one lay a mass of eggs. Observation is sometimes combined with experimentation. For example, a child might place a mealworm near a piece of apple and observe whether the mealworm moves toward, or away from, the apple. At the intermediate level, a teacher may ask students to do ten pushups and then record their elevated pulse rates. They would then discuss what they had observed about their pulses.

Third, students should be provided with experiences which require them to collect and organize information. Until they acquire much skill in notetaking and summarizing, teachers will need to provide an outline for the students. It should include questions to which the students must find answers (Raths et al., 1967, pp. 5 & 89). Fourth, students should be encouraged to raise their own questions and to pursue topics of interest to them (Ruggiero, 1988, p. 109). The "topic work" approach which is discussed in the following section of this chapter is an example of an approach to teaching which makes use of the suggestions just made.

Having students summarize, orally or in writing, various books, newspaper articles, movies, television shows, etc., is an activity which helps to prepare students for the topic work referred to in the above paragraph (Raths et al., 1967, p. 114). Journals are another activity which can contribute to the development of thinking among one's students, especially when students make frequent entries and teachers provide frequent and thoughtful feedback (Ruggiero, 1988, p. 112). Problem-solving is another activity which should be provided to students throughout their experiences in elementary school (Raths et al., 1967, pp. 96–98). Problem-solving is best introduced with warm-up exercises. Students who are used to achieving grades by memorizing and regurgitating information are likely to feel threatened by the more open-ended, problem-solving activities. Students need an opportunity to experience problem-solving in a nonthreatening situation which is not evaluated. Activities which invite students to be intellectually playful (e.g., writing captions for cartoons, or solving puzzles) will encourage children to use problem-solving in other situations (Ruggiero, 1988, p. 109).

Occasionally, a teacher may want to play the devil's advocate, that is, defend a position which no one else in the class will defend. This is done to stimulate discussion and further thought on the part of one's students, particularly when the teacher feels that her students are not considering both sides of an issue. This approach must be used cautiously, however, since students can be easily intimidated by seeing their teacher take a particular position on an issue. The teacher's role is usually one of moderator when students are discussing their opinions on issues. Certainly, the teacher, by playing the devil's advocate, will be able to get his students to consider another perspective. An unfortunate "side effect" of using this approach frequently might be that students will not express and defend their own ideas since they fear that the teacher will take the opposite position. Ultimately, one cannot develop thinking on the part of one's students without encouraging students to express their own ideas.

Teaching Thinking Summed Up

There are various approaches which can be used to go about teaching thinking. Concept attainment and inductive teaching are two of these approaches. There are also a variety of activities which can be used to develop thinking among one's students. Most important, however, are the goals which a teacher pursues and the types of interactions which a teacher exhibits with her students. When teachers pursue process goals—that is, goals which can be classified on the higher end of Bloom's taxonomy—students get much practice at thinking. When teachers pursue mainly content goals—that is, goals which can be classified on the lower end of Bloom's taxonomy—students get practice at acquiring information but they do not necessarily develop thinking skills as they do so.

When teachers use only those methods which are most effective for teaching content goals (e.g., presentation, mastery teaching, etc.), students will acquire lower level knowledge without learning how to critically examine such knowledge and without learning how to apply this knowledge to situations which demand its use in order to solve problems. On the other hand, teachers who stress problem-solving exclusively do their students a disservice by depriving them of the opportunity to acquire information which could be used as they pursue process goals.

As teachers pursue the development of process, or thinking, skills, they must make use of radically different teacher-student interactions. The teacher must abandon the role of expert and replace it with the more coach-like role of "facilitator." Teachers who desire to do this will do well to remember that students learn best when they invent, and use, their own ideas. This means that students must be encouraged to express and develop their own ideas at all times, even when the teacher is aware that these ideas are incorrect. By assisting students in the process of developing and testing their own ideas, even when these ideas are wrong, the teacher demonstrates a belief that process really is more important than content. The consequence of this approach is that students come to believe that their ideas really are important. And students who believe that their ideas are important take all ideas seriously and learn what they can to apply them. The more active role which students assume in such situations will be reflected in more independent and responsible behavior on their part. Teachers should be prepared for this behavior, and they will welcome and encourage it if they are truly committed to the development of thinking.

TOPIC WORK
(This section was written by Peter Frost and Robert Louisell)

Like thinking, **topic work** is known by a variety of names. "Thematic units," "project work," "integrated teaching," and "child-centered work" are some of the names by which topic work is known. In England the most common term for this style of teaching is "topic work."

Topic work differs from the typical American unit of study in that, for topic work, the teacher prepares the learning activities and gathers the resources himself. This contrasts starkly with traditional American schools, where the units of study are commercially prepared and teachers make use of them via a Teacher's Guide. Topic work, then, requires far more teacher preparation than a more traditional approach, but it also provides the teacher with far more autonomy in determining what is to be learned.

In order to carry out the topic work approach, large blocks of time must be scheduled from one day to the next in order to provide continuity so that students can work on the topics. Some British educators recommend that approximately 70% of each school day be devoted to topic work. Teachers who make use of the topic work approach usually take the time to list the skills which are being covered by a topic of study. In this way, teachers can determine which essential skills will not be covered by the topic. Teachers can then plan to provide instruction in these skills at another time.

Topic work strives to relate the content of a topic to the everyday lives of children. This is consistent with the recommendations of groups of American educators. (See, for example, the recommendations of the National Council of Teachers of Mathematics) (Schultz et al., 1989, pp. 27–29). There is a prevailing philosophy among schools which make extensive use of topic work that knowledge is learned best by children when it starts from what the child already knows and then moves outward beyond that with which the child is most familiar. This is often difficult to achieve when teachers are tied to an adopted textbook or set of curriculum objectives. But when children are exposed to new knowledge via topic work, the knowledge is often more meaningful.

For example, as part of one topic, students planned a ski trip. They were responsible for "costing out" the entire trip. They made the transportation arrangements, acquired the information about costs of ski lifts and rentals, etc. (Their teacher provided some of the data in rounded numbers so that computation would not become an overwhelming task.) During the course of their computations, the students were introduced to two-digit multiplication problems. Not all the students in this class were ready to learn this form of multiplication, so the teacher formed a group of students who were ready to learn this skill and he taught it to them. During the ski trip, some children became interested in the effects of wax and slope upon the speed of the skis. Upon their return to school, some students experimented further with problems related to the relative friction of the skis on snow under various conditions. The teacher who is committed to the topic work approach believes that students are far more motivated to learn when skills are integrated (as they are in topic work) than through separate lessons on topics such as "friction" or "two-digit multiplication."

In examples such as the one given above, it is not critical that the field trip be actually taken. The activities mentioned with this example (for example, "costing out" the trip, learning to multiply with two digits, testing the effects of various conditions on the relative speed of skis down a hillside, etc.) could all be carried out without actually completing a field trip. In fact, expense may prohibit teachers from taking such trips on a routine basis. What is important about this example, however is that students are imagining themselves to be participants in these trips. By inventing practical problems for their students (for example, planning a field trip to the local ski hill), teachers assure that the topic will come alive and create interest among their students.

In fact, topic work provides teachers with the opportunity to make topics come alive. For example, one class of students studied Kansas as part of a topic on *The Wizard of Oz.*[2] Maps of Kansas, summaries of Kansas history and life in Kansas, and even the speech accents of Kansas were some of the subtopics studied by the students during their topic work (see Figure 4.1). The school put on a production of *The Wizard of Oz* and the principal played the role of the scarecrow! When a whole school becomes involved in the study of a topic, and the production of a play related to that topic, it is certainly more difficult for a child to be indifferent to the information which is taught as part of that topic! On the other hand, if the same children had studied Kansas as an isolated social studies unit on farm life in Kansas, a unit in which they memorized important cities, crops, etc., how easy it would have been for them to sleep and daydream through the entire unit!

Another critical difference between topic work and traditional instructional units is that, in topic work, the child has a hand in planning what will be learned. The teacher includes the children in the initial planning stages for the topic, and throughout the topic of study, the child has at least some choices in terms of what he is to study. This is true even at the earliest levels of education in Britain (e.g., the British equivalent of our kindergarten and primary grades). This creates a sense of "ownership" in the students. Since they have a say in the course of study being pursued, the topic takes on a special meaning for them.

Topic work creates an ethos of quality. In classrooms where topic work is used consistently, there is an expectation that students will produce work which is of the best quality which they can produce. But the ethos of topic work extends to more than student work. It also applies to the quality of time which students will experience in such classrooms. In the best of those classrooms which use topic work, there is a premise at work that students will not be constantly occupied with "busywork" of questionable educational value.

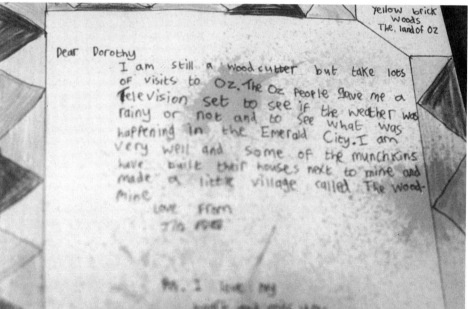

Figure 4.1 Samples of Student Work for a Topic Unit on Kansas

Teachers who have committed their classrooms to topic work must carefully balance the activities which they provide so that some activities are teacher-directed while others are only teacher-supervised or independently completed by the students. Obviously, teachers cannot lead more than one teacher-directed activity at any one time. It is a tricky business to supervise small groups, assist individuals who are working independently, and lead teacher-directed activities simultaneously. When beginning topic work in a classroom, therefore, it is important for teachers to reduce their teacher-directed activities as much as possible. This is the only way that a teacher can be expected to manage the complex classroom environment which will develop as topic work in the classroom unfolds. As the teacher becomes more skilled at handling the many things going on in his classroom, he can then begin to schedule more teacher-directed activities. It is equally important that the teacher develop a sense of independence and self-discipline among one's students when committing one's classroom to topic work. Without this quality, students will not carry out the variety of independent learning activities which are required by topic work.

In sum, the ethos of topic work applies to the entire classroom environment. The use of time and space, and the quality of student work all relate to this ethos.

A variety of elements are usually present in classrooms which have successfully developed this ethos. First, there is a noticeable respect between teacher and students in these classrooms. Children and teacher often work together, even in the planning of the topics. Teachers prize the work of their students. Teachers demonstrate respect for the work of their students by the seriousness with which they listen to children, read their writings, display their work, etc. Second, children work independently in such classrooms. One gets a gut feeling when in these classrooms that these classrooms are good places to be. Children seem happy and intellectually challenged. Third, teachers work together with each other for a variety of purposes in such settings (e.g., planning topic work). There is no competition among these teachers to compare results with their students or to "toot their own horns."

Topic work also emphasizes higher order thinking and process skills. The prevailing philosophy in topic work is that positive attitudes towards learning and general learning skills are more important than the acquisition of specific bits of information. People who concentrate on topic work talk about fostering a climate in which children discover the "joy of learning." While teachers who make use of topic work are not interested in exhaustively covering all the objectives of a particular curriculum, it would be a mistake to assume that these teachers are not interested in developing a concern for detail among their students. Rather, these teachers believe that specific details are learned best through the study of a topic. Through the study of a topic, details come to life in ways that they cannot when they are taught in isolation. Teachers who use the topic work approach believe in teaching as many basic skills as they can through this method.

For example, a study of England's role in World War II could be taught according to a list of important events. In topic work, however, the unit of study would probably be launched by a field trip to observe some local buildings which had been scarred by bombs. The teacher and students would then discuss what it might feel like to live in a city where one couldn't predict when bombs would land. Local artifacts from World War II would be brought into the classroom to be examined and discussed. Then the details of particular bombing sites in the world would be studied, appropriate children's books (fiction and nonfiction) would be read, etc. As children explored their topic, they would become more familiar with many of the most im-portant historical events of this war.

A traditional approach to teaching, especially one which emphasizes lower level learning, might expect children to acquire knowledge of all the names of rivers and key towns in each of the states of North America. A topic of study, however, would involve the students in the study of one typical town in one important state. The effect of the river on the town would be one of the subtopics. A key event related to this river might be acted out during the opening activity of the topic of study. By studying one town in depth instead of an entire list of towns superficially, the topic comes alive for the students. As they learn more about this town, they will be able to learn about other towns by comparing and contrasting them to one which they know well.

Unlike some other methods of teaching, topic work cannot be neatly summarized into a set of steps. Rather, topics provide teachers with a relatively loose structure which enables them to plan a continuum of learning experiences while at the same time avoiding excessive emphasis on specific bits of information. There are several character-istics which identify the best examples of topic work, however, and they can be summa-rized as follows.

Topic work
- avoids emphasis on isolated pieces of information. Instead, it develops connec-tions among its various learning activities—regardless of the subject areas from which these activities originate. Teachers develop their own topic work plans and they gather their own resources for them. In gathering learning resources, teachers make use of Teacher's Guides and textbooks but they do not become enslaved to them or feel obligated to deal with particular content which is cov-ered in them.
- develops a sense of "ownership" among teacher and students. They each have some say about what will be learned. Children's work (e.g., their writings, their art, etc.) is displayed throughout the classroom and school. Samples of best topic books are made available to everyone.
- fosters a collegial atmosphere. In topic work, teachers, students, parents, and principal all share their knowledge with each other. Teachers work together to develop a school policy for planning and evaluation, and parents have a ready access to the school and the topic work. Teachers tend to share rather than compete. The entire community is used as a resource for the topic.
- develops an ethos in which students develop independent work habits and learning skills. Students and teachers respect each other and prize each other's work and ideas. Students take their work seriously, and the learning is of high quality. The interaction between teachers and students is nonauthoritarian in the best topic work settings.
- makes use of direct, relevant experiences to teach concepts whenever it is pos-sible to do so. A variety of media (e.g., real life artifacts, movies, simulations, field trips, children's writings, etc.) are utilized.
- demands a flexible approach to grouping. This will be explained in greater detail in the topic work section of our chapter on instructional planning.

TEACHING TO LEARNING STYLES

During the 1980s, some schools began to train teachers in instructional approaches which address student learning styles. Many educators believe that efforts to address the various learning styles of children will improve the performance of students and their engagement in instruction. However, there is little agreement among learning style proponents about exactly what are the different learning styles which exist, nor is there much agreement on what their basic elements might be. In fact, leading authors in this field (Dunn, Gregorc, and McCarthy) present conflicting views and recommendations for instruction.

The major theme of the learning styles movement is that children are different and a single approach to teaching cannot be effective. Teaching based on learning styles focuses on the strengths of each learner rather than on her weaknesses. It tries to modify instruction in order to make learning as appealing as possible for different types of learners. Teaching based on learning styles assumes that children have different cognitive, affective, and physiological characteristics which affect their ways of perceiving and learning.

Learning styles include perceptual preferences (visual, auditory, and kinesthetic), orientation towards cooperation or competition, type of motivation (extrinsic, intrinsic), preferred degree of work structure (unstructured, structured), and environmental preferences such as temperature, lighting, background noise, type of furniture, etc.

Schools which have participated in teaching based on learning styles report increased student motivation and gains in standardized test scores. Their leaders claim that school dropouts have learning styles which are radically mismatched to the approaches commonly utilized in schools. Such students may learn best when they cooperate, are provided hands-on experience, or engage in high levels of interaction. Teaching based on learning styles makes teachers more sensitive to the strengths of individual students and the differences which exist among them. After receiving training in the learning styles of students, many teachers choose to collaborate to prepared instructional materials which address a variety of learning styles.

How can schools provide appropriate instruction which addresses the different learning styles of students? Some educators argue that students of the same learning style should be grouped together with a teacher whose teaching style is suited to the particular learning style of those students. While we believe that this approach is useful for some purposes, we also agree with those who say that all teachers need to become more eclectic and utilize instructional approaches which are appropriate to many learning styles. Further, children should also become more eclectic. They stand to benefit from instruction which stretches their range of learning modalities and enriches their cognitive, affective, and physiological repertoire. For example, students who are auditory learners can benefit from strengthening their visual and kinesthetic modalities.

Teaching based on learning styles helps teachers and students to understand each other and the ways they learn. As a result of this understanding, instructional materials and approaches can be modified to accommodate different learning styles and, ultimately, to individualize instruction. Teaching based on learning styles is diagnostic-prescriptive. It identifies the learning modalities of the students and their mastery of prerequisites, and it prescribes appropriate instructional approaches and materials.

One example of an approach to teaching which is based on learning styles is the 4MAT System developed by Bernice McCarthy in 1972. This is an eight-step cycle of instruction designed to address individual processing preferences which are attributed to brain dominances. McCarthy identifies a total of eight learning modalities. Teachers use the 4MAT system to employ instructional strategies which match the learning style with which each student is most comfortable. By following 4MAT's eight steps in planning, delivering, and evaluating their lessons, teachers address the different learning modalities which are usually present in the classroom. 4MAT is an eclectic approach which requires teacher and students to practice each of the eight learning modalities.

Another popular approach to teaching based on learning styles was developed by Rita and Kenneth Dunn. In this approach, the learning style of each student is identified through the Learning Style Inventory (Dunn, Dunn, & Price, 1975). The results of this inventory indicate which learning style each student prefers. Instruction is then matched to the student's preferred learning style.

While researchers have not found sufficient evidence to support the claims of those who advocate teaching based on learning styles, practitioners are very enthusiastic about the improvements which they have witnessed in their own classrooms. Although there is no clear agreement on what constitutes learning styles, there is agreement on the instructional benefits which can be derived from reflecting on the individual differences of students and from capitalizing on their strengths rather than emphasizing their deficiencies. As a result of the learning styles movement, educators are more aware of learning preferences among children and are more willing to diversify their instructional approaches in order to respond to these preferences. In our text, several aspects of learning styles are addressed such as intrinsic and extrinsic motivation, degree of structure in learning, and instructional settings.

NOTES

1. Personal conversation with Jack Easley, Fall, 1989.
2. Credit for this example goes to Deb Saunders, teacher, and her head teacher, Ron Oldale, both at Frogwell Primary School, Wiltshire (Chippenham), England.

GLOSSARY

declarative knowledge The content of any subject being studied; information, ideas, and concepts.

guided practice Supervised practice in which students work on material in which they have received recent instruction.

higher-order thinking Learning which can be classified in the highest three levels of Bloom's taxonomy (analysis, synthesis, and evaluation); problem-solving and thinking.

independent practice Practice in which students work on independently on material in which they have received recent instruction.

lower-order learning Learning which can be classified in the lowest three levels of Blooms' taxonomy (knowledge, comprehension, and application).

procedural knowledge Knowledge of skills or rules; "how to" knowledge.

Chapter
5

Planning for Teaching

DETERMINING WHICH SKILLS ARE "ESSENTIAL"

*D*ecisions about what skills and subjects should be taught to children in our society have evolved over a period from 1870 to the present (Ellis et al., 1988, p. 214), but today, general ideas about what an elementary school curriculum should be comprised of are almost universal throughout the United States. A typical elementary school curriculum is comprised of the following general skills and subjects: reading and language arts, mathematics, social studies, science and health, art, music, and physical education. State departments of education publish curriculum guidelines which list goals for each of these areas and recommend percentages of total school time which should be devoted to each of the areas. Local school districts also publish curriculum guides which usually list the basic objectives in each area and suggest activities which might be used to teach these skills.

The most commonly used source of information about instructional activities, however, is still the teacher's guide for the adopted textbook in each subject or skill area. The organization of the content of each of these areas is arranged according to a *scope and sequence* which specifies the topics (the **scope** of any curriculum is limited to certain topics) and **sequence** (these topics are arranged in some logical order by grade level or sequence of difficulty). Table 5.1 depicts a scope and sequence for a popular elementary science curriculum.

Table 5.1   SCOPE AND SEQUENCE (Merrill Science)

Level 1	Strand	Level 2
Chapter 8 Plant Parts: identification, basic functions.	Plants/ Simple Organisms	**Chapter 9** Plants grow; Plant changes: as they mature, seasonal.
Chapter 2 Body parts; Body coverings; Habitats.	Animals	**Chapter 1** Animal groups: insects, fish, amphibians; reptiles, birds, mammals; Seasonal changes.
Chapter 10 Description; Being responsible for your environment.	Ecology	**Chapter 10** Environmental changes: caused by nature, by people; Saving the environment.
Chapter 5 Body parts; Healthful habits; Safety; Mental health.	Human Health	**Chapter 5** Physical growth; Learning and acquiring skills; Safety.
Chapter 9 Properties of water and air; Water and air as components of weather.	Air, Water, and Weather	**Chapter 7** Properties of air; How air affects weather; Weather conditions.
Chapter 3 Dinosaurs; How scientists learn about dinosaurs. **Chapter 4** Properties of rocks, minerals, sand, soil.	Rocks, Minerals, and Land	**Chapter 2** Landforms; Bodies of water; Surface changes; Plant and animal extinction.
Chapter 6 Relationship of Earth and sun in space.	Space	**Chapter 8** Relationship of sun and Earth; Properties of sunlight; Shadows.
Chapter 1 Identification of properties using the senses; Solids; Liquids; Changes in matter.	Matter	**Chapter 4** Units of measure; Length; Volume; Weight; Time.
Chapter 7 Pulling and pushing forces in machines; Magnets.	Forces and Energy	**Chapter 3** Properties of sound; Useful sounds. **Chapter 6** Properties of heat; Temperature; Uses of heat.
Level 3	Strand	Level 4
Chapters 1–2 Seeds: definition, characteristics, germination, scattering of; Seed plants: characteristics, plant parts, life cycles.	Plants/ Simple Organisms	**Chapters 1–2** Green plants; Using plants as raw materials; Flowers; Seeds; Plant reproduction.
Chapter 11 Needs of living things; Producers; Consumers; Scavengers; Decomposers; Food chains and webs.	Animals	**Chapter 10** Behavior; Reflex; Instinct; Learned and social behaviors.
Chapter 12 Habitat: definition; Types of habitats; Conservation of habitats.	Ecology	**Chapter 9** Adaptations for survival; Body parts adaptations; Special adaptations.

Table 5.1 continued

Level 3 cont.	Strand	Level 4 cont.
Chapters 15–16 Cells: definition, characteristics; Tissues; Organs; Organ systems; Body defenses against disease; Diet; Drugs and poisons: effects on the body, safety.	Human Health	**Chapter 4** How we see; Eye problems; Eye care; Lenses. **Chapter 12** How we hear; Ear parts; Hearing. **Chapters 17–18** Good health habits: exercise, sleep, cleanliness, diet, nutrients, food groups, nutrition.
Chapters 9–10 Evaporation; Condensation; Clouds; Precipitation; Climate; Water cycle: stages, definition.	Air, Water, and Weather	**Chapters 13–14** Oceans and seas; Properties of ocean water; Ocean movements; Ocean life; Ocean floor features; Protecting the ocean.
Chapters 5–6 Minerals: definition; Igneous, sedimentary, and metamorphic rocks; Earth layers; Weathering; Erosion.	Rocks, Minerals, and Land	**Chapter 8** Using rock records; Fossil records; Using fossils.
Chapters 13–14 Apparent size of objects; Earth and moon characteristics; gravity, surface features; Moon exploration; Revolution; Rotation; Moon phases.	Space	**Chapters 5–6** The sun; Comparing stars; Solar eclipse; The planets: orbits, inner planets, outer planets; Asteroids; Comets; Meteoroids: meteors, meteorites.
Chapters 3–4 Matter: definition, properties, states; Matter changes state; Mixtures; compounds.	Matter	**Chapter 7** Earth's composition; Identification of minerals; Mineral properties; Rocks: mineral mixtures; Useful rocks and minerals.
Chapters 7–8 Forces: definition; Gravity: friction; Work: definition; Energy: definition; Simple machines; Compound machines; Safety.	Forces and Energy	**Chapter 3** White light; Reflections; Refraction; Color. **Chapter 11** Properties of sound; Behavior of sound. **Chapters 15–16** Parts of atoms; Static electricity; Current electricity; Magnets: behavior; Magnets and electricity.
Level 5	Strand	Level 6
Chapters 18–19 Plant patterns; flowers, leaves, color; vascular, nonvascular; vascular plant reproduction; Plant life cycles; Photosynthesis; Respiration; Transpiration; Deciduous trees and conifers.	Plants/ Simple Organisms	**Chapters 1–2** Features of life; Classifying organisms: five kingdoms; Scientific naming; Viruses; Monerans; Protists; Fungi.
Chapters 1–2 Classification of animals: invertebrates, vertebrates; Simple to complex invertebrates; Cold-blooded vertebrates: five groups; Warm-blooded vertebrates: two groups.	Animals	**Chapters 20–21** Cells; Mitosis; Meiosis; Reproduction in plants, animals; Heredity; Genetics; Dominant, recessive genes; Controlling genes.

Table 5.1   continued

Level 5 cont.	Strand	Level 6 cont.
Chapter 20 Forest types; Uses of forests; Threats to forests; Management of forests.	Ecology	**Chapters 16–17** Ecosystems; water, nitrogen, carbon dioxide-oxygen cycles; Food chains; Food webs; Community relationships: competition, predation, symbiosis; Habitat changes and population size; Endangered species; Biomes.
Chapters 7–9 Skeletal system; Skeleton: bones; Joints; Skeletal system disorders; Muscular system; Muscles; Caring for muscles; Nervous system; Jobs of Nervous system; Sense organs; Effects of drugs.	Human Health	**Chapters 10–12** Circulatory system: parts; Blood circulation; Blood types; Digestive system; Diffusion; Respiratory system: parts; Gas exchange and transport; Endocrine system: thyroid, parathyroid, adrenal, pituitary glands; Pancreas.
Chapters 5–6 Composition of atmosphere; Air pressure; Properties of air: energy absorption, wind, humidity, precipitation, clouds; Air masses; Fronts; Storms; Data collection; Climate: factors, types, microclimates.	Air, Water, and Weather	**Chapter 23** Water and air: important resources; Water treatment; Water and air pollution; Water and air conservation; Population growth; Environmental choices for the future.
Chapters 14–15 Earth's layers; Earthquakes; Plate tectonics theory; Volcanoes; Landscape changes: caused by running water, ice, wind; Mountain, plain, plateau formation.	Rocks, Minerals, and Land	**Chapters 13–15** Maps: using maps, types of maps; Continental drift theory: evidence; Plate tectonics theory: evidence; Dating rocks; Geologic history of Earth. **Chapter 22** Soil; Soil conservation; Refuse disposal.
Chapters 10–11 Measuring distances in space; Stars: types, sizes, colors, temperatures; Galaxies: types; Constellations; Movements of constellations.	Space	**Chapters 6–7** Vastness of space; Life cycle of stars; Nebula; Red giant; White and black dwarfs; Nova; Pulsar; Black hole; Big bang pulsating theories; Optical and radio telescopes; Rockets; Satellites; Space probes.
Chapters 3–4 Scientific method; Volume; Mass; Density; Weight; Atoms; Elements; Compounds; Mixtures; Changing states of matter.	Matter	**Chapters 3–5** Classification of matter; Composition of substances; Elements and periodic table; Compounds; Mixtures; Organic compounds; Inorganic compounds: acids, bases, salts, oxides.
Chapters 12–13 Motion; Forces: gravity, magnetic, electric; Newton's Laws; Work: definition, measurement of; Mechanical advantage; Simple machines. **Chapters 16–17** Potential and kinetic energy; Forms of energy; Energy transfer; Law of Conservation of Energy; Heat transfer; Energy conservation.	Forces and Energy	**Chapters 8–9** Fossil fuels: as resources, supplies, problems with; Fossil fuel alternatives: wind, water, geothermal, nuclear, solar energy. **Chapters 18–19** Static electricity; Current electricity; How energy is transferred; Electromagnetic waves.

As you can see, certain topics (e.g., electricity and magnetism, in the *Forces and Energy* Strand) are included in several grade levels. Jerome Bruner is responsible for articulating the concept of a "spiral curriculum" (Bruner, 1960), the idea that topics can be introduced in some basic way at one level and then presented repeatedly with increasing complexity as students reach higher levels in the curriculum.

In the past, some school administrators and school board officials have reflected a tendency to distrust the judgments of teachers about what should be taught. In response to this tendency, the publishers of textbooks and other instructional programs began to advertise "teacher-proof" programs during the 1970s, implying that the scope, sequence, lesson plans, and student activities were so well organized that "even a teacher couldn't mess them up." This uncomplimentary view of teachers is in direct contrast to another popular view which sees teachers as professionals who are best qualified to make decisions related to these matters.

Unfortunately, in many areas of the elementary curriculum (e.g., reading, mathematics, and science), teachers do not trust their own knowledge about these areas well enough to make really professional decisions about what should be taught or when a particular concept ought to be taught. Consequently, teachers often follow an adopted curriculum religiously, carrying out every lesson which can be found in the teacher's guide and using every workbook page or textbook page which is provided by the program. Lacking the theoretical knowledge which is necessary in order to make decisions about when to supplement or discard activities which have been included in the teacher's guide, and lacking a clear understanding of the goals of the entire curriculum in a particular subject or skill area, most teachers stick slavishly to the scope, sequence, lessons, and text of the adopted program.

However, these programs are not intended by those who publish them to be used as the entire curriculum for an instructional area. Rather, these programs are meant to provide a "core" of scope, sequence, and lessons which can serve as a framework upon which teachers can build. The publishers of these programs assume that, when teachers trust their own knowledge more than the knowledge represented in the teacher's guide, they will make decisions about which objectives and activities should be included or discarded. On the other hand, when teachers distrust their own knowledge in a particular area, they should fall back on the expertise which is represented in the teacher's guide for their adopted program.

When teachers stick slavishly to an adopted text or set of instructional materials, they tend to carry out the activities in an automized way with no real sense of purpose. Worksheet follows worksheet in an endless stream of activities dealing with objectives which often have a questionable relationship to the general goals of the curriculum in question. Teachers and students alike cannot see the forest for the trees. When the important educational goals receive less attention than the more specific objectives (which are intended to aid students in achieving these more important goals), teachers are less happy and their students are less educated than they might otherwise be. Student boredom may increase for two reasons. First, students are less likely to be aware of the value of what they are supposed to be learning. Second, when teachers lack a clear understanding of why they are teaching something, they are more likely to become bored themselves, and this in turn can communicate a lack of interest in the topic to their students.

So far we have summarized the basic subjects or skills which should be taught in elementary schools, and we have explained the process by which these subjects become organized into curricula. We do not intend that you become robot teachers who carry out "teacher-proof" curricula. However, in order to behave as professionals when making decisions about curricula, you will need two kinds of knowledge: 1) knowledge about the subject areas or skills which you are teaching, and 2) knowledge about the process of planning for teaching in any particular area. You should acquire the first of these in your college courses in liberal arts, sciences, and education. It is to this second type of knowledge that we now turn.

PLANNING FOR INSTRUCTION

During the 1930s, the "activity movement" became popular. This movement believed that children learn best when they are active and that they should therefore be engaged in activities and projects. However, some educators criticized this movement by pointing out that many activities seemed to be carried out in classrooms with no apparent purposes. When a parent or educator visits a classroom and asks, "What are these students learning now?", she has a right to expect an answer. To answer, "They are *doing* _____" (e.g., "making papier-mâché") does not answer the question (What are they learning?).

In reaction to this movement, Ralph Tyler, during the 1950s, proposed that educators clarify their educational purposes (Beane et al., 1986, p. 229). Instructional **objectives,** which stated *what* the students should learn (rather than what activities they would participate in) were the result. Although some educators still argue that, sometimes, activities ought to be identified *before* stating objectives (Zaborik, 1975 and 1976), most educators believe that the identification of instructional objectives is the first step in planning for instruction. We personally believe that either approach may be used in instructional planning and that the way which one organizes one's classroom, as well as the type of subject which one is teaching and the level at which it is taught are all factors which should affect decisions about which approach to use.

For example, in a nongraded setting, objectives will probably precede the choice of activities most of the time. In an informal setting, on the other hand, activities may precede identification of objectives. In teaching mathematics, objectives will usually precede the choice of instructional activity. But, in teaching science to young children, activities should often precede the identification of outcomes (objectives).

Because any teacher may use either approach to instructional planning, we have included two types of lesson plans, and two types of unit (long-term) plans in this chapter. But regardless of their ways of organizing classrooms and the subjects which they teach, all teachers will make extensive use of objectives during their teaching. It is to the use of, and composing of, objectives, that we now turn.

Using and Writing Objectives for One's Students

Objectives come in many types, and they answer a variety of questions, but for our purposes in this text, we can say that objectives answer two questions: 1) What will the student learn (know)? 2) What will the student do to demonstrate that he knows it? To avoid confusion, each of these questions must be answered fairly specifically. For example, the question, "What will the student know?" might be answered, "The student will know how to add." But this is not a very specific response. A teacher who reads this statement carefully may wonder, "Add what? Addends with only one digit? With two digits? Hundreds? Thousands? Millions?"

Obviously, a typical first-grade student can be expected to learn to add one-digit addends, but it would be ridiculous to expect him to learn to add with millions. It will take, at the minimum, at least a few years before he is capable of adding with millions, To be more specific, let's say, "The student will know how to add, using addends from 1 to 9." Now we have answered the question, "What will the student know?", and if we are teachers of children in the primary grades, we realize that this objective is probably intended for children in the 5–7 year-old range.

The second question, "What will the student do to demonstrate that he knows it?" is a more difficult question to answer. Imagine yourself as a teacher, trying to decide whether one of your students, Mary, knows how to add (using addends from 1 to 9). How can you know with reasonable certainty that Mary knows how to do this? Many teachers will mistakenly assume that, since Mary was in class on the day that this skill was taught, she now "knows it." Nothing could be further from the truth!

The only way to know for certain if Mary can add is to have Mary add. But what does this mean? Addition is a *mental* activity. Mental activity is unseen. Can a teacher take Mary's word for it that she is adding? Certainly not! It is the teacher's responsibility to know what her students can do. Can she give Mary addition problems to solve and watch her solving them? What will Mary be doing when she "solves" them? Suppose the teacher gives Mary an addition problem and Mary gets a puzzled look on her face and then begins to count, orally, on her fingers. What can the teacher take as evidence that Mary is really adding? For this objective, Mary must correctly solve addition problems. That is the only evidence that will demonstrate to the teacher that Mary can indeed add. She may do it in writing, with worksheets. She may take a written test. She may solve problems orally. But she must solve several of these simple addition problems and solve them correctly.

At this point, we can revise our objective and state it in the following way: Using addends 1–9, the student will successfully solve addition problems.

Notice that the answer to question #1 (What do you want the student to know?) disappears from the objective when you answer question #2 (What will the learner do to show that he knows it?). We no longer say, "The student will know how to add, using addends 1–9," because we realize that any child who can solve addition problems (with addends 1–9) *does* know how to add.

Notice also that the questions (numbers 1 and 2) related to any objective are always answered in terms of the *student—not* the teacher! This is so for a very good reason. We could state objectives for teachers. However, it is not the teachers that we are trying to teach. Teachers are responsible for teaching their students; not themselves. It makes better sense to state an objective in terms of the *learner* since it is the learner who must either achieve, or fail to achieve, his objective. Stating an objective in learner terms makes the teacher more accountable for the student's learning. It says in effect, "This objective is what I hope to help my student to accomplish, and when he has fully mastered this objective, student and teacher will have each done his jobs." This approach also makes the teacher more aware of the need to individualize since different students may be capable of achieving different objectives.

Whatever the objective, question #2 (What will the student do to demonstrate that he has mastered the objective?) must always be answered. Not answering it opens the door to penalizing students for thinking you wanted them to know something else. For example, suppose a beginning teacher stated as an objective for her first grade students that the student would "understand simple addition, using addends from one to nine." This seems clear enough, doesn't it? We know which addends will be used (one to nine). And we also know that the student only needs to understand *simple* addition. But what does this mean, to "understand" simple addition?

Suppose a student understands the process of simple addition; that is, he knows that to add, one must combine two sets of separate objects. Suppose, also, that he cannot yet count accurately. What if the teacher who wrote the objective administers a test to see who "understands" simple addition. Her test consists of a worksheet of 20 addition problems which must be solved, with no more than four mistakes, by her students. How will the student who cannot count perform? He will fail, but he "understands" simple addition!

Let's use another example. Suppose you are studying to become a teacher. Your professor tells you that you must "understand Descamps' principles of classroom discipline" (these are presented in chapter 9 of this textbook). Fair enough, right? You know where to find the information which you will be required to know (Chapter 9 of this book). What more could you need? Well, you might want to know what you will be required to *do* to prove you know it. Suppose, for example, that you read Descamps' 20 steps, or strategies, for classroom discipline, and you understand them all. Now, for a test, your professor asks you to *list* each of these 20 steps. Unfair! He didn't say you were going to have to *list* them. He only said you had to understand them.

Many educators believe that students have a "right" to know what they are being asked to learn and what they will be expected to do to demonstrate to their teachers what they know it. They consider anything less to be unfair. However, although this might apply to high school and college students, typical first grade children don't even know why they are in school. They have no idea why it might be unfair not to specify what they must do to prove their knowledge. But good instruction demands that their teachers take the trouble to specify this for themselves. Not to do so puts the student in a situation for which he can be the victim of his teacher's lack of clarity. A teacher may intend that a student demonstrate his learning through a particular action while the student has gathered the impression that he is supposed to perform a different action.

In addition to the problem of confusion between teacher and student, there is tremendous potential for confusion among teachers! Teachers who are part of a team-teaching arrangement, or even teachers who pass students on from one grade level to the next, may be using different performances to assess mastery of a particular objective. For the simple addition objective mentioned above, for example, one teacher may pass a student on for showing that addition is the combination of two sets while another teacher may retain that student because he cannot yet find sums.

There is, of course, a way to eliminate this confusion. It is to answer question #2, "What will the student do to demonstrate that he knows" whatever he is supposed to know. There are certain "action words" which, if used, will communicate what a student must *do* to prove mastery of an objective; that is, words like "solve," "list," "summarize," and "describe" (Mager, 1984, pp. 29–33). Other words, however, such as "understand" and "appreciate" are too vague and tend to confuse people. Statements that the student will "*understand* mathematics" or "*appreciate* music," for example, are too vague to be useful as objectives because they do not answer our question #2, "What will the learner *do* to demonstrate his knowledge?"

What *does* a student do when he understands mathematics? Solve problems? Devise problems? Read Einstein's treatise on relativity? The statement doesn't tell you! What does a student do when he appreciates music? Listen to it? Buy records? Perform it? (Mager, 1984, pp. 29 & 35) If you cannot answer our question #2, then your objective probably needs to be reflected upon and rewritten because each objective must state, first, what you want the student to *know*, and second, what the student must *do* to prove he now knows it.[1]

All this emphasis on what the student must *do* can be very counterproductive, however, if your objective does not also answer question #1, "What do you want the student to *know*?" For example, examine the following objective, written by a college student who was studying to become a teacher: The student will draw several pictures illustrating a personal experience with a friend.

This objective does answer question #2 (What will the student *do*?), but it neglects to answer our first question (What will the student *know*?). Does this future teacher want her students to "know how to draw pictures illustrating personal experiences with friends"? I doubt it, and this would be an objective of little worth to the student, if she did want them to know this. What probably happened when this prospective teacher wrote the objective was that she was thinking of an *activity* which she had in mind for her students to do. She didn't know what she wanted her students to *know*, but she knew what she wanted them to *do*. She also remembered that she was required to answer our question #2, "What will the student *do* to prove his knowledge?" So she told us what she wanted her students to do. However, this future teacher forgot that, when the student *does* something to prove that he has acquired new knowledge, it must really prove that the student has acquired some specific type of knowledge. Otherwise, her objective is open to the criticism which so many elementary teachers are open to; that is, that they mindlessly assign activities without any sense of purpose or objective.

We emphasize that there is a difference between an **objective** and an **activity**. An *objective* deals with *what the student will learn*. An *activity* deals with *how the student will learn*. When these two things are confused, instruction appears confusing also! Often, a poorly written objective describes an activity instead of answering questions 1 and 2 of this chapter. With many students of education, this mistake results from the belief that every lesson plan must have an objective. While many lesson plans *do* have an objective, the *lesson* is intended to teach the *objective*. Unfortunately, many beginners decide on their activity and then try to develop an objective to go with the lesson. This is like putting the cart before the horse! In any lesson which has an objective, *the lesson should be developed to help teach the objective*. But the converse is not true—objectives should not be developed simply to go along with lesson plans.

Put another way, most teaching in graded and nongraded settings alike should be done with objectives in mind. The curriculum has listed the objectives which the students ought to master. The teacher is responsible for choosing activities or lessons which will help the students to reach these objectives and master them. When a teacher states what she want the students to *do* but does not state what they will *learn* by doing it, this teacher does not have a clear objective in mind. This can be viewed as sloppy instruction which wastes the students' important time and contributes to their confusion. On the other hand, when students and teachers know what the students are supposed to be learning, students will be less confused and teachers will be more likely to select lessons or activities which help the students to learn it.

The sample objective above illustrated another important point for teachers and curriculum developers. When deciding on a statement of objective and while trying to answer our question #1 (What do you want the student to *know*?), it is important to ask another, related question: Is this knowledge worth acquiring? We believe an objective should state knowledge which is so important that all students at a particular level of school (elementary, middle, or high school) need that knowledge before commencing to higher levels. If it isn't that important, it certainly doesn't need to be included in the school-wide curriculum (whether that curriculum was prepared by commercial publishers or by the teaching staff in your school should have no effect on this criterion for determining the importance of an objective). Do all elementary students need to add, at a certain level of proficiency, before moving on to middle school? Most definitely! Do all elementary students need to be able to "draw several pictures which illustrate personal experiences with friends"? Most definitely not! Whether a child can do this will have no effect what-soever on his future happiness or success.[2]

For many years, educators favored so called "performance objectives." These included a standard and a condition for each objective. This resulted in overly narrow objectives which related to one lesson only. Such an objective might read: Given a drawing of a flower, the student will label in writing at least four of the five parts shown. (Beane et al., 1986, p. 232).

The problem with objectives such as the one above is that they are overly specific and therefore not fully worthwhile. It is not essential that every child label four out of five parts on a flower. What is important is that the child know the parts of the flower. How we test each child's knowledge is our own business as teaching professionals. The child *could* label the parts in writing, but the child might also simply *point to* each part and name it. Put another way, I am trying to teach the student the parts of a flower—*not* how to label them in writing for at least four out of five parts. The objective as stated above does not answer question #1 because it does not tell us what the student will learn. It *does* tell us what the student will *do,* but without answering question #1, this is misleading. Suppose I am a fourth grade teacher and a student walks up to my desk and identifies the parts on an actual flower. Suppose, further, that this child is a nonreader. He will fail the objective as it is worded above, yet he possesses the essential knowledge which the objective calls for. That is why it is a poorly worded objective.

But what happens when you can't state the objective according to our two questions but you know what you want the students to *do*? What if you want to provide a particular activity or experience to children and you really don't have a specific objective in mind for your students?

For example, you may want to take the students on a field trip to a science museum—not so they will acquire some particular knowledge, but simply to help them to become more familiar with the world of science and scientists. Or you may want to sing with your students or read to them—not so they will learn particular songs or stories, but so that they will come to appreciate songs and stories more. **Expressive objectives** are used in this type of situation. In this situation, the activity or experience truly is the important matter and the possible outcomes are left open-ended (Eisner, 1969).

Basically, there are two approaches to thinking about one's objectives for one's students, and these two approaches affect the type of lesson plan which one chooses to develop. The first type is sometimes referred to as the rational-linear approach (Arends, 1988, pp. 88–90). According to this way of thinking about lesson planning, a teacher first identifies the objective which she wants the students to acquire. Next, the teacher assigns some kind of activity which is intended to help the students to acquire this objective. This activity might be a teacher-directed lesson, an independent activity at a learning center, a guided practice activity with worksheets, or a cooperative learning task. Whatever the activity, its purpose is to help the student to achieve that objective which the teacher wants the student to achieve.

The other approach to thinking about objectives and lesson planning is called the nonlinear approach (Arends, 1988, pp. 88–90). In the nonlinear approach, the activity comes first. Then, certain outcomes occur, and these outcomes may lead the teacher to think of new objectives for her students. Expressive objectives fall into the nonlinear category of instructional planning.

Let us now summarize what we have said about objectives. First, *they answer two questions:* 1) What will the student know? and 2) What will the student do to demonstrate that he knows it? Second, they are stated in terms of the *learner—not* the teacher. Third, *expressive objectives* are used when the teacher does not have a particular outcome in mind for the student.

Making Lesson Plans

Lesson plans are a necessary and important aspect of teaching. Let's use this example from the life of a typical elementary teacher. She has planned her activity for her afternoon social studies period in general terms. She plans to show a film on "the old west." In her lesson plan book for the 2:00 P.M. space under Thursday's column, she wrote, simply, "Film: The Old West." Now it is 2:00 P.M. and her students have arrived from another classroom. She remembers what she has written in her lesson plan book and she realizes that she must obtain a 16 mm projector in order to show the film. She knows that there is only one 16 mm projector in her building and that this is usually stored in the library and loaned to teachers by the librarian. She hurries down to the library, but discovers that the librarian is on a late lunch break. Being enterprising, she looks for the projector in the place where it is usually stored, but she cannot find it. She then walks to the lunchroom where she finds the librarian. She informs her that the 16 mm projector is being used by a 5th grade science teacher in the building. Still hopeful, she goes to the 5th grade science teacher's classroom and asks if she can use the machine during that period. The teacher who is using the machine politely tells her that she would have been happy to rearrange her schedule to accommodate her need if she had only given her a day's notice. Returning to her own classroom, she mentally revises her plans, wondering what would be an appropriate and interesting lesson for this period. Ten minutes have passed, and she finds her classroom filled with students who are behaving in a somewhat rowdy manner, shouting and throwing paper objects at each other.

Teachers who do not prepare adequately for their teaching situations waste their students' time and distract their concentration. The teacher described above neglected one essential aspect of a lesson plan—*materials* needed. Note that in the lesson plans which follow, *materials* needed are always listed.

We have already pointed out that the objective which the teacher has in mind for students will dramatically affect the type of plan which the teacher develops. When the teacher has a specific objective in mind, either lesson plan format 1a (see Box 5.1) or 1b (see Box 5.3) is probably preferable. On the other hand, when the teacher has no particular objective in mind (or has an "expressive objective"), she will probably want to use our lesson plan format 2 (see Box 5.5). Each of these lesson plan formats, with examples from some of our elementary education students, are included in Boxes 5.1–5.6.

In lesson plan format 1a (see Box 5.1), teachers may choose to use either the *procedure* or *activity* heading **or** both headings in combination. In other words, under either the *procedure* or the *activity* heading, the teacher may describe what the teacher **and** the child will do. However, some teachers find it convenient to mentally separate their planning for themselves from their planning for their students. In such cases, they think first about what they must do in order to get the lesson going; then, they consider the more independent activities which they will assign to their students.

Box 5.2 is an example of a lesson plan which follows lesson plan format 1a. The teacher is an experienced teacher, and she has chosen to omit the *procedure*. Note that Annette includes a simple assessment in which her students illustrate, with drawings, different ways to make circuits with a battery, a bulb, and a wire.

As a general rule of thumb, lesson plans should not include more than one objective. It is difficult to teach more than one concept or skill at a time. A good lesson will usually emphasize that one objective which is the content of that lesson. If you, as a teacher, have more than one objective in mind, then you probably need more than one lesson to teach these activities.

Lessons do not last for any specified period of time. One objective may take 20 minutes to teach. Another objective may require several months of work before the students are able to master it. For the objective that takes only 20 minutes to teach, one lesson should be sufficient. But for the objective that takes several months for the students to learn, *many* lessons will be necessary.

A variety of factors can affect the mastery of an objective by a student. The rate at which students can learn a particular objective will vary with each student. Consequently, it is sometimes necessary to make use of individual lessons which can be independently completed by the students. (We call these "self-instructional lessons" in a later section of this chapter.) In group or whole-class teaching, however, we must keep in mind that some concepts and skills are far more difficult to learn than others (for *any* student) and will require much more time, and many more lessons, than objectives which are easier to learn.

Box 5-1 **Lesson Plan Format *1a***

Rationale (Optional) A rationale is something which orients your students towards the lesson which is about to take place. It could be a statement which tells the student what he is about to learn. It could also be something more "fancy"—intended to "catch the student's eye" and interest him in the content or materials of the lesson.

Objective Your objective is whatever you want your students to know. An objective does *not* state what the what the *teacher* will do. An *objective* focuses on what the *student* will learn.

Procedure What will the *teacher* do, during this lesson, to help the student to achieve his objective? Chronological "steps" might be listed here. For example:

1. Explain the concept of a complete sentence.
2. Give examples of incomplete sentences.
3. On the chalkboard in front of class, have students correct incomplete sentences .
4. Give directions for completing the student worksheet on complete sentences.

Activity What must the *student* do, during this lesson, to help himself so that he can achieve the objective? Chronological "steps" might be listed here, also. For example,

1. Participate in the teacher-directed part of the lesson.
2. Complete the student worksheet on complete sentences.
3. Compose one complete sentence about today's school lunch.

OR

1. The student will make two separate sets of objects, each set containing less than 5 objects.
2. The student will combine these two sets into one, new set.
3. The student will count the number of objects in the new set.
4. The student will repeat steps 1-3, placing different amounts in the two sets each time.

Materials Materials are any equipment, objects, writing implements, paper, etc., which will be needed by either teacher or students during the lesson. Examples might include textbooks, workbooks, paper and pencils or pens, paints, chalkboard and chalk, overhead projectors, movie projectors, video-cassette recorders, batteries and bulbs, etc.

Assessment (Optional) An assessment determines whether the student has acquired the objective which you gave for the lesson. An assessment of an elementary mathematics objective could be accomplished via a written test, completion of a set of worksheets by the student, or even the teacher's observation of the student as the student completes math problems on paper or at the chalkboard. All that is necessary is that the teacher actually judge whether the student has or has not reached the objective in question. When using an assessment, you should specify *how you* will assess your students; for example, "written test," "teacher observation," "student work sheets," etc.

Box 5-2   **Example of a Lesson Plan in Format *1a***
(**Written by Annette Cound**)

BATTERIES AND BULBS

Rationale   Open a class discussion with the following questions: "Have you ever thought about where light comes from? Who thinks they know how a light works? Can you explain it to us?"

Objective   The learner will explain the concept of a closed circuit

Activity

1. Class discussion of children's ideas about how a light works.

2. Divide the class into groups of 2.

3. Pass out 1 battery, 1 bulb, and 1 wire and ask the students to see if they can get the light to work.

4. Have groups draw a picture of how their set-up appeared when the bulb lit up.

5. Ask the students to speculate on why the wire in the bulb glows.

6. Help students to trace the path of energy with a diagram on the board.

7. Give each group another battery and wire. Have each group create a closed circuit using 2 batteries, 2 wires, and 1 bulb.

8. Draw the different ways to create a closed circuit on the chalkboard.

9. Review how the light works and what it means to have a closed circuit.

Materials   (class of 18)

20 flashlight batteries—D cells

12 flashlight bulbs

20 eighteen-inch length pieces of insulated wire, stripped on each end.

paper and pencil

Assessment   The learner will draw pictures of two different ways to light the bulb (making a closed circuit) — one way using 1 battery, 1 wire, 1 bulb; the other way, using 2 batteries, 2 wires, and 1 bulb.

In lesson plans, the assessment should always deal with the objective for that lesson. It is inappropriate—and unfair—to expect students to pass tests which deal with content that was not included within, or was only incidental to, the lesson. If you are trying to teach "Objective A" (whatever concept or skill objective A deals with), then you assess for "Objective A" and nothing else. In Annette's lesson, above, the assessment *is* related to the objective. If, however, she had assessed the student's ability to make light bulbs, she would have been guilty of assessing something which she had not taught.

Madeline Hunter (1982; see the section on "mastery teaching" in Chapter 4) has developed a variation of lesson plan format 1a. It is usually referred to either as the "seven steps" lesson plan format or as "Hunter's Mastery Teaching plan." In this text, we refer to it as format 1b (see Box 5.3). Box 5.4 is an example of a lesson plan which has been done according to format 1b.

As we have already said, the type of lesson which focuses on a particular objective is best summarized through either format 1a or format 1b. But when particular objec-

---

Box 5-3   **Lesson Plan Format *1b* (Hunter's Mastery Teaching Format)**

1. **Focus:** The teacher directs the attention of the students to the material to be learned (establishes set) and explains how this material will be learned and how it will be useful. (Objective and purpose)

2. **Input:** New information needed to fulfill the objective of the lesson is presented to students. This information may be acquired via a teacher explanation, group discussion, reading, observation, etc.

3. **Modeling:** Examples of the skill or knowledge which the students are expected to learn are presented. Students observe demonstrations which are conducted by the teacher, other students, or an expert.

4. **Checking for Understanding:** The teacher ascertains the students' understanding of the new material by asking questions or by having a few students demonstrate mastery. If the students have not mastered the skill at the minimum level required to be able to apply it, the teacher does not proceed to the next step.

5. **Guided Practice:** Students practice the new knowledge under teacher supervision, working individually or in cooperative learning groups.

6. **Independent Practice:** Once the students are able to perform satisfactorily during guided practice, the teacher assigns further practice to be done individually, either in the classroom or as homework. This assignment may vary for different students. For some, it may include enriching or challenging new material. For others, it may include remediation work which reinforces the minimum competency specified by the objective.

7. **Closure:** At the end of the lesson, the teacher seeks to extend learning by bringing disconnected elements of the lesson into a meaningful whole. During closure, students reach conclusions and insights about the material that has been studied.

Box 5-4   An Example of a Lesson in Format *1b*
(Hunter's Mastery Teaching Plan)

LATITUDE AND LONGITUDE

(Social Studies Lesson Plan For Grade 5)

Focus   The teacher shows the students a playing board for the game "Battleship" and asks them to tell what is the objective of the game (answer: to sink enemy ships by locating them through the use of coordinates). The teacher then states the objective of the lesson: to learn how to find points on a globe by using the coordinates of longitude and latitude.

Input   The teacher describes the concept "latitude" and its critical characteristics. The teacher then presents some examples and non-examples of latitude. The same process is followed to present the concept "longitude." The teacher then explains that latitude and longitude measures intersect at a point which is unique and different from all other points on the globe.

Modeling   Using a large globe, the teacher demonstrates how to find latitude and longitude points on the globe.

Checking for Understanding   The teacher asks questions to make certain that the students understand the concept of latitude and longitude. The teacher also asks several students to find latitude and longitude points on the globe.

Guided Practice   Working with smaller globes in cooperative learning groups, students are required to find particular places after having been given the latitudes and longitudes of these places. Next, the students are given the names of certain places and are expected to find their respective latitudes and longitudes.

Independent Practice   Students individually complete worksheets which require them to solve problems dealing with latitude and longitude. Students who finish their worksheets early are given more challenging problems. Students who appear to be having difficulty are grouped by the teacher so that she can go over the task with them together. These students are given remediation exercises to practice on their own.

Closure   The teacher asks the students for some of the practical applications of latitude and longitude (e.g., navigation, surveying, etc.). The teacher announces that, on the next day, a treasure hunt game will be played in which teams of students will be allowed to ask 20 questions about the latitude and longitude where the treasure is hidden.

---

tives are *not* the focus of the lesson, or when the activity itself is the most important aspect of the lesson, then format 2 (see Box 5.5) is more appropriate. Box 5.6 is an example of a lesson plan which has been done according to format 2.

Box 5-5 **Lesson Plan Format 2**

Activity This type of lesson plan begins with an *activity*—that is, something which you plan to have the students do—and has no particular objective in mind. Science lessons, especially at the early childhood level, frequently begin with an activity. A field trip is an activity which may have been planned with no particular objective in mind (Example: A walk in the woods adjacent to the playground).

Possible Outcomes Rather than state a specific goal or objective, this type of lesson plan lists the variety of learnings which might occur when students participate in this activity. Possible outcomes for a walk in the woods might include noticing the differences in densities of wildlife and plant life when comparing the playground to the woods, learning ways to estimate and determine the ages of trees, classifying leaves according to taxonomies, classifying leaves according to color or shape, etc.

Background Information (Optional): Usually, teachers can better prepare themselves for these types of lessons by learning about related topics. In preparing to take your class for a walk in the woods, for example, you might want to learn more about the means of determining ages of trees, taxonomies of leaves, how to examine small plant and animal life with a magnifying glass, etc. This information should be summarized in this section of your lesson plan so that anyone teaching the lesson (for example, a substitute teacher) will be adequately informed.

Materials Anything the teacher or students will need to carry out the activity should be listed here. If you are taking your class for a walk in the woods, you might want to bring along a magnifying glass, a North American pocketbook of trees, and a pocketknife.

Evaluation (Optional) In this type of evaluation, the teacher writes a brief account of the lesson. Usually, she will answer the following questions: What went well? What surprised me? What went poorly? Also, the teacher usually proposes changes for similar lessons in the future.

Any lesson plan, whether done according to format 1a, 1b, or 2, should have some degree of detail. Under the *activity* heading, for example, one would not write simply "field trip to the zoo" if that was the focus of one's activity. Rather, one would indicate that the activity is a field trip to the zoo and one would specify any details: for example, when the class would arrive, what areas they would visit first, next, etc., or what areas students would be allowed to choose to visit, etc. These details are especially important for student-teachers and beginning teachers.

We are not implying that teachers will always use this kind of detail in planning for their lessons. We do believe, however, that education students, student-teachers, and beginning teachers should consistently be required to develop plans at this level of detail. There is no doubt that many experienced teachers manage to consider each of the headings in our respective lesson plan formats without necessarily writing them

Box 5-6   **An Example of a Lesson Plan in Format 2**

THE PENDULUM

Activity

Step #1   The children will experiment at swinging a pendulum from various positions in order to try to knock down an object. If they succeed in knocking it down the first time, the object will be moved to a new location and the children will try to knock it down again.

Step #2   The next phase of the activity will be to have the children stand in only one position and predict where the object should be placed in order for the pendulum to hit it when it is released from that position.

Possible Outcomes

After a few experimental swings of the pendulum while trying to knock the object down, perhaps the children will realize that the pendulum has a definite arc, and also that the direction of that arc depends upon where the children stand when the pendulum is released. Hopefully they will realize that, in order for the object to be hit, it has to be located within that arc.

Materials

a long string

a block of wood

a milk carton

Source: Sue Brannon

Box 5-7   **An Entry Box in a Daily Lesson Plan Book**

	Monday	Tuesday	Wednesday
8:00			
9:00		Electricity: Circuits	
		Batteries, bulbs, & wires	

down or going into great detail about them. However, it is obvious to us that most student-teachers are overwhelmed by the process of planning for teaching because they do not have enough experience to anticipate all that must be done *before* a successful lesson can begin. Following the basic ingredients of our lesson plan formats should help beginning teachers to prepare successful lessons. As they mature, they must make their own decisions about how much detail to provide in any lesson plan. As they become experienced teachers, they may simply fill in lesson plan "boxes" such as the one included in Box 5.7. Hopefully, they will still be considering the other ingredients of a lesson plan, at least mentally, as they go about the business of preparing for instruction.

For the lesson depicted in Box 5.7, the teacher has an activity in mind for the students. They will use batteries, bulbs, and wires to make the bulbs light. If she were using lesson plan format 2, she would first describe the activity, then list possible outcomes, next mention any background information about electricity of which the teacher ought to be aware, and, finally, list the materials which she would need to provide. If she were using lesson plan format 1a, she would first state her objective (that the student will demonstrate or explain how a simple circuit works), then describe the activity, next list the materials which she would need to provide, and, finally, explain how she would assess whether the student had or had not achieved the objective. Instead of using either lesson plan format, she has simply listed the topic of her lesson (electricity: circuits) and the materials which she will need to carry out the lesson (batteries, bulbs, and wires).

SELF-INSTRUCTIONAL LESSONS

Sometimes students become ready to work on new objectives when it is inconvenient for the teacher to give these students a lesson. The teacher may, for example, be too preoccupied with students who are having difficulty with some other objective. In such situations, **self-instructional lessons** can be very useful. In self-instructional lessons, the content is explained, the students practice whatever skill is being taught and, finally, the students test themselves on how well they have learned the content in question (these tests are also **self-checking**). Such self-instructional lessons can be done by individuals or small groups but, in either case, the students involved must be capable of learning independently. This does not mean, however, that the students must be academically advanced. We have used self-instructional lessons with first-grade children who could not read (the explanation of the content, and the instructions for completing the lesson, were recorded on audiotape). Generally, the format for this unusual type of "lesson" is as it appears in Box 5.8

In Box 5.9, we have included an example of a self-instructional activity which was written for a group of teachers who were involved in a course to learn about media which could be used to develop classroom materials. Notice that all statements are written *to* the student, that is, as if the teacher were right there, talking to the students! Figure 5.1 provides an example of a self-instructional lesson which was written for children by one of our student-teachers.

Box 5-8 **Format for a Self-Instructional Lesson**
With Permission from W. R. Swyers

Title

General Statement

Task Statement

Materials Statement (Note: This is usually phrased "You will need: _____ ." It may not be necessary since all the materials should be provided)

Learner Activities

Self-Assessment

Key

Box 5-9 **A Self-Instructional Lesson for Teachers**
By Betty Swyers

SUBJECT: MOUNTING A PICTURE WITH STRAIGHT EDGES

Explanation

The GENERAL STATEMENT is called the "instructional set." It gets the learner all "set" for the task. It may be a motivating statement to get him enthusiastic or it could be some background information to "set the stage."

The TASK STATEMENT is your objective for the student, but it is written *to* the student.

LEARNER ACTIVITIES offer alternatives (options) that allow for variance in learning styles and instructional models.

These must include many types of instruction . . . films, tapes, pictures, listening, reading, role-playing, demonstration, real-life experiences, etc. (See "How Media Teach." Swyers. Feb. '72, p. 21, for more on instructional modes).

Actual Lesson

General Statement Did you know that you can mount pictures so that they will look as though they were done by a professional? Well, you can! And today you're going to find out how!

Task Statement You will choose a magazine picture that you especially like, and use the dry mounting tissue to mount the picture on a piece of 11" x 14" mat board.

Learner Activities

a. Look at the filmloop on "The Dry Mount Press."

b. Read the hand out "You TOO Can Mount Beautiful Pictures."

c. Look at the sequence pictures on pages 27–28 of the AV book on the teacher's shelf.

d. Look at the slides in the projector tray labled "Kid's Dry-Mounted Pictures," slides 1–17.

e. Watch someone who knows what he is doing and see how he used the press to mount the pictures.

continued

Card 4:
  Choose the words below which will be found on the dictionary page which has the guide words "quince" and "race." Do not use your dictionary.

stop	rabbit	rack	race
quince	pull	quiz	quiet

  Check the answers with the Key for card 4 (in the dictionary envelope in the file box).

Card 4 *Key*. You should have the words:

quince	rabbit	quiz	race

Card 5:
  Choose the words below which will be found on the dictionary page which has the guide words "curtain" and "cutting." Do not use your dictionary.

cat	cycle	curl	cutting
cute	custard	czar	cutup

  Check the answers with the Key for card 5 (in the dictionary envelope in the file box).

Card 5 *Key*. You should have the words:

cute	custard	cutting

Card 6: Self-assessment
Answer the following by filling in the blanks.
Part 1: Each page has _____ guide words.
   The first guide word tells the _____ word on that page.
   The last guide word tells the _____ word on that page.
Part 2: Use your Dictionary to answer the following.
   Find the guide words on

	First Word	Last Word
Page 96		
Page 289		
Page 436		
Page 454		
Page 490		
Page 565		

Figure 5.1 continued

Part 3:   Use your dictionary to find the following. Use the guide words on the page.

Word	Page	First Word	Last Word
ax			
castle			
garment			
island			
mob			
park			

Get Key Number 6 from the dictionary envelope in the box on the Teacher's

---

Card 6 **Key.**
Part 1:
Each page has 2 guide words.
The first guide word tells the *first* word on that page.
The last guide word tells the *last* word on that page.
Part 2:
Guide Words On

	First Word	Last Word
Page 96	bubble	buddy
Page 289	flower	fly
Page 436	line	lip
Page 454	malt	man-eater
Page 490	mouse	much
Page 565	pilgrim	pinch

Part 3:

Word	Page	First Word	Last Word
ax	52	awake	babies-breath
castle	116	cash	cat
garment	309	garden	gas
island	399	is	ivory
mob	481	mix	model
park	541	parent	parlor

Figure 5.1 continued

Modules and Units

Whether they are teacher-directed or self-instructional, lessons make up a large portion of any teacher's daily plans. But an endless stream of lessons would be pointless unless they fit into a large picture. Lessons are usually intended to help students achieve particular objectives, of course, and these objectives are included in a list of objectives for students in a given elementary or middle school. Frequently, these lessons (and the objectives which these lessons teach) contribute to long-term plans. Long-term plans may be developed by teachers or by school district supervisors. Many long-term plans are also developed for textbook publishers by curriculum authors.

Whoever develops these long-term plans, they are usually called either **modules** or **units.** We have included examples of each type of planning in our chapter here because we believe that each type is useful for different kinds of long-term planning.

Modules Modules are most useful when either of the following two conditions are met: 1) The teacher knows exactly which objectives he wants students to acquire, or 2) the teacher desires to individualize the delivery of the content so that individual students will learn whatever content they are most capable of learning. Box 5.10 depicts a planning format for modules.

In modules, the idea is that all the objectives for the module should be fairly closely related. A module on rules and laws might be good. A module on transportation might be good. But a module on rules, laws, transportation, parks, and recreation would be a disaster because it would be so broad that the objectives would barely relate to each other. Ideally, objectives for a module should be logically related or sequenced. For example, a module on simple addition might include the objective of making sets since students must be able to combine sets in order to learn to add.

Note that pre-assessments are utilized in modules. The purpose of a pre-assessment is that teachers should be able to identify the learning needs of their pupils. Once they have done so, they can make use of this information when forming instructional groups. However, some teachers choose to teach all their students together. In this case, a pre-assessment can make the teacher aware of the learning needs of her class in general.

Box 5.11 is an example of how one education student used the module format to make her long-term plans for the teaching of certain objectives which she wanted her students to acquire. The education major who wrote this module included ten lesson plans in her module. For the sake of brevity, we have included only three of her lesson plans in Box 5.11. The students whom she intended this module for were in grade 4.[5]

Note that the objectives for this module appear in the lesson plans for the module. This is no accident. When you develop a module, you start by listing the objectives which you plan to teach; then, you develop lessons to teach those particular objectives. Each of Katherine's lesson plans attempts to help students learn one of the objectives for her module.

Units of Topic Work[6] (This section was written by Peter Frost and Robert Louisell.) When compared to modules, **topic work** (discussed in Chapter 4) employs a more creative, interdisciplinary approach to teaching. We have said that modules should be used to plan instruction when one knows one's objectives exactly Topic work (sometimes called **thematic units**), on the other hand, should be used when one does not have precise objectives in mind. Instead, in topic work the teacher chooses a topic. Learning objectives are taught as part of a "theme." This "theme" must not be so specific as to limit the students' explorations to a narrow list of content which must be followed regardless of the interests of the students. Events that occur during the unit of instruction should be allowed to spark interest in other subject matter. Neither,

Box 5-10   # Modules Format
(with permission, W. R. Swyers)

Rationale   What is the purpose of teaching children these objectives? Why are the objectives for this module important for your students (or for any students)?

Objectives   What will the students know (that they didn't know previously) as a result of their participation in this module? Note that the focus is on *what the students will know* (not on what the teacher will say or do).

Prerequisites   Is there anything which the students must know, or be able to do, in order to participate successfully in this module? EXAMPLE #1—In a sixth-grade health module on reaction times, students were required to calculate averages for their reaction times. Since most students did not know how to determine averages, this was one of the objectives for the module. The ability to add and divide is a **prerequisite** for this objective (You cannot learn how to determine an average without knowing how to add and divide). EXAMPLE #2—The text being used in a fifth-grade social studies module has a readability level of fourth grade. The ability to read on a fourth grade level is thus a prerequisite for successful participation in this module.

Pre-assessment   How will you determine which of your module objectives have already been learned by any of your students? (It makes little sense to require anyone to spend time studying something which one has already mastered.) Teacher observations of students at work, conferences with other teachers or parents, samples of student work, and written tests are all appropriate sources of information for a pre- assessment. Include teacher comments, personal observations, and written tests used for your pre-assessment in your appendix. Be sure to indicate which objectives your pre-assessment deals with.

Learning alternatives   What will your students do to learn what you want them to learn? (How will they achieve the objectives of the module?) Learning alternatives can be *teacher-directed lessons, self-instructional lessons,* or *independent activities* directed by students.

Post-assessment   How will you determine which of your students have achieved what objectives in your module?

Remediation   What further learning alternatives will you provide for those students who have failed to achieve any of the objectives for your module? (What "second chances" will you give the student so that you can optimize his or her chance of mastering the objective?)

APPENDIX   Worksheets, handouts, tests, etc. Refer to copyrighted materials by publisher, title, and page numbers.

Box 5-11 **Example of a Module**

MODULE: MAPPING by Katherine Terrazas*

Rationale   Students need to know how to read a variety of maps for many different reasons. Perhaps they'll need to travel for business, or if they are lucky, for pleasure. In any case they will be better off knowing, ahead of time, the distances between locations, directions, altitude and political boundaries.

Objectives   The student will:

1. use a map to give directions on how to get from one location to another.
2. determine the direction of one map item from another.
3. use the guidelines on a map to locate different places.
4. use lines of latitude and longitude to locate different areas.
5. give the longitude and latitude of different cities worldwide.
6. use boundary lines on a map to distinguish the different countries and states or provinces from one another.
7. calculate the distance between two places by using the map scale of miles.
8. map out a travel route to a given destination.
9. construct a map.

Prerequisites   The students must have:

1. the ability to read at a third grade level.
2. the ability to write clearly.
3. some knowledge of the layout of his or her neighborhood.
4. the ability to do simple multiplication.

Pre-assessment   Hold a discussion on maps. Elicit from students any information they wish to contribute on the subject. Determine each student's mathematical abilities. The decision about which lesson to begin with will be based on an analysis of the responses given by the students.

Learning Alternatives   See lesson plans which follow.

Post-assessment   The final lesson of this module will be used as an assessment.

Learning Alternative (Lesson Plan) #1: Neighborhood Map

Rationale   We are a very mobile society. Many of us will someday travel to different places. We need to know how to get to these different places without relying on someone else to get us there.

Objective   Students will make a map of their neighborhood and give directions on how to get from one specific place to another.

(continued)

* In developing this module, Katherine consulted *Skills for Understanding Maps and Globes* by Kenneth Job and Lois Wolf. (Chicago: Follit. 1976)

Procedure   Inform students how maps were originally made. Explain how to use landmarks as guides.

Activity

1. Read to the students the story of how maps came to be (A Map Is Made).

2. Discuss with the class the necessity for maps.

3. Explain the use of landmarks as guides. Elicit the different landmarks in the neighborhood from students. Record these on the board.

4. Sketch a neighborhood map on the board. Include some fictitious landmarks. Have students orally practice giving directions.

5. Pass out 8½ x 11 newsprint and rulers.

6. Students are to draw a map of their neighborhood.

7. Students will write out directions to a friend on how to get from their house to school or to the store or on how to get from one friend's house to another's.

8. Have students exchange papers with a partner.

9. The partner should track the route on the map according to the directions.

10. Partners should not live too close to each other.

Materials

1. newsprint

2. rulers

3. markers

4. pencils

5. story on maps.

Assessment   Student should be able to track the route using the directions given.

Learning Alternative #5: Latitude and Longitude

Rationale   Guidelines are used on maps to help us find and locate places we want to know about. We use guidelines on city maps. On maps of larger areas we use lines of latitude and longitude.

Objective   The student will locate areas on a grid using latitude and longitude and mark areas with his initials.

Procedure   Use the grid on the chalkboard to find and locate areas.

Activity

1. Draw a grid on the chalkboard, marking lines of latitude and longitude. Each space should be about 3 in. x 3 in.

2. Explain the concepts of latitude and longitude. Demonstrate, on the grid, how to use directions of North, South, East and West along with latitude and longitude.

(continued)

3. Call on students to go up to the grid and locate an area. The teacher will provide the directions in latitude and longitude

4. After the student has located the correct area, have her initial it.

5. Show a map of the United States and have the students locate different cities. Students are to give longitude and latitude for these cities.

Materials   Chalkboard, chalk, large map of the United States.

Assessment   Assessment will by made by observing students. If reteaching is necessary, use the grid with small groups.

Learning Alternative #9: Road Maps

Rationale   Some day you may need to travel across the state or across the nation. In order to do this more efficiently, you will need to be able to read a road map. You also may go on vacation and you certainly won't want to get lost!

Objective   The student will map out a route which one could use to get from one city to another.

Procedure   Plan a vacation route.

Activity

1. Pass out a map of the state of Texas.

2. Hold a discussion with the class about planning a vacation. Focus the discussion on the necessity of reading maps.

3. Have the class study the map of Texas. Elicit responses as to where students would like to go.

4. Discuss the map's legend with the class.

5. Review how to calculate miles.

6. Pass out worksheet entitled "Road Maps."

Materials

1. maps of Texas

2. paper

3. pencils

4. rulers

5. worksheets

Assessment   Evaluation will be made on the vacation plan each group completes.

however, should it be so general that it does not provide some direction and unification to the instructional activities of the unit. For example, in one British school, the town in which the students lived became the topic of study. The unit included a treasure hunt through 42 sites of the town, including the Junior School, the fire station, the church, and a stone.[7] (See samples in Figure 5.2).

Planning of a topic work unit is usually done at three levels: **long-term, medium term** (weekly), and **daily**. **Long-term planning** refines and clarifies aims, key skills, and concepts which are to be emphasized during the topic unit. It also identifies resources and selects the opening activity which will launch the unit. Also, it specifies how students will be grouped and how the learning activities will be organized.

For example, the teacher will need to decide how to break up the long-term unit of study into smaller time frames. The teacher must make some estimate as to how long a topic unit might last. How much flexibility should she allow so that the unit can take more or less time than she has estimated? Will a topic of study which is expected to last six weeks be broken down into six weekly time frames? Three weekly time frames? Will each time frame last an entire week or only three to four days? What methods of instruction will be used? Whole-class discussions? Small group work based on interests? Small group work based on needs?

There is an "art" to good long-term planning which involves fostering an understanding in one's students that everything which one studies is related to everything else which one studies. This sense of integration pervades a good unit.

In schools where the topic work approach makes up the majority of the academic work of the students, the unit plan must be analyzed to assure that each of the essential subjects and skills areas will be dealt with throughout the topic. In England, language arts, math, and science are the three "core" disciplines which must be represented in a topic. In America, reading-language arts, math, social studies, and science make up the essential skills and subjects which must be taught (where physical education, art, and music are taught by specialists).

Of course, it is not always possible for teachers to insure that each discipline will be thoroughly represented in a topic. Some separate instruction in particular areas (e.g., math, reading, or science) may have to be scheduled on a daily basis in order to assure that all of the academic needs of the students are being met. In the United States, some teachers will opt to teach reading, language arts, and math during a half-day (e.g., mornings); then, topic work can be carried out in the afternoons.

Teachers also need to consider the balance of disciplines represented in their topic work throughout the year. For example, one topic may have a heavy science emphasis. This could be useful. However, if *every* topic unit placed heavy emphasis on science, wouldn't that mean that certain other subjects (e.g., social studies) were being ignored? Teachers who use the topic work approach routinely need to analyze their topics carefully with an eye for providing a balance among the elementary school subjects.

One way to keep track of which subjects are represented in a topic is to list the **key concepts** which will be covered during the unit. This list must be kept to a "manageable" minimum, however; otherwise, the unit begins to focus on a multitude of unimportant facts and lower-level learning eventually crowds higher-level thinking out of the picture. This defeats the purpose of topic work since one of its advantages is its ability to develop higher-order thinking in students.

Keeping the above thoughts in mind, a teacher can usually develop a good long-term plan for a topic unit by following the **seven stages of long-term planning**. Each of these stages is described below.

The Key To The Treasure

The Treasure Map

1. Junior School
2. The Old Police Station
3. Health Centre
4. Library
5. The Cycle Shop
6. The Cinema
7. The Fairways
8. The Pound
9. The Firs
10. British Telecom
11. Tourist Information Centre
12. The Fire Station
13. The Police Station
14. Tollgate Cottage
15. Little Thatch
16. Queensberry Bridge
17. Tumbling Bay
18. The Abbey Gates
19. Church
20. Funneral Directors
21. The Tree
22. The Veterans Club
23. Fairholme
24. Antrobus Arms
25. The King's Arms
26. Lloyds Bank
27. Cafe
28. Flower Shop
29. Prudential Estate Agents
30. The Bell Hotel
31. The Bakery
32. The Homebuyers Centre
33. Irene's
34. The Methodist Church
35. The New Inn
36. The George Hotel
37. Food Shop
38. The Cottage
39. Fairlawn Hotel
40. The Antique Shop
41. The Stone

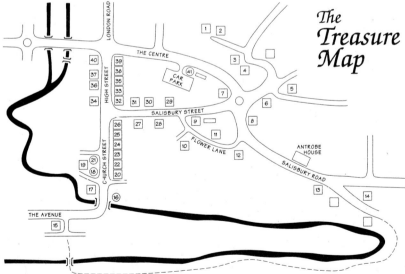

The Treasure Map

Figure 5.2 A British Town as a Topic of Study

First, one must **choose a topic** and **brainstorm** a web of ideas and tentative resources. The selection of a topic should be based on several factors. Teachers who listen to, and observe, their students, are usually aware of their students' interests. Because of this, certain topics (e.g., automobiles) may occur to them. Teachers with a few years of experience can usually recall topics which were "hits" in other years. Such topics are likely to experience success a second time around, especially if adjustments are made. Sources of ideas for topics which are frequently overlooked by teachers include their own personal interests. Most teachers have personal interests and hobbies which could easily be developed into excellent topic units. For example, one group of teachers visiting England from America spent most of their spare time at antique auctions. Yet, none of them considered developing a unit on this topic. As a topic, "antiques" is interdisciplinary (e.g., it includes much history, science process, and some

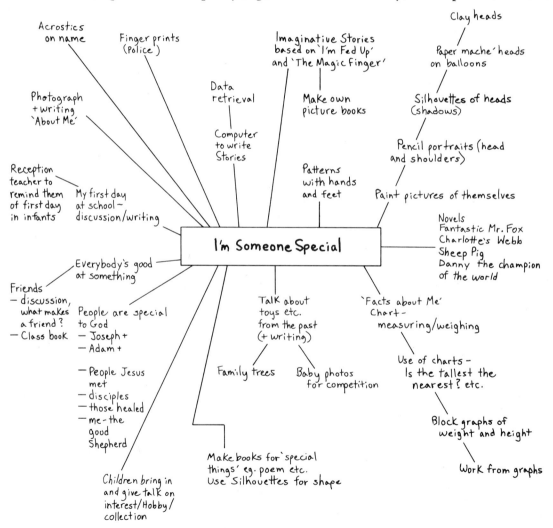

Figure 5.3 A Brainstorm Webbing for a Topic Unit

science content)—an almost ideally balanced topic. When teachers select unit topics on the basis of their personal interests, students are affected by their excitement about the topic and are motivated to participate fully in the unit. One must avoid selecting topics which are so comprehensive (e.g., the world) that they provide little guidance.

Shared brainstorm webs are done by listing and relating ideas (thus creating a "web") for a topic (see Figure 5.3). The ideas are freely listed and related. They are then examined.

In the **second stage** of long-term planning, content **webs are pruned** and **key themes are identified**. Some ideas may have to be discarded since dealing with too many ideas during a unit can create a sense of fragmentation. When teachers share in the development of their topic webs, their confidence is bolstered by their mutual support. Although teachers should create webs before beginning their topic units, it is also helpful to involve students in the process before the unit has been launched. It contributes to the student's sense of ownership and positively affects the student's interest in the topic. It also provides the teacher with information about which subtopics will be of most interest to one's students. In reality, although the teacher will have already developed a preliminary topic web, she should be flexible and ready to make changes according to what she learns from her students during the "shared brainstorm" session. In practice, the ideas of teachers and their students frequently coincide.

When a class attempts to identify **key themes**, related ideas are clustered in ways that make sense to the students. At times, this clustering is done according to concepts (e.g., "change"). Other times, a simple theme (e.g., "insects which walk") may be used to connect the ideas. At this point, new ideas may again be added and old ones discarded. A **pruned** web is the result. The teacher and children should also make an attempt to identify tentative resources which might be helpful in pursuing the study of these themes and concepts. At this stage, the teacher may also want to provide a list of subtopics from which the children will be allowed to choose.

The **third** stage of long-term planning is the **stage-by-stage progression**. This begins with a simple listing of the main activities or subtopics coupled with those skills which will be developed by these activities. The chart below illustrates this process.

Activity Progression	Key Skills

Suppose the teacher is about to begin a unit on "the environment," for example. She will be covering a variety of topics, but she will also be attending to her "core" subject areas. One of these areas will surely be math. What math concepts or skills might she choose to present as part of a topic on the environment? Shapes? If she chooses to teach about shapes, she will fill in part of her chart like this:

Activity Progression	Key Skills
Shapes	Mathematics: Geometry

Note that only main ideas about activities are listed here. The work on shapes could take two to four days or longer, but "shapes" (in the *activity progression* column) and "Mathematics: Geometry" (in the *Key Skills* column) is all that is needed to complete the chart. The content listed in the left-hand column can be analyzed in terms of whether it deals with lower-level or higher order types of knowledge, and plans can be revised according to the teacher's goals.

After the above chart has been completed, the teacher begins the **fourth stage** of long-term planning by carefully analyzing her topic plan for balance and depth. She completes another chart (see Figure 5.4). These charts deal with each subject area which the teacher intends to cover within the topic unit. In America, we can call this the "Subject Prediction Chart" because it predicts which topics in each subject will be

Subject Area:

SUBJECT PREDICTION CHART (SEPARATE CHART FOR EACH SUBJECT AREA)	
WEEKS ONE AND TWO	WEEKS THREE AND FOUR
★	
★ ★	
WEEKS FIVE AND SIX	WEEKS SEVEN AND EIGHT

★ In this space, list activities in words or phrases.
★ ★ In this space, list outcomes or objectives which the activities will teach.

Figure 5.4

covered. In Britain, it is referred to as a "Core Prediction Chart" because the chief subject areas in England are referred to as the "core" subjects.

For these charts, activities should be briefly described for every two weeks during which the topic unit will take place. More detailed plans will be included in the weekly and daily planning. As the teacher lists activities on this chart, each skill which is being dealt with by any activity is recorded (on Figure 5.5, *Skills Record*). In Britain, these are the skills which are listed as "attainment targets" by the National Curriculum. In America, the main objectives or outcomes of the school's curriculum (for each subject area) will be listed here. In either case (British or American), teachers are able to keep track of which skills are being taught during their interdisciplinary topic work.

In the **fifth stage** of long-term planning, the teacher makes a statement about how the students will be grouped. Will they be grouped according to abilities or achievement? Will they be grouped by mixed abilities as they are in "friendship groups"? Will each group participate in each set of activities for the topic unit? Or will some groups do all of the activities while others do only certain ones? Or will each group become "experts" in one aspect of their topic and share their knowledge in some way (e.g., class presentations, topic books, etc.) with their class as a whole? These things must be spelled out. It may not take more than a sentence or two to spell out the answers to these questions, but they must be answered.

In the **sixth stage** of long-term planning, **final preparations** are made. In this stage, the teacher searches for information and resources about the topic. No teacher can be expected to know everything about a topic, but a good teacher will gather information and identify resources. In doing so, she develops ideas for activities and selects information and resources which can then be made available to new students. Also, units frequently conclude with an integrated activity in which all students participate. For example, British Primary students concluded a topic unit on Kansas with a production of *The Wizard of Oz*. In the sixth stage, the teacher should be able to identify the concluding activity for the unit.

In the **seventh stage** of long-term planning, the teacher draws a **final web** and **completes the weekly planning for the first week** of the topic unit. The web can be used to record subjects covered during the topic unit. The weekly planning is necessary so that the teacher can launch the first week of the topic unit.

Medium-term, or weekly, planning must be completed prior to beginning any topic activities for a specific week. Weekly plans need not be planned too far in advance since they should be adapted according to what has transpired during previous weeks. Resources which are available for a specific week's activities should be identified in the weekly plan. A weekly plan might be completed in a simple chart such as the one on page 157.

The grouping decisions which have been made at the long-term planning stage must be more clearly explained at the weekly planning stage. For example, the teacher may have decided to alternate between whole class instruction and the use of small groups. Some teachers create "friendship" groups—that is, groups of mixed abilities who have selected each other because they work well together. These small groups are then "rotated" through different subtopics, since it is difficult to provide enough materials for each group to work on the same subtopic simultaneously. To avoid confusion, the teacher must specify the order or rotation for small groups in the weekly plan.

Skills Record

Class:	Age Range:	Topic:	Date:

A Observation	**B** Research	**C** Mathematical
① 2 ③ 4 5	1 ② 3 ④ 5 6	1 2 ③ 4 5 6 7 8
D Language (Oral & Aural)	**E** Language (Written)	**F** Creative & Imaginative
1 ② 3 4 5 6 ⑦	1 2 3 4 5 6 7 8	1 2 ③ 4 5
G Problem Solving	**H** Personal & Social	**I** Physical & Practical
1 ② 3 ④ 5 6 7	1 2 3 4 5 6 7 8	1 2 3 4 5 6

Figure 5.5

Weekly Planning Chart
By P. Frost

	Morning	Afternoon
M O N		
T U E S		
W E D		
T H U R		
F R I		

Resources:

Daily plans can take the form of the lesson plans already covered in this chapter. In general, activities are more important than objectives in a topic unit. Because of this, lesson plan format 2 is the most appropriate plan for use with a topic unit. An example of a topic unit plan is included in Appendix.

Evaluation of student work during topic work is covered in the chapter on evaluation.

NONACADEMIC AIMS AND GOALS IN TODAY'S SCHOOLS

There are many important aims and goals for students which do not necessarily fall under the heading "academic." For example, it is a widely accepted goal that students should develop a positive self-concept through their experiences in school. Many schools also list the abilities to think independently and use "processes" while solving problems as important educational goals for their students. Although we also believe that these goals are extremely important for today's students, we have chosen to present our opinions on these matters in other chapters, our chapters on classroom management issues.

There are also many authors who have employed creative classification systems which combine traditional subject area objectives with more innovative general goals. Berman (1968) has listed the processes of perceiving, communicating (this includes the traditional reading and language arts objectives but goes far beyond them to include the understanding of nonverbal messages and the interpretation of messages with a high emotional value), loving, decision-making, organizing one's own knowledge, creating, and valuing (The ability to choose ethical priorities). Swyers (1972) has listed "literacies" (e.g., intellectual literacies, career literacies, personal, social, and aesthetic literacies) which he believes encompass traditional and innovative objectives. More than 60 years ago, Dewey (1902, 1930, 1915) criticized our contemporary divisions of curriculum because they do not follow any logical order. Piaget (Piaget & Inhelder, 1969) stated that knowledge divides itself into three areas: physical, logical-mathematical, and social knowledge. Each of these authors, and many others besides, has had an influence on contemporary schooling. Nevertheless, we have chosen not to explain their ideas in detail because we believe only the most innovative of schools today makes use of their ideas to organize their curricula.

NOTES

1. Some educators like to specify the conditions and criteria for objectives ("conditions" tell under what circumstances the students will be required to prove their knowledge, and "criteria" tell how well the students will be expected to prove it), but we believe that this decision should be left to the teacher or teachers who will be involved in assessing the students.
2. The matter of "enabling objectives," which assist students in mastering objectives by breaking an objective down into component skills, will be taken up in our chapter on assessment and evaluation of students.
3. Sometimes it is not necessary to include a procedure and an activity in a lesson plan. This is because when you explain what the students must do (the *activity*) you may inadvertently explain what the teacher must tell his or her students to do. In this case, omit the procedure. Also, some lessons do not involve the teacher in any direct way. In this case, omit the procedure also.
4. Sometimes the learner activities for self-instructional lessons are written on individual index cards which can be laminated so that they can be used and reused extensively.
5. Written by Katherine Terrazas, El Paso, Texas.
6. Written by Robert Louisell in collaboration with Peter Frost of Bath College of Higher Education, Bath, England. Many of these ideas first appeared in *Making Sense of Topic Work and the National Curriculum* by Peter Frost and Ian Gyllenspetz (BCHE). 1991.
7. Amesbury document (Unpublished) by Peter Frost, Allison Jenkins, and Diane Roberts, Bath College of Higher Education, 1968

Glossary

scope The range of topics which are included in a curriculum.

sequence The order in which topics are taught within a curriculum.

objectives Statements about what learners ought to know after completing a school program.

expressive objectives Objectives which cannot be stated clearly because no particular knowledge is expected to result from the educational experiences which are being provided.

self-instructional lessons Lessons which are taught and corrected without the assistance of a teacher.

self-checking A feature of self-instructional lessons (students assess their own work).

modules Long-term instructional plans which are used when the teacher has specific objectives in mind.

thematic units Long-term instructional plans which are used when teachers do not have specific objectives in mind.

topics Thematic units.

Chapter
6

Assessing Student Learning

*I*n previous chapters, we have dealt with instructional settings, instructional techniques and methods, and instructional planning. However, each of these aspects of teaching is integrally related to the teacher's assessment of what his children know and how they have progressed in their learning. The most common term for this type of assessment is **evaluation.** In its most simple terms, evaluation is the collection of information to determine whether students know something.

When we use the term evaluation, most people think of tests. Although testing is one form of evaluation which is used frequently, any information might be used to determine whether students know something. For example, a teacher might observe a student performing a given task such as throwing a ball or writing a sentence. If this task represents an objective which the teacher has set for the student, then the student has demonstrated the ability to perform it. Since the teacher has observed the student performing this skill, he can conclude that the student knows how to do it. Or a teacher may have collected a portfolio containing samples of the child's work in a particular area (e.g., creative writing). This, too, could be used to assess a child's knowledge or progress. Any information which can help a teacher to determine whether or how well a child has learned something may be used for evaluation.

PURPOSES OF ASSESSMENT

Evaluation can take place *before* a student has been taught. When this is done, the purpose of evaluation is to **place** students in appropriate instructional activities. Evaluation can also take place *while* a student is being taught. Usually, we call this *formative evaluation.* Also, evaluation can occur *after* a student has been taught. In most cases, we call this *summative evaluation* (Bloom et al., 1971, p. 87).

To Place Students in Instructional Activities

Evaluation for the purpose of placement can prevent the occurrence of accelerated students becoming bored because they have already mastered the content which is being taught. It can also avoid the opposite problem of students becoming frustrated because they are being expected to master content which they are not yet capable of mastering (Bloom et al., 1971, p. 93). Instead of teaching all students the same content at once (the "lockstep" described in Chapter 2), students can be assessed for their knowledge of particular objectives and placed into instructional activities which match their needs (see Chapter 2, the section on nongraded settings, for this approach to instruction). Or students can be assessed for their general achievement in a particular subject area such as reading or mathematics. They can then be placed in specific groups for instruction in that subject area according to their achievement within it.

To Evaluate a Student's Progress in Learning

Formative evaluation is carried out while the student is involved in an instructional unit. The purpose of formative evaluation is to determine how well a given objective has been mastered and to identify which parts of the objective have not been mastered. It assesses whether a learner has mastered each step in a set of instructional tasks which lead to mastery of the objective. Formative assessments are intended to identify exactly where, in a unit of instruction, a student is experiencing difficulty. Because of this, formative evaluation is **criterion-referenced**. This means that each student is evaluated according to her mastery of a particular set of learning tasks or objectives.

When using formative evaluation, one must select a **unit of learning**. This could correlate with a unit of instruction or a chapter in a textbook or it could cover a specific unit of time (two to four weeks, at the elementary level). For example, an end-of-chapter test might be administered to determine how well the students have learned the content presented in the chapter. Or a test could be designed to assess how well the students have learned the content which has been presented over a specified period of time, say three weeks. A specific objective in the curriculum could also be used as a measure of one unit of learning. In this case, teachers would begin a unit of instruction on this objective and administer a formative assessment whenever they wanted to find out how many students had already attained the objective.

In formative evaluation, all the important elements in a unit are tested. This contrasts with summative evaluation. In summative evaluation, because of the extensive amount of learning material which is being assessed, only a sample of the important elements can be assessed.

In formative evaluation, one must set a satisfactory level of mastery in advance of administering a test. For example, if a teacher believes that 85% mastery on a test would indicate a satisfactory level of knowledge in order to advance to a new unit of learning, then 85% would be used as a criterion to determine which students would receive remediation and which students would move on to a new unit of instruction.

To Identify Special Difficulties in Learning

Diagnosis attempts to probe more deeply to identify the cause of failure when a student repeatedly fails in formative assessments. At this point, diagnosis is pursued for the purpose of developing a specialized plan for remediation.

To Assess Learning After Instruction Has Been Provided

The purpose of **summative evaluation** is usually to make a general assessment of how well the larger outcomes have been obtained over an entire grade or report period. A further purpose of summative evaluation is to grade pupils and to report to parents and school administrators. Depending on the type of instructional setting (i.e., nongraded, graded, etc.), summative evaluation can assess and report mastery of particular outcomes or it can assess how well a student has achieved in a particular subject area over a specified period of time.

REPORTING STUDENT PROGRESS

Instructional settings (discussed in Chapter 2), techniques (Chapter 3), and methods (Chapter 4) can each affect student learning. Because of this, teachers often attempt to "match" techniques, methods, and instructional settings to the needs of their students. In fact, each of the instructional settings described in Chapter 2 uses its own form of reporting student progress to parents and administrators. In this section of the chapter, we will describe reporting practices for each type of setting. In practice, one setting may employ some of the practices attributed to another setting. This is only natural since the settings we have described are only approximations which represent a range of school settings which are possible. Wide variations in reporting practices exist among individual schools and school districts.

Marking and Reporting in **Graded** Settings

Grades provide information about each student's performance. This information is made public and becomes part of the student's school record. Grades are used for administrative purposes (i.e., promoting a student to the next level) and to inform parents and others about student performance. Finally, grades are used to motivate students to learn. Grades, regardless of the endless debate about their worth, are taken very seriously by parents and students.

Teachers have two major roles in the classroom. First, they help students learn through instructional activities; second, they judge the quality of student work and assign grades. At times these two roles conflict, and it is difficult for teachers to assign grades to students, particularly when they know their students well.

There are several systems for assigning grades in traditional elementary settings. The most common system records student performance in the form of letter grades (A, B, C, D, F). Other systems use numbers (1 to 100) or notations (satisfactory-unsatisfactory). A few schools assign letter grades as early as the first grade. We believe that students should not receive letter grades until they are in the intermediate grades. Young children should receive descriptive notations such as "outstanding," "satisfactory," "improving," and "unsatisfactory" instead of letter grades.

Grades are periodically entered (every six or nine weeks) in report cards which communicate student progress and become part of the student permanent school record. Report cards usually describe student performance in academic areas and in conduct. They may also have a space for teacher comments about some aspect of student academic work or conduct (see Fig. 6.1).

Generally, each teacher is given considerable discretion and autonomy in deciding which procedures to use for the purpose of assigning grades.

Norm-Referenced Versus Criterion-Referenced Grading   A teacher may assign grades by comparing the performance of a student with the performance of other students (**norm-referenced grading**) or by comparing the performance of a student to some predefined standard of quality (**criterion-referenced grading**). Grading has traditionally attempted to categorize students in terms of their amount of learning as compared to that of other students. This is an example of norm-referenced grading.

In norm-referenced grading, also called "grading on the curve," the teacher arranges the students in order of their scores, or grading period marks, from highest to lowest. A certain percent of students are assigned As, Bs, Cs, etc. (For example, 7% A, 24% B, 38% C, 24% D, 7% F). The teacher decides what percent will receive each letter grade. Some teachers assign mostly As and Bs, while others give Bs and Cs or even Ds and Fs. Students receive a mark or grade based on their relative position within the class (i.e., their class ranking). This approach does not describe how well a student has done in terms of mastering the material which has been taught. In this system, students who perform better than most of their classmates receive the highest grades. This approach ensures that there is a distribution of grades across the various grading categories. Norm-referenced grading can be very appealing to students who usually score near the top of the class, but it can be devastating for students who score near the bottom of the class. This approach to grading emphasizes competition and discourages cooperation and interdependence among learners.

In criterion-referenced grading, the teacher compares each student's performance to a predefined standard which describes the level of mastery necessary to receive a particular grade. In the case of an elementary math test, the teacher may decide that students who master the material to the highest degree must answer nine out of every 10 problems correctly. Students who reach this level of mastery will receive a grade of A. If all the students reach this level, all of them will get an A. If none of the students reach this level, none of the students will receive a grade of A. Students are not compared to one another. Criterion-referenced testing encourages cooperation and

Name/*Nombre* ______________________

Effort/Character Development Scale
Escala de Esfuerzo y Desarrollo de Caracter

O — **Outstanding**/*Sobresaliente*
S — **Satisfactory**/*Satisfactorio*
I — **Improving**/*Mejorando*
N — **Needs Improvement**/*Necesita Mejorar*
U — **Unsatisfactory**/*No Satisfactorio*

GRADE PERIOD/*PERIODO DE CALIFICACION*

SUBJECT/*MATERIA*	1 Grade/*Grado*	1 Effort/*Esfuerzo*	1 Tutoring Recommended/*Se Recomienda Tutoria*	2 Grade/*Grado*	2 Effort/*Esfuerzo*	2 Tutoring Recommended/*Se Recomienda Tutoria*	3 Grade/*Grado*	3 Effort/*Esfuerzo*	3 Tutoring Recommended/*Se Recomienda Tutoria*	4 Grade/*Grado*	4 Effort/*Esfuerzo*	4 Tutoring Recommended/*Se Recomienda Tutoria*	5 Grade/*Grado*	5 Effort/*Esfuerzo*	5 Tutoring Recommended/*Se Recomienda Tutoria*	6 Grade/*Grado*	6 Effort/*Esfuerzo*	6 Tutoring Recommended/*Se Recomienda Tutoria*	ANNUAL AVERAGE/*PROMEDIO ANUAL*
Reading *Lectura*																			
English, Spelling, Handwriting *Lenguaje, Ortografía, Caligrafía*																			
English Language Development *Desarrollo del Idioma: Inglés*																			
Mathematics *Matemáticas*																			
Social Studies *Estudios Sociales*																			
Science *Ciencias naturales*	**Health** *Clase de higiene*																		
Health *Clase de higiene*																			
Physical Education *Educación Física*																			
Art *Arte*																			
Music *Música*																			
Days Absent *Días Ausente*																			
Request Parent Conference *Se Requiere Conferencia*																			

Teacher Conference Period *Hora de conferencia del maestro*	
School Telephone *Número de teléfono de la escuela*	

R — **Special Education Class**
R — Clase de Educación Especial

CHARACTER DEVELOPMENT
DESARROLLO DE CARACTER

WORK HABITS *HABITOS DE TRABAJO*	1	2	3	4	5	6
Listens to and follows directions *Escucha y sigue instrucciones*						
Completes work *Termina su trabajo*						
Works neatly *Trabaja aseadamente*						
Works independently *Trabaja independientemente*						
Uses time wisely *Usa su tiempo prudentemente*						

CITIZENSHIP *COMPORTAMIENTO*	1	2	3	4	5	6
Courteous and cooperative *Es cortés y cooperador*						
Takes care of property and material *Cuida útiles y materiales*						
Gets along well with others *Se lleva bien con los demás*						
Attitude *Actitud*						
Obeys school rules *Obedece los reglamentos de la escuela*						

Figure 6.1 Report Card From a Graded School (Courtesy of El Paso Independent School District, Used with Permission).

student interdependence in learning. It is the most commonly used grading system in elementary settings (Airasian, 1991).

Criterion-referenced grading may be used to assess academic learning, psychomotor learning (e.g., throwing a ball), or cognitive-psychomotor skills (e.g., making an oral presentation on topic research one has carried out). In the last example, performance prototypes of what constitutes an *A, B, C, D,* and *F* performance for the presentation must be identified beforehand. In the case of paper-pencil tests which are scored objectively, a range of correct responses is assigned to each grade (for example, 90 to 100 correct answers constitute an *A* grade, etc.) A criterion-referenced grading approach indicates how much of the material which has been covered has been learned by the student. A grade of *A* would indicate that the student mastered all or most of the material studied. A grade of *D* would indicate that the student did not master much of the material studied.

What to Grade and How Much It Should Count   Once a teacher has decided whether to use a norm-referenced or criterion-referenced approach to grading, he must next decide exactly which assessments will count towards grades for the grading period in question. The teacher must also decide how much value or weight should be given to each assessment that will be counted. The class work and projects which a teacher uses to determine a final grade for a report period should consider only student performance in the subject and not other factors such as student conduct and attitude. Separate grades can be given for conduct and attitude so that parents can be informed about these matters.

Some teachers will count only performance on objective tests towards a grade. Other teachers will include in-class and out-of-class projects or homework. The decision of what to count depends on the type of subject. Social Studies lends itself to a variety of student assessments (i.e., tests, essays, class and community projects, role-plays, etc.), while spelling will rely mostly on written exercises. When a variety of performance indicators is available, the teacher should make use of this diversity instead of relying on a single type of performance indicator. The greater the variety of types of evidence considered, the less likely it is that the student will be penalized by not being good at a particular type of assessment. For example, a student may do poorly on multiple-choice tests but performs well on essay assignments. Including both types of assessments in the determination of the grade will reduce the chance that the student will receive an unfair grade.

Deciding how much each assessment will be counted in the determination of a grade involves several considerations. Should a test count as much as a project? Should an in-class project count as much as an out-of-class project? Should homework count as much as quizzes? How much should a group report count? Usually, the teacher should assign more weight to assessments which provide more complete information about student learning (a test or project) than to assessments which measure less comprehensive learning objectives (a quiz or homework). When assigning weights to individual assessments, it is advisable to use ratios which are easy to compute (for example, tests and projects can count twice as much as class logs, etc.)

How to Compute Scores and Assign Grades   Once a teacher has assigned different weights to the student performances which are being counted toward a grade, it is important to convert these performances into numerical scores. These numerical scores should add-up to a maximum total of 100 points, or a multiple of 100, so they can be easily converted to a scale of 100. For example, in the area of language arts, a teacher may assign 100 points to each of the following items: two projects, one essay, one research paper, and the class notebook. The teacher may also assign 50 points to each of two spelling tests. The total number of possible points is 600. The scores of each student are added and divided by six in order to come up with scores on a 100 point scale (see Figure 6.2, Language Arts Scores).

If the grades are assigned using a norm-referenced approach, the teacher arranges the students in the order of the scores from highest to lowest and assigns grades according to a predetermined formula (e.g., x% of As, x% of Bs, etc.). If the grades are assigned using a criterion-referenced approach, the teacher checks the scores of each student against a predetermined table of grades (e.g., students with 90 to 100 points receive A, those with 80 to 89 points receive B, etc.)

When assigning *norm-referenced* grades, teachers make a series of decisions which can be summarized in the following steps (Airasian, 1991):

1. Decide the "grading curve" (What percentage of students will receive As, Bs, etc.)
2. Assign numerical values to the work of each student.
3. Arrange the total scores of the students in numerical order from highest to lowest.
4. Assign grades to students according to the order in which they appear in the class grade distribution and decide whether small adjustments should be made based on other considerations such as proximity to the next grade boundary.

When assigning *criterion-referenced* grades, teachers make a series of decisions which can be summarized in the following steps (Airasian, 1991):

1. Decide what work will count toward the grade and how much weight it should have.
2. Decide what performance standards to apply (What is an *A* performance, a *B* performance, etc.)
3. Assign numerical values to the work of each student according to the predetermined performance standards.
4. Convert the numerical values obtained by students into grades and decide if small adjustments are to be made based on other considerations such as proximity to the next grade.

One further note about marks in graded settings is in order. Although we have described norm-referenced and criterion-referenced approaches to reporting, **it is our firm belief that criterion-referenced evaluation is the only appropriate approach to reporting in elementary school settings**. We especially apply this belief to reporting in the primary grades. Children in the **primary grades** (grades 1–3) should not be compared to each other in progress reports. Even in the **intermediate grades** (grades 4–6), earlier marks should *not* be averaged. Rather, formative eval-

SAMPLE OF TEACHER GRADE BOOK

Grade: **5–A**
Subject: **LANGUAGE ARTS**
Grading Period: **#1**

	Note book	Proj 1	Essay	Spell Test*	Proj 2	Paper	Spell Test*	Total Score	Average	Letter Grade
Acosta	100	92	90	50	85	100	50	567	95	A
Anderson	100	60	65	38	96	100	45	504	84	B
Cox	100	100	80	48	100	100	45	573	96	A
Elliot	85	100	88	50	100	100	48	571	96	A
Gorbet	100	100	98	48	100	100	45	591	99	A
Kyle	100	100	90	46	60	100	43	539	90	A
Lyons	100	100	94	50	100	100	48	592	99	A
Montes	100	100	92	50	80	100	45	567	95	A
Paschal	100	60	85	48	90	100	48	531	89	B
Powell	100	100	65	38	40	55	38	436	73	C
Reyes	100	100	98	50	100	100	50	598	100	A
Shaw	100	100	75	50	55	100	40	520	87	B
Thurman	100	100	98	50	100	75	48	571	96	A
White	75	100	85	50	90	100	45	545	91	A
Yates	90	100	88	44	100	100	38	560	94	A

*Spelling tests count 50 points each. All other items count 100 points for a possible total of 600. The average is obtained by dividing the total score by 6.

Figure 6.2 Language Arts Scores

uation should be used to identify areas of student success and need. Reteaching should then be done to give students every opportunity to achieve mastery of the required objectives (Bloom et al., 1971, p. 133).

Discussing Grades with Parents   Report cards do not communicate much to parents about the academic and personal growth of their children. A face to face meeting between teacher and parent(s) should take place each time that report cards are given. A teacher-parent conference helps explain the grades in the report card and answer parent questions. There are certain preparations a teacher must make before the conference take place. First, the teacher must clarify what is the major objective of the meeting (what does the teacher want the parent(s) to do as a result of the visit). The teacher must also gather samples of student work and assessments which will document the child's progress (or lack of it) and share this information with the parent(s). Finally, the teacher must come up with a specific plan of action for the parent(s).

The conference should follow a simple format in which the teacher: 1) welcomes the parent(s) and says something nice about the child, 2) summarizes the academic and personal progress of the child as indicated in the report card, 3) answers questions and accepts the feelings of parent(s), 4) shares information to underscore the need for action (either improvement or celebration), 5) invites parent(s) to team up with the teacher and support continued growth of the student, 6) proposes a joint plan of action, 7) makes arrangements for further follow-up through visits or phone conversations, and 8) thanks the parent(s) for supporting the child and the school.

Having parents come to conferences about the progress of their children is not always easy. Some schools take an assertive position stating that all parents must volunteer for some school-related activity. A list of possible activities is mailed to the parents with the request that they check the type of volunteer work in which they will participate. These schools report increased involvement on the part of parents. When all parents participate in at least one school activity, it is easier for teachers to schedule conferences to discuss the progress of their children.

Reporting Student Progress in **Nongraded** Settings

We have already described, in Chapter 2, how children are grouped according to their instructional needs in nongraded settings. In nongraded settings, then, it would be ridiculous to compare students to each other by a ranking system. Ranking children in comparison to each other contradicts the basic philosophy of nongraded education. It also communicates misleading information. When children are compared to each other, parents may jump to incorrect conclusions about their children's abilities.

For example, children in a particular third grade class may all be reading at the 75th percentile or better according to national norms. In such a class, if traditional, norm-referenced, grading procedures are used, one of these children might receive an "A" in reading while another student might receive an "F." In another class, where most children read at the 50th percentile or less, the same child who received an "F" in the last example would receive an "A." A child's rank in a class of college-bound children may only be average, yet she could still rank in the 90th percentile nationally.

Obviously, parents are not assisted in evaluating their children's capabilities by misleading information such as marks or grades which are based on comparisons to other children. Rather, the best way to report student progress in a nongraded setting is to describe the child's progress in terms of objectives attained, objectives which the child is currently working on, general social skills and habits, special problems and concerns, etc.

Reporting objectives attained is a form of criterion-referenced evaluation. Sometimes it is referred to as **objectives-referenced** evaluation. This approach to reporting can consider a child's history as it has developed in her classroom or over the period of years that she has been in school. It takes the child out of an unrealistic, competitive environment and places the child in comparison with something attainable—that is, her own intellectual baseline. Such reports are more honest because they communicate to the parents what is actually happening at school. Box 6.1 is a sample of a report card from such a school.

Note that the report on mathematics is a narrative summary of outcomes or objectives which the student has either achieved or is presently working on. Some nongraded reports prefer to include these outcomes in a checklist format within the report itself. Although this does not contradict nongraded practices, we dislike this approach. Parent are not all well-versed in the different degrees of difficulty which outcomes can represent. Consequently, the effects of such reports can be quite different than that intended. Although teachers intend that parents will be well informed about what is being learned at school, parents may reduce such checklists to a counting of outcomes achieved. Some parents may even award a specific amount of money for each outcome achieved in the same way that parents in graded settings have awarded money for each A or B. In contrast, a narrative keeps parents informed without lending itself to easy misinterpretation.

However, we do believe that such checklists of outcomes should be shared with parents during **parent conferences**. They should be kept in a **portfolio** which includes any relevant information about the child's learning for that report period. Portfolios contain samples of the child's **best work** in each of the subject or skill areas being taught. They should be maintained for each area of the curriculum and should be shared with parents at conferences. Portfolios can often include more information about a child's learning than either a traditional, graded report card or a nongraded, narrative report. We recommend combining a nongraded, narrative report with a student portfolio, however.

What does a portfolio include? Usually, a portfolio includes the following: 1) Samples of the student's work which have been selected by the teacher or the student, 2) Observational notes which have been made by the teacher, 3) Periodic self-evaluations (especially when the students are older children), and 4) Progress notes which have been contributed by the student and teacher (Valencia, 1990).

Examples of items contained in a portfolio include: pieces of children's written compositions in various stages of completion; samples of a student's handwriting; checklists of outcomes for the area of the curriculum in question; unit projects; student responses to reading assignments; samples of the child's art work. Photographs or video-tapes of children's productions can even be included! Anything which communicates student progress is acceptable. However, it is important that portfolios be fairly selective. Otherwise, there is a danger that they will become a "junk box" which no one examines and which communicates nothing. When teacher and student exercise care in selecting examples which represent a child's progress in a given academic area, however, portfolios can tell a very complete, and succinct, story.

This approach to reporting student progress matches the philosophy of nongraded education. In the traditional approach to graded instruction, students are all given the same instruction for a given period of time. Under this approach, if the students vary in

Box 6-1 **Example of a Report from a Nongraded School**

Communicative Arts (Reading, Writing, Spelling, Listening, Speaking, Handwriting, Word Attack, and Comprehension)

Mary Jane is now a strong reader. She is acquiring mastery of word attack skills (needed to decode unknown words) and reads with excellent comprehension and expression. Her vocabulary is well-developed. Mary Jane also shows an interest in reading, and frequently chooses stories or non-fictional books which are obviously of special interest to her. She exercises careful choice of books to be read, and this is unusual in a child her age.

Her story-writing is always interesting. Her spelling is good for her level of development. Her comprehension activities ("work cards") are thorough and demonstrate perception about stories and characters. She is presently working on the comprehension skill of choosing the topic sentence of a paragraph. Her written work ranges from very neat to messy. She is an excellent learner, completes assignments, and is well behaved.

—Mr. Johnson

Mathematics

Mary Jane has made very good progress in math this year. She has mastered place-value for tens and ones. She can add and subtract regrouping for two-digit numbers. She understands places to thousands. She has had experiences with measurement in linear, square, and cubic relations (length, area, volume) using the metric system. She also has had some activity assignments using the standard American units (pints, quarts, etc.). A good math student who thinks and applies her knowledge.   —Mr. Johnson

Social Studies and Science

The major emphasis in the social studies area has been the study of families and their needs. Similarities and differences in homes and family structures were explored. This led to the study of home construction, map reading and description of position.

A variety of science units have been offered: your child has been allowed to choose those of interest to her.

Physical Education, Music, Art

Experiences provided in these area have included:

Music—recognition of rhythm, and tonal patterns, listening and singing.

Phy. Ed.—large muscle coordination (running, dodging, throwing and catching).

Art—discovery of painting and sculpture through the use of a variety of art materials.

GENERAL COMMENTS

Mary Jane continues to experience success in all activities of the school day. She is polite and courteous with all whom she works with and is respected by her peers.

She is sensitive yet has little difficulty adapting to new situations. She does her best at all times. She receives suggestions with a good attitude.

Mary Jane has made fine progress this year.   —Ms. Kramer aptitudes as children typically do, some students will learn well (and receive good report marks) while others will learn poorly (and receive poor report marks). However, if you expect that each student can, eventually, master the objectives (as nongraded schools expect), all students **will** master the objectives if they are given enough time to do so (Bloom et al., 1971, pp. 44–46). To accomplish this, the teacher must vary the instruction according to the aptitudes and needs of students and his evaluation must reflect this philosophy.

What is the best way to report in nongraded settings? First, review your objectives for each student for the report period in question. Ask yourself, "Which objectives has this student achieved? Which objectives is she still working on?" Report the child's progress in these terms. For example, in mathematics, if the child has mastered beginning addition and subtraction, say so in a clear and simple sentence; for example, "Marie has learned to add and subtract with results of 10 or less." If the child is beginning her study of place-value, say so; for example, "She is now learning about the place values of tens and ones." Then add any useful comments about your student's work habits, etc.; for example, "Marie is a pleasure to work with because of her positive attitude. She is always interested in learning new material." Or "Jane has told me several times that math is not her favorite thing to do."

Some people believe that nongraded schooling, because it does not award marks or "grades" for student progress (e.g., A, B, C, D, F) communicates lower expectations to students than graded settings do. In other words, they believe that since there are no comparative marks awarded, students have no incentive to work or learn. Nothing could be further from the truth! Teachers in nongraded settings communicate high expectations for their students, **but they do so according to the students' capabilities to learn**. Because students are taught at levels at which they are capable of succeeding, students are highly motivated and demonstrate positive attitudes towards learning.

Progress report in nongraded settings communicate positive information about the child's achievements. This follows through with the philosophy of instruction which is evident in nongraded settings. Parents who receive descriptions of their children's progress are likely to show approval to their children. Nongraded progress reports do not report only positive information about students, however. All important information is communicated in these reports. If a student is experiencing behavior problems, academic problems, or social difficulties, that student's teacher will briefly describe the nature of the problem in the appropriate section of the report allowing for narrative comments about these matters. This information is extremely important for parents and future teachers.

Reporting Student Progress in **Informal** Settings[1]

British teachers are not as concerned as American teachers are with keeping track of and reporting the progress of each child in every subject area. Perhaps the integrated approach of topic work prohibits teachers from focusing on the progress of each child for particular skills. Or maybe the creative approach of topic work makes it more difficult for teachers to concern themselves with the systematic collection of information about each child. Teachers in informal settings resist precise measurement of learning because they are philosophically opposed to dividing knowledge into separate compartments or objectives. Also, the mixed-age grouping arrangement, in which teachers often work with children over a period of two to three years, may enable teachers to get to know their students more closely than in typical American settings and may thus make the systematic collection and documentation of student progress less important.

In many British schools, **general reports** about activities and studies completed during the course of a topic unit are common. In this type of report, teachers enter comments about *class* progress, subtopics covered, and activities on which the class spent extended time or effort in their records of specific topic units.

One could also look at displays of student work in and around the classroom as a form of reporting on class and individual learning. As we have mentioned in Chapters 2 and 4, teachers in informal schools devote a great deal of effort to displaying the work of their students (e.g., on the walls, through bookmaking, etc.), and parents and other visitors are able to get good insight into what is happening in the classrooms via these displays.

But **individual progress** is also documented in several ways in these settings. The chief means of documenting and reporting student work is through profiles and portfolios. A **profile** is a cumulative record of student accomplishments over several years. Input from the child's teachers, parents, and the child herself is used to include everything from samples of the student's handwriting and compositions to photographs of students participating in creative dramas or school productions. **Portfolios** are similar to profiles, except they cover a smaller span of time (one report period) and can therefore include more examples. Samples of the child's work, photographs, anecdotal records about what the child learned or did, etc., can be included in portfolios. A fairly detailed picture of the child's learning can be reported via a portfolio. (See the comments on portfolios included in the previous section on reporting in nongraded settings).

Whatever the reason for the different attitude towards evaluation of students which is demonstrated in British settings, American teachers in *any* setting (including an informal setting) must communicate specific information about student progress in the basic skills; in particular, they must communicate information about student progress in the areas of reading and mathematics. Some teachers in informal settings keep a cumulative record, for each student, of math skills which have been mastered (similar to the management "keysort" cards described in the section on nongraded education in Chapter 2).

To report student progress in reading, teachers in informal settings sometimes keep checklists on which they "tick off" those skills or attitudes which they have observed. Teachers may also keep a notebook of personal observations about a student's strengths, problems, and interests in reading. In such a notebook, a teacher may also keep a record of specific books which have been read by each student. Sometimes this information (i.e., a list of books which have been read by a particular student) is recorded by the student herself and is included in the student's portfolios. Student response journals, which include students' written responses to particular books, are also included in such portfolios. Because teachers in informal settings espouse a philosophy which encourages students to take responsibility for their own learning, students are involved in the preparation of their evaluative reports.[2]

Teachers in informal settings also rely heavily on parent visits and "open house" events to communicate to parents about what is happening in school. In the past, parents came to observe children working in school for an afternoon during the fall. Then parents came to school for a formal conference in the evening at which teachers shared student portfolios and discussed each child's work with her parents. Some informal schools also employ narrative reports. However, one head teacher in a British Primary School told me that her school eliminated narrative reports two years ago when they moved to an "open access" policy of allowing parents to visit the classrooms at any time during the school day. This same head teacher had organized an evening during which parents and children participated in learning activities together at school. She is changing her school reporting procedure to one in which parents visit the classroom in groups of five for one-half day and then return for half hour parent conferences a few weeks later. This procedure will be repeated four times per year.[3]

Reporting Student Progress at **Alternative Heights**

Reporting at Alternative Heights consists of a combination of narrative reports and portfolios in each area. The narrative reports have sections for **student** *and* **teacher** comments. For the learning activities period (morning) during which reading-language arts and maths skills are taught, an evaluation of student progress is completed and a portfolio of student work is assembled by the student. (See Figure 6.3 for an example of an evaluation for this period.) Narrative reports and portfolios are also developed for each class that a child takes during the afternoon classes which she has selected. (See Figure 6.4 for an example of an evaluation for one of these classes.)

Parents attend conferences four times yearly at Alternative Heights. The first conference occurs at the beginning of the year. At this conference, the teacher, parents, and child discuss concerns and goals for the year. The child and her parents also select classes for the academic quarter to follow. During the following conferences, the teacher, parents, and child discuss academic and social progress as they peruse the child's portfolios and evaluations. They also select classes for the following academic quarter. Conferences are a relaxed but professional event in which parents and child honestly discuss the child's likes and dislikes, strengths and areas of difficulty, with the teacher. Many parents leave these conferences with a feeling of pride in the work which their child has completed and a sense of satisfaction that they have selected Alternative Heights as a school for their child. Few parents could leave a conference about a traditional, graded, report with as much insight into what their child is actually learning in school.

TESTING

Standardized achievement tests, standardized diagnostic tests, and teacher-made tests can each be used to identify learning problems of students or to assess student performance.

Standardized achievement tests can indicate the existence of a problem. **Standardized diagnostic tests** give detailed information about a student's knowledge in a variety of subskills. When a student does poorly on a diagnostic test, responses in

(Wendell Carroll, St. Paul Open School)

Evaluation of morning work in room 206 with Wendell, fall quarter, 1989

Name ——————————————————— Advisor ———————————————————

The schedule for our mornings except Thursdays is:

      8:40– 9:25   reading and writing,
      9:25–10:10   PE instruction alternates with math work,
    10:10–11:10   individual projects or continued work on goals,
    11:10–11:15   clean-up and listen to a bit of *Where the Red Fern Grows*.

On Thursdays, about half of the students have used most of the morning on an airplane designing and building project with a parent, Aaron Petersen. The other half has continued work on individual goals.

This group has, in general, been very cooperative, helpful to each other, focused on appropriate work, and eager to learn. All have been encouraged to bring some of their work home often so that parents can see the fine work that's being done.

I have read the following during open classroom during the past two months: ——————————

——

——

——

The best of what I have read was ——————————————————————————————————

It was good because ———————————————————————————————————————

——

——

In Math I have worked on the following: (Circle those you've worked on, then under each give an example of your work.)

        ADDITION   **SUBTRACTION**   **MULTIPLICATION**

   DIVISION   **GEOMETRY**   **FRACTIONS**   **DECIMALS**   **GRAPHING**

I've been using the ——————— math text. I've completed the work and understand what I'm
                   color

doing through chapter ———— , page ———— .

Figure 6.3 Evaluation for Learning Activities Period in an Alternative Heights Setting. (Courtesy of Wendell Carroll, Teacher, St. Paul Open School, Used with Permission).

HEROINES & HEROES
with Don and Melissa

Fall Quarter
1990 - 1991

A multi-disciplinary approach to the subject
of Heroes and Heroines.
Dealt with mythological, comic book,
historical and contemporary heroism.
We read together, shared in group discussions,
did research and wrote reports. Students had time
most days for some work on individual or small
group projects.
Projects included reading, writing, drawing,
D & D, and mural-sized reproductions with an
opaque projector. As a group we made clay figures
and painted them.

STUDENTS RESPONSE

Who is your all-time favorite hero and why? _____

Example of "everyday life" heroism _____

My clay figure _____
My projects _____

My best experiences _____

For me the class _____
Don & Melissa's Comments

Figure 6.4 An Evaluation for an Afternoon Class at St. Paul Open School. (Courtesy of Don Paden, Teacher, St. Paul Open School, Used with Permission).

any subskill can be analyzed. Unfortunately, diagnostic tests are not available for each area of the curriculum. At the elementary level, diagnostic tests are published in the areas of reading and mathematics. Simple **teacher-made tests** can be designed to diagnose particular learning problems in students. Students with similar problems can then be grouped for instruction. Reporting to parents and future teachers can then refer to mastery of particular objectives (Bloom et al., 1971, p. 101).

Teacher-Made Tests

There are three major purposes for testing in the classroom: 1) to acquire information about the effectiveness of instruction, 2) to give feedback to students about their progress, and 3) to assign grades. It is our opinion that teacher-made tests should be used in the primary grades only for the purposes of formative evaluation and placement. In other words, testing in the primary grades should be used in order to place students in appropriate instructional activities for their needs or to assess whether students have mastered particular objectives on which they have been working. Testing for the purposes of assigning grades should not take place until intermediate grades. Also, in primary and intermediate grades alike, teachers frequently administer tests to large groups or the entire class. When errors on a test occur for a majority of the students in a class, the teacher should investigate these errors and reteach the entire class (Bloom et al., 1971, p. 136).

Standardized tests and commercially published tests do not help teachers to obtain information about the effectiveness of their teaching, nor do they help teachers to verify student mastery of specific skills and content. Since commercially prepared tests are not able to address the peculiarities of specific learners and classrooms, teachers have to develop their own instruments or procedures to assess what has been learned by their students.

What factors should determine the assessment measures or tests which teachers develop? There are three major factors to consider when preparing teacher-made tests:

1. The level of learning objectives, according to Bloom's taxonomy, which will be evaluated (knowledge comprehension, application, analysis, synthesis, and evaluation (see Chapter 3 for further information on this topic). Some types of objectives are easily measured by paper-pencil tests, while other objectives are not.
2. The age and developmental status of the learner. Four year olds may be able to match similar kinds of objects (or pictures of objects), but they will not be able to write an essay about an object.
3. The state of the art in testing and the test-making skills of the teacher designing the test.

What should teacher-made tests measure? Teacher-made tests should measure the objectives covered in a series of lessons or a unit. A teacher-made test should assess only those objectives which it purports to test. No other objectives should be assessed.[4] Whatever the student is required to do on a test should match the level of knowledge of the objective(s) being tested. If the objective emphasizes the recollection of facts, the test should be designed to measure memorization. If the objectives are aimed at the use of skills, the test should verify skill mastery.

The first step in the preparation of a test is to study the list of objectives covered and to attempt to classify these objectives according to Bloom's taxonomy. In Chapter 3, we recommended that teachers address various levels of Bloom's taxonomy when covering content and working on skills. As you compile the list of objectives covered in a unit, you will probably find that they address several levels of Blooms's taxonomy. You then must design a test which measures the acquisition of these different types of objectives. The test should not assess objectives at the knowledge level only if the learners have been expected to master application, analysis, and synthesis objectives. *The test must measure the types of objectives covered in the unit or lesson.* An experienced school administrator is able to tell what type of learning is taking place in a classroom by examining the tests or measuring instruments designed by the teachers (unless the teacher is a good instructor who prepares bad tests). Tests which do not assess the objectives covered in the lesson or unit are poor tests, regardless of how good the items may seem.

What types of tests should teachers prepare? When teacher-made tests are discussed, there is a tendency to think that the only types of tests prepared by teachers are paper-pencil tests. Multiple choice, true-false, short-answer, and essay tests are paper-pencil tests.

Paper-pencil tests are usually good for measuring declarative knowledge (content) and some procedural knowledge (skills). They are good vehicles for verifying acquisition of content at different levels of Bloom's taxonomy. But paper-pencil tests are not very good for assessing the mastery of certain skills which involve cognitive and psychomotor activities such as making graphs, reciting a poem, conducting a science experiment, singing a song, and putting a puzzle together. Mastery of some cognitive-psychomotor skills cannot be ascertained by paper-pencil tests. In those situations, teachers must find other ways to measure performance. Another limitation of paper-pencil tests is that they assume that learners are able to read and write. Obviously, multiple-choice tests are not appropriate for five year old students. Teachers of young children must be able to develop assessment measures which are appropriate for their students.

Throughout this book, we have endorsed a cooperative, rather than a competitive, approach to teaching and learning. Again, we recommend that teacher-made tests and grading for elementary students be criterion-referenced (i.e., evaluating the student's mastery of the objectives) rather than norm-referenced (i.e., comparing the performances of students to each other). There seems to be little justification in the elementary school for ranking and comparing students frequently. Students develop at different rates during their childhood. When comparisons among students are made, it is assumed that the participants are at the same level of cognitive, emotional, and psychomotor development. However, this is simply not the case. In Chapter 10, we will explain how competitive grading negatively impacts motivation among many students. It is generally agreed that children during their elementary schooling are expected to develop skills and knowledge which will be the basis for further study in secondary school and college. What is important is that elementary school students master the desired learning objectives by the time they make the transition to the middle school. This achievement should be assessed mostly through the use of criterion-referenced measures. An emphasis on comparing students who are developing at different rates makes as little sense as basing claims of superiority on the fact that a child has learned to walk sooner than another child.

A significant amount of time in the elementary school is spent on the teaching and learning of basic skills. This type of learning, procedural knowledge, addresses the "how to" of a discipline. Many of the skills taught in elementary schools are of a cognitive nature. Reading comprehension skills, computation skills, and grammar skills are examples of cognitive skills. Other skills are of an affective nature. How to resolve conflicts and get along with others are primarily affective skills. Finally, there are psychomotor skills. Psychomotor skills require significant motor performance (and at times they also require significant cognitive performance). Playing a musical instrument, singing a song, drawing, dancing, putting a puzzle together, working with science equipment, reading a poem, presenting a speech, coloring, and doing handwriting exercises are examples of psychomotor skills. Time is also spent in the elementary school on learning subject matter, the "what" of a discipline. This type of learning is called declarative knowledge. In the following sections, we will discuss how teachers can evaluate psychomotor and oral skills.

How to Evaluate Psychomotor and Oral Skills   There are two major approaches a teacher may use to evaluate the acquisition of psychomotor and oral skills in the classroom: 1) Observation of student performance, and 2) Evaluation of student projects. These approaches may also be used to evaluate the academic progress of young students who are not able to read and write.

Teacher **observation of student performance** is an assessment approach in which the student performs the desired skill in the presence of the teacher. The student, for example, lines up three cards with drawings of a seed, a young plant and a full grown tree in the correct chronological sequence. The teacher observes the student performance, gives feedback to the student and keeps a written record of the child's performance, if appropriate.

Teachers may conduct observations in a holistic or in an atomistic manner. A holistic observation approach is utilized when the teacher gives a score or feedback based on preestablished prototypes of how an outstanding, average or deficient performance looks. Before the observation takes place, the teacher carefully describes the different levels of performance. If these prototypes are well described, the students are able to conduct an assessment by themselves.

For example, when eleven year old students are asked to make an oral report on research which they have carried out on a particular topic, the teacher describes the factors which go into an ideal presentation. The student's knowledge of her topic, organization of her presentation, enunciation, voice projection, and enthusiasm are all factors which could be considered in this case. The teacher would describe the ideal presentation, making sure to comment on each of these factors. A student whose presentation closely matched the ideal presentation described by the teacher would receive a perfect mark. A student whose presentation was slightly less than ideal would be assigned a "very good" mark. A student who displayed weaknesses in some of the factors while showing strength in others would receive a mark of "fair." A student whose presentation did not meet minimum standards would receive a "needs improvement" mark.

The other method of teacher observation is the atomistic, or analytic observation, approach. Analytic teacher observations require that a task analysis be conducted in order to identify the major subtasks involved in the student performance. In the case of five year old students throwing a beachball, for example, the teacher identifies the movements required to perform the task of throwing a ball. Next, the teacher develops a checklist which lists each of the movements which are essential to the performance of this task, that is, the initial position of the feet, arms and upper-body, next, how the feet, upper-body and hands push the ball, and, finally, the position of the feet when the throw is completed. These positions are demonstrated to the students. As students perform the action of throwing, the teacher assigns checkmarks for each of the various subtasks. After the child has performed the action of throwing, all checkmarks are considered and an assessment of the performance is made.

In the example of older students making an oral presentation on their research, subscores would be assigned for each subtask and these subscores would then be totalled to determine a total grade for the presentation if the teacher was using an atomistic approach. Another manner of assessing student mastery of a skill is through the **evaluation of student products** which demonstrate to the teacher that the student has acquired the skill. In the case of handwriting skills, for example, samples of student handwriting make it possible for the teacher to assess mastery. Science, social studies, or language arts projects may also be used to assess student progress.

Student products may not require skill in reading and writing. They may turn in products at the iconic or representational learning mode such as drawings, models, construction paper products, puppets, silly putty products, etc.

The same principles involved in holistic and atomistic observations apply to the evaluation of projects. The teacher may identify prototypes which represent different levels of performance for a project or do a task analysis and assign scores by subtasks. In either case, it is very important to communicate to students the criteria and procedures

Figure 6.5 Reprinted with permission: Tribune Media Services.

utilized in the assessment of their work. In many nontraditional and traditional classrooms, students keep a portfolio with samples of their work. The teachers utilize these samples to make instructional decisions and to report progress.

How to Evaluate Progress Using Paper-Pencil Instruments   Many student learnings may be assessed through paper-pencil instruments or tests. Objectives which cover comprehension or critical-creative thinking are examples of student learning which can be evaluated through paper-pencil tests. Paper-pencil tests are called **objective tests** when the answers of students can be compared and quantified to yield a numerical score. Paper-pencil tests which are not easily quantified are called **subjective tests**.

There are several types of paper-pencil testing instruments. The most commonly used are: matching (pictures, words, numbers, concepts); short-answer; essay; multiple-choice; and research papers. In the following sections, we will describe how to use these different forms of paper-pencil measures.

Matching Items   In matching exercises, students are asked to connect two or more items according to a particular criterion. For example, given a list of words, students match those which are nouns, those which are adjectives etc. By matching, students demonstrate that they have mastered some concepts, such as the concept *noun,* or the concept *adjective.* The principle behind matching exercises remains the same, to connect items which have something in common in order to demonstrate that the concept has been understood.

Matching items may vary in their degree of abstraction. There are matching exercises done with pictures. In this case, students are given drawings or pictures of objects which are to be connected according to a preestablished criterion. For example, students may be asked to sort pictures of fruits, vegetables, dairy products and meats into four piles. These types of matching exercises are excellent means of assessing understanding and mastery among young children. They measure the comprehension, application and analysis levels of Bloom's taxonomy.

There are also matching exercises which are done with words and numbers. These tasks require a more abstract level of performance on the part of the students. Matching words and numbers evaluates the acquisition of knowledge, comprehension, application, and analysis objectives. Finally, there are more complex matching exercises which go beyond connecting symbols into connecting concepts expressed through paragraphs and mathematical formulae.

When matching items are included in paper-pencil tests, they are presented in two columns which list the sentences, words, numbers or drawings. The object of the question is to successfully match the items in one column with the items in the second column according to a given criterion. The instructions should clearly state on what basis the association or matching is to be done. The length and complexity of the items presented in the columns will depend on the stage of development of the student. The number of items in the right column should be greater than the items in the left column in order to avoid giving clues about correct answers by enabling students to eliminate other possible answers. An example of a simple matching items test is included in Box 6.2, to the right.

Box 6.2 **Example of Matching Items Test**

Look at each type of food in the left column and find one *example* of it in the right column. There is only one correct example of each type of food. Enter the number of the correct examples in the blanks provided on the left column.

_____ Fruit   1. Soup

_____ Vegetable   2. Turkey

_____ Dairy product   3. Pizza

_____ Meat   4. Banana

                             5. Dessert

                             6. Corn

                             7. Egg

Short-Answer Items   As children develop basic reading and writing skills, they are able to give brief written explanations to questions presented in a paper-pencil test. Short-answer items are of two kinds: convergent and divergent. In a convergent question, all students are expected to answer in the same manner by recalling, describing, or applying material previously covered in class. Examples of short-answer convergent items are:

What kind of animal scared Little Red Riding Hood? (A Knowledge level question)

Why did the wolf disguise himself as the grandmother? (Comprehension)

Are there any adjectives in the name Little Red Riding Hood? (Application)

The other kind of short-answer item is the divergent, or open-ended, question. In an open-ended question, students are expected to answer in different ways according to their perceptions and values. The students analyze, synthesize, and evaluate the material initially covered in class. Examples of short-answer divergent items are:

Why do you think that Little Red Riding Hood entered her grandmother's house? (Analysis)

How would you change the Little Red Riding Hood story if you were the author? (Synthesis)

Should this story be read to young children? Why? (Evaluation)

Short-answer convergent questions verify lower level thinking and allow the teacher to give marks in an objective manner since all students are expected to give the same answer. Short-answer divergent questions foster higher level thinking and become the building blocks for future essay questions. The scoring of these questions is less quantifiable, since at times there are no wrong answers to the questions.

Essay Questions   Essay items are questions which require a more elaborate discussion of a topic, usually at the comprehension, analysis, and evaluation levels of Bloom's taxonomy. Essay items, like short-essay items, may be convergent or divergent. In a convergent item, the response is restricted to what the teacher expects the learner to discuss. In a divergent or open-ended item, learners are free to express their own ideas and view, exploring interpretations when the responses are compared with a pre-determined correct response.

A question which asks the students to describe the character of the protagonist in a book discussed in class may be scored objectively since a predetermined response for the question exists in the minds of the teacher and students who paid attention to the class discussions. Essay questions of a divergent kind, such as when students are asked to discuss what difference would it have made in the plot and dialogue of a story if the protagonist would have been a young woman instead of a man, may not be scored objectively. Divergent essays are scored in a less objective manner since there is no predetermined prototype to compare the answer with and since the students will write essays which will be very different from one another.

Essay questions address higher order thinking levels. They may ask students to compare, summarize, analyze, create, and judge information. Essay questions are excellent for assessing ability in self-expression and original thinking. They also help verify the degree of understanding a student has about a topic and probe deeper than other measures such as multiple-choice items. One weakness of essay tests is that they do not cover a representative sample of all the material studied. As a result, significant learning areas may be missed by the test. To avoid this potential weakness, a teacher may ask several shorter essays instead of one long essay.

The wording of an essay question should be precise, pointing out specific processes to be carried out. Words like compare, contrast, refute, and judge should be used. Students should be allowed plenty of time to complete their essays since the teacher wants to find out if the student can answer the essays. If a test is going to affect grades, all students should be given the same questions without providing students with the opportunity to choose among several questions. Having all students respond to identical questions facilitates comparison.

Multiple-Choice Questions   Multiple-choice items have two parts, the stem and the choices. The stem presents the question to be answered. The choices are the possible answers. The student's task is to select the correct answer from the possible answers listed. The number of possible answers offered is usually five. But when using multiple-choice items with younger students, the choices may be as few as three. Multiple Choice items may be written to cover material at the knowledge, compre-hension, application, and analysis levels of Bloom's taxonomy. These items can be answered quickly and may be electronically scored. A large number of multiple-choice items may be answered during a class period. By presenting a large number of items, the test is able to cover a broad amount of material and students are tested on the most important areas studied.

When writing multiple-choice items, it is recommended that the stem be pre-sented in the form of a complete question, such as "What is the area of a rectangle 6 ft. long and 3 ft. wide?" The stem should be brief and unnecessary wording should be avoided. On the other hand, all necessary information must be included in the stem. Usually the stems are numbered 1, 2, 3, etc. and the choices are labeled with letters (a, b, c, d, e).

Choices are made up of a correct response and distractors. As much as possible, all choices should seem plausible, at least to students who haven't mastered the content. In the application item presented above, all choices to the question about the area of a rectangle should be numbers expressed in square feet. It would be undesirable to include other units of measure such as watts, ohms or decibels. The correct answer must be clearly a better answer to the stem than the distractors. If two choices can be defended as correct, the item should be modified or discarded.

Multiple-choice items which test knowledge and comprehension are usually easier to write than items which test application and analysis. When writing a multiple-choice test, teachers should study the list of objectives covered in the unit and decide which objectives need to be assessed by knowledge and comprehension items and which ones need to be assessed by application and analysis items. A small number of multiple-choice items would diminish the validity of the test. Thirty items or more are desirable in order to insure that the test measures a representative sample of the material learned. Examples of multiple choice items are included in Box 6.3.

Research Papers   Research papers are another way to assess student progress and mastery of the material covered in a discipline. They assume more maturity on the part of the student and do not lend themselves to precise comparisons since each student or group of students may choose a different topic or treat the same topic in a different manner. Research papers are more complex products than essay questions. They are prepared over several days in which the students have access to library and community resources. These projects are ideal for fostering higher level thinking. The aim of a research paper could be to analyze, summarize, judge or create. These projects may be carried out individually or by teams of students using cooperative learning approaches. Although not easily translated into comparative measures, these projects are excellent indicators of student learning and progress. A portfolio of individual projects throughout intermediate and middle school grades could be an excellent tool to demonstrate student capabilities and achievements, particularly in the case of students who are not good at taking standardized achievement tests.

When to Use Which Assessment Items   You have been exposed to a variety of means of evaluating progress in the elementary school. The next question is "When do I use each of these approaches?" As we indicated at the beginning of the section, the stage of intellectual development of the learners, the levels of the objectives to be assessed, and your personal skill in preparing evaluation items will influence your decision on how to assess. The following charts, Tables 6.1 and 6.2, indicate our own opinions about what assessment approaches are reasonable according to intellectual development and grade levels.

Standardized Tests

Standardized tests are used so that educators can compare the performance of a student or group of students to the performance of a group which has already taken the

Box 6-3   Examples of Multiple-Choice Items

Recall:

Which Indian group made the first calendar in the Americas?

    a. Apache

    b. Inca

    c. Mezquito

    d. Cherokee

    e. Aztec

Comprehension:

Why did the Pueblo indians live in adobe houses?

    a. Because they were larger and accommodated more people.

    b. They were easy to defend from enemy attacks.

    c. Adobe houses could be built quickly.

    d. They provided protection from winter cold and summer heat.

    e. Because they were inexpensive to build.

Application:

In which area did the Maya and Aztec indian cultures originate?

    a. East of the Mississippi River.

    b. Mesoamerica

    c. South of the Amazon River.

    d. New Mexico

    e. The Andes Mountains.

Analysis:

Why do you think Cortez burned his fleet of ships before starting the conquest of Mexico?

    a. Because they were old and in need of repair.

    b. He didn't want the indians to capture them.

    c. To force his troops to fight harder and succeed.

    d. So he could ask the King of Spain for new ships.

    e. Because he did not plan to use them again.

Table 6.1 SUGGESTED USE OF ASSESSMENT MEASURES ACCORDING TO COGNITIVE DEVELOPMENT STAGES

	Preoperational	Concrete	Formal
Observe student performance	X	X	X
Student work products	X	X	X
Matching pictures	X	X	X
Matching words/numbers	X	X	X
Matching statements		X	X
Short-answer items		X	X
Essay questions			X
Multiple-choice items		X	X
Research papers		X	X

Table 6.2 SUGGESTED USE OF ASSESSMENT MEASURES ACCORDING TO GRADE LEVELS

	PK	K	1	2	3	4	5	6
Observe student performance	X	X	X	X	X	X	X	X
Student work products	X	X	X	X	X	X	X	X
Matching pictures	X	X	X	X	X	X	X	X
Matching words/numbers	X	X	X	X	X	X	X	X
Matching statements			X	X	X	X	X	X
Short-answer items						X	X	X
Essay questions						X	X	X
Multiple-choice items					X	X	X	X
Research papers						X	X	X

test. The group to which students are compared is called the **norm group**. The performance of the norm group is the *standard* or frame of reference which is used to determine the relative standing of anyone else who takes the test. Standardized tests also use standard content and procedures. This means that a given standardized test must test identical content regardless of where it is administered, when it is administered, or to whom it is administered. Sometimes a standardized test will include multiple test forms so that students who take the test a second time will not be able to remember the answers from the first test. Even when multiple forms are used, however, standardized tests deal with the same content. Standardized tests also include a test manual for the test administrator, who is usually a classroom teacher. This is done so that every child who takes a particular standardized test will receive the same instructions when taking the test.

Standardized tests have advantages and disadvantages which must be considered when one is deciding whether to make use of standardized or teacher-made tests. Standardized tests are excellent for evaluating educational development in basic skills or instructional objectives which are common throughout the country. They are also useful for documenting student progress over a period of years. Frequently, however, an individual class or school has objectives which are not common to the rest of the nation. When this is so, teacher-made tests, or comparable assessments, should be used. Likewise, when a teacher desires to assess student progress from day to day, or to assess student mastery of the objectives of a particular unit of instruction, teacher-made assessments will be more appropriate. Also, some areas of the elementary curriculum, such as science and social studies, have a rapidly changing content. In such cases, teacher-made assessments are probably more useful than standardized tests (Gronlund, 1985, pp. 266–267).

Standardized tests offer a further advantage in that they have been carefully constructed by experts. These test authors have taken pains to make sure that their tests offer a high degree of reliability and validity. **Reliability** refers to the *consistency* of the test results. For example, if the test is given on two or more separate occasions, and each student gets very similar results from one test-taking to the next, then the test would seem to have a high degree of reliability. Reliability is important in the administration of tests because, as teachers, we want to be confident that we are really measuring the knowledge of our students rather than accidental deviations in their performance (Gronlund, 1985, p. 56).

Validity refers to the accuracy with which the test measures whatever it purports to measure. More precisely, it refers to the appropriateness of the interpretation of the test results. For example, an elementary mathematics test may accurately measure computational skill but may not measure mathematical reasoning as well. In this case, the results of the test will be highly valid for indicating computational skill but the same results will probably not have much validity for mathematical reasoning. Will the results be valid for predicting future success in mathematics? That depends. Test-makers use their expertise to estimate validity by collecting evidence that the test is valid for specific purposes. If the authors of the test intended its results to be used for predicting future success in mathematics, then they estimated its validity for this purpose. Assuming their validity estimates were high, educators can feel justified in using the test results for this purpose. However, if the authors of the test did not have this use of test results in mind when they estimated validity, then the results are not valid for this use (Gronlund, 1985, pp. 57–59).

Most standardized achievement tests are norm-referenced since their purpose is to determine an individual's relative standing when compared to a norm group. Because of this purpose, and because they frequently assess a student's achievement in a variety of skill areas, these tests are *surveys* of the child's knowledge in the skill areas being tested. In other words, such tests do not include many items for any particular objective being tested. In fact, some achievement tests may include as few as one or two test items for a particular objective being tested. This means that a student could make a simple mistake, such as accidentally marking an incorrect answer, and fail that objective on the achievement test. But since achievement tests don't measure success on particular objectives, this is an acceptable practice. Achievement tests measure success in general skill areas (e.g., reading, language arts, mathematics, and study skills)—*not* on specific objectives.

Some publishers of standardized achievement tests have begun to publish **instructional tests**. While achievement tests may be able to tell us that a particular student is achieving poorly in reading or mathematics, they are unable to identify the strengths and weaknesses of that student within a specific skill area (e.g., reading or mathematics). Instructional tests are intended to help teachers identify a student's particular strengths and weaknesses so that a plan of instruction can be developed for the child. In this case, more test items are included for each objective than are included in a typical achievement (i.e., survey) test. Nevertheless, these tests usually include only a few test items for any given objective and accidental mistakes could still mislead a teacher into misinterpreting the results of a test.

The best advice we can offer teachers who desire information which they can use to make instructional decisions is to develop their own, teacher-made tests. Although these tests may be less reliable or valid, they are designed to test specific learning outcomes and can be used for the purpose of making decisions about instruction. Standardized criterion-referenced tests are also available for this purpose, but their validity and reliability is questionable because the authors of most of these instruments have not provided information about these matters. Finally, when teachers believe that particular students have difficulty in specific skill areas (e.g., reading or mathematics) and they believe that using teacher-made tests will not provide adequate information with which to assist the students in question, then teachers must turn to standardized diagnostic tests. In many cases, these are administered by instructional specialists such as a special needs facilitator, a reading specialist, or a school psychologist.

Abuses in the Interpretation of Standardized Tests   Although standardized tests have many uses, there are many potential abuses of these tests, and we feel a professional obligation to discuss some of the most common ones. Standardized tests were originally developed for the purpose of comparing large groups of students (Perrone, 1977). For example, school districts, or even entire states, can compare their test results to the norm group for the nation and obtain information about the relative ranking of their students in particular subject or skill areas. In practice, this is one of the ways that standardized tests are used. However, there is much potential for abuse in this approach as the following hypothetical examples demonstrate.

Suppose, for the moment, that an elementary school principal wants to compare the effectiveness of two third grade teachers, Mr. Wilson and Mrs. Duffy. Mr. Wilson is using a traditional, basic reader approach to instruction while Mrs. Duffy is experimenting with the more innovative, whole language approach. But when the tests results are returned from the scoring center, Mr. Wilson's students have achieved much higher scores. This school principal concludes that Mr. Wilson is the more effective teacher, and when his superintendent instructs him to fire one teacher due to budget cuts, he fires Mrs. Duffy.

However, Mrs. Duffy employs an attorney who, in turn, employs the services of an educational psychologist. This educational psychologist discovers that although Mr. Wilson's students did attain higher scores on the test, they had higher scores during the test administered on the previous year as well. Mrs. Johnson was teaching these students during that year—*not* Mr. Wilson. This educational psychologist compared last year's test results with this year's test results for each of Mr. Wilson's and Mrs. Duffy's students. He subtracted each student's score on last year's test from his or her score on this year's test and thus arrived at a "gain score" for each student. He then averaged these gain scores for both Mr. Wilson's class and Mrs. Duffy's class. To his amazement, Mrs. Duffy's students had achieved an average gain score of two grade equivalents in reading whereas Mr. Wilson's class had only achieved an average gain of one grade equivalent. Mrs. Duffy's attorney presented this information at a hearing of the school board, and the board reversed the principal's decision, reinstating Mrs. Duffy and dismissing Mr. Wilson.

Now, of course, Mr. Wilson will employ an attorney. When he does so, his attorney will also engage the services of an educational psychologist. This educational psychologist will discover that, although Mrs. Duffy's students have achieved better gain scores, *they were expected to achieve better gain scores because they were much more intelligent* (as measured by the standardized intelligence tests which were administered during a previous year). In fact, students had been homogeneously grouped in this school. Out of four third grade classrooms, Mrs. Duffy's students had extremely high intelligence scores (and could thus be expected to achieve large gains) while Mr. Wilson's students had very low intelligence scores (and could thus be expected to achieve very small gains). When Mr. Wilson's attorney learns about this, he will engage the services of a PhD in tests and measurements. This PhD will use a technique called "factor analysis" to estimate the expected average gains for each class based on the average intelligence scores of each class. He may find that Mr. Wilson's students were only expected to achieve an average gain of one-half of a grade-equivalent. That would mean that Mr. Wilson's students are achieving a higher than expected gain. What will he find for Mrs. Duffy? What if her students are also achieving higher than expected gains?

In the same way that two teachers can be unfairly compared, so can two schools, or even two school districts, be unfairly compared. The intelligence of students makes a large contribution to student achievement. Experts in the area of tests and measurements have developed means to factor out the effect of intelligence on test scores, but school districts and newspapers which report school or school district test scores do not typically make use of these techniques. Socioeconomic background has also been established as an important contributor to student achievement (Hodgkinson, 1988). Again, newspaper reporters and school district personnel frequently neglect to consider this factor when they report test scores.

Suppose Urban Center School District has a magnet middle school and its test scores show excellent gains from year to year. Does this indicate an excellent school program with excellent teaching? Not necessarily. Parents must volunteer to send their students to magnet schools. Parents who choose to send their children to a magnet school may have a special interest in education. Children who attend magnet schools may come from high socioeconomic backgrounds. Each of these factors may have more to do with gains in test scores than either the teaching or the educational program at the school. Standardized tests may have been developed so that educators can make comparisons, but the interpretation of their results requires some careful thought and specialized training. The assistant principal of this magnet school demonstrated either that he had not acquired this specialized training or that he was not inclined to careful thought when he released the test scores to the local newspaper with the statement, "These scores demonstrate that magnet schools are educationally superior to traditional middle schools."

Another newspaper decides, through its editorial staff, to have one of its reporters write a story comparing the Wealthy Heights School District to the Urban Poverty School District. Test scores are to be one of the chief means of comparison. However, children from Wealthy Heights come from high socioeconomic backgrounds. Children from Urban Poverty come from low socioeconomic backgrounds. The news reporter neglects to take this important factor into account when he concludes that Wealthy Heights offers a superior school program.

In sum, we must be very careful about reaching conclusions based on test score results. Test scores from standardized tests may be used to interpret *general achievement* in specific skill areas for individual children. They may also be used to compare large groups of students *if contributing factors are given fair consideration*. Unfortunately, many in our society, including school administrators and teachers, are not adequately aware of the potential abuses in interpreting the results of standardized tests.

NOTES

1. Bob Louisell gratefully acknowledges a summer conversation with Ms. Shirley Palmer, Wiltshire Schools, England, who helped him clarify many questions which he was asking about evaluation and reporting in British Primary Schools.
2. Thanks to Dave Heine for discussing the ideas of this paragraph with me.
3. Conversation with Ms. Shirley Palmer, Wiltshire Schools, England, Summer, 1990.
4. Of course, since much knowledge is cumulative, tests can rarely avoid testing prerequisites. For example, an addition test on combining sets will inadvertently test a child's knowledge of sets since the child must know how to make sets in order to add.

GLOSSARY

criterion-referenced evaluation Evaluation by comparing the performance of a student to some predefined standard of quality.

evaluation The collection of information to determine whether students know something.

general reports Reports of student progress which are not individualized but which report on the progress of an entire class instead. Usually, these reports summarize class learning during a specific topic unit.

instructional tests Standardized tests which attempt to identify a student's strengths and weaknesses within a specific skill area (e.g., reading or mathematics). Usually, these tests are a revised form of a standardized achievement test.

intermediate grades The upper grade levels of a traditional elementary school (grades 4-6).

norm group In standardized tests, the group which has already taken the test and which is used to determine the relative standing of anyone else who takes the test is called the **norm group.** The performance of the norm group on the test is the *standard* by which all others who take the test are ranked.

objective tests Paper-pencil tests for which the answer of students can be compared and quantified to yield a numerical score.

objectives-referenced evaluation Evaluation of student learning based on mastery of specific objectives.

portfolios Individual packets, one per student, in which is included any sample of children's work, tests, teacher observations about a child, or anything else which can communicate progress in learning for the child in question.

primary grades The lower grade levels of a traditional elementary school (grades 1-3).

profiles Individual packets, one per student, in which is included samples of children's work, tests, teacher observations, etc., which can communicate important information about a student's progress over an extended period of years (e.g., the elementary school years).

reliability The consistency of test results from one occasion to the next. A high degree of reliability indicates that tests-takers are likely to earn similar scores on two administrations of the same test.

standardized achievement tests Standardized tests which are used to assess student performance, identify the existence of learning problems in individual students, or to compare the performance of large groups of students (e.g., school districts or states).

standardized diagnostic tests Standardized tests which are used to give detailed information about a student's knowledge in a variety of subskills. When a student does poorly on a diagnostic test, responses in any subskill can be analyzed.

standardized tests Tests which use a norm group and which make use of standard content and procedures. A standardized test must test identical content regardless of where it is administered, when it is administered, or to whom it is administered.

subjective tests Paper-pencil tests which are not easily quantified.

teacher-made tests Tests developed by teachers to assess the performance of their students. These tests may assess knowledge of particular objectives or knowledge of a general topic or unit of instruction. They can be used to diagnose particular learning problems in students, to group students with similar instructional needs, or to assign evaluative marks for the purpose of reporting pupil progress.

validity The accuracy to which a test measures whatever it purports to measure; more specifically, the appropriateness of using the test's results for a particular interpretation.

Chapter
7

Classroom Management: Establishing the Socioemotional Environment

*C*hapter 7 describes skills for managing the socioemotional dimensions of the classroom. In particular, it focuses on how to foster positive relationships among teachers and students. Chapter 8 deals with the instructional, physical, and record-keeping dimensions of the classroom. It discusses classroom procedures and rules, how to manage records, supervise paraprofessionals, and work with parents. Chapter 9 presents a system to manage student behavior and address discipline problems.

In the previous chapters, emphasis has been placed on teaching. When thinking about teaching, teachers must consider many things: the nature of children, personal philosophies, a variety of instructional settings, techniques, methods, and instructional planning. The role of the teacher in the instructional dimension is a proactive, rather than a reactive role. The teacher is expected to be in charge, plan, organize and direct the organizational "symphony" played in the classroom. Teacher preparation programs spend a significant amount of time preparing candidates for this role. But in order for learning to take place, there are several things, besides teach, which teachers must do. These activities are sometimes classroom management tasks, and they include establishing, maintaining, and managing the socioemotional environment, the teaching-learning environment, and the physical environment of the classroom. They also include managing clerical tasks and student behavior.

To successfully perform classroom management tasks, classroom management skills are needed. Teacher preparation programs often neglect the development of classroom management skills. As a result of this lack of emphasis, many candidates learn these skills through modeling during student teaching and through trial and error later in their own classrooms.

The purpose of Chapters 7–10 of this book is to help future teachers develop classroom management skills. The role of the teacher in the classroom management dimension must also be proactive rather than reactive. Teachers cannot wait for students to set the behavior norms of the class, or the work procedures, or the work expectations, or the rewards and consequences. Teachers must, as classroom managers, be in charge and direct the symphony.

In order for teachers to be proactive in classroom management, they must master skills in establishing a positive classroom climate, a productive learning environment, a pleasant physical environment, and they must learn to manage clerical tasks and student behavior. As you study the various sections of each chapter and begin to develop classroom management and discipline skills, it is important for you to realize the importance of being a proactive teacher, regardless of individual personality characteristics. An effective teacher does not wait for students to be quiet before starting the lesson. This waiting could take forever. The effective teacher may ask easy review questions and get the lesson on the way without having to utilize desist behaviors. An effective teacher does not wait for students to become frustrated with the amount of material to be covered in a test, but an effective teacher does listen actively to the perspectives and feelings of students.

Effective teachers do not allow student behavior to become annoying; rather, they assertively communicate their needs and explain how they are personally affected by their students' behaviors. Effective teachers do not allow for student talk to disturb class work. Instead, they may move the students away from each other or request a change of behavior privately. Effective teachers do not judge and criticize students who are not performing a desired task; rather, they describe to the students what they are not doing well. Effective teachers do not avoid students who are off-task; rather, they move close to them and use body language to redirect the students to their task. All of these teacher behaviors have one thing in common: the teacher is proactive rather than reactive in the use of classroom management skills.

The socioemotional environment is one of the most important matters related to the success of a teacher. It deals with four major dimensions: **human relations, rewards, expectations,** and **values**. A classroom can be lacking in high quality physical features—even a roof, but it cannot lack a healthy socioemotional environment if learning is to take place. Learning takes place in a socioemotional context, a setting made up of a social group of students and their individual emotions. Unless teachers know how to foster a healthy socioemotional environment, all their good teaching techniques and instructional efforts may be wasted, for many students will not focus on learning due to the fact that their socioemotional needs in the classroom are not being met. When the emotional needs of teachers and students are not met, the capacity for teaching and learning is significantly reduced (Gordon, 1974). In this chapter, we will deal with each of the dimensions which affect the socioemotional environment.

- Human relations
- Classroom rewards
- Self-concept and expectations.
- Values

HUMAN RELATIONS

Human relations in a classroom are composed of interactions between teachers and students and interactions among students. The degree of these interactions may vary according to teacher styles and subjects taught. For example, there is greater interaction while teachers are conducting small group work or class discussions than when students are engaged in seatwork or reading silently. But if there is a characteristic essential to teaching and learning, it is human interaction. Regardless of the role of the teacher—that is, source of information, facilitator, coach, evaluator—interaction between teacher and learner is essential to learning. Few occupations require as frequent and sustained a degree of interaction all throughout the day. A very important component of teaching is to interact with students and guide the interactions of students with each other in the classroom. Individuals who dislike to interact frequently with children will have to acquire a quick liking for it if they are to be successful elementary teachers.

Whenever twenty children and a teacher come together, we have a social interaction situation. In a social gathering, the host is responsible for structuring the activities of the event. In a classroom, the teacher is responsible for structuring the activities. In a classroom, also, the teacher is responsible for structuring the *interactions* that occur during the day. Teachers who are successful at creating a good social environment in the classroom exhibit the following human relations skills:

1. **Communication** skills.
2. **Conflict resolution** skills.
3. **Establishing a positive climate**.
4. **Fostering a sense of individual importance**.
5. **Fostering a sense of belonging**.
6. **Team work** skills.

Communication Skills

Teachers communicate with students verbally and nonverbally. The way teachers use language affects their human relations significantly. Teacher language may be descriptive or judgmental, accepting or unaccepting, assertive or hostile. Through language, teachers convey a myriad of messages to students about their potential, how well they are liked by the teacher, their worth, their shortcomings and talents, the interest of the teacher in their personal problems and those of their families, etc.

Teachers also communicate similar messages through their body language. It is almost impossible to fake communications for a sustained period of time. Sooner or later, particularly under stressful situations, our true feelings come through and are apparent to the students. So the first area for teachers to work on when improving communications with students is to develop positive and caring attitudes toward each of them. It does not matter how skillful a teacher is in listening or using descriptive rather than judgmental language; if the teacher has a negative view of the student, this will creep through carefully prepared statements and will be perceived by the student or any other careful observer.

Teachers should develop a professional philosophy of hope and caring: hope that, with effort and time, students can be helped to learn and improve themselves; caring, as their professional call. Teachers are members of a helping profession dedicated to caring for the welfare of each student. As teachers succeed, this philosophy is reinforced. Conversely, as teachers fail in the classroom, they begin to gradually lose this hope and caring and become burnout workers unable to help many children learn and grow. To avoid failure in the classroom, teachers need to develop skills in relating to students, and, particularly, in communicating with students through language which is descriptive, accepting, and assertive. There are **four types of communication** the teacher must master: 1) **descriptive** language, 2) **accepting** language, 3) **assertive** language, and 4) "body" or **nonverbal** language.

Descriptive language indicates to students what is presently happening. Students can modify their behavior after receiving a message in descriptive language from the teacher. For example, if the teacher says, "Adrian, that noise from your pencil tapping is distracting me," the language used by the teacher describes to Adrian what is happening and points out its effect. Judgmental language, on the other hand, labels behavior. For example, in "Adrian, can you stop being so nervous?" or "Adrian, you are so insensitive to the needs of the class!", the language applies to off-task classroom behaviors as well as it applies to on-task behaviors.

"Adrian, your essay has many descriptive images. It shows that you are mastering the use of simile and metaphors," uses descriptive language. "Adrian, your essay is outstanding!" utilizes judgmental language. Cangelosi (1982) recommends that teachers restrain themselves from even thinking in judgmental language terms: "smart," "messy," "slow." Teachers must avoid labeling students, even in their minds, and think of students in terms of tasks and circumstances. Descriptions such as "reads prose well," "does not clean up work area," "requires more time to complete task" should be used. Student displays of misbehaviors are not necessarily a reflection of a character flaw. A student can easily change present behavior, but cannot easily change a character trait. If students conclude that they are "behavior problems" or "poor in mathematics," they are less likely to apply themselves and try to behave appropriately or work enthusiastically on math problems. As years of judgmental language go by, students accumulate "failure labels" in their minds and tend to give up. Terms like "slow learner," "lazy," "stubborn," "dumb," "mean," and "selfish" take their toll. Descriptive language overcomes this past history and emphasizes present learning objectives that are specific and feasible for the student. Teachers are not called to be character judges, but to help students improve their achievement and behavior through small, daily, learning steps.

Accepting language is characterized by an ability to identify and accept student feelings. Teachers adept in the use of accepting language listen to what students say about how they feel and inform the students that they recognize and accept those feelings. Active listening (Gordon, 1974) is a form of accepting language. The teacher actively listens and accepts the feelings of others. The teacher recognizes that students have a right to their feelings and communicates to the students that their feelings are accepted. "I hate reading!", "Susie is stupid," "teachers are so dumb" are messages students send indicating they are upset about something. Teachers skillful in the language of acceptance identify the feeling and verbalize it for the student. Teacher responses to such statements might include, "You do not like reading," "You are disappointed in Susie," and "You believe that teachers do dumb things." This acceptance places the responsibility for the situation back on the student and shows the students that the teacher accepts them regardless of how they feel. As a result of this acceptance, students feel understood and develop a sense of closeness with the teacher. In turn, they assume more responsibility in solving their school and personal conflicts. The opposite of accepting language is the language of unacceptance, which Gordon (1974) calls a communication roadblock. Instead of identifying and accepting student feelings, teachers who use the language of unacceptance respond to statements in which students describe their feelings by criticizing or advising the students in question. As a result of this, students feel misunderstood and distant from their teachers and blame the teacher for their problems rather than taking responsibility for them.

Assertive language is characterized by teachers stating clearly what they want students to do and how their off-task behaviors affect them. There are two types of assertive language. One type communicates to students which behaviors are desirable and positively affect the work of the teacher. "When students pick up the art supplies at the end of the lesson, I am able to start the next lesson quickly" is a type of "I message" in which the teacher communicates desirable behavior *before* it is to occur. The other type of assertive language communicates to students how off-task behaviors affect the teacher. "When students leave the art supplies all over the tables at the end of the lesson, I have to spend time picking them up, and I am unable to start the next lesson on time." This is a type of "I message" in which the teacher communicates the impact of undesirable behavior *after* it occurs.

Teachers, then, may use assertive language in a proactive manner, before behaviors take place, or in a reactive manner, after behaviors take place. In either case, the teacher describes the student behaviors which affect her. She describes the impact which these behaviors have on the performance and feelings of the teacher. We call this "assertive language" because those teachers who employ it make their needs clear to the students, as professionals and as human beings. When they want things done in a certain way, or when students behave in an undesirable manner, teachers immediately communicate to the students how their needs can be met or are not being met.

This type of communication makes teachers easy to understand and predict. There is no second guessing. If the teacher wants something, it will be expressed, and if the teacher does not want something to continue happening, it will also be expressed. The manner in which teachers communicate how student behaviors affect them is descriptive, matter of fact, present-oriented, and addresses facts and circumstances. It uses descriptive rather than judgmental language. There is no attempt to produce guilt. The objective is to communicate individual needs so the student, or students, may know what the teacher desires or what is bothering the teacher. Most students, once they know their behavior affects the teacher, will modify it, in order to please, and avoid annoying the teacher.

At times teachers are reluctant to communicate their needs to students. Teachers may believe that their feelings must remain private and not be disclosed. When students have difficulty understanding how their behavior affects the teacher, it is difficult for the students to relate to the teacher. They may be perplexed and confused. "Why wouldn't teachers say what they want and what bothers them?" Indeed, why not? Teachers must use assertive language and state their needs so students are able to modify their behavior accordingly. If teachers fail to express their needs and to communicate how the behaviors of students affect them, they are adopting a role which leads to reactive behavior. The students will take the initiative to test for limits, since limits are not established by the teacher. Or the students will try to irritate the teacher since the teacher does not express what irritates her. Through a trial and error process, students try to discover the limits as well as the emotional world of their teacher. This interferes with classroom work and saps the energy of the teacher. The tables are turned in these classrooms and the students initiate interactions. They "serve the ball" while the teacher adjusts responses to the students initiatives. This is reactive classroom management.

Body language is another form of communication in the classroom. It is composed of the gestures, facial expressions, eye movement, voice inflections, and physical positions teachers adopt. While it is possible to fake verbal statements, it is very difficult to fake body language. In the event of conflicting messages between verbal language and nonverbal language, the students will believe our body language rather than our words. For example, a teacher may state to the class that she is very happy with the progress they are making in mastering reading comprehension skills, but the students may detect a lack of enthusiasm in her voice and a dullness in her eyes. They may notice that her body is half-turned away from the students as the statement is made. "Naaah!" many of the students will conclude; "she is not happy." On the other hand, Mrs. Ortega wants Adrian to stop tapping his pencil. She comes close to Adrian, bends over, looks at him in the eyes, and says in a slow and low voice, "Adrian, please stop tapping your pencil." Adrian will listen to the teacher's words, check the body language and think "Yeaah! She means it." When teachers fail to come close to students and to look at them in the eyes while requesting a change of behavior, the verbal language may be appropriate, but the nonverbal language is inadequate and communicates a lack of will and determination. As teachers verbally express their classroom needs, they must accompany these verbal statements with congruent body language (Jones 1979). Eye contact, lowered speech, and physical proximity are the most effective nonverbal statements teachers can make when relating one-on-one with students. When working with the whole class, the eyes of the teacher should make contact periodically with the eyes of individual students, and the body should be erect and facing the students as much as possible.

Of course, the cultural attitudes of one's students must also be taken into account. If a Native American child has been taught, according to his family and culture, that it is impolite to look at someone directly in the eye, the teacher must respect this cultural value. Cultural attitudes must always be taken into account.

Obviously contradictory verbal and nonverbal messages must be avoided; for example, telling the class that their behavior must stop while smiling. One way of improving body language is to increase the amount of periods of silence when communicating verbally. Pause frequently to look at students in the eyes. When needing to request a change of behavior, use gestures to convey your instructions. Point, signal, stop talking and look at, or slowly walk toward the student. Many requests for students to get back on-task may be done nonverbally (see Chapter 9). Remember, students pay attention first to nonverbal messages and second to verbal ones. It is not so much **what** effective classroom managers say to students, but **how they say it** that matters. While we have discussed the use of body language for communicating your needs to students, we also use it to communicate approval, encouragement and support through smiles, movement of the head, clapping, thumbs-up, etc. These nurturing nonverbal messages are quick and effective, and they reach many students at the same time.

Conflict Resolution Skills

When the needs of students and teachers in a classroom are not met, a conflict exists. Regardless of how well organized a classroom is, how the rules and procedures might have been cooperatively designed by the teacher and students, or how smoothly things run, sooner or later conflicts between the needs of teacher and students, or teacher and an individual student, will occur. Unless these conflicts are satisfactorily resolved, the socioemotional environment of the classroom will suffer.

Examples of conflicts between teacher and students are: when the teacher is planning a field trip with students and the students opinions about where to go are totally divided; when the teacher needs the students to come back from P.E. on time and students need to drink water from the only fountain available; when the teacher needs to cover a certain amount of material and the students find it to be too much; when the teacher needs the students to pay attention and the students find the activity very boring; and when the teacher expects the students to master a skill and the students are frustrated because they do not understand it.

Examples of conflicts between the teacher and an individual student are: when the teacher needs to start the lesson and a student comes late from another class in which the student is doing extra work; when a student is late in the morning several days in a row; when the teacher reviews homework on a daily basis and a student is frequently late in turning in homework; when a teacher needs the attention of the class and a student interrupts to tell something to a friend; when a teacher likes to have projects neatly presented and a student has illegible handwriting; when a teacher wants students to sit still and a student is not able to sit still; when a teacher likes an orderly classroom and a student leaves things out of place; when a teacher wants all students to take turns doing sample problems on the chalkboard and a student dislikes working in front of the class.

How do teachers go about resolving conflicts in the classroom? Gordon (1974) states that teachers usually follow one of three possible approaches: 1) make the students comply with the teacher's needs at the expense of the students' needs (**Method I**); 2) comply with the students' needs at the expense of the teacher's needs (**Method II**); 3) seek a way to meet the needs of both sides through communicating with them and exploring mutually satisfactory solutions (**Method III**). In Method I, the teacher wins and the students lose. In Method II, the students win and the teacher loses. In Method III, both sides win and no one loses.

In reality, it would be impossible to resolve all classroom conflicts through a method III approach. It also would be almost impossible to find a teacher who resolves conflicts all the time through Method I. Most teachers oscillate a little between Method III and Method I. But students can easily identify those teachers who "are fair," (predominantly Method III) and those who "don't care about the students" (predominantly Method I). Method II is found less often in the classroom as the dominant approach to conflict resolution since it eventually would lead to chaos. Teachers who frequently yield to the students' wishes without solving their own needs become frustrated and ultimately shift to a harsh Method I approach to regain control and save their jobs. Teachers who shift from Method I to Method II frequently are inconsistent and difficult to predict.

What is the impact that conflict resolution approaches have in the behavior of students? When the teacher wins and the students lose (Method I), it is easy to predict that students will be less motivated. They will also be resentful, rebellious, passive, in need of close supervision, and will lack initiative. When the students consistently win and the teacher consistently loses (Method II) as a dominant approach, the students will become selfish and increasingly demanding, and less learning will take place. When both the teacher and the students win and no one loses (Method III), the students become more motivated. They like the teacher and they need less supervision. Real learning obstacles are removed, more learning takes place, and the teacher likes the students.

How is Method I carried out? The teacher states the way things are to be done. The students may bring out their point of view in the conflict, and the teacher may appear to listen politely, even smile, and counter the students arguments; but finally, it is resolved "the teacher's way." The teacher wins and the students lose. This does not have to be done in a hostile manner. As a matter of fact, some teachers are very skillful at appearing to listen to the students' and even allowing them to express themselves for a while; but finally, the teacher's way prevails.

How is Method II carried out? The teacher states the way things are to be done. The students begin to complain and express their point of view. The teacher may gently present the other side, but the students do not listen, and press to have it resolved "the student's way." The teacher finally says "O.K.!" The students win and the teacher loses.

How is Method III carried out? The teacher states the way things are to be done, and the students bring up their point of view. The teacher recognizes that there is a conflict of needs and follows this sequence:

1. She communicates her needs to the students.
2. She asks the students to express their needs.
3. She asks the students to come up with possible solutions to the conflict which would satisfy the needs of both sides.
4. She agrees with the students on one solution.

At times, after going through the process of exploring solutions, none is found which is satisfactory to both sides. Then the teacher may tell the students that they have to do what was originally proposed. The students are likely to accept the "teacher's way" now since it is obvious to them that no satisfactory alternative could be found.

Conflicts also occur in the classroom among students, and the same three approaches may be used to solve them. Once the students experience Method III in their interactions with the teacher, it will not be difficult for them to use it among themselves. The teacher can also mediate disputes through a Method III in which each side wins and no one loses.

Classroom needs conflicts may be seen as opportunities to get students involved and responsible for the events in the room. Once the students have participated in exploring solutions to a conflict, and have decided on one solution, they are likely to perceive this solution as theirs. A sense of ownership, groupness, and teaming will be developed through the resolution of differences. As a result of joint problem solving, motivation increases and better solutions and approaches will be identified in the classroom. After all, students are also experts in learning.

Establishing a Positive Classroom Climate

The classroom climate is directly related to the attitudes, values, learning experiences, and interpersonal interactions which exist in the classroom. There are four major variables which contribute to the nature and quality of the classroom climate:

1. *Teacher affect:* the degree of warmth, friendliness, acceptance, and personal interest established by the teacher.
2. *Support for learning:* the degree of success that the students experience in learning, help provided by the teacher and peers, and opportunities to make mistakes which are afforded in the classroom.
3. *Degree of enjoyment:* the extent to which experiences are pleasant and interesting, the threat of failure or embarrassment is low, and humor and enthusiasm permeate the daily activities.
4. *Focus of control:* the degree to which the teacher directs things versus the amount of opportunities for student self-direction and autonomy.

As a result of the mixture of these four variables in different degrees, the classroom climate, although different from room to room, can generally be classified as: 1) **positive,** 2) **business-like,** 3) **"just-a-job",** and 4) **negative.**

A **positive** classroom climate emphasizes both academic and effective outcomes. In a positive classroom climate, the teacher is committed to helping students learn basic skills and to develop self-concept, creativity, and citizenship values. Teacher warmth and affect is evident. The teacher is friendly, the students like the teacher, and the teacher likes the students. Support for learning is high. Students receive abundant assistance. Learning activities are designed in a manner that insures a high degree of success by each student. Students dare to make mistakes knowing that teacher and peers will be supportive. The degree of enjoyment is also high. Students are involved in fun activities. Students are not overly threatened by tests and anxiety levels are low. Learning is engaging and students succeed at it. The focus of control is balanced. There are plenty of teacher directed experiences, but there are also abundant opportunities for students to be self-directing or to participate in decisions about classroom matters. In a positive classroom environment, students and teachers appear busy and engaged in work. They express themselves freely, look happy, and work as a team. Obviously, different teachers will have different degrees of affect support, enjoyment, and control, according to their individual styles. An observer could visit several outstanding classroom situations and find different types of positive classroom environments.

A **business-like** environment is one in which the learning dimension is emphasized and the affective dimension purposely ignored. This type of environment is predicated on the belief that schools are to teach subject matter and that attitudes, values and feelings do not belong in the classroom. The teacher will relate to students in a "business-like" manner and will avoid sharing personal experiences, feelings, or beliefs. The teacher may be a very warm and caring individual, but these characteristics are not expressed in the classroom. The affect dimension is neutral in such classrooms. Students are treated with courtesy and respect, but the teacher remains aloof. She redirects students who pursue a close relationship with their teacher by emphasizing learning tasks. Support for learning insures that students receive assistance and that the learning activities are helpful, but it is the responsibility of the student to succeed. The classroom work environment is very likely to be competitive. Those students who have greater ability, or put forth more effort, succeed, and those who have less ability or put forth less effort do not succeed. The degree of enjoyment is moderate. School is a place to work hard and prepare oneself for a career. There is distrust toward learning activities which are not academically oriented. The focus of control is teacher centered. The teacher is in charge of teaching and the students are responsible for following directions and learning.

It is difficult to accept the validity of "business-like" classroom environments in primary grades. They do exist in intermediate grades and middle school. When visiting such classrooms, some students will appear busy and engaged in learning while others will only go through the motions of working. An aura of seriousness will permeate the room, and there will be little self-expression on the part of the students. Some students who are succeeding will appear happy, while other students who are failing will appear detached. There will be order and respect in the classroom.

A **"just-a-job"** environment is characterized by lack of attention and effort on the part of the teacher. For whatever reason, teaching and learning are not the focus of interest and energy of the teacher. The teacher goes through the motions but fails to perform as a professional. The teacher may be burned out or distracted by outside activities, or she may have given up due to lack of professional ability or a very difficult classroom assignment. The end result is a classroom without energy, direction, and learning. The professional rituals are followed, that is, subject matter is covered, grades are assigned, parent-teacher conferences are held. But for the teacher, it is just-a-job which is not to be taken seriously, which ends at 3:30 p.m. everyday, with slow starts on Mondays and wasted Fridays, class days which precede holidays, etc.

The affective dimension in these classrooms can range from high to flat. Some just-a-job teachers are very warm and friendly to students in order to avoid complaints or criticisms. Others are not interested. Support for learning is minimal. Lessons are poorly planned, little supervision is given, student work is not seriously evaluated, and performance standards are mediocre. Enjoyment is not related to learning tasks. Students are bribed with films, games, free periods, music listening time, etc. As a matter of fact, students get the message that learning is a duty to get over hurriedly in order to enjoy other extracurricular activities. The focus of control is student-centered. The students manipulate back and forth, and through complaining, establish the amount of work to be done and how and when it is to be done. Since the teacher does not have clear goals for the classroom and wishes to avoid conflict, it is easy for the students to impose their point of view or to spend significant amounts of time negotiating what is to be done and how their work is to be assessed. When visiting these classrooms, the teacher will appear to be working at the desk while students are reading from the text, answering questions from the text, working on a ditto, or studying for a quiz. A perceptive observer will notice hidden off-task behaviors on the part of the students and a lack of caring on the part of the teacher. The ringing of the bell will bring relief to all. Class is over, the day is over, the week is over, school is over! Such a learning climate requires immediate administrative intervention.

A **negative** climate may be high or low in its emphasis on learning outcomes, but the socioemotional atmosphere is negative, hostile and threatening. Name calling, screaming, rudeness, lack of respect for individuals, lack of respect among students, fear of the teacher, fear of tests, and high anxiety are all negative aspects of classroom climate which may be present. Support for learning is poor in such settings. The teacher does not like many students and does not spend time helping them succeed. Some students may get help and attention, but a significant number go ignored or denigrated. The degree of enjoyment is nonexisting. A large number of students hate the teacher and the class. The focus of control is teacher-centered. There are no opportunities for students to express their points of view and needs. Such a situation can not be tolerated. A negative socioemotional climate is not acceptable in an elementary school. Teachers who establish negative classroom climates must receive immediate attention and help. The side effects of a negative learning climate on young students are very serious. A perceptive visitor to such classrooms will notice that the teacher may refrain from using negative language but will be unable to hide body language, looks and facial expressions, and many children will appear subdued and shy.

Fostering a Sense of Individual Importance: Love and Acceptance

Young students need to feel that they are important to the teacher, regardless of their abilities, looks, ethnicity, race or socioeconomic status. They need to perceive a commitment on the part of the teacher toward their growth and success. They need to see the teacher as a supporter and special friend who has been placed in the classroom to help them along the long road of becoming a successful citizen. They do not need a judge who is constantly evaluating them. The teacher should be more a coach than an umpire. All students must feel they have the full interest and caring of the teacher, and that each of them, one by one, count and are very important to the teacher.

The teacher's career should be dedicated to helping each student to develop. The teacher should accept each of them as they come to the classroom and set a plan of action to help each student succeed. The teacher should be more impressed with individual effort than with ability. The teacher's job is to elicit as much effort as possible from each student. When students perform well, they are loved, and when they perform poorly, they are loved too. When they try hard, the teacher is happy, and when they do not try hard, the teacher is sad. The teacher has a vision for each one of them.

There is a need for the talents of each one of them on this earth. The teacher cherishes the diversity of her students and accepts their limitations. She does not see them as finished products, but rather she sees them as gems to be polished until they shine.

The teacher should have great respect for all hard working individuals; the janitor, the cook, and the gardener, as well as the hard working doctor, business executive, and engineer. The serious teacher sees our task on this earth as one of fulfilling individual potential under given circumstances. The teacher has a message of hope for the future which can be accomplished through competence and learning in the classroom. The teacher is a guide, friend and coach. When students fail and lose, somehow the teacher fails and loses too. The teacher is not in the classroom to pit the students against each other in a competition. The job of the teacher is to make each student a winner. Having losers does not make the classroom have higher standards nor does it make the winners more deserving.

How do teachers make students feel important and accepted? Teachers should find time everyday, in self-contained classrooms, to talk briefly to individual students and listen actively to them in order to learn about their circumstances. Teachers also should frequently canvas the room with their eyes and briefly look at individual students in their eyes. Teachers should move around the room during individual and group activities and come in contact with individual students through a question about their work, a smile, or a pat on the shoulder. When students come into the classroom, the teacher may stand by the door and greet them individually by name or with a smile and eye contact.

The teacher should give frequent feedback to the students on their work, using descriptive language. She should also listen to her students and accept their feelings. When students are having difficulties, the teacher may make arrangements for tutorial sessions with other students or spend extra time with struggling students. Above all, teachers must examine their values toward student achievement and develop a teaching philosophy which emphasizes the importance of individual student effort and perseverance over ability. Since individual ability is a difficult trait to change, teachers should focus on individual effort and perseverance. These are traits which can be developed. All students will try their best and be proud of their achievements, placing little emphasis on comparing themselves to others when the philosophy of the classrooms is "each student is respected for effort and individual talents."

Fostering a Sense of Belonging

Students are members of a classroom group, a school, and a neighboring community. As students relate within each of these groups, particularly the classroom, they have a need to feel they belong. The teacher is responsible for fostering this sense of belonging in the classroom, and she is also responsible for helping the school staff and student body leaders make every student feel proud and accepted in their school. Never is the need for helping students feel they belong more important than during the first days of school, particularly in the early grades. Students new to school may encounter difficulty in adjusting and making friends. On the other hand, many returning students, who are not new to the school, may also have difficulty adjusting. They may feel alienated and resentful as a result of their accumulated school failures. These students may feel like strangers in their own classrooms and even hate school and teachers. In some schools, accentuated economic differences among students, or ethnic and racial differences, make some groups of students feel alienated or marginal. They are "not in," left out, not popular, not members of the in crowd. This need for acceptance is heightened in preadolescence and early adolescence.

How do teachers help students feel they belong as members of the class? Instructional activities which require frequent group interaction, such as group projects, tutorials, and cooperative learning experiences, help students get to know each other. Cooperative learning activities, in particular, force students to relate to each other, and, as a result, to accept each other. Other actions teachers may take are: to model friendliness and treat all students with love and acceptance, without having special friends or enemies; to display the work of students and have a picture of each student on the bulletin board; to rotate important classroom jobs so all students get to participate.

How does the teacher foster a sense of belonging within the school and community? By having students team up with other teachers, parent volunteers, and community members in school and community-wide projects such as refurbishing the school grounds, or having a school fair, or a parent night. In this way, students get to contribute with other students and adults for the betterment of the school and the community. These types of activities produce tangible positive results which the students can be proud of and claim responsibility for, and from which they derive a sense of ownership and belonging. Instead of feeling like guests or strangers when they walk the halls of their school, the students perceive the school as their own in much the same way as they would if they were at home. Likewise, when students help in community clean-up activities, or distribute flyers, or sell postcards for a worthy cause, they interact with adults and achieve a sense of belonging in the neighborhood while beginning to develop civic leadership qualities and values. A very important task for teachers is to help students make the transition from close human interaction of the home to the broader interaction of the classroom and to the more complex social settings of the school environment of the community.

Team Work Skills

In order to maintain a positive socioemotional atmosphere in the classroom, teachers must have team work skills. The schooling of children is not the result of isolated efforts produced by very talented teachers; it is the result of the contributions of many individuals. Central office personnel, school administrators, teachers from other classrooms, librarians, clerical staff, support services staff, community leaders, and, particularly, parents contribute to the education of each student. Teachers who are skillful at utilizing the support provided by these various offices and individuals will model skills in human relations, will have classrooms which adults will want to help out in, and will provide an enriched socioemotional environment for students. Conversely, teachers who like to conduct a solo performance and who ignore the wealth of support available around them, tend to model egocentric behavior and lack of interaction skills with other adults. How can a teacher ask students to learn to work with each other and get along with other students and adults if the teacher does not get along with the principal, janitor, office secretary, central office supervisor, community leaders, and parents?

Teachers should practice the same human relation skills they teach their students when they interact with other adults in the school. Teachers also need to participate actively in school and community activities, sharing the load. It is difficult to work well with others when we do not do our part, taking on responsibilities in committees and school duties. Effective human relations among professionals and adults are based on fulfilling our obligations beyond the minimum and in caring for each other. Teachers ought to set examples of involvement and work cooperatively with other adults. It is difficult to require things from our students which we fail to do ourselves. Students can learn very quickly the double standard found in most ineffective bureaucracies: that is, work hard until you get to the top and then watch and tell others to work. Children may wonder why they should listen to the teacher and cooperate with each other, giving their best effort, when the teacher does not cooperate with other adults or give a good effort. Teachers must foster a sense of individual importance and belonging not only among their students but among adults who work with them. Besides, children are not the only individuals who are in need of love and acceptance in the school. Administrators, faculty members, staff, and community members are also in need of respect, love, and acceptance. This love and acceptance is expressed through team work and collegiality. It is very unlikely that a teacher will establish a positive socioemotional environment in the classroom while relating poorly with members of the larger social environment of the school.

CLASS REWARDS

All classrooms have a reward dimension. When students engage in desired behaviors, they are rewarded, through intrinsic or extrinsic means, and when students engage in undesirable behaviors, they are deprived of rewards or experience consequences for their actions. Learning activities are also a great source of rewards for students. Until lately, the learning reward dimension of the classroom had not been widely discussed. But since the introduction of cooperative learning, a greater awareness and discussion of the possible classroom reward dimensions has occurred. Johnson and Johnson (1985) and Stallings and Stipek (1986), among others, have studied the effects of competitive, cooperative, and individualized learning approaches on student attitudes and achievement. Researchers have identified three types of learning environments which are produced according to the manner in which students interact with each other. Students may compete to see who is best; students may work cooperatively, exhibiting concern for each other's learning; and students may work individualistically toward a goal, without concern for the goals of others.

Effects of Competitive Learning Environments

Competitive learning environments tend to discourage students who are not performing successfully. These environments divide the students into winners and losers and emphasize comparisons and extrinsic motivation. Students measure their progress in terms of the progress of others, regardless of individual abilities and effort. Students who cannot keep up become discouraged. An overcompetitive environment promotes lack of concern for the success of others. It may even discourage students from spending time assisting and helping other students who do not understand the material.

In the field of sports, careful matchings of size and abilities are made before students engage in competition. No one shouts victory when a bigger and stronger player defeats a smaller and weaker one, or when the varsity team beats the freshmen team. Furthermore, after a few defeats, the freshman team will refuse to come to the field and the varsity team will have lost interest in this type of unmatched competition. In the competitive classroom, however, the attitude seems to be, "Let the best students win!" As a result, a few students win most of the time and a few students lose most of the time. This last group of students finally drops out.

Competition in sports and business is frequently balanced by cooperation. Teams of individuals with different talents work together to be the best. Team members support each other and value each other's diversity and different abilities. In the competitive classroom, it is "Every man for himself!" There is no team and there is no cooperation. Students learn to work alone and to ignore the needs of others. Those students who are overcompetitive become lonely and are frequently anxious that someone better than they will appear. They come to love tests because they confirm their superiority. They feel that they cannot have a true measure of their worth unless they are competing and being tested. They have become victims of the system and live in constant need to match and compare themselves with others. They cannot find peace and company with other students since other students are potential competitors. And they have not learned this ruthless way in the American field of sports or business. They have learned it in the primary school classroom! Overcompetitive learning contexts severely damage the socioemotional environment of the classroom.

Effects of Cooperative Learning Environments

Cooperative learning environments tend to promote more learning than competitive or individualistic experiences. Those students who perform in the lowest of three levels in the classroom appear to gain the most in cooperative settings while the middle and upper third achieve less dramatic gains (Johnson & Johnson, 1985). Cooperative learning experiences seem to promote the following: higher motivation to learn, particularly intrinsic motivation; higher levels of self-esteem; greater acceptance of differences; and improvement of interaction among students of different ethnic backgrounds and among nonhandicapped and handicapped students.

Effects of Individualistic Learning Environments

Individualistic learning environments are those in which students work, for the most part, at their own pace and by themselves toward the attainment of basic skills and subject matter knowledge. The curriculum is presented through individualized instructional materials, and the students interact with learning materials or one-on-one with the teacher. In this type of learning environment, students develop a strong sense of individual responsibility and direction. Students must assume responsibility for their own learning and make commitments to master their objectives. They must decide how much time and effort to put forth in order to accomplish this. Individualized instruction develops strong intrinsic motivation and autonomy in students.

It must be evident to the reader that all three types of learning environments—cooperative, individualistic, and competitive—have beneficial effects on students and on the socioemotional environment of the classroom. The classroom learning activities should provide a balance of cooperative, individualistic, and competitive situations. Teachers should consider deemphasizing competitive contexts, however, especially in the primary grades. When students are placed in a competitive context, success should be measured by the sum of several criteria rather than by academic achievement only. Critical thinking, writing style, artistic presentation of the learning material, creativity, and originality are some of the factors to keep in mind when assessing individual student performance. While individualized learning and cooperative learning have been introduced through seminars and courses, competitive learning is the approach which has been traditionally utilized in many classrooms. The main fault with competitive learning environments is the narrowness of their aim, that is, academic achievement, as measured by the teacher or standardized tests, frequently at the expense of student creativity, divergent thinking, and artistic expression. They reflect a lack of awareness of the variety of ways to learn and achieve

Types of Rewards and Their Effects

The learning reward structure is not the only factor which affects the reward dimension of the classroom. The teacher, through the use of rewards and consequences for student behavior, influences the nature of the classroom climate. Deci and Ryan (1985) and Stipek (1988) warn about the possibly negative effects of extrinsic rewards which may erode intrinsic motivation and reduce motivation to participate in the activity once the extrinsic rewards are eliminated. Nevertheless, teachers in elementary classrooms sometimes feel the need to use extrinsic rewards in order to stimulate students to engage in some activities which do not seem appealing, or because some students do not seem to respond, at first, to intrinsic rewards.

Intrinsic rewards are those derived from the activity itself, for example, the pleasure of learning, becoming more competent at something, or solving a challenging problem. Extrinsic rewards may be intangible or tangible. Intangible rewards consist mainly of giving attention to students through verbal recognition or display of their work. Tangible rewards consist of symbols such as certificates, happy faces, stickers or, material rewards such as small toys, books, games, pencils, and food. Intangible rewards are easier to give. Symbols require some time to prepare and involve modest cost. Material rewards are costly and difficult to provide on a frequent basis.

The types of rewards teachers use affect the socioemotional climate of the classroom. Intrinsic rewards are self-renewing, place little demands on the teacher, and foster student autonomy. Extrinsic verbal and social recognitions contribute to a positive climate, and, if used moderately, do not reduce student autonomy. Extrinsic symbolic rewards shift the focus of control from inner motivation and the enjoyment of learning toward receiving something for working, for example, stickers. Material rewards may erode the positive climate of the classroom since students will eventually require more and more tangible incentives in order to work. "What do I get for doing this work?" and "What's in it for me?" will be asked more frequently as students become more demanding.

Types of Consequences and Their Effects

Consequences for inappropriate classroom behavior have a very significant impact on the socioemotional climate of the classroom. There are three major types of consequences: **natural** consequences, **logical** consequences, and **penalties**.

Natural consequences are the natural results of an action. For example, if a student plays with food and soils her skirt, she spends the remainder of the day walking around the school with a soiled skirt. If a student uses a new pen to dig a hole on the playground, his pen is no longer new. If a student is rude to a friend, her friend will not associate with her any longer. If a student has not completed an assignment, he will not be able to answer questions when the teacher calls on him. All these are natural consequences of student behavior. Natural consequences are the best deterrent to inappropriate behavior because they occur automatically, without the intervention of the teacher.

Logical consequences are utilized when natural consequences do not occur. For example, a student may scratch the surface of her desk and not care about having an ugly looking desk. Or a student may be rude to another student and not care about losing the friendship of the other student. Or a student may neglect to complete an assignment yet have no concern about what the teacher or the rest of the class thinks. Logical consequences are enforced by the teacher. The student who scratched the desk top will have to stay after school to sand it and varnish it. The student who was rude to another student will have to write a brief letter of apology. The student who did not complete the assignment will have to stay after school to complete it. A student who ruins the bathroom wall with graffiti may have to repay, on reasonable weekly installments, the cost of the paint and labor needed to refurbish the wall. Logical consequences are individualized and time consuming. Teachers can not always use them. When neither natural nor logical consequences are effective, penalties are utilized as deterrents to inappropriate student behavior.

Penalties are not naturally or logically linked to the misbehavior. But because penalties are unpleasant, they function as deterrents. Staying after school, referral to the principal, loss of recess, being forced to eat lunch alone, and demerits are some examples of penalties. Penalties are most efficient at the beginning of the school year when the teacher does not have time to assign logical consequences to student misbehavior. They are also effective with unruly groups of students. As soon as a positive socioemotional and working climate has been established in the classroom, teachers should shift from using penalties to using logical consequences.

The main factor in the distribution of rewards in the classroom should ultimately be the student. The student must learn to derive intrinsic rewards out of learning activities—to enjoy learning activities for their own value. Students must also learn to seek social rewards provided in the classroom such as the esteem of teacher and peers which can be won by behaving in conformity with their expectations. Students must also learn to avoid the negative consequences which are associated with the violation of classroom rules and peer behavior norms. The teacher is a very important factor in the distribution of rewards. The teacher can help students find meaning and satisfaction in their work. She can also provide verbal rewards or more tangible rewards such as stickers or popcorn. Peers are also a source of reward or punishment since they accept certain behaviors and reject others. The teacher must exert influence on the norms of behavior that peers establish in the classroom.

Through a balanced use of competitive, cooperative, and individualized learning approaches, as well as through the appropriate use of rewards and consequences, effective teachers establish and maintain a positive classroom atmosphere.

SELF-CONCEPT AND TEACHER EXPECTATIONS

The socioemotional climate of the classroom is influenced by the sum of the feelings and perceptions of individual students. How individuals feel about learning, how they feel about the teacher and their peers, and how they perceive the teacher's views about them, are critical factors in determining the affective climate of the classroom and the achievement of students. In the section about human relations skills, emphasis was placed on the quality of human interactions within the social dimension of the classroom. In this section, emphasis is placed on the student's self-concept and the teacher's expectations for each student. We will discuss how student performance is affected by: 1) how students view themselves, 2) how parents view their children, 3) how teachers view their students, and 4) how students view each other.

The views that students have about themselves, or **self-concepts,** are the result of their histories of success and failure. They are also a product of how significant others have viewed them throughout their early years (Combs & Snyggs, 1959). Research shows a relationship between self-concept and academic achievement (Purkey, 1970). The successful student has a relatively high opinion of himself and is optimistic about the future. The unsuccessful student tends to feel less confident about himself and less adequate than others. This view of self influences school achievement, and school achievement influences one's sense of self-worth.

All students walk into the first day of school with a "history" which may be positive or negative. If students have succeeded at mastering life tasks, such as getting along with others, playing, and learning, they will walk into the classroom with a predisposition to continue mastering the challenges that school will present. When students have somehow failed at mastering many of life's tasks, or the school doesn't play by the same rules they learned in their home and neighborhood, they walk into the classroom with a low opinion of their abilities and a predisposition to look at challenges as invitations for further failure and confirmation of their lack of worth. The longer the history of failure, the greater the predisposition to look at learning tasks pessimistically. "I am not good at reading," "I am not very smart," and "I am bad at math" are examples of attitudes which can result. Conversely, those students with a history of success will have a high opinion of themselves as learners and a strong sense of personal worth.

Most individuals tend to protect their sense of worth. They may take personal responsibility for their successes, but will attribute their failures to external conditions beyond their control (Covington, 1984) and will employ creative strategies to preserve their sense of worth when faced with failure situations. Students decrease their degree of school failure by minimizing their degree of participation. Or they "do not try" so that their failure will not imply that they are not capable of succeeding. Students seem to prefer the disapproval of the teacher to the attribution that they are not capable when confronted with learning situations where they might fail (Covington et al., 1980). Another strategy for avoiding the feeling of failure and incompetence is for students to set unattainable goals. Failing at doing the impossible does not imply low ability, while failing at any easy task suggests lack of ability. Another strategy is to assure success through cheating, or to attempt only very easy tasks, or to have very low aspirations.

The perceptions which students have about themselves are also influenced by the views that significant others, such as parents and teachers, have of them and their abilities. Students with a history of home and school support, whose parents and teachers have had positive perceptions about their abilities and have accepted and loved them for their own worth, have a better view of self than students whose parents and teachers have put them down frequently, or have expressed doubts about their worth.

The views of parents about their children are also a result of a history of success and failure. Parenting skills are a great influence on the early experiences of children and their self-concept, that is, on whether the child succeeds frequently or fails frequently. Some parents are more skillful than others at teaching their children life skills. Their language is descriptive, accepting and assertive. These parents provide home environments in which children have opportunities to experience challenge, respect, autonomy, warmth, and success. Other parents lack parenting skills and provide early opportunities for rejection, disrespect, dependence, and failure. The children of all these parents come to the classroom with their individual histories of success and failure, and with individual expectations that are shaped by their parents' views of them. Some of these parental views will influence children for the rest of their lives and become self-fulfilling prophecies.

Can teachers and schools make a difference? Although Coleman concluded, in 1966, that environmental factors impacted the futures of children more than the efforts of schools, the effective schools movement of the late 1970s and early 1980s has demonstrated that teachers and schools can make a difference even when children come to school with a negative history and a negative view of self.

Teacher expectations may also be self-fulfilling. Positive teacher expectations about student achievement is a variable that separates teachers whose students attain significant gains from teachers whose students do not achieve as much (Brophy & Evertson, 1976). Students who are perceived by teachers as high achievers receive different treatment than students who are perceived by teachers as low achievers. Teachers smile at high achievers more often, look at them more frequently, stand closer to them, interact more with them, give them more material to learn and more difficult assignments, call on them more often, wait longer for them to answer, provide more detailed feedback, express dissatisfaction when they perform poorly, and praise them more frequently (Brophy & Good, 1974; Rosenthal, 1974; Rist, 1970). Students whose teachers have high expectations for them receive many more opportunities to learn than students whose teachers have low expectations for them. Students whose teachers have high expectations for them also receive greater emotional support than students whose teachers have low expectations. Teacher support for students influences student achievement indirectly by affecting the beliefs that students have about their own abilities and their likelihood of success.

Teacher expectations are, to a significant degree, based on the past performance and behavior of their students (West & Anderson, 1976). Once initial interpretations about children's learning and behavior are developed, it is difficult for teachers to correct them. Furthermore, information contrary to a particular expectation may not be noticed, even if it is present. Teachers interact hundreds of times a day with children (Jackson, 1968). It is easy for teachers to miss information which contradicts their expectations. Once expectations are developed, teachers tend to behave as if they were true. And by behaving as if the expectations were true, they assure that they are fulfilled. After a few cycles of success or failure, students begin to be affected both by the amount of learning opportunities they receive and by the labels they begin to assign to themselves. The teachers' expectations become more firm, and so do the students' perceptions of self as good learners or poor learners. At the point when both teacher and student have developed a self-fulfilling prophecy for their individual behaviors, it is very difficult to change perceptions and resulting actions. As time passes, the student who is perceived as successful by the teacher, and accordingly, by self, will do better, and the student perceived as mediocre will do worse.

When a teacher "inherits" a student who has been labeled a failure, and who behaves in ways which perpetuate failure, it will not be easy to change such a self-fulfilling prophecy, particularly if these failure experiences also exist at home. If the teacher is unable to turn events around and the student continues to do poorly, the situation will become worse as time passes by. In a few short years, such students will be ready to drop out of school in order to avoid such experiences of failure and to protect their sense of self-worth.

How can teachers turn histories of failures around? They can do it step by step, day by day, and with a lot of effort, hope and acceptance. It is impossible to convince a student that five years of failure in reading are not an indication of poor reading skills. It is even more difficult to convince him that he could eventually become a good reader. They only way to restore confidence is to prove to students that they can take one step and master a particular skill, take another step and master another skill, etc. School history has to be thrown out the window. Every day has to be a new day. Nothing can be done about the past, but "today we can learn" (Glasser, 1969).

It is impossible for teachers not to form expectations, or to have only high expectations for all their students. Teachers cannot easily control their expectations since these frequently develop without teachers being aware of them. But teachers can control their behavior within their own classrooms. They should give students opportunities to achieve to their highest potential. Stipek (1988) has four recommendations for teachers to avoid the effects of negative expectations:

1. The initial impressions of skill level and learning ability which the teacher formulates should be based on reliable information.
2. Teacher expectations should be flexible and fluid.
3. Teacher behavior toward low and high performing students alike should not differ unless there is a good reason for this to occur.
4. Teachers should not give up on a student.

Peer expectations are seldom discussed, although it is broadly recognized that peer influence is an important factor in the behavior of individual students. Peer expectations toward other students are formed partly as a result of what peers hear the teacher say about that student, how the teacher interacts with that student, and how the peers assess that student. Teachers may influence the perceptions of peers about a student in both positive and negative ways. As a general rule, teachers should relate to individual students privately, recognizing the fact that each student is different and develops at a different rate and manner. Corrections should be made as much as possible in private, while compliments may be given in public. In this manner, the teacher enhances the image of each student in front of other students.

The peer group can reinforce and magnify the impact of the beliefs of a teacher on a particular student. This holds true both for positive and negative beliefs. Many students experience negative self-fulfilling prophecies from their teacher and also experience this with their classmates. Conversely, high achieving students frequently receive a large dose of positive expectations from their classmates as a result of what the peer group notices about the expectations and behaviors which the teacher holds for those students. Effective teachers make sure that the peer group becomes a positive force in the classroom, supporting the learning of each student, rather than a destructive force which reinforces failure and helps further demoralize individuals. Cooperative classroom environments are a way of fostering positive peer support.

When peer group expectations and values run counter to the expectations and values of the school, the peer group becomes a tremendous negative force. Students who do well academically are harassed. In these circumstances, to behave is "not cool," and to undermine the efforts of the teacher is "cool."

Students who come from depressed and poor urban areas at times exhibit this form of alienation and hate toward the values the school stands for. These students see school as the enemy, and they see teachers as the instruments of an unkind society. Schools located in socioeconomically depressed neighborhoods with high rates of unemployment and crime cannot operate on the assumption that students come to the classroom to learn and follow rules. These school have to "sell" their value to the children, and to their parents, who themselves may have had negative personal experiences in the past which made them distrustful of schooling and teachers. Establishing an appropriate socioemotional climate and a positive personal feeling for each student is important in every classroom; but, in schools attended by socially disaffected children, it is the cornerstone, without which no other goals can be attempted and attained. When students feel that they are loved and accepted, they are more likely to try harder and succeed.

But children from socioeconomically depressed neighborhoods are not the only ones who come to school disaffected. There are many children from all types of socio-economic environments who come to school emotionally disabled, lacking appropriate social skills and attitudes toward learning, and feeling neglected and unaccepted. It is paramount that elementary teachers provide classroom environments which are emotionally supportive and offer fair opportunities for all students to achieve. Adults do not like to lose and find themselves without support. They tend to avoid activities in which they might become losers. Children do not like to lose, either, nor, do they like to find themselves without the support of the teacher. But, unlike adults, children cannot escape the classroom. To fail day after day, to go home feeling like a loser, and to have to return the next day to lose again, is a tough destiny for a child. Elementary classrooms must be places where the feelings of children are uplifted, not torn apart. Few experiences can be more damaging to the feelings of children than low teacher expectations and repeated failure.

VALUES

Since its early beginnings, American education has made the development of values among learners one of its major purposes. The Puritans in New England saw schooling as a place where children would learn to read the Bible and be strictly disciplined to become productive members of the community. A century later, the founding fathers saw education as the means to prepare a civilized citizenry which would make democracy feasible. In the nineteenth century, when common schools became firmly established, children from a variety of ethnic backgrounds and languages came to school to learn the American language and the American culture. In this century, until the 1950s, schools emphasized the development of the whole child, that is, the intellectual, moral, and physical sides of the child.

Since 1950, an essentialist view of education, which claims that children need only learn the subjects which are necessary for successful work in society, has emphasized the intellectual development of students and frowned on the teaching of values, which are supposed to be the responsibility of the home. This approach has challenged the traditional view of American schools as places where children are helped to develop morally, and has gradually gained public support, particularly among conservative groups. Presently, a division of opinion exists among the American public in terms of the purposes of schools. While many continue to support the goals of developing the whole person, others oppose any curriculum which deviates from the teaching of academics. The back to the basics movement of the late 1970s and 1980s exemplifies this way of thinking. The proponents of this emphasis are usually citizens who have become disaffected and distrustful toward schools and who are critical of the the achievement of students in American schools as they appear to be falling behind others students from industrialized nations.

Regardless of the controversy over the teaching of values, teachers have known for a long time that they teach values, explicitly or implicitly. A great part of the early elementary curriculum is dedicated to socializing children, for example, teaching them to respect others and their property, how to share, how to be honest, work hard, and not cheat. Whether they do or don't want to, teachers teach values about learning. Students learn to pursue knowledge for its own sake or in order to get the rewards given by the teacher. There are values taught about human nature. Students learn to trust or distrust people, to be egocentric or to cooperate. There are values taught about the appropriateness of self-disclosure. Students learn that feelings are to be kept to oneself, or that it is okay to share feelings. And there are values taught about socioeconomic status. Students learn that those with money and influence get their way, or that all students are treated fairly.

As teachers work, their individual style, professional competence, view of life, degree of courtesy, and ethics are modeled day after day for the children, who tend to imitate these behaviors. These experiences to which children are exposed, which are not necessarily prescribed in their program, are called the "hidden curriculum." It is impossible to teach academics without impacting the beliefs, emotions, and values of children. The essentialist view that only subject matter must be taught in schools is unrealistic. Schools produce affective outcomes as well as cognitive outcomes.

Teachers must be very aware of the existence of this hidden curriculum and make sure that it becomes explicit rather than implicit, conscious rather than subconscious, purposeful rather than aimless. As teachers plan for instruction and identify learning objectives, they must take into account the affective outcomes which will be part of the lesson, examining them in order to make sure they are appropriate for their particular groups of students. Teachers must not only ask themselves what content or skills the students will learn as a result of a particular lesson. They must also ask what affective outcomes, beliefs and values will be reinforced as a result of any lesson. By addressing the affective domain of learning, teachers minimize the unexamined impact of the hidden curriculum on children.

As you can see, we firmly believe that values should be addressed in the educational program of the school. But how do teachers foster the development of values? We have already identified the most powerful approach: teacher modeling. The behaviors of the teacher will be carefully observed and learned by many students.

In order to better understand how to foster the development of values, it is important to distinguish between two types of values: **core values** and **personal values.** The values on which we all agree—liberty, honesty, justice, private property, and work ethics—are considered *core* values of our culture. They are incorporated into our historical, legal, and judicial documents, and can be traced to our folklore and literature. National heroes have lived lives which exemplify these core values. Few would object to the development of core values among children in the classroom. There are other values on which it is more difficult to reach societal consensus: they may be called *personal* values. They represent individual interpretations of the core values. Religious preferences, moral choices, political and economic views, for example, are based on core values, but they become personal values when individuals make different decisions and choices based on them.

It is obvious that schools must promote the development of core values without prescribing the choice of personal values. Core values may be taught while personal values may not. What can teachers do to help students develop core values? How can core values be promoted in the classroom? The following six practices should help teachers to do this.

1. Stressing classroom practices which respect the rights of others, freedom, equality, honesty, and independence of thought.
2. Studying the history and traditions of the nation and emphasizing the values which have guided it.
3. Reading about individuals whose lives exemplify our core values.
4. Studying the American legal and judicial system.
5. Discussing the values portrayed in literary works and news media.
6. Studying the values of societies different from ours.

Personal values can not be promoted in the classroom in the same manner that core values can be promoted. While core values may be taught, personal values must be developed by the student. How can teachers help students develop their personal values? They can teach them the process of valuing without prescribing the outcomes. The classroom, then, becomes a rich environment in which discussion about values occurs and students learn to make their own choices. The teacher identifies value conflicts which appear in literature, history, the fine arts and sports, and has the students study the conflicts and evaluate the choices made by literary or historical characters. This type of critical thinking coincides with Bloom's evaluation level on the taxonomy (1956) which calls for using standards or criteria to make judgments about the value of an idea or event.

Another approach to foster the development of personal values is the "values clarification" process designed by Raths, Harmin and Simon (1978). They suggest that, to foster the clarification of personal values in children, teachers should

1. Encourage students to make value choices, freely.
2. Help students think of alternatives to a conflict.
3. Help students reflect on the consequences of each possible choice.
4. Encourage students to identify what is important to them.
5. Provide opportunities for students to act in accordance with their choices.
6. Help students become aware of behavior patterns in their school life.

The teacher may use classroom conflicts, as well as situations found in the materials studied, to build a consciousness of values and help children to identify what is important to them. Some programs include values clarification exercises which present the pupils with moral dilemmas to be resolved. We recommend that core and personal values be fostered within the context of the curriculum and through daily classroom events rather than through specially designed values clarifications exercises. Above all, teachers must constantly be reflecting on the values they are modeling in order to bring the hidden curriculum to a conscious and purposeful educational level.

GLOSSARY

accepting language Language which identifies and accepts a student's feelings (about learning, the teacher, or other students).

active listening A form of accepting language in which the teacher actively listens and accepts the feelings of others.

assertive language Language in which the teacher clearly states what she wants students to do or how particular student behaviors affect her.

core values The values on which we all agree in our culture; for example, our ideas about liberty, justice, and private property.

descriptive language Language which communicates to students what is happening.

extrinsic motivation Motivation brought on by forces outside oneself; for example, motivation for rewards—or fear of punishment—coming from persons other than oneself.

hidden curriculum Values to which children are exposed in schools even though these values are not articulated in the school curriculum. For example, teachers often transmit their personal values as they interact with their students in school.

I message A form of assertive language in which teachers communicate to students how their off-task behaviors affect them.

intrinsic motivation Actions which are performed by persons because they believe such actions to be valuable in themselves.

judgmental language Language which attaches evaluative labels to student behaviors.

logical consequences Consequences which are enforced by the teacher when natural consequences do not motivate a student to change behavior. Logical consequences are always related to the inappropriate behavior which the teacher is trying to get the student to stop performing; for example, the student who writes on the wall will be required to clean that wall.

method I An approach to conflict resolution in which the teacher wins and the students lose.

method II An approach to conflict resolution in which the students win and the teacher loses.

method III An approach to conflict resolution in which both teacher and students have their needs met.

natural consequences The natural results of actions; for example, if a student plays with food and spills food on his shirt, he will go through the rest of the day with a dirty shirt.

off-task behavior Student actions which cannot be classified as classroom activities which are approved by the teacher.

penalties Consequences which are enforced by the teacher when neither natural or logical consequences motivate the student to change behavior; for example, requiring a student to stay after school for talking when talking was not allowed.

personal values The individual interpretations of core values; for example, religious beliefs or political opinions.

proactive classroom management An approach to classroom management in which the teacher prevents possible problems through positive interventions.

reactive classroom management An approach to classroom management in which the teacher waits for problems to arise before intervening.

socioemotional dimension That aspect of classroom life which deals with social interaction and the emotions of the students and the teacher.

win-win A form of conflict resolution in which both parties come out of the disagreement with some of their needs met.

Chapter
8

Classroom Management: Considering the Teaching-Learning Environment

THE TEACHING-LEARNING ENVIRONMENT

*A*ccording to one study, elementary school teachers have over 500 exchanges with students each day! (Doyle, 1986, p. 394) Elementary classrooms are a fast-paced environment which require teachers to perform a variety of tasks. Some of these tasks may have little or no bearing on actual instruction. In a study of selected classrooms, one educational researcher discovered that only about half of the acts of the teachers whom he studied had anything to do with instruction! (Doyle, 1986, p. 399) The rest of the teachers' actions were related to organizing and arranging instruction, dealing with misbehavior, and handling individual problems. Teachers spend a high percentage of their time *managing* the teaching-learning environments in their classrooms.

How Teaching and Management Are Related

Most people would assume that effective classroom management is necessary in order for teaching and learning to occur. However, few people seem aware that teachers also make use of their teaching actions to achieve better control (Doyle, 1986, p. 394). While studying the classroom behaviors of a first-year teacher, Louisell discovered that teachers may sometimes use questions for the purposes of focusing the attention of their students and achieving better control (Louisell, 1979). In a study of teaching in junior high school classes in which disruptive student behavior occurred frequently, another author found that successful managers tended to push the curriculum. These teachers preferred to discuss school work with their students rather than to talk about misbehavior (Doyle, 1986, p. 411).

Classroom management and teaching appear to occupy a "two-way street." Teachers need to effectively manage their students in order to facilitate a positive teaching-learning environment. However, teachers are expected to manage their students effectively regardless of how well they teach them. While it is true that good management will facilitate teaching and learning, it is also true that focusing on academic tasks can help a teacher to achieve control of his students. In some cases, focusing on academic tasks may even help the teacher achieve control at the expense of good instruction. For example, a student may finish her classroom assignments early because she knows the content very well. However, the teacher may assign this student more work, dealing with the same content, because he wants to keep her busy and "out of trouble."

The best way to sum up this confusing relationship is to say that elementary teachers do things in their classrooms for at least two reasons. First, they want to accomplish some instruction. Second, they want to achieve control of their students. Sometimes these two goals relate to each other. When they do relate, a teacher can use one goal to achieve the other. Sometimes these two goals do not relate to each other. When they do not relate to each other, they may be in conflict. This is what happened in the example above in which a teacher assigned extra work to a student in order to keep her from getting into trouble. Doyle sums up the relationship between management and learning by saying that they are two goals which coexist in the same classroom (Doyle, 1986, p. 395).

How Teaching-Learning Environments Are Kept Going

Whether a teacher is attempting to help his students learn or is simply trying to control them, he must direct a stream of activity which includes interactions among the teacher and his students. This stream of activity includes several key strategies. These strategies, and their relationships to each other, are depicted in Figure 8.1, below (Louisell, 1979).

One can debate whether teachers control their students so that they can teach them something or whether they may sometimes teach their students something so that they can control them. Both of these arguments could be correct at different times! However one answers this question, we will all agree that elementary teachers do try to **teach something** (Box 1). In order to teach whatever it is that they are trying to teach, they **provide experiences** (Box 2). These experiences may take the form of lessons, activities, or field trips. They may involve teacher supervision or they may involve some type of independent work on the part of the student. When teachers provide these experiences, they do so because they intend to help the students learn what the teachers are trying to teach them. At least, that should be the teacher's reason for providing many of the experiences which he provides.

If the experience which a teacher has provided is self-motivating for one's students, then they will readily attend to it. However, if the experience is not self-motivating to any of the students, then the teacher will have to expend some effort attempting to **get the student(s) to attend** (Box 3). Once the student is attending, a whole series of teacher behaviors (Boxes 4–11) must be utilized in order to keep the teaching-learning situation going.

But students do not always stay involved with the experience which has been provided by the teacher, and when they are not involved with it, problems with management and instruction inevitably occur. Management problems occur because students who are not occupied productively will sometimes distract others. Instructional problems occur because students who don't stay involved with the experience will probably not learn what the teacher is trying to teach them. Because of each of these concerns, the teacher must direct some of his efforts towards **keeping the students involved** (Box 4) and **keeping track** of what each of the students are doing (Box 5).

Keeping track (Box 5) requires that the teacher be aware of which students have completed the experience which has been provided, which students are involved or not involved with it, etc. This behavior often necessitates another strategy on the part of the

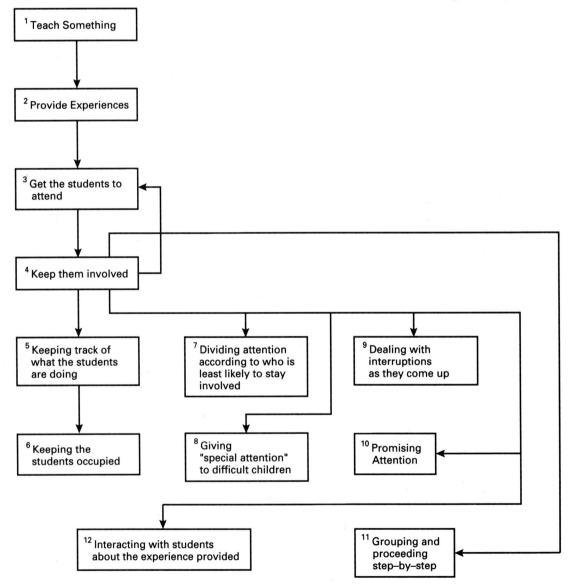

Figure 8.1 The Teacher's Management Concerns

teacher, **keeping the students occupied** (Box 6). Students who have finished an assigned activity must be given something else to do so that they will not become a distraction to other students in one's classroom. Also, it is the teacher's responsibility to teach these students well. If they have completed the experience which has been provided, they are probably ready to tackle a more challenging task.

Citing Kounin's study on classroom management, Doyle explained that a teacher's ability to monitor or keep track of one's students is a key to successful classroom management. Kounin found that teachers whose students had high levels of work involvement and low levels of misbehavior were aware of what was going on in the classroom, were able to communicate that awareness to students, and were able to keep track of two or more events at the same time (Doyle, 1986, p. 414). According to another study, teachers monitor three types of things: 1) Groups, 2) Student conduct or behavior, and 3) The pace, rhythm, and duration of classroom events. Doyle also says that while teachers may monitor individuals, they do this by focusing on groups and observing whether the behaviors which they expect to occur are in fact occurring.

We have discussed the various ways in which teachers group their students elsewhere in this book. The grouping arrangements which a teacher makes use of in his classroom can affect his classroom management. Whenever a teacher divides his class into subgroups or assigns activities which are to be completed independently, the teacher is faced with the problem of how to divide his attention. Some teachers **divide** their **attention by giving it first to those children who are least likely to stay involved** (Box 7). By doing this, the teacher helps to insure that no students will get off task or create distractions for others.

Although we do not recommend this practice, many teachers—especially beginners—**give special attention to their most difficult students** (Box 8). Like the strategy depicted in Box 7, this (Box 8) strategy also helps to prevent students from creating a disturbance. One must be careful about using this strategy, however. Although it has the potential to reach and help students who have not been succeeding in the school environment, it also has the potential to create resentment among students who have been cooperative and involved all along!

When teachers make use of groups and independent activities for classroom instruction, interruptions are bound to occur. Students will need to seek help from their teachers and ask questions about their assignments. How should a teacher handle these interruptions? Some teachers **deal with interruptions as they come up** (Box 9). By handling interruptions in this way, they believe that they are preventing distractions. As one first-year teacher said:

> When somebody interrupts, I feel that the person I'm helping is going to be there with me, and, if I don't help the person who's interrupting—it could cause more problems (Louisell, 1979, p. 80).

But this approach has its own problems. Some children are less assertive than other in seeking help from the teacher. These children could be neglected by such an approach. As one experienced teacher said:

> If I just let the kids come up and see me, then there are going to be, like, six kids that are going to dominate my time. . . . Some of the kids that will need me . . . they'll [just] sit there. So, rather than have these six kids keep me tied up wherever I'm standing, I want everybody to stay put. I can come around, identify problems quickly . . . (Louisell, 1979, p. 82).

Promising attention (Box 10) is a strategy which teachers employ as they try to juggle the various activities which are going on simultaneously in their classrooms. By promising future attention to a student ("I'll be with you in just a minute"), the teacher helps to keep students involved with their schoolwork even though he is unable to help them at the moment when he gives this promise. Of course, if a teacher consistently fails to deliver on these promises, students will cease to take his promises seriously and classroom management problems will result. Doyle found that teachers tend to become involved with an activity and stay involved with it until it can continue without their involvement. In the meantime, students are usually expected to wait until the teacher is free. They are also expected to do something to fill that waiting time (Doyle, 1986, p. 405). Promising attention may be a teacher's way of reinforcing that expectation.

Regardless of how you decide to divide your attention, deal with difficult students, or handle interruptions, you should be aware that you will have to deal with these problems routinely when you are teaching in a classroom. Perhaps the strongest reason why traditional teaching approaches have survived for so long has to do with the way that grouping as a whole class circumvents so many of the problems identified in Boxes 5–11.

When a teacher **takes the whole class through a lesson step-by-step** (Box 11), or page-by-page, it is far easier for him to keep track of what the students are doing (Box 5). After all, each one of them is supposed to be doing the same thing! Since they each do the same thing at the same time, there is no need to keep students occupied when they have finished early (Box 6). They *can't* finish early! Attention does not have to be divided between groups (Box 7), interruptions will be less frequent (Box 9), and the teacher will not have to promise attention (Box 10) in order to "buy time" and keep his students on task until he is able to assist them. No wonder so many teachers prefer the graded approach to the nongraded!

But for those teachers who provide a multitude of experiences for different students during the same time segment because they are attempting to be responsive to the individual needs of their students, the strategies depicted in Boxes 5–10 are inevitable. In addition, one more strategy may be necessary. In Box 12, teachers **interact** with their students **about the provided experience**. They may do this with individuals or with small groups. They may do so very briefly in order to check on a student's progress or provide a brief explanation about the task. Or they may do so extensively in order to discuss details related to the content which the students are studying. This strategy helps the teacher to keep track (Box 5) and to keep the student involved. It also helps the teacher to "stretch" the student's goals, understandings, and expectations. For example, by discussing content with their students, teachers may be able to make them aware of details or concepts which they had not previously considered. Even during activities as simple as supervised seatwork, some management studies have indicated that effective teachers monitor their classes thoroughly, inspect individual papers frequently, and "generally hover over the work and usher it along" (Doyle, 1986, p. 416).

The Teacher's Management of Time

With experience, elementary teachers acquire the ability to estimate and manage their time. Beginning elementary teachers try to do the same, but they have usually not had enough experience to estimate very accurately. For example, college students majoring in elementary education typically experience difficulty managing time during the practicum. Some students plan lessons which they expect to take about 25 minutes but discover, when they actually teach the lessons to their students, that the lessons take only three minutes! In this case, the unfortunate education major has 22 minutes during which he must keep his students occupied. (Box 6 of Figure 8.1). Just as frequently, the opposite occurs. The student has planned a lesson which he believes will take about 25 minutes when in reality he needs several days to complete the lesson.

Louisell (1979) has described an outstanding beginning teacher who nevertheless had to struggle with her management of time. This teacher was conducting a language experience lesson during which the students drew pictures to depict their Halloween trick-or-treat experiences. The teacher called each student to her individually to talk about his or her drawing. While listening to her students, the teacher then took dictation from her students, writing their words verbatim underneath their drawings. She listened to each talkative child and wrote what was said. With the less talkative ones, she prompted them with questions until they volunteered more information. During the beginning of the lesson, each child had three or four sentences recorded underneath his or her picture. As the lesson continued, however, this teacher allowed less time for each student to talk. The number of sentences recorded was reduced to one. Finally, with the last student, the bell for outdoor recess rang. The student wanted to continue telling his teacher about his picture. The teacher asked this student to try to "remember it in your [his] head" until the next day.

The teacher whom we have described was an excellent beginning teacher. Like most beginners, however, she could not estimate accurately how long a given activity might take to accomplish with a class of six year olds. She knew, however, that her cooperation with other teachers would require her to finish her lesson at a designated time. For the last 10–15 minutes of her lesson, she had been racing against time in an effort to complete an interesting lesson in time for her students to be able to go out to recess. There is nothing wrong with what she did. With experience, she will acquire an ability to more accurately estimate the amount of time which will be needed in order to complete a given activity.

We know of no way to accelerate this teacher's development of the ability to estimate and manage time. We do know, however, that you will need to pay careful attention to your estimates of time during your first few years of teaching. Even experienced teachers often estimate incorrectly, but their estimates are far more accurate than those of the beginners whom we have described. The best advice we can give you on this topic is to make careful estimates prior to beginning a lesson and then be flexible about adapting your teaching when you discover that you have estimated incorrectly.

The Socialization Process

Earlier in this chapter, we pointed out that instruction is not the only goal which teachers pursue in their classrooms. For example, they must also focus on their classroom control. In addition to these goals, we must add a third goal, one which occupies elementary teachers more than most people realize. In fact, all teachers spend much of their time teaching students to be responsible and to behave appropriately in classrooms (Doyle, 1986, p. 396–397). Teachers are preparing their students to successfully participate as adults in their society. Instructing children in particular skills (e.g., how to read) and information (e.g., Sacramento is the capital of California) is only one aspect of this large task.

The whole process of preparing children to function successfully in their society also involves the transmission of certain cultural values. For example, before they participate successfully in their adult society, children must learn to be responsible about completing work and completing their work to the best of their ability (Louisell, 1979). Of course, children don't typically master these types of things until they *are* adults, but teachers are nevertheless expected to begin teaching children about these things during their first days of school. This process of accustoming children to the values and procedures of our culture is usually called the **socialization process** (Stake and Easley, 1978). When used in this context, the term has nothing to do with providing opportunities for children to socialize with each other. It simply means that teachers are teaching their students about how things are done in their adult world.

It would be incorrect, however, to assume that teachers consciously set out to teach their students about participating in the world of adults. Rather, in order to manage a classroom in such a way that students participate in activities and get assignments done, teachers must socialize their students (Doyle, 1986, p. 413). Also, teachers unconsciously emphasize cultural values while they interact with their students in the classroom.

The Importance of Routines

Even on the first day of school, teachers who manage their classrooms effectively plan something for their students to do (Doyle, 1986, p. 411). Some teachers involve their students in placement tests and "getting to know you" activities. Some teachers give lessons on rules and procedures. Some teachers do all of these things. During the first several weeks of school, teachers and students are involved in a process which one educational researcher has called "grooving" (Smith and Geoffrey, 1968). This term refers to two things. First, the teacher is accustoming the students to the rules and routines of the classroom. Second, the students are teaching the teacher about their own needs and how they are used to functioning in classrooms. Teacher and student adjust to each other during this period and settle into a groove in which routines and rules help the classroom to run itself. Another educational researcher has argued that routines make classroom activities less susceptible to breakdowns during interruptions because the students know what they should be doing and when they should be doing it (Doyle, 1986, p. 412).

This means that procedures for virtually every classroom eventuality—that is, going to the bathroom, taking attendance and lunch count, participating in reading and math groups and completing assignments, going out to recess, etc.—must be spelled out to the students or otherwise taken care of. Some teachers have general rules which allow students to make decisions about most of these matters. In many classrooms, teachers assign particular responsibilities, such as lunch count and attendance, to their students.

All elementary teachers must frequently send notices home to parents with their students. Every teacher will take care of this in his own way. One teacher may hand each child a notice as they go out the classroom door. Another teacher may have the students pick up these notices from some designated place in the classroom. One first-grade teacher whom we know has a "mailbox" system. At the end of the day, she dismisses her students in small groups. When a group is called, each student in that group puts a chair on top of his or her desk (so the janitor can easily sweep) and walks over to an individual "mailbox" where notices are picked up to be taken home.[1]

At the beginning of any school day, many teachers "preview" the events of that day. After taking morning attendance and completing a daily calendar activity with her students, another teacher whom we know conducts a ten-minute class activity during which she and her class fill in the events of the day on a blank schedule. All activities and assignments are entered on this schedule, and students consult this schedule throughout their school day.[2]

Students complete many assignments during a school day, and teachers may not have time to read or grade these assignments until the end of the day. Some teachers collect the assignments at particular points in the school day. If there is individualization of instruction and students are completing their assignments at different times of the day (or if students are completing different assignments), collection of assignments can be a confusing task. Another teacher whom we know solves this problem by setting out boxes on the counters of her classroom and designating them for particular assignments. Each student knows where to put their assignment when it is completed, and the teacher knows where to find her students' work at the end of the day when she has no time to look at it.[3]

Some kindergarten teachers make an instructional lesson out of these daily tasks. For example, one kindergarten teacher asks her class of students, "Girls and boys, how many children belong in our class?" After they respond with "Twenty!," she asks them, "How many are in class today?" After counting, the children respond with "Nineteen!" She then asks her students, "Who is missing today?" (Kamii, 1985).

Another teacher in a traditional graded classroom is interrupted by his principal just as the students return from morning recess. As he talks with his principal, the students begin to get noisy and one student throws an eraser at another. First he turns to the class and asks, "Boys and girls, what do we do everyday after recess?"

"Spelling!" the children reply.

"Then get out your spelling books and begin working," responds the teacher.

Of course, this teacher will also have to deal with the individual who threw the eraser because it violates one of the rules of his classroom. But in the meantime, his students have returned to their work, the potential for disruption has been avoided, and the teacher is able to complete his conversation with his principal. This was all accomplished because the teacher was able to remind his students of a routine which had been established during the first few weeks of school.

In sum, from the first day of school, teachers must accustom their students to the rules and routines of their classroom. These will vary according to the ages of the students, the policies of the school, and the personal preferences of the teachers. When the students of any classroom understand what these rules and routines are, they are easier to manage. When they are uncertain of rules or routines, there is potential for disruption. Each teacher must make his own decision about what rules and routines will be necessary. Every teacher should communicate these rules and routines clearly and frequently.

In nongraded schools and in some informal schools, students are assigned to the same teachers for more than one year in succession. In these settings, accustoming students to rules and routines is much easier for two reasons. First, the students are already familiar with the teacher's rules and routines. Second, older, more experienced students can help beginning students to adjust to the classroom rules and procedures.

Managing the Physical Environment

At times, teachers walk into their new classrooms and leave them as they are, without making any changes in the arrangement of furniture, storage space, or wall space. These teachers end up adjusting their teaching to the physical arrangements of the classroom. Obviously, it should be the other way around. The physical environment of the classroom should be arranged to support the learning activities presented by individual teachers. As the curriculum changes, or the learning needs of the students change, the physical arrangement of the classroom will require modifications. The physical environment has a strong influence on the amount of learning which takes place in the classroom, and on the attitudes of students and teacher. A good physical environment is inviting, efficient, and supports the efforts of both teacher and learners as they work. A poorly designed physical environment becomes an obstacle which teachers and students must overcome as they try to teach and learn.

The major goal a teacher must keep in mind when designing the physical environment of the classroom is to prevent undesirable student behaviors and to foster student learning by the arrangement of desks, furniture, storage areas, equipment, and materials. Effective teachers increase work efficiency, order, and student attention through good classroom organization. These teachers change the physical conditions which may negatively impact the behavior of students in order to avoid delays, distractions, and undesirable student behaviors.

When organizing the physical dimension of the classroom, the teacher must keep in mind the following considerations: 1) Visibility, 2) Accessibility, 3) Flexibility, 4) Comfort, and 5) Aesthetics.

Visibility   It is important that the students can see, from where they are sitting, the area or areas in which instruction takes place. They should not be sitting too far, for example, to read a chart, or bothered by the reflection of the sunlight on the chalkboard, or have their view blocked by the overhead projector. It is also important that the teacher be able to see all students, at all times from the areas in which the teacher works, that is, desk, chalkboard, small group areas, etc.

Accessibility   Frequently utilized instructional materials and equipment should be stored in areas easy for students to reach, where they will not have to request teacher assistance. The room should be arranged in a manner which provides easy access to the pencil sharpener, teacher's desk, work stations, sinks, storage cabinets, and doors. Traffic patterns must be designed in a manner which does not create congestion or disturb the work of other students.

Flexibility   Work stations, desks, tables, and chairs should be easy to rearrange and move according to the instructional needs of the teacher and students. For example, in most self-contained classrooms, teachers shift instructional activities several times during the day, for example, from a short presentation to individual seatwork, or to small group discussions, or to teacher-led large group discussion, or to reciprocal peer tutoring, or to a role play activity. The classroom floor space must be arranged in a manner which facilitates the rearrangement of furniture to accommodate these instructional activities. Sitting in rows appears to increase the amount of individual work produced by students (Bennett & Blundell, 1983), while a circle arrangement of desks produces the best results for discussions (Rosenfield, et al., 1985).

Comfort   It is difficult to concentrate and be productive in a classroom that is too cold or too warm, in which there is too much light or not enough light, where outside noise makes it difficult to hear what the teacher or other students are saying, where the students are sitting too close to each other, where there is no place for students to place their books and materials, or where students have to stand up to see a film. Most classrooms are small when we consider that over twenty children and one or more adults will spend almost seven hours a day in them for nine months of the year. Given this congested condition of humans and furniture, the teacher must be very pragmatic and efficient in the organization of the classroom. Form must follow function. And function mandates that adjustments be made so the physical arrangement is congruent with the type of instruction taking place while at the same time providing a comfortable environment for students and teacher.

Aesthetics   The aesthetic dimension of the classroom consists of those features a teacher adds to the existing physical structure and furniture in order to create an environment which is pleasant and conducive to work. This dimension reflects the personality and values of the teacher, and it conveys to students how the teacher feels about teaching and learning. Teachers, having different personalities and styles, choose to express themselves differently in the manner in which they arrange the classroom. Some teachers are austere and focus all the attention on the learning materials. Other teachers seek to create a very stimulating environment. Particularly with young children and students who lack opportunities for comfort and aesthetics at home, it is very important to have classrooms which are inviting and convey messages that learning is fun and school is beautiful. This effect is attained through the use of art objects, learning materials, plants, furniture, and music.

Since the classroom is the place where a teacher spends seven hours a day for nine months of the year, it is important that it be comfortable and appealing, not only to the students but to the teacher. The decoration of the classroom should involve the ideas and efforts of students as well. The teacher could appoint a rotating or permanent committee in charge of assisting in the decoration and displays. In the case of very young students, the teacher may involve some of the parents in this task. A very valuable sense of ownership and pride will result from these efforts. It is far better that the classroom appearance be the result of student and parent efforts, even when the results may not be outstanding, than to have a better homes and gardens type of classroom solely arranged by the teacher. As the students take pride in the looks of their class-rooms, their learning attitudes will be positively affected, and they will develop aesthetic values and respect for school furniture and materials.

The improvements of the classroom's looks may be attained through inexpensive materials and borrowed objects at the beginning of a teacher's career, and eventually through gradual purchases with the assistance of the P.T.A. or school funds. Art objects, plants, special furniture, and music are some of the items which constitute the aesthetic dimension of the classroom.

Art objects may include photographs, replicas of original paintings, sculptures, and framed samples of outstanding student art work, weavings, and drawings. Live plants may be acquired and cared for by the students. Additional furniture, such as an old rocking chair and small carpet for an area to be used for leisure reading or story-time, adds a special touch to the room. Some schools allow teachers to paint the walls of their classrooms in colors other than the institutional gray or light green. In one school we know, children paint the windows with tempera. It is a great community project to have students, parents and teachers come in during the weekend and paint a classroom with bright colors of their choice. It will not be difficult to keep those walls clean because the children will take pride in them and see the classroom and school as their own. Background music may be played sometimes during quiet time to add relaxation and enjoyment to the learning activity. Hopefully the students will also participate in the selection of the music and "host" particular listening times. This would be an excellent opportunity to enrich the musical background of the students and their liking for a variety of musical experiences.

What does the aesthetic dimension have to do with learning academic subjects? By providing an inviting aesthetic environment, the attitudes and behaviors of students will be positively affected. One is less likely to lose one's manners in an art gallery than in a graffiti soiled subway station. By creating an aesthetically pleasing classroom environment, teachers make a statement about their expectations for learning and behavior. This fosters the development of aesthetic values in children.

MANAGING RECORDS

There are two types of records which teachers must keep: records of student progress, and inventory lists of materials, equipment, and textbooks.

Student records keep track of academic as well as social development, and communicate this information to students, parents, and school officials. The most common student records are: the grade book, individual folders, cumulative folders, and report cards. Information about the students is included in these records as a result of informal or standardized tests, class projects, and teacher observations of student performance. The grade book contains information about student academic performance, daily attendance, and social behavior. Individual folders contain samples of student work, quizzes, tests, list of books which have been read, feedback comments from the teacher, and, when possible, a progress chart indicating the objectives mastered and the objectives to be mastered. Cumulative records of student performance throughout elementary and secondary education are kept on each student in the school office. Information about students scores on standardized tests, social development, and extracurricular activities is entered on a yearly basis on a form which is added to this folder.

The amount of student work accumulated throughout a day can be overwhelming for the teacher to review. Teachers must find ways to avoid taking home large stacks of paper at night. They need to correct student work during the school day, by incorporating the review of papers as part of the lesson, by having students check their own work, or by having student monitors help in the checking of papers. Not all student work needs to be graded and entered in the grade book. A large portion of student work should be done for the purpose of practicing and attaining mastery and should not count for a grade. When teachers grade papers, they should return them the next day in order to provide quick feedback to students. If piles of back papers begin to accumulate, a teacher should consider finding help from students, reducing the number of projects to be graded, or developing quicker ways to check the papers.

Besides keeping student records, teachers must sometimes maintain inventory lists for classroom materials and furniture, for example, number of textbooks assigned, number of dictionaries and encyclopedias available, audiovisual equipment, constructions paper, supplies, and number of desks, tables and chairs. These inventory lists are prepared before classes start and are updated periodically.

SUPERVISING PARAPROFESSIONALS

Paraprofessionals are adults who assist the teacher in the classroom, that is, paid aides, college students majoring in education, and community volunteers. They help with the preparation of instructional materials, clerical tasks such as the recording of grades, taking care of animals, monitoring tasks, etc. Frequently they also provide some instruction. The number of paraprofessionals a teacher may use in the classroom depends on the type of instruction taking place. When teachers have small group instruction or learning centers, several adults may be utilized. When instruction is teacher centered, more than two paraprofessionals may be cumbersome.

As teachers carefully structure the rules and routines of their classrooms in order to maximize teaching effectiveness, they must also provide explicit role definitions for each paraprofessional, that is, what authority the paraprofessional has, which tasks are to be performed, and which tasks are not to be performed, etc. Paraprofessionals are trained on the job. They learn basic instructional techniques, management skills, and clerical tasks. The teacher must make sure that these skills are developed through modeling and supervised practice. Abundant and supportive feedback should be provided. Paraprofessionals need to perceive themselves as useful, accepted, and appreciated. It is the teacher's responsibility to structure work in a manner which makes paraprofessionals succeed in their classroom tasks.

NOTES

1. Thanks go to Julie Lembeck of St. Cloud Public Schools for sharing this idea with us.
2. Thanks go to Margie Miller, of the Becker Public Schools, for sharing this idea with us.
3. Credit goes to Deb Koopmeiners of St. Cloud Public Schools for this idea.

Chapter
9

Classroom Management: Managing Student Behavior

*I*n this chapter, a 20-step system to manage student behavior is described. The 20 steps are based on the research literature of classroom behavior theorists such as B. F. Skinner, William Glasser, Thomas Gordon, and Lee and Marlene Canter. Before introducing the 20-step system, we will present a brief review of the research on classroom management and a summary description of the classroom discipline approaches which provide the foundation for the system.

Brophy and Rohrkemper (1981) studied the perceptions of teachers about what causes student misbehavior and found that teachers tend to identify factors outside themselves as causes of misbehaviors. Teachers frequently pointed at students as the only causes of misbehaviors, ignoring other factors such as the appropriateness of the curriculum or their teaching methods. The reluctance of teachers to consider themselves as possible sources of discipline problems makes it difficult for teachers to change. Teachers will not change their own behavior when they think of the students as the only ones who must change.

Kounin (1970) found that more effective and less effective classroom managers alike tended to address student misbehavior with similar strategies. If they use the same intervention strategies, what makes them better or worse classroom managers? Their prevention activities and their instructional activities were significantly different, and these apparently determined their classroom management effectiveness. Brophy (1982) reviewed the research on classroom organization and management, and concluded that conducting class in an alert, smooth fashion substantially diminishes student misbehaviors. This confirmed the prior findings of Kounin.

Cotton and Savard (1984), in a review of studies on discipline and motivation, concluded that classroom conditions which provide students with opportunities for academic and social success tend to diminish student misbehaviors. Jones (1979) found that while most teachers fear discipline crises such as fighting and open challenge to authority, severe discipline problems seldom occur, even in hard to handle classrooms. He found that most student misbehavior consists of students talking to other students or students walking about the room without permission.

Jones suggests that teachers should address possible student misbehaviors by setting limits, using nonverbal language effectively, utilizing incentive systems, and giving help efficiently. Weber (1984) examined the strategies that experienced teachers utilized to maintain a positive classroom environment and found a high degree of agreement on six approaches to improve classroom discipline: using positive reinforcement, applying logical consequences, establishing and maintaining group cohesiveness, establishing and maintaining productive group norms, exhibiting unconditional positive regard, and using time out.

For the past two decades, a number of scholars have proposed approaches or models to improve classroom discipline and increase student learning. The most influential of these have been B. F. Skinner (1968), T. A. Harris (1969), W. Glasser (1969), T. Gordon (1974), and Lee and Marlene Canter (1976). Each of these authors developed a unique approach to classroom discipline and teacher-student interaction. The 20-step system which is presented in this chapter combines the strategies developed by these authors. In the following paragraphs, these unique approaches, which are the main sources of the 20-step system, are briefly described.

Behavior Modification approaches were originally developed by B. F. Skinner (1968) and were later adapted for classroom use. This method states that student behavior can be changed if the circumstances surrounding the behavior are appropriately modified. The primary goal of behavior modification is to change student behavior. This method places little importance on finding the causes of behaviors. Rather than labeling children as educationally deprived, teachers must discover what is happening in the classroom environment to perpetuate undesirable student behaviors and how this environment can be changed to bring about desirable behavior.

According to Skinner, all human behavior can be explained as responses to environmental stimuli. Students behave well because adults and the school environment have rewarded correct behaviors and have not rewarded incorrect ones. Students behave poorly because adults and the school environment have rewarded incorrect behaviors and not rewarded desirable ones. The behavior of a student is shaped by its consequences. If a behavior is rewarded, it is likely to be repeated. If a behavior is not rewarded, it is less likely to be repeated. Reinforcement, which is usually perceived as originating in the environment rather than within the individual, can be tangible or social; for example, food, stickers, teacher praise. According to Behavior Modification theory, students will avoid experiences which are painful or not pleasing and will seek experiences which are rewarding and pleasing. Most elementary teachers recognize reinforcement as an important element in promoting desirable student behavior.

Transactional Analysis, popularized by T. A. Harris (1969), proposes that individual behavior is guided by one of three possible ego states: parent, adult or child. Each ego state has positive and negative qualities. The parent state may be nurturant or authoritarian. The child ego state may be characterized by playfulness or defiance. The adult ego state is the least emotional, and the most rational and reasonable. Interpersonal problems tend to occur when teacher and students interact at different ego states, for example, when the teacher is operating at the adult level while the student is responding at the child level. Or the teacher may operate at the negative parent state and the student may respond at the negative child state. These incompatible interactions can form a pattern or game which detracts from good communication.

Teacher-student interactions at the adult to adult levels are the most likely to promote satisfactory communication and harmony in the classroom. Our 20-step system of classroom discipline uses Transactional Analysis to foster desirable interaction between teacher and student. The teacher should avoid "parent to child" interactions, and utilize, as much as possible, "adult to adult" exchanges. When "adult to adult" interactions are not possible, the teacher should use "nurturant parent to adult" exchanges. Transactional Analysis principles help the teacher remain in a professional and composed role while interacting with students.

The **Reality Therapy-Schools Without Failure** approach introduced by William Glasser (1965 and 1969) emphasizes that students should be aware of their own behavior and committed to a plan for succeeding. Glasser wants teachers to help students become aware of why things go wrong for them at school, to eliminate situations where students are likely to fail, and to increase success experiences in the classroom. This approach calls for a caring adult who gets involved with the growth of students and who will not let them abandon their commitments for self-improvement. Such a teacher will not give up on one's students and will confront students with the natural and logical consequences of their behaviors. Students must find ways to deal with the world the way it is. Glasser calls this "reality therapy." At the same time, Glasser states that many student problems originate in the school system and that the system must change the conditions under which students fail. He wants "schools without failure." Glasser encourages teachers to reflect on their own behavior toward students, to start each day with a fresh approach, and expect a better tomorrow. Glasser believes that students want to experience success and wish to have feelings of self-worth. He thinks that the role of the teacher is to help the student recognize the obstacles, make a plan for success, and enforce natural and logical consequences if the student's commitment is not fulfilled. A limitation of the Glasser approach is that it is time-consuming and requires individualized attention for each student.

T.E.T.: Teacher Effectiveness Training, by Thomas Gordon (1974), states that when teacher and students communicate about what is bothering them, and about how their behaviors affect each other, there is more time spent on learning and less time wasted on discipline. The objective of T.E.T. is to improve relations between teachers and students by communicating and resolving conflicts in a manner that is fair to both sides. When this happens, no one loses. Gordon perceives the classroom as a place where both teacher and students are responsible for the quality of learning. In T.E.T., the use of teacher authority is minimized as much as possible, and the students' needs for autonomy and responsibility are enhanced. One of the main goals of T.E.T. is that the teacher help students learn how to solve their own problems. An important role of the teacher is to be a supportive, noncritical facilitator of student responsibility and self-direction.

Assertive Discipline, by Lee and Marlene Canter (1976), states that teachers have the right to teach and no student has the right to interfere with the classroom instruction. Assertive Discipline has predetermined rewards for good behavior and consequences for misbehaviors. Teachers take charge and make sure the students adapt to their expectations. This approach to discipline is influenced by Assertiveness Training and Behavior Modification. The teacher makes a classroom discipline plan, stating a few basic rules and several consequences for following or not following the rules. The emphasis is on rewards and consequences. Assertive Discipline has become very popular in the past few years. The Canters report that their system reduces misbehavior by 80 to 90% in most classrooms. Assertive Discipline provides a system in which teachers, parents, and administrators agree on the same standards of behavior. It transfers the responsibility for behavior from the teacher to the student. It is easy to learn and easy to implement.

THE 20-STEP SYSTEM OF DISCIPLINE

The 20-step system of discipline is an eclectic approach which brings together, in a hierarchical arrangement, the behavior management strategies developed by Skinner (1968), Harris (1969), Glasser (1969), Gordon (1974) and Canter (1976). The system is designed to accommodate differences in teachers' styles and philosophies as well as differences in the maturity and moral development levels of the students. The system provides teachers with a structured set of alternatives from which to choose in responding to discipline situations in the classroom.

In an attempt to solve the problem of classroom discipline at the elementary level, many schools have adopted one of the well-known classroom management models—Assertive Discipline, Behavior Modification, Reality Therapy, or Teacher Effectiveness Training. Such efforts to institute a particular behavior management model usually involve considerable effort and funds. All too often this also produces frustration and poor results. A common complaint from teachers is that the imposed model does not match with the philosophy or style of individual teachers. Another typical complaint is that it does not allow for sufficient adaptation to meet the wide range of social and moral development of young children. Teachers often prefer to apply these models to particular circumstances, believing that no model can work effectively in every situation.

The 20-step system (Descamps & Lindahl, 1988) was developed so that teachers can more successfully adapt the good points of each of the classroom models which we have just described. The behavior management system presented in this chapter offers the teacher a system and a set of alternatives from which she can select while attempting to meet the perceived needs of the individual student and the characteristics of the classroom situation at a particular time.

The 20-step system of behavior management categorizes student behavior into four types, each with a progressively more negative impact upon classroom discipline. Each type of behavior is paired to a corresponding level of response containing several steps, or alternatives, from which the teacher may choose. The **four types of targeted**

classroom behaviors are: **desirable, minor disruptions, unacceptable,** and **severe.** The **teacher responses** which should correspond to desirable student behaviors are called **prevention** steps. **Redirection** steps match student minor disruptions. **Consequence** steps are applied when students' behaviors are unacceptable, and **team support** steps are used when student behaviors fall under the severe category.

The type of behavior exhibited by the student influences the type of response the teacher will use. If the student behavior is desirable, the teacher's primary concern is one of prevention of undesirable behaviors in order to maintain a positive atmosphere and maximize the amount of time and energy devoted to learning activities. When minor disruptions occur, the teacher's attention may shift to redirection, seeking to bring back the student to a productive mode of behavior without imposing negative consequences for the infraction. This is best accomplished by interacting at an "adult to adult" level with individual students, without involving the attention of the peer group in the exchange. When students break classroom rules, they engage in unacceptable behaviors. In this situation, the teacher imposes consequences. These actions may be particularly useful in working with students who seem motivated by reward and consequence approaches. Finally, in those occasions when severe behaviors take place and all teacher efforts seem futile, team support steps must be utilized. In such situations, the teacher seeks outside assistance from another teacher, the student's parents, or a school administrator.

Within each of the four types of responses—prevention, redirection, consequences, and team support—there are a variety of alternatives from which the teacher may choose. They do not have to be utilized according to any prescribed order. The earlier steps assume a better classroom situation and more motivation on the part of the learners. The later steps assume a greater need for teacher authority. The steps may be used sequentially, or the teacher may skip steps as needed (see Box 9.1). The teacher may also shift to later or earlier steps as the particular student behavior and the situation require. The teacher's personal style, the student's personality, the success of past efforts to discipline the student, and the circumstances surrounding the behavior should all be considered in determining which step is most appropriate.

In the remainder of the chapter, an explanation of the following topics will be presented: how to establish standards of behavior; how to match teacher responses to student behaviors; prevention steps, redirection steps, consequence steps, and team support steps; and conditions necessary for the 20-step system to work.

How to Establish Standards of Behavior

In the classroom, as in any social setting, students need to know what is expected of them, that is, what behaviors are desirable and which ones are minor disruptions, unacceptable, or severe. Some students perceive behaviors as simply good or bad, lacking the sophistication to distinguish degrees of desirability or undesirability. For the purposes of the present approach to discipline, behaviors are categorized under four types: 1) desirable, 2) minor disruptions, 3) unacceptable, and 4) severe.

At the beginning of the year, in a classroom designed to foster responsibility and participation, the teacher involves students in an exercise to discuss which behaviors fall under each category. As a result of this discussion, four lists (one per category) are prepared citing examples of each type of behavior. All students should be able to identify classroom behaviors by type. Some examples are:

Box 9-1 **20-Step System of Discipline**

PREVENTION STEPS.
The teacher:

1. Provides effective instruction.

2. Helps students experience more success than failure.

3. Recognizes and rewards desirable behavior.

4. Sends a preventive "I Message" communicating desirable behavior.

5. Gives early attention to potentially disruptive students.

6. Changes circumstances that may produce misbehavior.

7. Uses physical closeness to prevent misbehavior.

REDIRECTION STEPS.
The teacher:

8. Ignores minor disruptions and recognizes desirable behaviors.

9. Sends nonverbal message requesting change of behavior.

10. Asks for status or rule to redirect behavior.

11. Requests a change of behavior.

12. Isolates the student to keep minor disruption from escalating.

13. Sends an "I Message" communicating the effects of undesirable behaviors.

14. Conducts a "Method III" conference: a no-lose conflict resolution approach.

CONSEQUENCE STEPS.
The teacher:

15. Conducts a Glasser conference to develop a behavior improvement contract.

16. Implements a class "Assertive Discipline" plan.

TEAM SUPPORT STEPS.
The teacher:

17. Sends the student for "time out" to another classroom.

18. Involves the parents in changing student behavior.

19. Involves the principal in changing student behavior.

20. Requests that the student be removed from the classroom.

Type	Student Behavior
Desirable	Works on assignment
Minor disruption	Taps desk with pencil
Unacceptable	Does not bring materials to class
Severe	Repeated failure to turn in assignments

It is also important to communicate what teacher responses are to be expected for the different types of behaviors. For example, desirable student behaviors are likely to elicit teacher praise and reinforcement, but minor disruptions will prompt the teacher to redirect the student back on task. Unacceptable behaviors will have predictable and preestablished consequences, such as loss of privilege or staying after school. Severe behaviors will be addressed by involving other professionals or parents. It is advisable that teachers involve students in deciding what types of consequences should be applied to different types of behavior.

Teachers who do not have clear standards of behavior for their students are very likely to be unpredictable, inconsistent, and unfair. This initial confusion and lack of direction will open the door for students to test their limits until chaos reigns or until standards are identified through trial and error. In either case, the result will be a loss of respect toward the teacher, who will be perceived as weak and unprofessional. Conversely, teachers who have clear standards and are predictable from the first day of class make students feel that a competent person is in charge, that there is a purpose to school, that things are done with fairness, that no time will be wasted in testing who is the boss and how much students can get away with, and that the teacher is a professional.

If the standards are clear but the consequences are too lenient, a loss of respect and credibility will occur. If the consequences are too harsh, resentment and dislike for the teacher and school is likely to follow. The fairest manner of deciding on consequences is to meet with the total group, or a selected sample of students, and discuss possibilities until a satisfactory set of consequences is selected.

How to Match Teacher Actions with Student Behaviors

As a general rule, the type of student behavior determines the type of step the teacher should apply. Desirable behaviors call for prevention steps; minor disruptions are addressed through redirection steps; unacceptable behaviors require consequence steps; and severe behavior is handled through team support steps. There are several alternative steps within each category: seven prevention steps, seven redirection steps, two consequence steps, and four team support steps.

Type of Behavior	Type of Step	Step Number
Desirable	Prevention	1-7
Minor disruption	Redirection	8-14
Unacceptable	Consequences	15-16
Severe	Team Support	17-20

The teacher chooses from the type of step, or step category, the step that is most likely to help the student. Before a decision is made about what step to implement, the teacher must have as much information as possible about the variables impacting the behavior of the student. The following areas should be assessed:

- The student's stage of moral development. Stages of moral development include: fear, rewards, peer acceptance, law and order, and social-contract (Kohlberg, 1975).
- Student behavior goals. These might include: attention seeking, power, revenge, display of inadequacy (Dreikurs et al., 1982).
- The prevalent student need. Any of the following needs may prevail: physical, safety, belonging, adequacy, and self-actualization (Maslow, 1962).
- The socioeconomic and cultural conditions of the child's home environment.
- The student's school performance history.

The more the teacher understands the behavior of the student, from as many diagnostic approaches as possible, the more assured the teacher will be of the validity of the steps chosen to improve the student's behavior. The experienced teacher makes these assessments rapidly and sorts out possible variables until she is satisfied that the step which she has chosen is a good match to the needs and conditions of the student. For example, a student influenced by peers will not benefit from a public admonition as much as from a private one because he may get positive reinforcement for behavior which is undesirable in the teacher's eyes. Or if the safety needs of a student are threatened because the student fears an attack by a gang after school, it will be useless for the teacher to emphasize the need for careful attention to seatwork.

Prevention Steps

Prevention steps are utilized by the teacher when desirable student behaviors occur in the classroom. These are the most important steps in classroom management. The teacher sets up circumstances which help students succeed and prevent them from failing or getting into trouble. A positive climate is established in which the teacher takes a proactive rather than a reactive role. The teacher initiates and sets classroom conditions which make students want to work. In this environment of quality teaching and positive interaction, students experience success and find learning and relating to the teacher a rewarding event. Outstanding teachers confine most of their classroom management interactions to the prevention strategies. As a result, there is more time dedicated to teaching and learning because teachers anticipate problems before they occur (Kounin, 1970). Many teacher actions which are intended to improve the quality of instruction affect the classroom climate positively and prevent student misbehavior. There are seven prevention steps which the teacher may use to maintain a positive climate in the classroom and prevent misbehaviors. Steps 1 and 2 address the quality of instruction and indirectly diminish misbehaviors. Steps 3 through 7 are specifically designed to prevent misbehaviors.

The teacher:

1. Provides effective instruction.
2. Helps students experience more success than failure.
3. Recognizes and rewards desirable student behavior.

4. Sends a preventive "I Message" communicating desirable behaviors.
5. Gives early attention to potentially disruptive students.
6. Changes circumstances that may produce misbehaviors.
7. Uses physical closeness to prevent misbehavior.

Step 1: The Teacher Provides Effective Instruction   Students who know what is expected of them and what tasks are to be mastered, who are busy covering extensive and challenging content, who interact frequently with the teacher through questions, and who are given periodic feedback on their mastery of tasks, have greater academic achievement and are more likely to have a positive outlook toward schooling than students in classrooms where effective instruction is not provided (Brophy and Good, 1986). Effective instruction helps students develop a sense of purpose and makes them impatient with other students who slow down academic progress with misbehaviors. Conversely, when there is little work going on, when the teacher does not communicate a sense of purpose and does not deliver a quality lesson, or does not seem to care, students are likely to become discouraged and find classroom time a disappointing experience. If instruction does not engage the attention of the students, other topics will become the focus of their interest. Unless students are very alienated, it can be said that the better the lesson is, the less students misbehave; likewise, the worse the lesson, the more students will misbehave (Kounin, 1970). One of the first questions teachers should ask themselves when their students are frequently unruly is, "How is my teaching?"

The following characteristics of effective instruction have been validated by research findings (Brophy and Good, 1986) and may be used by a teacher to verify that Step 1 is being implemented.

A teacher who provides effective instruction:

a. Posts class rules and expectations.
b. Communicates lesson objectives.
c. Keeps students on task and covers material extensively.
d. Provides opportunities for students to participate actively.
e. Asks questions which produce many correct answers.
f. Provides feedback on student progress during instruction.

Step 2: The Teacher Helps Students Experience More Success Than Failure   Student success is considered to be one of the most important variables influencing achievement (Bloom, 1976; Skinner 1968). No one likes to lose, and to lose repeatedly is devastating to our sense of adequacy (Maslow, 1962). According to behavior modification theory, when the activities we engage in produce positive results we are likely to continue doing them. The better the results, the more likely we are to engage in them (Skinner, 1968). Conversely, the more we fail, the less likely it is that we will engage in those activities. It would be rare to find students hating a class in which they are doing well. So if we want children to hate learning, let's make sure they do poorly and are unable to master the tasks expected of them. And if we want kids to love learning and schooling, let's make sure they master the tasks expected of them. The issue is not one of lowering standards but rather of adjusting the difficulty of tasks and the time allotted in such a manner that students attain mastery (Bloom, 1976;

Brookover et al., 1982). For example, if the exit standard is x, good instructional practice will gradually increase the difficulty of intermediate tasks which students are able to perform until they can do x. "At risk" students, particularly, need this approach so they will not become discouraged and give up their education. When "at risk" students master the learning tasks, they will feel good about themselves, they will like school, and they will develop a sense of educational purpose.

If a student has failed, for years, at learning in general, what can we expect that student to do but hate school and be disruptive? For failing students, the system is the enemy which makes them feel inadequate. Unless these students fight the system, they will lose their self-respect. Many times, students who fail are not lacking in ability; rather, something has gone wrong in their schooling or lives. Teachers who do not help students succeed are like doctors who do not help patients get well.

The ratio of successful experiences over failures in the classroom should be high. For seatwork activities, for example, Brophy and Good (1986) suggest a success rate of 90 percent. This means that, ideally, out of every ten tasks attempted during seatwork, the student will get nine correct and one wrong. This is particularly important in the early grades when students are learning basic skills. The younger the students are, the more important it is for them that the success ratio be high. Once students have developed a high self-concept as learners, they will tolerate, temporarily, lower success ratios. Certainly, teachers cannot maintain a 90% student success rate in many classroom activities. But as the success rate declines, the motivation and achievement of the students will also decline.

The teacher who helps students experience more success than failure:

a. Establishes a cooperative learning environment.
b. Adjusts learning tasks to students' ability levels.
c. Provides extra assistance to those having difficulty.
d. Provides many opportunities for practice.
e. Creates an environment in which it is okay to make mistakes.
f. Prepares individualized plans for those not succeeding.

Step 3: The Teacher Recognizes and Rewards Desirable Student Behavior

The ultimate reinforcer for students will be a successfully completed task and knowing that they are increasing in their competence and knowledge as human beings (Stipek, 1988). This sense of success is fostered through Steps 1 and 2. But to attain mastery requires sustained effort and time. Most students need frequent reinforcements and depend on the teacher for encouragement and nurturance, particularly when they are not being successful at mastering their tasks. Learning is at times stressful, and students get easily discouraged. Young students especially need adult praise frequently.

Providing feedback to students about their progress in learning is the teacher behavior most consistently related to student achievement (Bloom, 1976). Teacher praise is most effective when given to students for having put forth high effort or good performance (Brophy, 1981). Praise must have credibility by being descriptive and by giving information to the students about what they have accomplished. Praise given indiscriminately, without having been earned by the student, may actually have a negative effect on students' confidence and motivation. Teachers must give feedback and praise students for their academic achievements or efforts, and for their behavior. Some students, because of past failures, tend to discourage very easily. They will need greater amounts of encouragement. Other students, because of past experiences of success and acceptance, tend not to discourage easily. They have confidence in their own abilities. These students will need less encouragement in the form of verbal praise, and will benefit from being challenged.

Teachers sometimes utilize extrinsic rewards in order to stimulate students to engage in some activities which do not seem appealing. Deci and Ryan (1985) warn about the possible negative effects of extrinsic rewards, which may erode intrinsic motivation and reduce motivation to participate in classroom activities once the extrinsic rewards are eliminated.

The teacher who recognizes and rewards desirable student behavior:

a. Smiles at students.
b. Praises students privately.
c. Recognizes students publicly.
d. Provides tangible rewards.

Step 4: The Teacher Sends a Preventive "I Message" Communicating Desirable Behaviors Often students fail to behave appropriately because it is not clear to them what the teacher expects them to do, or because they do not realize the impact that their behavior has on the teacher. Teachers who make clear, through explicit rules, how students are supposed to behave may still have a difficult time getting them to comply because the students do not know how their behavior impacts the teacher personally. Being young and unaware of the perspectives of others, students fail to see how a teacher is affected when they follow their own impulses and desires. It is hard for many students to imagine the teacher feeling disappointed or discouraged by their misbehaviors or lack of appropriate behaviors. Students sometimes fail to see teachers as humans, and teachers may be partly responsible for this since they sometimes avoid disclosing information about themselves and maintain a business-like atmosphere in the classroom.

For example, at lunch time, students feel restless and they may display this restlessness in the way that they walk down the hall on the way to the cafeteria. They feel a need for acting up a bit. They know that they are not supposed to do it according to the rules, and that the teacher will enforce these rules, but they do not know how the teacher is affected when other teachers and students observe the behavior of her class. If they knew that it is very important to their teacher that they behave in front of other groups, and that when they do so the teacher feels competent and energized, then they would be more motivated to behave properly than they are by the fear of a reprimand or consequence. Frequently, students want to please the teacher: it is important, then, that the teacher inform them specifically of valued behaviors.

The "I Message" communicating desirable behaviors is an adaptation of T.E.T.'s "I Message" (Gordon, 1974). As a prevention step, teachers disclose beforehand to their students the impact that a desirable behavior has on their performance and feelings. In the lunch example, before leaving the room, the teacher would say, "Class, it is really nice when you behave appropriately during lunch. This makes me very proud of you." The preventing "I Message" is based on the assumption that humans do not like to hurt others and are inclined to treat them the way they like to be treated. This is particularly true when the teacher treats students with respect, kindness, and love.

The teacher who sends preventive "I Messages":

a. Describes the student behavior that is desirable.
b. Describes the effect of this behavior on teaching and learning.
c. Describes the feeling that this behavior produces in the teacher.

Step 5: The Teacher Gives Early Attention to Potentially Disruptive Students There are, at times, a few students in a group who have greater difficulty than other students in finding a sense of belonging and purpose. These students have frequently experienced failure at home and school. As a result, they are "turned off" to learning and teachers. They enter the room with a negative attitude and have little to cherish about what is going on in the classroom. The teacher must give early attention to these students, in the form of greetings and compliments, before the lesson starts, since they will do little that can be praised later, and may be misbehaving. These students may not do anything academically that deserves praise or recognition.

The teacher starts the day at the door, greeting all students and looking in particular at the potentially disruptive students in their eyes as if to say, "Welcome, this is a new day, let's forget about the past, let's work and succeed today, I am your friend" (Glaser, 1969). These students are not used to having teachers approach them in this way. By now, everyone knows they are negative and hostile students, and teachers stay away from them. As a matter of fact, these students avoid their teachers too, sitting as far as possible from the teacher's desk. The stereotype is perpetuated by both sides.

"Teachers are the enemy!" thinks the student.

"This student is a pain!" thinks the teacher.

It is the teacher's task to break this cycle so the student begins to think, "Not all teachers are a pain. Some are nice."

Once a teacher shows concern and relates closely to a student, without making it embarrassing in front of the peer group, it will become increasingly difficult for that student not to reciprocate and behave. The teacher may have to be patient and continue to greet and smile even when the student may be distrusting and reluctant to reciprocate, but eventually the teacher's caring will prevail and make a difference in the child's life. It is hard to resist positive attention from such an important figure as the teacher.

The teacher who gives early attention to potentially disruptive students:

a. Makes eye contact, smiles, and says hello.
b. Walks toward the student and chats privately.
c. Compliments the student in private.

Step 6: The Teacher Changes Circumstances That May Produce Misbehavior This step may be found in most plans for classroom management. Before attempting to change the behavior of students, the teacher should modify the circumstances in the physical, social and academic realms of the classroom (Skinner, 1968). This step requires a proactive teacher who does not wait for things to happen but rather shapes the learning environment to prevent difficulties. Outstanding teachers spend more time changing their own behavior than attempting to change their students' behavior, and conversely, ineffective teachers spend little time in changing their own behaviors and a great amount of time trying to change their students' behaviors. For example, in the case of a kindergarten teacher, the use of Step 6 would suggest that the teacher will spend time, before the arrival of the children, preparing the room, removing objects which may be dangerous, arranging a play area with toys and coloring materials, finding records with nursery rhymes, etc. An ineffective teacher would wait for the children to arrive and then would begin to prepare the room. We all know what happens in these circumstances. The children become proactive, and the teacher reactive. The teacher has to do a lot of work to be in charge of a classroom. The question is: Does the teacher do it in a preventive fashion, or does the teacher wait for students to take charge and then react?

The teacher may change circumstances in the physical, social and academic realms of the classroom. For example, if students are distracted by playground activity, the teacher may lower the window shades or turn the students' desks away from the windows. If several students tend to talk among themselves, the teacher will rearrange the seating to prevent talking. If there is the likelihood of a fight on the playground, the teacher may keep one of those two who may fight nearby during recess. In the academic realm, the teacher may change the order of events or the nature of activities in a lesson to prevent disruption or boredom.

How does a teacher know what circumstances to change or rearrange? Mental reflection is a most important component of teaching. Effective teachers reflect after each activity, asking themselves, "What went well?" and "What needs to be improved?" These teachers constantly monitor their performance through self-analysis and feedback elicited from others. Professionals engaged in this process of self-appraisal will continuously monitor and modify their performance and seek the assistance of a qualified supervisor. Such professionals grow and improve and become more knowledgeable about what circumstances need to be modified for particular students or groups. Nonreflective teachers repeat their errors continuously and may exhibit the same ineffective performance in their fifth year of teaching that they exhibited in their first year. Instead of quiet self-appraisal, many ineffective teachers engage in compulsive venting and justification. Meanwhile, effective professionals reflect and attempt to design new approaches to address similar circumstances more successfully the next time.

The teacher who changes circumstances that may produce misbehavior:

a. Makes changes in the physical environment, that is, materials, furniture, etc.
b. Changes the position of students.
c. Removes distracting objects.
d. Changes the order or nature of instructional activities.

Step 7: The Teacher Uses Physical Closeness To Prevent Misbehavior

The closer that a teacher is to a student or group of students, the more likely the students are to behave appropriately. The opposite is also true. When a teacher is away from students, they are more likely to engage in undesirable behaviors. Traditionally, in the upper grades, teachers have presented their lessons from the front of the room and have not moved around the classroom. Step 7 calls for the teacher to remain physically close to students as a way of fostering intimacy and avoiding misbehaviors.

An effective teacher who cares about students projects an image of friendliness and leadership. These two components are essential. The students must feel at ease around the teacher, but they must also respect the teacher as an instructional leader and a professional responsible for fostering their growth and learning. The students must associate the teacher with their own self-improvement. The power of teachers emanates from their instructional leadership and not from fear of punishments. The student should not perceive the proximity of the teacher as a threat. The teacher is a mentor for the students. When around the teacher, students should perceive themselves as more secure and adequate. The teacher is also a role model of a self-actualized adult: competent, involved, enjoying work, and in charge. In Step 7, the teacher becomes a tool. By being close to students, the teacher fosters desirable behaviors and prevents undesirable behaviors.

The teacher who uses physical closeness to prevent misbehavior:

   a. Walks toward or stands by students who are likely to misbehave.
   b. Canvasses work areas frequently, making eye contact with students.
   c. Relocates potential trouble makers so they are near the teacher.

Redirection Steps

Redirection steps are used by the teacher when minor disruptions occur. According to Jones (1979), over 90% of student misbehaviors consist of minor disruptions. Redirection strategies are desist messages which assume that most learners will cease minor misbehaviors once the teacher intervenes. There are no consequences linked to redirection steps. By interacting at an "adult to adult" level (Harris, 1969), the teacher hopes to have the students assume responsibility for their class behavior and perform in a desirable manner (Gordon, 1974). Redirection steps are, as much as possible, individualized messages given in a low voice and without involving the peer group. The interaction is characterized by coming close to the student, making eye contact, speaking in a low voice and prompting the student to change behavior (Jones, 1979). Redirection steps maintain a positive classroom atmosphere, free of consequences or penalties, and quickly redirect students to continue working without disrupting others. This approach is the one mature adults utilize in their interactions. It is easy to use redirection steps and immediately return to prevention steps. Redirection steps have no negative connotations. There are seven steps the teacher utilizes to redirect student behavior.

The teacher:

   8. Ignores minor disruptions and recognizes desirable behaviors.
   9. Sends a nonverbal message requesting change of behavior.
 10. Asks for the status or a rule to redirect behavior.
 11. Requests a change of behavior.
 12. Isolates students to keep minor disruptions from escalating.
 13. Sends an "I Message" communicating the effects of undesirable behavior.
 14. Conducts a "Method III" conference: a no-lose conflict resolution.

Step 8: The Teacher Ignores Minor Disruptions and Recognizes Desirable Behaviors This step applies both to individual students and to groups. When working with only one student, the teacher may ignore a minor disruption, wait for a desirable behavior to occur, and then praise the student for it. When working with a group in which some students are engaged in desirable behaviors while others are engaged in minor disruptions, such as not starting seatwork, the teacher praises those students behaving in a desirable manner and ignores those who are not behaving as expected.

The consistent implementation of Step 8 establishes a positive socioemotional climate in the classroom. The teacher sees the good in the students, and as a result of this perception, students behave as expected. The teacher gets caught in this cycle of reinforcement and is upbeat and happy with the group. The students, in turn, respond well to a happy and optimistic adult who see the best in them. Praise becomes abundant and failure scarce. A high success ratio exists in the classroom. As students succeed they need less discipline interventions from the teacher. Conversely, a teacher who is very quick to notice the flaws of the students produces a negative socioemotional climate in which students perceive the teacher as a nagging, frustrated individual, unable to relate to children. Students end up disliking the teacher and, possibly, the subject taught. Criticism will abound and praise will be scarce. As students fail, the teacher will find a great need for correction and discipline.

Step 8 focuses the attention of the teacher on the good things that are going on in the classroom (Skinner, 1968). It assumes that unless an unacceptable behavior occurs, the teacher's attention should be on the positive events. Obviously, if a behavior is disruptive to the functioning of the classroom, the teacher will address that behavior. Examples of minor disruptions in a group setting which may be ignored in order to recognize desirable behaviors are: students getting off to a slow start, looking at the ceiling, dropping pencils, not finding the appropriate page, or making comments in a low voice.

Effective teachers are proud of their ability to find good happenings rather than the ability to catch the smallest infraction. Step 8 can sum up a whole philosophy of teaching and life: there are those who notice the flowers, and those who notice the dirt in which the flowers grow.

The teacher who ignores minor disruptions and recognizes desirable behaviors:

a. Focuses attention on desirable behaviors rather than undesirable ones.
b. Recognizes individuals who are behaving appropriately.
c. Ignores individuals until they begin to behave appropriately.

Step 9: The Teacher Sends a Nonverbal Message Requesting a Change of Behavior When students are engaged in minor disruptions and require redirection, the teacher attempts to get the students back on task with the least expenditure of class energy, attention, and time possible. A gesture, communicating to the student the need to get back on task, is least distracting to other students. The teacher must have one objective in mind: to redirect behavior. Words are distracting to other students and embarrass the student to whom they are directed. Words remind students of the many admonitions they receive at home and have learned to shut off. Given a choice between a nonverbal and verbal message, humans give more credence to the nonverbal message.

Nonverbal messages are desist messages which are imperceptible to the majority of the class. They do not detract from a positive classroom atmosphere by focusing student attention on what is wrong. Ideally, the teacher should come close to the student, and, making eye contact, point or make a gesture which communicates what the teacher wants. This strategy allows the teacher to be the center of communications with as many individual students as needed while the peer group is excluded from the interaction. Messages between teacher and student alone, without the participation of the peer group, are more likely to be accepted and acted on. Conversely, messages sent in a public forum and witnessed by peers are less likely to produce the desired results. This is particularly true of preadolescents. As students get older, they will prefer to antagonize the teacher rather than to alienate their peer group. Examples of nonverbal redirection messages are to point at a book the student is supposed to be using, at a desk where a student is supposed to be sitting, an object that is to be put away, or to gently guide a student toward a work area.

The teacher who sends nonverbal messages requesting changes of behavior:

a. Communicates, through gestures, the need to change behavior.
b. Approaches the student, stares, and points at work to be done.
c. Moves the student toward the appropriate area, gently.

Step 10: The Teacher Asks for Status or a Rule to Redirect Student Behavior Redirection strategies increase gradually in terms of degree of teacher intervention and directness. Step 8 attempted to redirect students to their tasks by focusing attention on the desirable behaviors, a totally indirect strategy. In Step 9, the teacher requested a change of behavior using a nonverbal message. Step 10 is another teacher effort at redirecting student behavior in an indirect manner: using a question rather than a request. Instead of saying to a student, "Please start your assignment," the teacher asks, "How is your assignment coming along?" Instead of saying, "Please go back to your seat," the teacher says, "Where are you supposed to be now?" Instead of saying, "Please raise your hand when answering questions," the teacher asks, "What is the rule for being recognized when questions are asked?" This approach would not work with students who are very young or new to the school and are unaware of rules and procedures.

An order or request tends to be less effective than a question in redirecting student behavior. The reason is that in our society, we give high regard to autonomy. Individuals would rather change behavior on their own than be told to do it. When the teacher requests redirection of behavior through a question, the student is given the opportunity to retain a certain sense of autonomy by answering the question and then acting on it. The student is an active participant in this interaction with the teacher, and not a passive recipient of an order or request. The teacher then may thank the student for changing behaviors. The interaction has three parts. First, the teacher asks the question. Second, the student responds. Third, the teacher waits for the student to initiate change and then thanks the student.

A procedural question involves the student in an "adult to adult" interaction (Harris, 1969) and promotes student ownership in the management of the classroom. The teacher is asking students about their participation as contributing and responsible members of the group. Step 10 is even more effective if the students themselves participate in the identification of classroom rules and procedures. Procedural questions provoke reflection and foster moral development. The students become more aware of their actions, and their source of control is gradually shifted from dominant adults, or peers, to themselves.

The teacher asks the students:

a. "How is your work coming along?"
b. "What are you supposed to be doing?"
c. "What is the rule about…?"

Step 11: The Teacher Requests a Change of Behavior   This step consists of a polite request in which the teacher asks the student to perform the desired behavior. The emphasis of the strategy is still on gently redirecting the student toward a desired behavior, but in this case, it is done in a more direct manner. The teacher says, "Please do this" or "Please continue your assignment." All attention is placed on the desired behavior without any mention of the undesirable behavior which is to be changed.

By using "please," a polite request approach, the teacher maintains an "adult to adult" interaction avoiding treating the student like a child (Harris, 1969). These requests are done in low voice, as privately as possible, in a matter of fact tone of voice. They are designed to redirect behavior, not to embarrass or establish authority.

Step 11, although less likely to provoke reflection on the part of the student than Step 10, is a quicker tool. It gets the message across faster when time is a factor. Effective teachers use a mixture of Steps 10 and 11. The circumstances and judgment of the teacher determine which strategy to use. Notice that a polite request is different from an order. A management style in which the teacher frequently orders the students around will strip them of their sense of autonomy. Of course, orders are appropriate in the case of an emergency or when the student exhibits unacceptable behaviors such as those which will be discussed later.

The teacher who requests a change of behavior:

a. Asks the student to perform the desired behavior, politely and making eye contact.
b. Thanks the student when the behavior change occurs.

Step 12: The Teacher Isolates a Student to Keep Minor Disruptions from Escalating   The teacher must have a designated place in the room where students can be placed in "time out" until they are ready to return to class activities. This is not a punishment or embarrassment place, but on the contrary, this is a good, protective place, where a student can slow down and get away from the distracting influence of other class members and get back on track, avoiding further trouble. Step 12 offers the students an opportunity to stop, reflect, and work privately before joining the group again. Many teachers ask students to indicate when they are ready to return to their seats.

The teacher who isolates students to keep minor disruption from escalating:

a. Informs the students that the minor disruptions must stop.
b. Moves the students to a "time-out" area.
c. Returns the student to his seat when the student is ready to work properly.

Step 13: The Teacher Sends an "I Message" Communicating the Effects of Undesirable Behavior   The "I Message" (Gordon, 1974) is an effort on the part of the teacher to communicate to the students the effect that their disruptions have on the classroom performance and on the feelings of the teacher. The rationale for this strategy is the same as the one for Step 4 (Teacher sends a preventive "I Message" communicating desirable behavior). The difference between Step 4 and Step 13 is that in Step 13 a minor disruption has occurred while in Step 4 no misbehavior has taken place.

The "I Message" is an effort to make students aware of the effect of their behavior. The teacher discloses oneself. It does not assign blame to anyone. It should be shared without anger. It is a friendly effort to inform another person about how that person is affecting the teacher. A teacher may feel uncomfortable disclosing personal feelings to students and choose not to use 13, but students benefit from interacting with teachers as complete individuals who share their feelings. Most students will avoid hurting a competent, caring teacher. Step 13 will not help an incompetent teacher who fails to promote learning in the classroom. The students will grow impatient with this teacher, and will find it difficult to care for someone who does not care enough about them to be prepared and deliver quality instruction.

"I Messages" can be used with the whole group or with individuals. "I Messages" to the whole class usually refer to group behaviors which slow down progress or make it difficult for the teacher to teach. For example, when students leave material in disarray at the end of an activity and the teacher has to pick them up, the teacher says, "When I have to spend time picking up and arranging books after a session, I feel discouraged." "I Messages" which are directed to individual students are the most likely to produce a change of behavior in a student because they are shared in private, one on one. For example, when a student fails to complete an assignment, is loud while working in groups, or is falling asleep in class, the teacher may share with the student the effect these behaviors have on her.

When delivering an "I Message," the teacher must describe the student behavior which is creating a problem and the impact of this behavior on the teacher's performance and feelings. It is important to share primary feelings which describe our condition (e.g., "discouraged," "inadequate," or "disappointed") rather than secondary feelings, which surface after primary feelings have not been resolved (e.g., "frustrated" and "angry"). It is easier for the student to hear that not having an assignment ready makes the teacher feel discouraged than to hear that it makes the teacher feel angry.

An excessive use of "I Messages" would suggest that the teacher is falling into a reactive, rather than a proactive, role in the classroom. If this happens, the teacher should consider increasing the use of prevention steps. Students will not respond well to a teacher who is constantly sending "I Messages," as this person will appear out of control and this will eventually promote a negative classroom climate.

The teacher who sends an "I Message" communicating effects of undesirable behaviors:

- **a.** Describes the student behavior that is disruptive.
- **b.** Describes the effect of the behavior on teaching and learning.
- **c.** Describes the feeling that this behavior produces in the teacher.

Step 14: The Teacher Conducts a "Method III" Conference: A No-Lose Conflict Resolution   Step 14 consists of a conference in which the teacher and student communicate the effects their behaviors have on each other and explore alternatives to their conflict until a satisfactory solution is agreed upon. This exchange is handled in a context of parity, at an "adult to adult" level, assuming that both teacher and student need to know about the way in which their behaviors affect each other in order to modify them in such a way that neither person is negatively affected. For example, in the case of a student who comes late to school, the teacher will share the trouble this creates, and the student will share how he has no control over the situation since his mother gets up late to drive him to school. Both teacher and student will explore possible solutions. The teacher should let the student do most of the exploration of possible solutions since it is very important for the student to achieve parity in this conference and be empowered by the teacher to become more responsible for his actions. It is called a "no-lose" conference because both the teacher and the student agree on a mutually satisfactory solution.

In order to conduct this conference, the teacher may need to use active listening skills. In active listening, the student is sharing his point of view and feelings. Active listening, as presented in T.E.T. by Thomas Gordon (1974), is a process by which the teacher identifies the feelings the student is experiencing as he talks, and accepts these feelings and repeats them to the student. As a result of the exchange, it should be clear to teacher and students which feelings are being experienced.

Although Step 14 is designed as a redirection tool to address minor disruptions, many teachers have found this strategy to work well with more serious discipline situations. Hard core problem students, who are not responding to consequences and penalties, are at times receptive to a no-lose conference in which power is absent and the teacher relates to them, in private, as reasonable adults.

The teacher who conducts a "Method III" conference:

a. Shares the effect of the disruptive behavior.
b. Asks the student to share his or her side.
c. Asks the student to identify possible solutions to the conflict.
d. Invites the student to agree on a solution and make a commitment.

Consequence Steps

The teacher uses consequence steps when unacceptable behaviors continue to occur and redirection strategies have failed to make students take responsibility for their actions. Consequence steps are teacher interventions which result in the students experiencing consequences for their behavior. For example, a student who does not complete work may be asked to stay after school to do it. Under this type of step, it is assumed that the less mature students will resist changing their behavior unless consequences are applied. There are two consequence strategies the teacher may use.

The teacher can:

15. Conduct a Glasser conference to develop a behavior improvement contract.
16. Implement a class "Assertive Discipline" plan.

These two consequence steps emphasize two very different roles for the teacher and the student. Step 15, in which the teacher conducts a Glasser conference to develop a behavior improvement contract (Glasser, 1969), calls for an involved and caring teacher who interacts with the student privately in order to facilitate designing an individualized plan for success. The teacher invites the student to participate actively in accepting responsibility for his behavior, in exploring solutions, and in making a commitment to change. There are logical consequences attached to the contract as an expression of the seriousness and commitment of both student and teacher. This type of interaction is one of "caring parent to adult" (Harris, 1969).

Step 16, in which the teacher implements a class Assertive Discipline plan (Canter & Canter, 1976), calls for an assertive role on the part of the teacher and a passive role on the part of the student. In this strategy, the classroom rules and consequences for desirable as well as undesirable behaviors have been posted. The teacher's role is to carry out the plan in a business-like manner. The student's role is to comply with the plan. While Step 15 requires time and a private place to interact, Step 16 takes very little time and is done in public.

Which approach is chosen by the teacher will be influenced by the age of the children, their maturity, the size and responsiveness of the group, the types of misbehaviors, the time of year, and the professional style of the teacher.

Step 15: The Teacher Conducts a Glasser Conference to Develop a Behavior Improvement Contract Glasser's contract is a plan for student improvement aimed at succeeding (Glasser, 1969). This step is more appropriate for intermediate grades and less likely to work with pre-schoolers. The teacher interacts with the student, asking questions, in order to get the student to recognize what he should be doing, and to make a commitment to change. The teacher relates to the student in a warm, helpful manner, getting involved and not giving up. The teacher cares about the student and wants to help the student improve. The conference may be structured around **five questions**.

The **first question** is **"What were you doing?"** The teacher invites the student to reflect on the behavior and accept responsibility by describing it. The **second question** is **"How did that help you learn?"** The teacher has the student make a value judgement about the desirability of behaving in such a manner. The **third question** is **"What were you supposed to be doing?"** The teacher has the student describe the desirable behavior for that particular time. The **fourth question** is **"What are you going to do about this?"** The teacher invites the student to consider possible solutions or ways of behaving which will make the student more successful. The **fifth question** is **"What should happen if you do it again?"** The teacher explores possible consequences with the student in case the contract is not carried out.

The consequence should relate to the infraction as much as possible. In other words, the teacher should apply logical consequences. For example, if a student fails to do an assignment during seatwork, a logical consequence will mandate that the assignment be completed after school or be done at home. If a student disrupts class, the consequence may be that the student write an essay about the importance of education and the effects of not completing school. If a student talks during band practice, the consequence may be to come earlier to practice the tuba. To walk around the track ten times carrying the tuba would be inappropriate because this is a punishment—not a consequence.

Some students have difficulty coming up with possible consequences for their misbehaviors. This may indicate a home background in which fine distinctions about the degree of severity of behaviors have not been established. The child may have been punished in the same manner regardless of the type of infraction committed. This child will particularly benefit from exploring alternative consequences to misbehaviors and will hopefully learn that not all behaviors have the same degree of seriousness.

Other students, particularly in the upper grades, refuse to respond to these questions or react to them with protests, denials, and excuses. In such cases it is recommended that the teacher remain silent for a while and, making eye contact, repeat the question in a low and caring voice.

The teacher must remember that the five questions should be used to structure the conference, but not to create an interrogation session in which the teacher tries to intimidate the student or make clear who has the power in the classroom. The conference is an effort to help the student come up with a contract to improve behavior. It does not provide the interaction parity of Step 14 in which both student and teacher share their feelings, but it seeks to create the opportunity for the student to be empowered through a more structured interaction and the addition of consequences. As a result of Step 15, students should become more responsible for their lives and gradually need less teacher supervision and assistance in solving their behavior and academic problems.

The conference takes just a few minutes, but should be conducted in private and with sufficient time to interact with and listen to the student. The student should not fear coming to the conference. If the misbehavior occurs again, the teacher applies the consequences and negotiates a new contract.

The teacher who conducts a Glasser conference asks the student:

a. "What were you doing?"
b. "How did it help you learn?"
c. "What were you supposed to be doing?"
d. "What are you going to do about this?"
e. "What should happen if you do it again?"

Step 16: The Teacher Implements a Class "Assertive Discipline" Plan

Assertive discipline (Canter & Canter, 1976) is a school-wide approach to the implementation of classroom rules and consequences in which other teachers, administrators, and parents participate. A list of desirable classroom behaviors and consequences is posted in each classroom. When students fail to behave, the teacher checks their name. For each check there is a preestablished consequence. As more checks are accumulated, the consequences may involve contacting parents or going to the principal's office. The developers of the system insist that it is as important to reward desirable behaviors as to check negative ones.

Assertive Discipline is most effective the first few weeks of the academic year when the teacher needs to take charge of discipline, or with a particularly difficult group of students. The method also works very well with small children when the teacher consistently rewards desirable behavior. It is our opinion that as the students become older, the method is less effective and limits growth in student responsibility and initiative. Unlike Steps 14 and 15, which emphasized the learning of conflict resolution skills and student responsibility, this method makes the students remain dependent on the teacher to solve classroom behavior problems.

The teacher who implements the class "Assertive Discipline" plan:

a. Applies the same rules and consequences to all students.
b. Puts checks on the board or in a notebook every time a student breaks a rule.
c. Communicates in a firm, low-profile manner.
d. Applies consequences consistently.
e. Rewards desirable behaviors frequently.

Team Support Steps

Team support steps are used when student behaviors become severe and all efforts followed by the teacher seem futile. In these situations, the teacher seeks outside help from another teacher, the parents and the principal. At this point, an effort is made to broaden the consequences of student behavior from the classroom to the home and the school. If outside help is asked too frequently, the teacher may be perceived as unable to manage the classroom. There are four team support strategies a teacher may use. The teacher can:

17. Send students for "time out" to another classroom.
18. Involve parents in changing student behavior
19. Involve the principal in changing student behavior.
20. Request that the student be removed from the classroom.

Step 17: The Teacher Sends a Student to "Time Out" in Another Classroom   When students become very difficult, it is helpful to send them to another classroom, where they are unfamiliar with the teacher and students, until they settle down and are ready to return to their own classroom. Two teachers can work out an arrangement by which they may send students to each other's rooms. This is a severe measure that should not be used frequently. Only one student at a time should be sent to another class and for no longer than a half day or a day. The teacher referring the student is responsible for structuring the conditions of "time out" through a written contract in which the work to be completed is described. When the contract conditions are met, the student is returned to the classroom. If a student misbehaves while in another classroom, the principal is contacted.

The teacher who sends students for "time out" to another classroom:

a. Works out an arrangement with another teacher for a "time out" exchange.
b. Draws up a contract detailing work to be completed before returning to class.
c. Requires the student to stay out until contract conditions are met.
d. Sends any student who misbehaves while in the other teacher's classroom to the principal.

Step 18: The Teacher Involves Parents in Changing Student Behavior
There are two ways to involve parents in helping the teacher change student behavior: a telephone conference, and a face to face conference in which the student is present. Both conferences are similar. They should be scheduled ahead of time. To prepare for the conference, the teacher must identify what student behavior needs to be changed and what the parents can do about it. The teacher will also need data or samples of student work to support statements that the student needs to change performance.

There are seven steps that can be followed in a teacher-parent conference. The teacher:

a. Says something nice about the student when greeting the parents.
b. Describes the student behavior that needs to be changed.
c. Accepts the parents' feelings and opinions about the situation.
d. Shares data documenting the need for change.

    e. Suggests a plan for parents to follow at home in helping the student.

    f. Asks parents to summarize the plan.

    g. Reports to parents weekly on student progress.

When contacted by a teacher, many parents feel anxious and inadequate about the job they have done raising their children. To hear something nice about their child is reassuring and conveys to them the idea that the teacher cares and that there is hope for their child.

Describing the behavior which needs to be changed should be done without looking for psychological, socioeconomic or cultural interpretations. The task of the teacher is not to describe why the child is having trouble learning or whose fault it is, but to communicate what kind of difficulty the child is experiencing.

Parents will react in different ways to the teacher's statement about their child's problems. Some parents will be surprised and annoyed. Some will blame the teacher or school. Some will want more information or proof. Some will declare themselves helpless. It is important that the teacher accepts these feelings. When a parent feels upset and the teacher accepts the feeling by saying, "You are upset about…," the parent is more likely to cooperate and respect the teacher as a professional.

It is important for the teacher to document statements with samples of student work or other types of descriptive data. Parents should be treated as rational adults and not like children who should take the teacher's word without explanations.

The action plan that parents will carry out at home is the most important component of the conference. The plan should be practical, easy to follow, and should not require specialized knowledge on the part of the parents. Most plans will suggest that the parents supervise the child's study time, or provide rewards and consequences for school behavior.

It is important that the parents summarize the plan to make sure they have understood it. Calling in the child is an effective way to give the parents an opportunity to verbalize the plan and show the child that parents and teacher are working together toward his or her improvement.

A weekly follow up, through a written note or phone call, will reinforce the parents' efforts and give them feedback on their child's progress.

The involvement of parents in the schooling of children should start at the beginning of the academic year. At that time, teachers should send a letter to them describing their academic goals, assignment procedures, classroom rules and consequences, consultation times, and procedures. In this letter, the teacher should emphasize the important role parents play reinforcing the work of the school by making sure that their child completes assignments and follows procedures.

Step 19: The Teacher Involves the Principal in Changing Student Behavior

There are times when severe behavior on the part of the student is such that the teacher must ask the principal for help, particularly if the parents have not been supportive or available. Because the principal in an elementary school cannot do much more than an effective teacher in providing consequences for misbehavior, a teacher does not usually go to the principal requesting further consequences. What new consequences can a principal apply that the teacher as an effective professional cannot? The principal will help, primarily, as a member of a professional team, by getting involved and supporting the teacher. The teacher must not be all alone addressing difficult discipline problems.

It is suggested, then, that the principal be used as a source of guidance and support, rather than as the person who administers the consequences. The teacher should administer the consequences. If the student is assigned detention after school, the teacher should be the person supervising detention. If teachers do not have time for working on discipline with problem students, the school schedule, grouping practices, and teacher team organization should be studied and modified to allow for these tasks.

What types of help may a teacher get from the principal? Professional advice, validation of a course of action, identification of possible new approaches, and referral services are examples of the types of assistance which a principal can provide. The other type of help which a principal may provide is to consider removing the student from the classroom so that he can be assigned to another teacher, placed in an alternative program, or suspended. There are students who respond to some teachers better than others. Assigning a troubled student to another teacher could solve the problem. This will be discussed in Step 20.

The most important assistance the principal can provide to teachers who have problem students in their room is to keep informed of the situation, consult frequently with the teacher, be aware of the procedures the teacher is following to solve the problem, and support the teacher's actions. The principal, after being informed and agreeing to a course of action, must support the teacher's actions and let the student and parents know that the teacher is acting under the principal's authority.

The teacher who involves the principal in changing student behavior:

a. Consults the principal about actions to address student behavior.
b. Obtains the principal's support for the plan of action.
c. Keeps the principal appraised of progress.
d. Communicates to student and parents that the principal supports the teacher's actions.

Step 20: The Teacher Requests That the Student Be Removed from the Classroom After the teacher has sought assistance from other teachers, parents, and the principal, if the discipline problem continues, the teacher documents the frequency and impact of the behavior and requests that the student be removed from the classroom and get sent to another classroom, an alternative program, or be suspended from school. Since the teacher has involved the principal in the process, it will not be difficult to have the principal's support once all reasonable attempts and efforts fail to improve the situation and it is clear that other students are being negatively affected. The parents will not be surprised since they have been contacted earlier and asked to assist in the solution of the problem. In a well developed process, a conference could be set up in which the supporting team members (teacher, support teachers, parents, and principal) would discuss the disposition of the case.

The teacher who requests that a problem student be removed from the classroom:

a. Documents the measures taken attempting to improve student conduct.
b. Documents the frequency, severity, and effect of misbehaviors on others.
c. Meets with the support team to recommend a course of action.

CONDITIONS NECESSARY FOR THE 20-STEP SYSTEM OF DISCIPLINE TO WORK

For the 20-step system to work, four conditions must exist: 1) the goals and values of the school program must be reflected in the discipline approaches used in the classroom; 2) the role of the teacher as a professional must be clearly established; 3) the role of the student must be defined according to the school mission and goals; and 4) a school discipline approach must be aimed towards helping students grow into more advanced ways of behaving.

The Goals and Values of the School Program

If one important school goal is the development of civic-minded, responsible citizens, the classroom discipline interventions must be congruent with this goal. Discipline systems that foster passivity, lack of responsibility and ownership must be used only as last resort, for as short a time as possible, and with as few students as possible. The school's hidden curriculum is seldom so evident as with the handling of discipline. An emphasis on punitive discipline or an approach in which the student is treated as a "child" does not facilitate the development of the responsible citizen. By studying a school's adopted discipline plan and philosophy, an observer will be able to predict the amount of student motivation and sense of autonomy that exists in the building.

The Role of the Teacher

A teacher who is regarded as little more than a semiskilled worker, without professional autonomy to make instructional and procedural decisions, will be a poorly motivated individual without much inspiration to offer as a role model. This teacher will tend to pass on authoritarian approaches to students and treat them as the teacher is treated, without allowing for student involvement in decision making and without providing opportunities for choices in learning. This teacher may become alienated and convey a sense of helplessness and lack of purpose with the students.

Teachers must be "professionals" with sufficient autonomy to make curricular and disciplinary adjustments and decisions, and with freedom to deliver an educational program that benefits the student. Above all, teachers must be in charge of their professional lives as much as is possible. They should have a say in budget, hiring of personnel, and the allocation of resources and facilities. In turn, these teachers, when they are not debilitated by state department of education mandates or central office or school building restrictions, will convey to students a sense of direction and purpose.

Semiskilled workers perform tasks which require little decision making and adjustment. They follow formulae which are described in very minute detail, and apply these formulae daily, to all students, regardless of circumstances, as if working with students would be similar to working with glass in a bottling factory. Unlike physical matter, students are not a constant to which a set procedure can always be applied. Professionals working within the guidelines and knowledge base of their professions address their task in a problem-solving manner, performing differently according to the particular circumstances of each case. Classroom management requires professional actions—not semiskilled worker performance.

The Role of the Student

It would be unusual for a school not to emphasize the development of social and civic skills. In a democratic society, students should be given as much responsibility as possible for their own education. Students should participate in the identification of class rules and consequences, the assignment of seats and materials, the identification of some learning experiences and evaluation procedures, and in the implementation of the discipline system. This active and involved role of students fosters the development of self-directed, responsible citizens. Conversely, if the student is not given responsibilities and is passive in the schooling process, motivation will be low and the "student as child" personality will be perpetuated until it eventually becomes "citizen as child."

A School Discipline Approach Must Be Aimed at Helping Students Grow into More Advanced Ways of Behaving

A teacher may prescribe penalties or use assertive discipline which tends to foster passivity on the part of the learner, but only as needed, and having in mind a goal of growth. If the months go by and the teacher continues to use punitive or passive behavior management approaches, there should be concern about the amount of student growth which is occurring and the effectiveness of the discipline approach being used. For example, a teacher who keeps students after school over and over throughout the year should question the effectiveness of these measures.

SUMMARY

The proposed 20-Step System of Discipline for early childhood and elementary teachers provides an eclectic tool to address four different types of behaviors in the classroom: desirable behaviors, minor disruptions, unacceptable behaviors, and severe behaviors. The type of behavior exhibited by the student determines the type of step the teacher will use in response. If the student's behavior is desirable, the teacher's primary concern is one of **prevention** of undesirable behavior to maintain a positive classroom climate and maximize the amount of time and energy devoted to learning activities. When minor disruptions occur, the teacher's attention may shift to **redirection**, seeking to return the student to a productive mode of behavior without imposing consequences for the infraction. This is best accomplished by interacting at an "adult to adult" level with individual students without involving the peer group. When students engage in unacceptable behaviors, the teacher may choose to impose **consequences**. This strategy may be particularly useful in working with students who depend on the teacher for direct guidance. Finally, in those occasions when behaviors become severe and all efforts followed by the teacher seem futile, **team support** steps may be utilized. In such situations, the teacher seeks outside assistance from another teacher, the parents, and the principal or assistant principal.

Within each of the four types of strategies (prevention, redirection, consequences, team support), there are a variety of steps from which the teacher may choose and which follow no prescribed order. The earliest strategies assume a greater maturity on the part of the student; those which come later assume greater need for teacher domination. The steps may be used sequentially or the teacher may skip steps as needed. The teacher also may shift forward or backward, as long as the steps match the student's type of behavior and level of development. The teacher's personal style, the student's personality, the success of past disciplinary approaches with that student, and the specific circumstances surrounding the misbehavior should all be considered in determining which of these alternative steps is most appropriate. A detailed list of the 20-steps, with the teacher behaviors which are characteristics of each step, is presented in Box 9.2.

Box 9-2   **20-Step System of Discipline**

PREVENTION STEPS
  The teacher:

1. PROVIDES EFFECTIVE INSTRUCTION

    a. Posts class rules and expectations.
    b. Communicates lesson objectives.
    c. Keeps students on task and covers material extensively.
    d. Provides opportunities for students to participate actively.
    e. Asks questions which produce many correct answers.
    f. Provides feedback on student progress during instruction.

2. HELPS STUDENTS EXPERIENCE MORE SUCCESS THAN FAILURE

    a. Establishes a cooperative learning environment.
    b. Adjusts learning tasks to students' ability level.
    c. Provides extra assistance to those having difficulty.
    d. Provides many opportunities for practice.
    e. Creates an environment in which it is OK to make mistakes.
    f. Prepares individualized plans for those not succeeding.

3. RECOGNIZES AND REWARDS DESIRABLE BEHAVIOR

    a. Smiles at students.
    b. Praises students privately.
    c. Recognizes students publicly.
    d. Provides tangible rewards.

4. SENDS A PREVENTIVE "I MESSAGE" COMMUNICATING DESIRABLE BEHAVIOR

    a. Describes the student behavior that is desirable.
    b. Describes the effect of desirable behavior on teaching and learning.
    c. Describes the feeling that desirable behavior produces in the teacher.

(continued)

5. **GIVES EARLY ATTENTION TO POTENTIALLY DISRUPTIVE STUDENTS**

    a. Makes eye contact, smiles and says hello.
    b. Walks toward student and chats privately.
    c. Compliments student in private.

6. **CHANGES CIRCUMSTANCES THAT MAY PRODUCE MISBEHAVIOR**

    a. Makes changes in the physical environment: materials, furniture etc.
    b. Changes the position of students.
    c. Removes distracting objects.
    d. Changes the order or nature of instructional activities.

7. **USES PHYSICAL CLOSENESS TO PREVENT MISBEHAVIOR**

    a. Walks toward or stands by students who are likely to misbehave.
    b. Canvasses the work area frequently, making eye contact with students.
    c. Relocates potential trouble makers so they are near the teacher.

REDIRECTION STEPS
The teacher:

8. **IGNORES MINOR DISRUPTIONS AND RECOGNIZES
    DESIRABLE BEHAVIORS**

    a. Focuses attention on desirable behaviors rather than undesirable.
    b. Recognizes individuals behaving appropriately.
    c. Ignores misbehaving individuals until they begin to behave appropriately.

9. **SENDS NONVERBAL MESSAGE REQUESTING CHANGE OF BEHAVIOR**

    a. Communicates through gestures the need to change behavior.
    b. Approaches the student, stares, and points at work to be done.
    c. Moves the student toward an appropriate area, gently.

10. **ASKS FOR STATUS OR RULE TO REDIRECT BEHAVIOR**
Asks the student:

    a. "How is your work coming along?"
    b. "What are you supposed to be doing?"
    c. "What is the rule about ...?"

(continued)

11. REQUESTS A CHANGE OF BEHAVIOR

   a. Asks the student to perform the desired behavior—politely, making eye contact.
   b. Thanks the student when a behavior change occurs.

12. ISOLATES STUDENT TO KEEP MINOR DISRUPTION FROM ESCALATING

   a. Informs the student that the minor disruption must stop.
   b. Moves the student to "time-out" area.
   c. Returns the student to seat when the student is ready to work properly.

13. SENDS AN "I MESSAGE" COMMUNICATING EFFECTS OF UNDESIRABLE BEHAVIORS

   a. Describes the student behavior that is disruptive.
   b. Describes the effect of the behavior on teaching and learning.
   c. Describes the feeling that this behavior produces in the teacher.

14. CONDUCTS A "METHOD III" CONFERENCE: NO-LOSE CONFLICT RESOLUTION APPROACH

   a. Shares effect of the disruptive behavior.
   b. Asks the student to share his own side.
   c. Asks the student to identify possible solutions to conflict.
   d. Invites the student to agree on a solution and make a commitment.

CONSEQUENCE STEPS
The teacher:

15. CONDUCTS A GLASSER CONFERENCE TO DEVELOP A BEHAVIOR IMPROVEMENT CONTRACT

   Asks the student:

   a. "What were you doing?"
   b. "How did that help you learn?"
   c. "What were you supposed to be doing?"
   d. "What are you going to do about this next time?"
   e. "What should happen if you do it again?"

(continued)

16. **IMPLEMENTS A CLASS "ASSERTIVE DISCIPLINE" PLAN**

    a. Applies the same rules and consequences to all students.
    b. Makes checkmarks on board or notebook every time a student breaks a rule.
    c. Communicates in a firm, low-profile manner.
    d. Applies consequences consistently.
    e. Rewards desirable behaviors frequently.

TEAM SUPPORT STEPS
The teacher:

17. **SENDS THE STUDENT FOR "TIME OUT" TO ANOTHER CLASSROOM**

    a. Works out an arrangement with another teacher for "time out" exchange.
    b. Draws up a contract detailing the work to be completed before the student may return to class.
    c. Requires the student to stay out until the contract conditions are met.

18. **INVOLVES THE PARENTS IN CHANGING STUDENT BEHAVIOR**

    a. Says something nice about the student when greeting parents.
    b. Describes the student behavior that needs to be changed.
    c. Accepts the parents' feelings and opinions about the situation.
    d. Shares data documenting the need for change.
    e. Suggests a plan for parents to follow at home in helping the student.
    f. Asks the parents to summarize the plan.
    g. Reports to the parents weekly on student's progress.

19. **INVOLVES THE PRINCIPAL IN CHANGING STUDENT BEHAVIOR**

    a. Consults the principal about actions to address student behavior.
    b. Obtains the principal's support for a plan of action.
    c. Keeps the principal appraised of progress.
    d. Communicates to the student and parents that the principal supports the teacher's actions.

20. **REQUESTS THAT THE STUDENT BE REMOVED FROM THE CLASSROOM**

    a. Documents the measures taken attempting to improve student conduct.
    b. Documents the frequency, severity, and effect of misbehaviors on others.
    c. Meets with support team to recommend course of action.

GLOSSARY

active listening Careful, accepting listening; for example, when a teacher listens carefully to a student and accepts his or her feelings.

adult to adult interaction Interaction in which teacher and student both relate rationally to each other.

at-risk student A student who is likely to drop out of school.

group norms Unwritten rules of conduct for a group. For example, cohesive classroom groups may not engage in gossip. Different groups have different norms which may be positive or negative (as is the case with gangs).

parent to adult interaction Interaction in which the teacher relates to the student as the authority in the classroom while the student responds rationally.

parent to child interaction When the teacher relates to the student as the authority in the classroom and the student responds in an immature manner.

positive reinforcement Teacher actions which follow a desirable student behavior and which increase the likelihood that the behavior will be repeated, for example, teacher praise.

procedural question A question which refers to classroom rules and procedures.

time-out When students are removed from a classroom activity and placed in a quiet place for a short time until they can control and redirect their own behavior. Time out should not be used as a punishment. Rather, it should be used to intervene, when necessary, to prevent further trouble.

Promoting Student Involvement in Classrooms

MOTIVATION: HOW TO PROMOTE STUDENT INTEREST, EFFORT, AND GOOD PERFORMANCE

*W*hen asked, "What is the greatest challenge in the schools today?," many teachers respond, "the students' lack of motivation." In an era when the school dropout rate ranges from 25 to 45%, promoting student motivation becomes a priority. Teachers may be very knowledgeable about subject matter and instructional techniques, but if they do not know how to get kids involved in learning, their efforts are wasted.

Motivation can be broken down into six types of student behaviors or dimensions (Stipek, 1988; Hunter, 1982):

1. **Attention:** This can be defined as any instance in which the student chooses to focus on the instructional activity rather than on other noninstructional behaviors.
2. **Time on task:** Evidence of this behavior is provided when the student spends sufficient time engaged in the learning activity.
3. **Effort:** This is demonstrated when the student works intensively, investing the energy and ability required by the task.
4. **Feeling tone:** This can be assessed if the student appears happy, self-confident, and eager in the learning situation.

5. **Extension:** Examples of this include situations in which the student goes beyond the standards required by the activity; for example, the student reads about the subject during free time or solves extra problems.

6. **Performance:** When the student masters the task, performance has been demonstrated.

Satisfactory performance of a learning objective does not necessarily indicate that a student is highly motivated. At times, very talented students get bored with the task, and while they are able to complete the task successfully, they lack motivation. In classrooms where a large number of students are having difficulty mastering the material, it is easy to overlook the learning needs of talented students who are not learning according to their potential. Such students are often lacking in the attention, time on task, effort, feeling tone, and extension dimensions of motivation. Those students who achieve, but are experiencing motivation problems, can go unnoticed by the teacher. They find school boring and may be "at risk" of dropping out.

There are ten ways through which teachers can increase motivation in the classroom (Stipek, 1988; Hunter, 1982). They can:

1. Make the learning tasks challenging.
2. Deemphasize testing and grades.
3. Provide assistance without overprotecting.
4. Shift from extrinsic to intrinsic rewards.
5. Use praise appropriately.
6. Have high expectations for each of their students.
7. Provide knowledge of results.
8. Promote success for all class members.
9. Increase, in students, the perception that they control the learning situation.
10. Change the classroom goal-reward structure.

Making the Learning Task Challenging

In order to satisfy the needs of students to achieve competence, learning tasks must be perceived as contributing to the development of mastery and skill. Learning tasks should be challenging. Tasks which are too easy or too difficult are not motivating. Each child must be given tasks which are challenging enough to require effort and which, without requiring too much assistance, result in increased mastery (Stipek, 1988). It is very difficult for teachers to provide each student with a task which is at once challenging and likely to result in success. In order to help teachers individualize tasks, schools should use flexible arrangements for grouping students; for example, those described in the section of Chapter 2 which dealt with nongraded schools.

Learning tasks need not only be challenging; they must also be varied. Having a variety of instructional experiences promotes novelty and student interest. A routine that becomes repetitive and predictable, whether in lesson preparation or seatwork and assignments, decreases student motivation.

The manner in which teachers present a task and the feeling tone communicated affect the students' attitudes toward the lesson. If learning tasks are presented as games, for example, the students' motivation will be greater than when tasks are presented as subject drills. If teachers are enthusiastic about their subjects and look forward to seeing their students learn, they will establish a positive feeling tone and make a difference in the students' motivation to participate in the lesson.

Deemphasizing Testing and Grades

When students are concerned about being tested or receiving a grade, they choose less challenging tasks, express less pleasure as they solve a problem, and appear more anxious, than students who are not being tested or graded (Harter, 1978). External evaluations can inhibit students from choosing challenging tasks and can lower student motivation (Maehr & Stallings, 1972). Reminding students frequently that they will receive a grade does not help them develop interest in learning; instead, it develops their interest in the grade. Extrinsic motivation based on grades ceases to affect the student once the rewards are removed. But intrinsic motivation, or working because it makes one feel competent, is self reinforcing; the more competent one becomes, the more one strives toward greater competence.

Grades are required in schools and can provide information on the progress of students and their mastery of learning tasks. But grades do not need to be emphasized. Some motivation theorists would like to see grades eliminated. They would like students to be given specific feedback about their mastery of various learning objectives as is done in nongraded schools. When students express concern about grades, teachers should redirect their attention toward the task to be mastered.

Providing Assistance Without Being Overprotective

Students frequently ask for teacher help in order to complete learning tasks. Assistance should be given if needed, in a manner that allows for the student to take some credit for the completion of the task (Stipek, 1988). A student feels less proud and competent when helped more than is necessary. In the long run, once children learn that the teacher will come to the rescue, a loss of persistence and effort results. Too much help may have as bad an effect on motivation as too little help. A poor product, completed solely by the student, may be more beneficial (in terms of motivating future effort on the part of the student) than an excellent product for which the student can not claim ownership.

Shifting from Extrinsic to Intrinsic Rewards

Offering extrinsic rewards to students seems, initially, to increase the amount of time they spend on a learning task, but as the rewards are withdrawn, students lose interest in the task. It appears that when rewards are given, students eventually perceive the rewards as the reason to engage in the activity (even if without the reward they would have also been motivated to do the task). Once students perceive rewards as the reason to do the work, they will not work until the rewards are offered (Stipek, 1988; Morgan, 1984).

When should teachers give rewards? There are many tasks that, because they are initially unappealing to students, may require the use of rewards to get them done; for example, writing neatly. In this case, rewards are used as means to get students started on a task. In the case of tasks that can be achieved and are challenging, teachers should emphasize the value of the task, shifting the attention of the students to the intrinsic value of the activity and the attainment of mastery and competence. The students will hopefully see the activity as valuable in itself and will not need rewards to perform it. The teacher must focus the attention of the students on the importance of the task and how good it feels to master it and be competent.

Rewards, if not used to introduce students to uninteresting tasks, should be given for tasks which all students can achieve, should be contingent on effort or good performance, and should give students useful feedback about the value of their work.

Using Praise Appropriately

Teacher praise, a form of extrinsic reward, is most effective when given to students for having put forth high effort or good performance (Brophy, 1981). Praise must have credibility, that is, it must be descriptive and give information to the students about the value of their accomplishments. Sometimes negative, nonverbal expressions contradict verbal praise, and, as a result, communicate to the student that the praise which has been given is not sincere. Praise which is given noncontingently or insincerely may actually have a negative effect on the confidence and motivation of students. Praise, at times, is only given to these self-confident students who elicit it from the teacher while many less confident children are overlooked. Ironically, children with low confidence are the ones in greatest need of teacher praise. Effective praise reinforces the efforts and accomplishments of a wide range of students and provides opportunities for celebrating success.

When a teacher praises a student for a well written story by using only an evaluative comment, "Jane, your story is excellent," the message has failed to give information to the student about the value of her accomplishment. "Jane, your story shows that you have mastered the technique of description very well, and you are ready to move on to the use of metaphors," is a more complete form of praise, one for which the teacher focuses the attention of the student on the value of competence, not on being one of the best students in the class.

Having High Expectations for Each Student

Teacher statements make a big impact on students' beliefs about their competence. Teachers can attribute a student's failure to lack of ability or to lack of effort. Since students have no control over their innate abilities, teachers should attribute failure to low effort and lack of practice. When teachers attribute student failure to low effort, the message implies that the student has sufficient ability to master the task if effort is applied. Attributing failure to lack of ability may undermine the student's sense of adequacy. At times, attributing success to high effort could also lead to the conclusion that the student lacks ability. Obviously, one of the most damaging statements a teacher could make is, "You were lucky, you got it right." This implies that the student lacks both ability and effort (Stipek, 1988). Teachers must be very careful that the statements they make about their students' work reflect positive teacher expectations rather than pessimistic views of the students' potential.

Children whose teachers expect all of their students to learn achieve at a higher level than children in classrooms where teachers do not hold high expectations

(Edmonds, 1979). Expectations can bias the interpretations teachers make about student performance. If a student who is believed to be very intelligent performs poorly, lack of effort or attention may be interpreted as the reason. If a student believed to have low ability performs poorly, lack of ability may be the interpretation. As a result of initial expectations, self-fulfilling prophecies develop, and students are likely to behave as they are expected to behave. Teachers must be constantly on guard against interpreting students' behaviors according to low expectations. Stipek (1988) lists four suggestions to help teachers avoid the consequences of negative expectations: 1) expectations should be based on valid information, 2) expectations should be dynamic and flexible, 3) teachers should avoid treating high and low ability students differently, and 4) teachers should not give up on a child.

Stipek's second suggestions (keep expectations dynamic and flexible) relates back to the philosophy of a nongraded school (discussed in Chapter 2). Each child must be successful at her own learning if she is to stay motivated. When we recommend that teachers have high expectations for their students, we are **not** implying that teachers should set standards so high as to create failure for their students.

We wish to add, as a parenthetical note, that nongraded schools deviate from this recommendation, but they do so in a positive way. Rather than holding all students to equal standards of achievement, nongraded schools hold all students accountable for their potential. Thus, if a student has mastered simple addition, she is now ready to tackle simple subtraction or two-digit addition. Another student may have already mastered two-digit addition. That student is ready to learn how to add with regrouping (carrying). Each student, however, faces uniformly high expectations in the sense that she is expected to move on and achieve whatever she is capable of achieving next.

Providing Knowledge of Results

Students are better motivated to continue working on a task when they are frequently told how well they are performing in specific and immediate terms. This topic was discussed in detail under "feedback skills" (see Chapter 3).

Promoting Success for All Class Members

Success means the extent to which students can accurately perform a task or complete an assignment. Completing a high percentage of tasks successfully makes students feel good about their ability to learn and increases the likelihood that they will apply themselves with persistence and effort in subsequent tasks. Teachers must plan lessons which promote a high rate of success for all members of the class. Success rate in seatwork activities should approximate 90%, particularly in the early grades (Brophy & Good, 1986).

How can teachers promote high rates of success for all students? Individualizing learning tasks, setting attainable performance standards, and utilizing mastery learning and cooperative learning strategies are some of the approaches which will help to promote this. We dealt with these approaches in the chapter on teaching methods. Nongraded school settings (discussed in Chapter 2) also help to foster success.

Increasing Student Perceptions of Control

Student interest in learning activities increases when teachers relinquish some of their control and provide opportunities for students to choose among tasks (Morgan, 1984). Children's perceptions of control over learning situations increase when they are allowed to participate in decision making. As students increase their perception that they control their learning environment, their interest and achievement in school also increases.

Teachers promote student perceptions of control and autonomy by giving students some choice about the amount of material to be covered, the level of difficulty, how that tasks are to be completed, when they are due, and how much they count. As students perceive themselves as more active participants in decisions about learning, they develop a greater sense of responsibility and ownership about what goes on in the classroom. Wang (1983) found that elementary students complete more tasks when they have some control over the task. Teachers who are skillful at motivating their students provide instructional situations which afford students the opportunity to exert control over what they are learning. This fosters a sense that they are participating because they want to participate. The informal and alternative settings described in Chapter 2 are examples of settings which promote student perceptions of control. Topic work (see Chapters 4 and 5) is an example of an instructional method which promotes a sense of student control.

Changing the Classroom Goal-Reward Structure

Competitive classroom goal and reward structures emphasize making comparisons among students and creating win-lose situations for them. **Cooperative** goal-reward structures emphasize interdependence and make individual effort, rather than ability, a primary goal in the classroom. A third type of classroom, where tasks are assigned to each student on an individual basis as they demonstrate mastery of previous tasks, and where each student works at her own pace, follows an **individualistic** orientation (Johnson & Johnson, 1985). Cooperative and individualistic classroom goal-reward structures increase whole class productivity, particularly when students are given choices and a sense of control over their learning. Competitive classroom goal-reward orientations inhibit motivation, unless the members of the class are individuals of equally high ability since, in this situation, success is a result of effort. A competitive approach among students of various ability levels does not encourage high effort from students of high ability since they compete with students of lower ability. Competitive approaches can be devastating to low ability students since they will seldom experience success under these conditions. When grouped together, high and low ability students benefit more from a cooperative learning approach, or from a mastery learning program, or a combination of both types of programs, than from a competitive learning structure.

GROUP PROCESS SKILLS: HOW TO ORGANIZE, FACILITATE, AND MONITOR SMALL GROUP WORK

A very common activity in elementary classrooms is small group work. Teachers divide the class into smaller groups and assign tasks which the students are to complete together, learning from each other and helping each other.

Advantages of Small Groups

We have already discussed some of the instructional advantages of using small groups in the classroom. In Chapter 2, we described various types of small groups which might be formed in a classroom, for example, achievement groups and skill groups. Small groups afford teachers the opportunity to meet individual needs of students and to teach more effectively. In addition to these instructional benefits, however, there are several other advantages afforded by the use of small groups (i.e., subgroups of the entire class) in one's classroom.

Some student behaviors, such as responsibility and cooperation, cannot be taught through teacher presentations. In order to attain them, the students must engage in activities or experiences which, after many occurrences, will affect their attitudes and, eventually, their spontaneous behavior. These educational outcomes, such as citizenship or communication skills, are at least as important as academic learning. In order to develop these behaviors, the students must have opportunities to practice them. Small group work is one of the best vehicles to afford students these opportunities.

Through small group work, students learn to interact with each other, to listen and wait for their turn to talk, to express their own views and respect the views of others, to make decisions which take into consideration the needs of others, to resolve conflicts through compromise, to be responsible for carrying out their own tasks within a group, to develop leadership, to work as a team, to value members of another race, ethnic group, or gender, and to relate to peers who have a diversity of talents and handicaps.

Small groups require that students assume responsibility for their own learning, learn problem solving skills, and develop critical thinking abilities. They also promote the understanding of subject matter and the learning of concepts and facts. Since small groups are mostly student directed, they increase the feeling on the part of the students that they have some autonomy and are able to make choices. This creates a very motivating instructional activity. Some students who do not actively participate in a large group setting become more involved and vocal in small groups. These are some of the advantages of having students work in small groups. They cannot be achieved in a teacher-directed learning format.

Role of the Teacher

The teacher's role in working with small groups is a complex one. The teacher has to structure the class work in advance in a manner that helps develop the prerequisite skills and climate for small group work. Throughout the unit, the teacher maintains an active role in planning, organizing, and assessing progress. Once the groups are given their tasks, or have decided on their tasks (depending on their maturity level), the teacher assumes a supervisory role and observes the students at work. The teacher relinquishes authority to the group and ceases to be the center of attention. Now the teacher talks to individuals or small groups rather than to the whole class.

Small group work requires a climate of acceptance and a democratic leadership style in the classroom. Students who feel inhibited or not welcome to express their views are not ready for small group work. Likewise, students who are overdependent, needing constant teacher reassurance and assistance, will have difficulty working with peers unless the teacher has gradually prepared them for group work. Very young children are limited in their capacity to work within groups, especially when that work demands cooperation among peers.

Learning how to work in groups and how to function in different group roles is not easy for many students. The teacher must help students learn how to contribute to group planning and decision making, define and clarify problems, organize to complete a task, distribute assignments, and assume leadership roles. It requires time to prepare students gradually to become skillful members of groups. These skills must be taught by the teacher just as any other academic subject or skill must be taught.

Forming Groups

Groups are more than just some quantity of students brought together for learning purposes. A group exists when there is sense of identity, mutual trust, respect, and team effort among the members. Group work is characterized by students exchanging ideas, actively learning, and actively participating and putting forth effort toward the attainment of a specific goal or task. Teachers foster the development of group spirit by creating a classroom climate in which ideas, agreements, and disagreements are accepted. In such a climate, student-to-teacher and student-to-student communication is emphasized, team efforts toward the achievement of attainable objectives are facilitated, and increased autonomy and self-direction are fostered (Schmuck & Schmuck, 1983).

Group size is an important variable which influences the degree of student participation and the ability of the group to achieve its task. Group size varies from student pairs and trios to groups of about six to nine students.

Group membership is decided by the teacher, depending on the nature or purpose of the group. For example, tutorial groups require joining students who have achieved high and low mastery of the material. Interest groups, on the other hand, may bring together students of similar backgrounds. Most groups are best formed by dividing students in such a way as to make each group become a micro-representation of the class. At times, teachers use student sociograms as one source of information to divide students up into groups. (See Figure 10.1).

The lifetime of a group may be very short (as when it meets only once) or rather long (as happens when it is assigned to a task for several days or weeks). Obviously, long-term group membership assignments require careful thought, while short-term groups may be arranged randomly. Likewise, the preparation of instructions, materials, evaluation procedures, areas of work, and work schedules will be rather elaborate for long assignments but very simple for short assignments.

Group Decision Making Methods

There are four major ways in which groups in the classroom can make decisions: 1) by **consensus**, 2) by **majority vote**, 3) by allowing a member of the group to function as an **"expert"**, and 4) by vesting the group leader with the **authority** to make decisions for the group. The most effective way of group decision-making is by consensus, where all members agree to a decision. Consensus-decision making takes more time than other methods. It requires that group members see their differences of opinion as a challenge to come up with better alternatives. In consensus-decision making, discussion

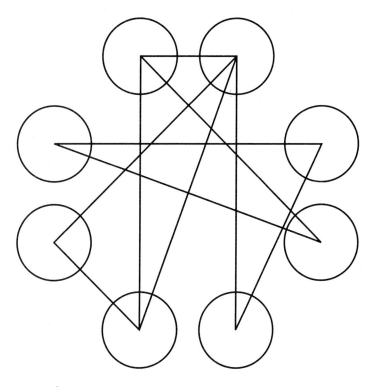

Figure 10.1 A Sample Sociogram

is not closed until all members are satisfied with a solution. Consensus decisions foster group communication, trust, and cohesion.

When groups are very divided on issues, and consensus is almost impossible, decisions may be reached by majority vote. Votes representing half of the group membership plus one constitutes a majority. This approach is less time consuming, but fosters less critical and creative thinking and could undermine the cohesiveness of groups of young students if used too frequently.

A decision by an expert member may be used as a way to expedite group progress and divide responsibilities. In this method, the group agrees to follow this approach and identifies a member who will be responsible to make decisions for a particular area and to explain the decision to the group. For example, a committee which is preparing a play may select an expert member to make decisions about the lighting and sound, another to make decisions about costumes, etc.

Decision making by authority occurs when the group members empower the group leader, or chair, to make all the decisions without consulting the members. This approach to decision-making, although very common in business, has less place in the classroom. It is designed to emphasize product efficiency rather than the quality of the process. But process is the objective of educational groups. This approach eliminates the democratic process from classroom groups.

Areas of Group Work

Teachers may structure small group work in three major areas: academic work, social problem solving, and student interests. Academic group work may consist of discussions, inquiry activities, cooperative learning teams, group projects or tutorial work. Social problem solving groups discuss student or group behavior, classroom management issues, and school issues. Student interest groups address topics relevant to the lives of students. These topics may not be clearly related to the academic objectives of a subject, but they relate to contemporary issues and allow students to enrich their education with projects and discussions.

Organizing Small Groups

Once the students in the class feel accepted as individuals and are free to express their points of view, the teacher may put them to work in small groups. A gradual initiation into groupwork can be attained by giving a demonstration with one group while the rest of the class looks on. After this first group demonstrates readiness, the teacher may initiate a second group or allow all class members to work in groups. The younger the students, the more it is recommended that groups be formed and added in gradual increments, and that the teacher work closely with each new group until they work in groups satisfactorily. When organizing small groups, teachers follow five steps. Teachers:

1. Explain the group's task and make sure that all students understand it.
2. Establish the leadership structure of the group.
3. Have appropriate materials available.
4. Help the group decide on a plan of action.
5. Communicate criteria for the evaluation of group performance.

Explaining the group's task and making sure that all students understand it is the first step to follow when organizing a group. The task is usually decided by the teacher unless the students are mature and ready to be given some degree of choice in its selection. For short term group meetings, the teacher assigns the task. For long lived groups, the students should be given opportunities to have input into the selection of the task, and the task should be broken down into subtasks. For example, a group which meets once a week for six weeks to prepare a science project on dinosaurs should be assigned specific sub projects to complete during each meeting. Examples could include listing sources, selecting types of dinosaurs to be studied, completing individual assignments, outlining individual reports, reviewing individual reports, editing the final draft of the report, preparing the art props, etc. By helping the group identify subtasks and time lines, the teacher assures an efficient work structure and a greater sense of purpose and direction.

Group tasks should be interesting, feasible and specific. The end product should be tangible, that is, something that can be read or viewed or listened to by the rest of the class. If the task is to "discuss the four types of decision-making methods described in the handout," it will be difficult for the teacher to evaluate the progress of the group, and the group will have difficulty agreeing on what needs to be done. The group will not have any tangible product to submit. On the other hand, if the task is defined as "discuss the four types of decision-making methods described in the handout and rank order them in order of preference," the group will have a specific task and will turn in, at the end of the session, a list with their rankings. The instructions for group work should be clearly stated and written on the chalkboard or on material given to the students. When students keep asking the teacher, "what are we supposed to be doing?," it is usually an indication that the instructions were given orally instead of in writing.

Establishing the leadership structure of the group is the second step to follow when organizing group work. The teacher selects the student group leaders on the basis of leadership abilities already demonstrated in classroom situations. Students who are good thinkers, responsible, respected by peers, and articulate, usually make good group leaders. The student leaders will be responsible for keeping the group on task, regulating the work pace, facilitating compromises among group members, maintaining harmony, involving all members, and helping the group evaluate progress toward its goal. Leadership is a learned skill, so the teacher should eventually rotate this responsibility in order for many students to have an opportunity to practice. The teacher should give special instructions to group leaders and should include a series of steps for them to follow as they guide the group through its work. This especially applies to nine to ten year old students. As the students get older and more experienced in group work, the leaders and members of the group can be given more latitude. For example, the teacher might allow members to select their leaders. Another important member in a group is the recorder. This student assists the leader in clarifying issues and keeping track of tasks, pace, and progress. The recorder keeps a record of the group's work and is responsible for describing the results of this work to the rest of the class at the end of the period.

While the teacher assures, through the appointment of a leader and a recorder, that the group work will be structured in certain ways, it is very important that it be made clear that the success of the group is the result of the efforts and contributions of all of its members. The leadership structure, including the teacher as a background resource, is designed to facilitate the participation of all group members. Only a democratic work climate, where the voice of each student counts and where each group member feels equally valuable, will yield the process outcomes listed at the beginning of this section. An autocratic leadership approach may work well for organizations in the business sector, but in a learning environment, the processes of participating, listening to each other, and reaching consensus are as important as the accomplishment of the group task. Schools are supposed to prepare students to participate in the life of a democratic society. Where else but in small group sessions can students practice the skills of democratic living?

Having appropriate materials available so students can carry out their task is the third step to follow when organizing group work. If, for example, the group is to research a topic, the teacher must have checked with the librarian to make sure that plenty of books are available on the subject and the teacher must also have made arrangements either for students to visit the library or for the books to be brought into the classroom. If the group is to manipulate or make objects, the materials must be available in the room or be reasonably easy to procure at home. The topic or task chosen determines the type and quantity of materials needed. If materials or sources are scarce, it is likely that the students will become frustrated or participate without much interest. A wealth of materials assures opportunities for students to do quality work. If there is a lack of materials for a particular topic, the teacher should choose another topic for which appropriate materials exist.

Helping the group members decide on a plan of action is the fourth step in organizing group work. In the case of short term groups, the teacher decides the role of each group member and whether a buzz group or a brainstorming group process should be followed. But in the case of long-lived groups, the students must have a say in how the group will go about attaining its goal. The teacher could facilitate these decisions by providing the group leader with a series of questions about possible approaches which the group might consider. A more experienced group should be allowed to develop its own procedures. Long-term groups must devote the first sessions to planning and organizing activities: How do we do it? Who does what? When do we complete each subtask? What materials are needed? How do we insure that the subtasks get done? Etc? In these cases, the first subtask or product for the group to submit should be a detailed plan of action which describes the procedures to be followed and the responsibilities of each group member. Students should be given an increased degree of choice as they become more experienced in decisions about procedures and individual assignments. Individual assignments should be appropriate to the abilities and special talents of each member. The tasks should offer opportunities for many different talents to be displayed. Some students are good at gathering information; others are artistic; still others have talent for keeping the whole group working and bringing all the parts into a whole. As group plans are developed, all members must be given an opportunity to contribute and to utilize their talents to a maximum so the final product is perceived by all group members to be the result of their efforts.

Communicating the criteria for the evaluation of group performance is the fifth step to follow when organizing group work. Students need to know, in detail, how the teacher is going to evaluate individual and group contributions and how the quality of their work is going to impact their class grades. A reward structure that reinforces cooperation among group members, rather than one which reinforces competition, is essential if group members are to work as a team. The value of individual effort and diversity of talents should be stressed. All members contribute as much as they can toward the group goal, regardless of their individual characteristics. In a sense, this is like a tug of war contest in which each member of the team pulls as much as possible, regardless of one's size and strength. Hopefully, all members contribute according to their particular talents. Team sports provide a good example of how different individual talents can be utilized in different roles in order that teams will succeed.

Team sports emphasize intragroup cooperation in order to win intergroup competition. This approach could be followed in the classroom, provided that the groups are formed with an eye towards equality among the groups. But during most of the group activities, it seems advisable to play down the competition among teams and to measure team success by pitting the teams against preestablished criteria, that is, make teams compete against themselves by meeting the performance criteria to the best of their abilities. Slavin (1983) recommends that a point system be developed to determine and reward team performance. Each team member receives "individual improvement" points in addition to raw scores. The team score is the result of the sum of the individual scores divided by the number of team members. Teams could earn different awards or certificates which matched various scores. By knowing ahead of time the number of team points required to receive a certain recognition or certificate, team members would be motivated to do their best.

Evaluating groups working on academic tasks is more difficult that evaluating groups working on social problem solving tasks. In social problem solving groups, the evaluation focuses on the processes rather than on the products. The degree of student participation, the quality of the discussion, solutions presented, individual commitment, etc., are some of the things which should be assessed. Grades or rewards are not associated with this type of group work.

In the case of academic group work, group processes are only one of the areas for which assessments are needed. The quality of work, amount of effort, and the rewards which students should receive must also be considered. If grades are utilized, all the group members may get the grade they received as a group, or the group may recommend a grade for each one of its members (based on preestablished criteria). Or each member may submit documentation of his or her individual assignment and be graded by the teacher. As was discussed in the section on motivation, grades can get in the way and shift the classroom goal-reward system from a cooperative to a competitive orientation. If the teacher is required to grade one's students, or if he desires to do so in order to communicate information about the quality of student performance, group work grades should constitute a small percent of a student's total grade for a subject area. Group efforts are best recognized by displaying the results of group work in prominent places where all students and visitors may see them. Teachers may also have the students make presentations of their reports to the class, and, if possible, important guests. Results may also be publicized through a class bulletin or newsletter.

There are seven criteria which the teacher may use to evaluate the effectiveness of group work (Danforth Foundation, 1988, p. 251). They can be phrased in the form of the following questions:

1. Is the group task clear and deemed important by all members?
2. Do group members feel free to express themselves?
3. Are responsibilities shared?
4. Are group decisions reached by consensus?
5. Are good communication skills practiced?
6. Is group progress monitored periodically?
7. Do individual and group products meet performance standards?

The teacher should provide feedback to the group members in terms of their progress towards the attainment of the task, their use of group processes, their interaction skills, and their individual contributions.

Prerequisite Skills for Group Interaction

In order for students to function successfully in groups, they must be proficient in the use of communication skills and conflict-resolution skills. Students must know how to listen to the ideas of other students and accept a variety of points of view. They must also know how to express their own views and feelings, how to speak succinctly, how to talk in turns, how to seek alternatives which resolve group conflicts in a **"win-win"** manner, and how to work as a team. These skills may be taught through the use of a "fish bowl," group demonstration, or through role play exercises.

Six Types of Small Groups

In the following section, six types of small groups will be described. They are: 1) fish bowls, 2) brainstorming-consensus groups, 3) in-basket groups, 4) buzz groups, 5) task groups, and 6) classroom meetings.

Fish Bowl   The fish bowl is a type of small group, formed by about seven students and the teacher, which meets in a circle in front of the rest of the class. It has two major purposes: one, to serve as a demonstration and training tool on how to participate in a group; the other, to control a group discussion of sensitive topics, which may get out of hand if the teacher is not in direct control of the interaction. The fish bowl is also useful when the teacher would like to have small group sessions but the physical setting makes this impossible.

The fish bowl is an excellent training tool which can be used to demonstrate the functioning of many types of small groups, including the other five types which will be described in this section. When the fish bowl is used for training purposes, the teacher usually takes the role of group facilitator and leader. But some teachers prefer to remain outside the fish bowl and act as a stage director, asking the group to cut (i.e., stop) for a moment to give instructions, request a change of direction, or focus on a particular skill that has just been performed.

The members of the class who are not active participants in the fish bowl are frequently given the role of observers, with an assignment to provide feedback on particular aspects of the interaction. Some fish bowl arrangements provide an empty chair, which allows any of the members of the class to temporarily join the group to make a statement or ask a question and then return to the role of observer. This measure affords those students who become very involved in the fish bowl interaction an opportunity to briefly participate.

The length of the meeting seldom exceeds twenty minutes since the teacher must allow time to reflect on the session at the end of the period.

A classroom climate of acceptance and trust is essential for students to risk participation in a demonstration fish bowl. The teacher must utilize very positive feedback, praising the students for their assertiveness and effort, and frequently reminding the students that "If they do *not* make mistakes, the teacher is out of a job." Students must perceive mistakes as natural and be reinforced for having the courage to make them in the process of trying to learn. Teachers must model this acceptance of mistakes as a necessary component of learning by frequently pointing out their own errors as they work in the classroom. In order for students to learn group interaction skills, they must be willing, like actors on stage (with the help of the teacher), to try several times until the performance is successful.

Brainstorming-Consensus Group Meeting   Brainstorming is a small group technique used to gather ideas to solve a particular problem. A brainstorming session lasts no more than ten minutes. Once a large number of ideas has been generated, the group classifies or groups them, and discusses them until consensus is reached about their order of desirability. Brainstorming, as the image suggests, is a storm of ideas generated by the group. In order to maximize the production of ideas, certain rules are followed: 1) criticisms, explanations, or judgment are not allowed, 2) freewheeling of ideas is welcomed, 3) combinations and improvements of ideas are desirable, and 4) quantity of ideas is the main goal.

Brainstorming is used in the classroom when there are situations which require a variety of solutions to be entertained. For example, possible project topics, aspects of a project, books to read, or how to improve the looks of the room might be some of the matters considered. Students will be surprised by the number of great ideas that a brainstorming session can yield in a few minutes. Brainstorming frequently precedes decision making by consensus.

Consensus means agreement arrived at by those concerned about a particular problem or a solution. Consensus is best sought when the participants have trusting relationships and a sense of belonging to the group. Consensus cannot be imposed. When groups are presented with a problem and need to arrive at a solution, it is obvious that there will be differences of opinion. An agreement to reach solutions through consensus is a commitment to maintain a sense of community and fellowship among group members. It is also a challenge to come up with better solutions which satisfy everyone. Consensus decision making takes longer, but it fosters quality of decision making and insures a sense of togetherness and belonging.

During brainstorming, the group generates many solutions without making any value judgments about them. Then in the consensus seeking phase, the ideas are grouped by clusters, or considered one by one, and those that are obviously unworkable are eliminated. The clusters of ideas are combined into coherent statements, and the most promising statements are considered. Arguments are given in favor or against each idea. Some modifications and improvements may be suggested as a result of the discussion. During this interaction, some members begin to change their minds, and this brings the group closer to agreement. Discussion continues as group members continue to voice their views. The group is challenged to refine and further modify some of the most workable solutions until all members are satisfied. The consensus part of the activity may last as much as thirty minutes, depending on the complexity of the problem to be resolved.

Brainstorming-consensus group activities are excellent tools for problem solving. They also increase communication and conflict resolution skills and build a sense of fellowship and collegiality among group members. The structure of the sessions does not require much direct leadership. Someone must record the ideas suggested during the brainstorming session and a facilitator must lead the consensus seeking discussion. This is a very engaging group activity which fosters participation, initiative, and a democratic climate among class members. Brainstorming-consensus may be done in a fish bowl setting to demonstrate for the class how the activity is carried out.

"In-Basket" Group Exercise The "in-basket" group activity is a variation of brainstorming. Instead of seeking solutions for a group problem, the objective of the activity is to provide ideas about how to resolve a classroom problem. The individual requesting ideas could be the teacher or one of the students. In either case, the person briefly describes the situation or problem and asks, "What can I do?" A brief time for clarification is allowed during which group members may request more information. Next, the group members voice suggestions in brief statements, following the rules of brainstorming. Once enough possible courses of action have been suggested, the member that requested assistance closes the session by thanking the group.

A student, for example, may be having difficulty with her assignment for a group project. That student might request an "in-basket" activity to get some help. She would describe the situation and ask, "What can I do?" Some members of the group might ask a few questions to make sure they understand the problem. Then the group members would begin to offer suggestions in a brainstorming fashion while the student would listen and take notes, remaining quiet during the idea production stage. Finally, the student would thank the group. The ultimate decision that this student makes may never be disclosed to the group. The role of the group members is to help, by broadening the range of alternative solutions which might be considered while allowing the individual member to go through the decision making process privately.

The "in-basket" meeting can last from fifteen to twenty minutes. Teachers will benefit from using this technique to receive suggestions about instructional problems and classroom management issues.

Buzz Groups   Buzz groups are discussion groups made up of a few students that meet briefly to discuss a topic during the course of a lesson. Buzz groups provide an opportunity for students to express their views on the material presented and to reflect critically on it. The assignment for the group should be one that can be carried out in a short period of time, usually, no more than twenty minutes. After the groups discuss the topic, each group recorder presents a summary of that group's work to the rest of the class. These groups bring variety to the classroom and involve the students in an active learning mode by allowing for verbal interaction and problem solving efforts.

Task Groups   Task groups meet several times for the purpose of attaining a particular goal. Each group member has a significant contribution to make towards the group assignment. The characteristics of a well organized group, discussed earlier, apply specifically to task groups: clarification of the task, establishment of a leadership structure, availability of resources, procedures to follow, individual assignments, time lines, and criteria for evaluation of group performance. Task groups may have many applications, that is, academic projects, tutoring, or special projects.

Classroom Meeting   The classroom meeting (Glasser, 1969) is an approach designed to develop a caring social group which becomes increasingly self-disciplined and committed to the improvement of behavior. The classroom meeting involves the whole class in an open discussion of academic issues, classroom behavior, or other topics of importance to the entire class. The class is seated in a large circle for a period of 20 to 40 minutes, and the teacher leads the group as the students attempt to share the responsibility for learning and behavior by resolving their problems within the classroom.

Although the classroom meeting may not be a small group meeting, it emphasizes the student interaction and problem solving processes which are common to small groups. The classroom meeting is an excellent tool to help class members develop the communication, interaction, and conflict resolution skills which they will rely upon whenever they become involved in small group work. It is a kind of fish bowl in which all members are inside.

The meeting usually has four parts: a) an initial activity in which all members share their feelings about the problem by taking turns around the circle, b) a discussion in which the teacher asks questions to provoke the students to express their views, c) an exploration of alternative courses of action, and d) a final activity in which each student makes a public commitment to action.

GLOSSARY

cooperative learning A teaching method which emphasizes the role of students as teachers of one another.

external reward A reward which is given to students by another person, for example, a sticker, teacher praise, etc.

internal reward A reward which students derive directly through their participation in an experience, for example, the enjoyment of reading a good story.

sociogram A compilation of lists in which students privately identify those students whom they most like. This information is used by teachers when they plan social interaction in their classrooms.

win-lose situation A conflict between two parties which is resolved in such a manner that one party's needs are met but the other party's needs are not met.

win-win situation A conflict between two parties which is resolved in such a manner that both parties have their needs met.

Chapter
11

Developing a Teaching Style

*T*his last chapter of the book is designed to assist future teachers in making decisions about their teaching style. The chapter may also be used as a review of the major issues covered throughout the text. In previous chapters, different approaches to classroom organization, use of subject matter, instructional planning, teaching, evaluation, classroom management, and behavior management have been presented. Your preferences in the use of these approaches will constitute your teaching style.

First, we would like you to choose and make rational decisions after having studied the options. We have often observed that teachers do not teach according to what they have learned in teacher preparation programs; rather, they teach as they were were taught when they were students. Obviously, effective doctors do not treat patients according to the manner in which they were treated as young patients. We hope you do not teach the way you were taught; rather, we would like you to make informed professional decisions based on the knowledge presently available to our profession.

Your choices will be influenced by four major factors: 1) The existing professional knowledge, 2) the educational philosophy of the school to which you are assigned, 3) the students whom you are teaching, and 4) your personality type. (See Figure 11.1)

An effective teaching style is flexible and makes adjustments according to particular teaching contexts. Nevertheless, it is important for you, after reflecting on the options

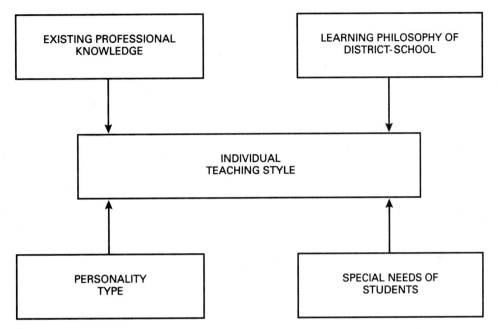

Figure 11.1

available, to identify what type of teacher you would like to be. We are going to present eight areas which contribute to a teaching style. Within each area, several dimensions will be presented. Your task is to determine which orientation you prefer (within each dimension) and to examine this preference to make sure it is congruent with your professional knowledge and the needs of schools and children today.

You may have an unexamined preference, for example, about how to organize students for instruction. It may be based on your past experiences as a pupil or as a parent. In Chapter 2, you studied different ways of organizing classrooms. You now know enough to begin to examine your teaching preferences and make informed professional choices about this dimension. Do you prefer a graded classroom setting because this is the only way of organizing learners that you have experienced, or have you carefully thought about the implications of this choice before deciding that you prefer this type of setting? Or do you prefer a team-taught, nongraded setting because you hated your school experiences in a graded classroom and you wish to move as far away as possible from what you experienced? Is this reaction an examined choice?

Are there any other options you are not examining? We hope this chapter will help you make informed choices as you reflect upon your teaching style. The eight major areas which make up a teaching style are:

1. The organization of schools, teams and classrooms for instruction, that is, instructional settings.
2. The organization, selection, and presentation of subject matter.
3. The focus and delivery of instruction.
4. Instructional planning

5. Evaluation
6. Classroom climate
7. Motivation and control.
8. Behavior management

Instructional Settings

Instructional settings can be grouped along a continuum. At one end of the continuum are schools made up of age-graded, self-contained classrooms. Nongraded schools are at the other end. Between these two extremes, you can find schools using various combinations of graded and nongraded approaches. For example, you might find an elementary school in which parents may choose either a self-contained, age-graded classroom or a nongraded classroom for their child. (Different wings of the school building might be designated for each of these two approaches.) Or you might find a school which uses a nongraded organization for the intermediate grades. In consultation with teachers and parents, administrators make decisions about how schools are organized. Teachers must feel comfortable with the approach which has been selected if they are to be productive, happy, and remain at that school site.

Continuum 1
Grouping of Students in Elementary Schools

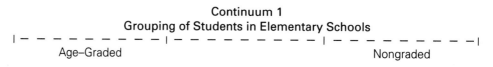

Age–Graded   Nongraded

What type of approach to school organization would you prefer? A self-contained, graded setting? A departmentalized, graded setting? A team-taught, multiaged, nongraded setting? As you reflect on these questions, look at Continuum 1 and place an *x* at the point on the continuum where you believe your personal preference is best represented.

Another organizational dimension to consider, when describing teaching style, is how students are grouped within a classroom. Regardless of what type of instructional settings they find themselves in, teachers have several options when grouping students for instruction. At one end of the continuum is homogeneous grouping. For this approach, the teacher groups the students by achievement (usually in reading and mathematics), forming three or four groups which range from very high achievers to low achievers. The students remain in these groups throughout the year and little change in group membership occurs. This is the least flexible approach to organizing students within a classroom. At the other end of the grouping continuum would be heterogeneous, multiaged grouping. Students would be grouped in small groups which reflect the composition of the whole class, or team, in terms of achievement, ethnicity, race, and gender. There are a variety of combinations in between these two positions on the class grouping continuum. An eclectic, or middle, position would be to group students either homogeneously or heterogeneously depending on the learning task.

Continuum 2
Student Grouping Approaches in the Classroom

Homogeneous Grouping   Eclectic   Heterogeneous

What are your student grouping preferences? The school district which employs you may determine the type of school setting in which you work, but you will decide how to group students within your own classroom. What approach to grouping students do you prefer? As you reflect upon these questions, look at Continuum 2 and place an *x* at the point in the continuum where you believe your personal preference is best represented.

The Organization, Selection, and Presentation of Subject Matter

Subject matter, or content, may be organized in different ways in order to be taught to students. At one end of the continuum, the subjects are distinct from each other (reading, spelling, writing, arithmetic, social studies, science, etc.). On the other end, subject matter is brought together in an interdisciplinary approach as it is in **topic work**. In between these two approaches, there are a variety of combinations. An eclectic, or middle position is to combine the various knowledge and skill areas into **clusters**. The **communications cluster** would include reading, writing, spelling, oral communication, and related skills. The **fine arts cluster** would include art, music, dance, photography, creative dramatics, etc. In sum, subject matter may be organized and taught as separate unrelated subjects, as clusters, or through an interdisciplinary approach such as topic work.

Continuum 3
Organization of Subject Matter

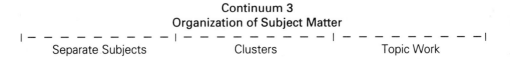

| Separate Subjects | Clusters | Topic Work |

How will you organize subject matter in your classroom? Will you choose a separate subject approach for all disciplines? Will you use a combination of separate subjects and clusters? If so, which subjects will you teach separately and which ones as clusters? Will you use the topic work approach? Will you use topic work to teach all subject and skill areas? As you reflect upon these questions, look at Continuum 3 and place an *x* at the point on the continuum where you believe your personal preference is best represented.

A second dimension of the subject matter area is selection. What subject matter should we teach to children in the elementary school? Should we emphasize basic academic skills? Or should we strive to expose children to the best of our cultural and academic heritage? Should the emphasis be on learning by experience to solve problems rather than on the learning of specific content? Should children be able to choose what they want to learn on the basis of their personal interests? Looking back on education over the past fifteen years, we can see that schools have experienced a revived emphasis on the basic skills. Previous to this, learning processes and student choices had been emphasized. During the period when schools were stressing basic skills, our cultural and academic heritage received less attention from the elementary school curriculum. Yet it is by exposing children to the best of our cultural heritage (e.g., art, music, stories and fairy tales, experiments in science, etc.) that we are able to develop truly educated people. What do you think should be taught in our schools? The curriculum continuum for this topic is a complex one. At one end of the continuum is the emphasis on basic skills. On the other end of the continuum is a curriculum resulting from the choices of students as they pursue their personal interests.

Continuum 4
Selection of Subject Matter

| — — — — — — — — | — — — — — — — — | — — — — — — — |

| Basic Skills | Cultural and Academic Heritage | Thinking Processes and Valuing | Personal Interests of Students |

In language arts, should elementary students learn primarily basic skills in language arts, or should they be exposed to classic fairy tales and children's books? Should students be allowed to decide what to study within a subject or skill area? Which curriculum emphasis do you favor? Do you view the elementary school curriculum as comprised of basic skills which will prepare students for more advanced studies, or do you favor a more eclectic approach? If so, which combination of approaches do you prefer? If a skills-oriented text is selected for your class, how will you enrich such a textbook? If given an opportunity, would you choose a textbook which emphasizes the reading of classic folk and fairy tales and places emphasis on thinking and valuing? If you were interviewed for an intermediate grade teaching position, how would you describe your views on the selection of curriculum? On which side of the continuum do you believe your personal preferences are best represented?

A third dimension of the subject matter area is the continuum which deals with the teacher's beliefs about learning. Some educators define this issue by asking whether teachers should proceed from "part to whole" or from "whole to part." Will you emphasize specific skills and bits of information (parts) as the initial step in the pursuit of learning? Or will you emphasize understanding (whole) as the initial step and then move to the learning of specific skills and information? Or do you prefer an eclectic approach in which you mix both positions? The teaching of phonics through basic reader activities is sometimes done in such a way as to be an example of starting by the part (phonics) in order to teach the whole (comprehension). Do you prefer to teach reading by focusing first on the parts before moving on to emphasize understanding the whole? Or do you prefer an approach such as "whole language" which exposes the learner to the whole first (e.g., an interesting story) and moves on to the acquisition of more specific skills?

Continuum 5
Presentation of Subject Matter

| — — — — — — — — | — — — — — — — — | — — — — — — — |

| Parts to Whole | | Whole to Parts |

Look at Continuum 5 and place an *x* at the point on the continuum where you believe your personal preference is best represented.

Methods of Instruction

A teaching style is significantly influenced by the manner in which instruction is carried out. There are three major dimensions which one must consider when identifying one's instructional style: focus of delivery, levels of thinking, and types of activities.

The first dimension to consider when describing instructional methods is the focus of delivery preferred by the teacher. The delivery of instruction may be represented as individually taught or as collaboratively taught. In teacher-centered instructional delivery, the teacher becomes the main source of interaction for the students. Collaborative instruction, on the other hand, is when other teachers and members of the community are a significant source of interaction for the class. The students may also be included in the delivery of instruction when collaborative approaches are used.

Which delivery orientation do you favor? Will you have a teacher-centered approach to instruction or will your students also play an important role in the delivery of instruction? Will you involve other teachers and adults in your instructional activities? There are two major emphases possible: teacher-centered and student-centered. Naturally, the focus of instruction changes periodically. But most teachers have a dominant focus. If different teachers are observed for several consecutive periods, it will be noticed that some of the teachers spend most of the time being the center of the instructional activities while other teachers have the students spend most of the time working in groups or by themselves. For Continuum 6, place an *x* at the point on the continuum where you believe your personal preference is best represented.

Continuum 6
Focus of Delivery

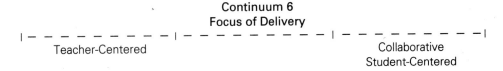

Teacher-Centered   Collaborative
                                                                     Student-Centered

Which instructional focus do you prefer? Can you think of a professor in your teacher preparation program who used a student-centered approach? What approach was used in your favorite course? Are there reasons why either approach might be effective at the elementary level but ineffective at the college level?

A second dimension to consider when describing instructional approaches is the type of learning activity used. There are three major types of learning experiences which teachers provide when engaged in instruction: symbolic, representational, and enactive (see our *Types of Instruction* chart in Chapter 3). Instructional activities which emphasize the use of symbols are those in which learners are listening or reading materials. Activities which emphasize the use of representations appeal to the senses and imagination of the learners by presenting pictures and other visual and auditory stimuli. When students engage in simulations or actual experiences, they are learning by doing.

Continuum 7
Types of Learning Experiences

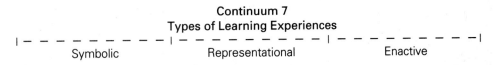

Symbolic   Representational   Enactive

One goal of instruction is to help learners to develop intellectually. To achieve this cognitive development, young learners need to be exposed first to an abundance of experiences at the enactive levels of our *Types of Instruction* chart. It will not be until the middle school grades that most learners will make the transition into formal operational thinking. Instruction in the primary grades cannot require that level of thought.

Learning experiences at the enactive and representational levels should predominate in the elementary grades because these types of experiences are an appropriate match to the intellectual development of the children during this period. When you prepare a social studies lesson or a math lesson for primary children, what types of learning experiences will you choose? Will you emphasize symbolic activities? Will you emphasize enactive experiences? Or will you combine both? Look at Continuum 7 and place an *x* at the point on the continuum where you believe your personal preference is best represented.

A third dimension to consider when describing instructional style is the type of thinking promoted by the teacher. Reproductive thinking is found at one end of the thinking continuum and productive thinking at the other end. Through the pursuit of recall, comprehension, and application objectives (see our explanation of Bloom's taxonomy in Chapter 3), teachers promote reproductive thinking. On the other hand, analysis, synthesis, and evaluation objectives engage students in productive thinking (also called critical-creative thinking).

Continuum 8
Types of Thinking Promoted Among Students

| — — — — — — — — — | — — — — — — — — — — | — — — — — — — — — |
    Reproductive Thinking   Productive Thinking

What orientation do you favor when teaching? What types of learning objectives will you emphasize in your language arts lessons? In your mathematics lessons? In your social studies and science lessons? In the arts? What percent of your students' learning time will be spent teaching critical-creative thinking? Teachers who adhere closely to text book activities promote the type of thinking that the text emphasizes. Texts tend to emphasize lower level objectives. If the text covers lower order objectives, the learners will be thinking at the reproductive level unless the teacher adds activities specifically designed to foster productive thinking. As a teacher, you must carefully study your classroom textbooks and identify the type of student thinking which they promote. You must also examine your own instructional activities for the same reasons. What type of thinking will you promote among your students? Look at Continuum 8 and place an *x* at the point on the continuum where you believe your personal preference is best represented.

Another dimension to consider when describing instructional style is the type of productive thinking fostered. There are two major ways of promoting productive thinking; one is convergent and the other is divergent. In convergent thinking, the teacher guides the students through analysis questions until they reach a prespecified learning. The teacher knows where the questions are leading to and skillfully guides the students in their discovery of a concept. In divergent thinking, there is no prespecified outcome. The teacher herself is not quite sure of the outcome. This type of thinking is open-ended and is generated through synthesis and evaluation objectives. The students are able to tell the differences between convergent and divergent thinking activities. In one, the teacher knows the answer and the students must find it. In the other, the students and the teacher search for answers. In between these two points, there is an eclectic position in which the teacher promotes both convergent and divergent thinking.

Continuum 9
Types of Productive Thinking

|— — — — — — — — — —|— — — — — — — — — —|— — — — — — — — —|

Convergent Thinking   Divergent Thinking

Which approach to productive thinking would you prefer? In which lessons will you use mostly convergent thinking? In which lesson will you use divergent thinking? In which lessons will you use both? Please, look at Continuum 9 and place an *x* at the point on the continuum where you believe your personal preference is best represented.

A last dimension to consider when describing instructional style is the variety of methods used by the teacher. At one end of the continuum, teachers may show little or no variety in their use of methods. This position is endorsed by teachers who are very predictable and adhere to a particular teaching method which they find very effective. The method may be mastery teaching, mastery learning, presentation or cooperative learning, etc. What characterizes these classrooms is that the same method is used most of the time. At the other end of the continuum, we find great variety in the use of instructional methods. Students in these classrooms are exposed to frequent changes in teaching methods used.

Continuum 10
Variety in the Use of Teaching Methods

|— — — — — — — — — —|— — — — — — — — — —|— — — — — — — — —|

Same Teaching Method   Many Teaching Methods

If you find a teaching method that really works with students, will you stick with it for the whole year? Or do you prefer some variety? Do you prefer a significant degree of variety in learning experiences? Which end of the continuum do the textbooks adopted by your local school district emphasize? Will you be able to implement the type of teaching variety you desire by using these textbooks? Which degree of variety in the use of teaching methods do you prefer? Look at Continuum 10 and place an *x* at the point on the continuum where you believe your personal preference is best represented.

Approaches to Planning

While there seems to be little controversy among education professionals about how to implement instructional methods, when it comes to approaches to planning for instruction, opinions are divided. University teacher educators pay great attention to planning processes while many practitioners in the field are able to fit a lesson plan in the small box of a planning book. Experienced teachers seem to carry detailed planning schemata in their minds and are able to bring these schemata forth without having to write the steps of a lesson in a detailed manner. For some teachers, planning involves religiously following every page of the Teacher's Guide for the textbook. In this case, teachers only need to write down a page number of their Teacher's Guide and this constitutes the lesson plan.

There is certainly a significant discrepancy between the perspectives of university educators and those of practicing teachers on the issue of planning. In university teaching, there is plenty of time to develop detailed lesson plans. In actual elementary classrooms, however, teachers are busy teaching most of the day and have little opportunity to plan. In most elementary schools, the daily schedule of teachers involves five or more teaching periods and one planning period. A few schools are starting to rearrange the schedule of teachers to afford them two periods of planning.

In our text, we have taken the position that planning is a very important component of teaching and that novice teachers need to spend a significant amount of effort planning their lessons until they become accomplished teachers. We do not believe that following the textbook page by page is an effective way of addressing the learning needs of students, but we do understand how difficult it is for teachers to create their own instructional activities when they have a limited amount of time allotted in their schedules for instructional planning.

The first dimension to discuss, as you explore your planning style, is related to the sources of your lessons. Are you going to rely on the textbook as the only source for your lesson plans? This approach represents one end of the sources of planning continuum. The other end is represented by lesson objectives, activities, and materials which are created by the teacher. There is a middle position in which some of the lesson objectives, activities, and materials are gathered from the textbook or from the district's curriculum guide while others are developed by the teachers.

Continuum 11
Sources of Lesson Plans

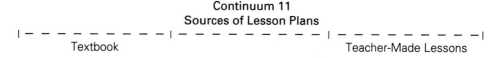

Textbook   Teacher-Made Lessons

Which sources of planning do you favor? If you find an excellent textbook or curriculum guide, are you going to rely exclusively on it? Or do you prefer to develop your own lessons? What are you going to do if a textbook does not match your students' learning needs? Look at Continuum 11 and place an *x* at the point on the continuum where you believe your personal preference is represented.

Another dimension which describes the planning style of a novice teacher is the degree of detail. Lesson plans may be general or very detailed. Which approach to planning do you prefer? Are you comfortable, as a new teacher, with writing two or three lines to outline your lesson? Or, do you need more detail? Does it help your teaching when your lesson plans include detailed sample questions, examples and problems to practice?

Continuum 12
Degree of Detail in Lesson Plans

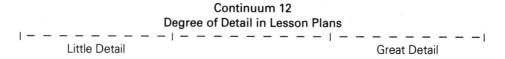

Little Detail   Great Detail

Please look at Continuum 12 and place an *x* at the point on the continuum where you believe your personal preference is represented.

Another dimension in planning is one of compliance with the plan. Will you, as a teacher, follow the lesson as it was planned? Or will you deviate from the plans as the circumstances of the classroom require it? How much are you willing to deviate? How frequently are you going to deviate from the lesson plan?

Continuum 13
Degree of Compliance with Lesson Plan

| — — — — — — — — | — — — — — — — — — | — — — — — — — — |

No Deviation from Plan   Great Deviation from Plan

Look at Continuum 13 and place an *x* at the point on the continuum where you believe your personal preference is represented.

When teachers plan lessons, they follow different paths. Some teachers center their teaching on behavioral objectives for which the learning outcomes are predictable and verifiable. Other teachers emphasize expressive objectives or activities for which learning outcomes are not predictable or verifiable.

Continuum 14
Types of Objectives

| — — — — — — — — — | — — — — — — — — | — — — — — — — — |

Behavioral Objectives   Expressive Objectives

Which orientation do you prefer? Will you follow an objectives approach to planning and teaching? Will you abandon objectives completely and plan only activities or expressive objectives? Will there be some long-term instructional plans for which objectives will be more appropriate? Will there also be units for which expressive objectives will be more appropriate? How would you assess outcomes for expressive objectives? Which types of objectives do you prefer? Please look at Continuum 14 and place an *x* at the point on the continuum where you believe your personal preference is represented.

Approaches to Evaluation

The evaluation of student progress is another important area which describes the style of a teacher. Evaluation and grading practices influence student motivation and the effectiveness of a teacher. The first dimension to consider when describing the evaluation style of a teacher is the degree to which evaluation is emphasized. This emphasis can be determined by the frequency of quizzes and tests given which count toward a class grade. The opposite approach is one which deemphasizes the importance of tests.

Continuum 15
Degree of Emphasis on Evaluation

| — — — — — — — — — | — — — — — — — — — | — — — — — — — — |

High Emphasis on Evaluation   Low Emphasis on Evaluation

Which end of the continuum do you favor? Do you believe that you will help your students learn more by giving frequent tests and exams? How frequently will you administer tests? Or are you, on the other hand, inclined to give feedback about progress toward mastery and competence without giving many tests? Or do you favor a combination of both approaches? Please look at Continuum 15 and place an *x* at the point on the continuum where you believe your personal preference is represented.

Some elementary schools do not give grades for student performance. These schools provide descriptions of progress towards specific learning objectives. Each student receives information about his or her progress in a particular subject or area. Other schools give letter grades to students in order to communicate to them and to their parents how well they are performing in a subject.

Continuum 16
Grading System

| — — — — — — — — | — — — — — — — — — | — — — — — — — — —|
Letter Grade   Description of Progress

Which grading approach do you prefer? Do you believe that letter grades communicate the quality and effort put forth by the student? Do you prefer to avoid letter grades and write a descriptive statement of the student's progress or to plot this progress on a learning continuum? Do you prefer a combination of both approaches? Please look at Continuum 16 and place an *x* at the point on the continuum where you believe your personal preference is represented.

Some students are very good at taking tests. Other students do not do well on tests, regardless of their ability. When evaluating student progress, teachers may use tests as the only measure, or they may use a variety of measures besides tests. For example, a teacher may assign points for individual and group projects, creativity, assisting other students with tutoring, participation in role plays, or for extra work, as part of the class grade. Performance in paper-pencil tests may count only as a part of the total grade.

Continuum 17
Sources of Evaluation

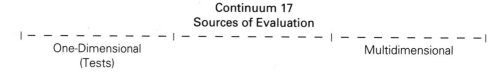

| — — — — — — — — | — — — — — — — — — | — — — — — — — — —|
One-Dimensional   Multidimensional
(Tests)

How much value will test grades have in your classroom? Will you have a multidimensional approach to evaluation? Or do you believe that tests should be the core of evaluation? Which side of the continuum do you prefer? Look at Continuum 17 and place an *x* at the point on the continuum where you believe your personal preference is represented.

Another dimension of evaluation is the point of reference utilized to determine progress. Learner progress may be assessed by determining how a student performs in comparison to the rest of the group or by evaluating the performance of students against a set of predetermined criteria. One is called norm-referenced evaluation; the other is called criterion-referenced evaluation. Norm-referenced evaluation emphasizes comparison of performance among students. Criterion-referenced evaluation emphasizes the attainment of particular goals by each student. In norm-referenced evaluation, the student finds out how he ranks in the group. In criterion-referenced evaluation, the student finds out how much he has progressed and how much more he needs to learn to fulfill the learning objective.

Continuum 18
Types of Evaluation

| — — — — — — — — | — — — — — — — — — | — — — — — — — — —|
Norm-Referenced   Criterion-Referenced

Which approach to evaluation do you favor? Will you give out information on student work and test results so students can figure out how they stand in comparison with their peers? Or will you emphasize individual progress against predetermined standards? Please look at Continuum 18 and place an *x* at the point on the continuum where you believe your personal preference is represented.

Finally, teachers have a choice of types of test items and examinations they can give to students. Some teachers prefer objective test items (i.e., multiple choice, true-false, etc.), while other teachers prefer short answer essay questions and essay questions. Which type of test item will you use? Objective test items? Essay questions? A combination of both?

Continuum 19
Type of Test Items

| — — — — — — — — — | — — — — — — — — — | — — — — — — — —|

Objective Test Items   Essay Test Items

Please look at Continuum 19 and place an *x* at the point on the continuum where you believe your personal preference is represented.

The Type of Classroom Climate Established

The classroom climate is a result of the socioemotional and learning atmosphere which is established by the teacher and the students in the classroom. One dimension which describes classroom climate is the degree of teacher affect. How much does the teacher express warmth and friendliness? To what degree does the teacher accept individual students and show an interest in what happens to each child? At one end of the teacher affect continuum are the teachers who keep their feelings to themselves. These teachers emphasize communications about learning matters only and do not talk about their feelings or their students' feelings. At the other end of the continuum are teachers who express their feelings freely and who accept their students' feelings and discuss them. These teachers are interested not only in the academic progress of students but in their personal lives. They notice when students are happy and when they are sad.

Continuum 20
Degree of Teacher Affect

| — — — — — — — — — | — — — — — — — — — | — — — — — — — —|

Low Emphasis on Feelings   High Emphasis on Feelings

Which side of the continuum do you favor? Will you place a low emphasis on feelings in the classroom? Will you give them high emphasis? Will you get involved emotionally with your students or will you remain detached? Place an *x* at the point on the continuum where you believe your personal preference is represented.

Another dimension of classroom climate is the degree of success students experience and the way mistakes are dealt with by the teacher. At one end of the continuum, we find classrooms in which students are penalized for their mistakes. These classrooms have a high degree of student failure. The tasks are seldom mastered by the students.

Students are conscious of mistakes and feel embarrassed if their answers are wrong. When students do not know how to perform a learning task, it is up to them to catch up. On the other end of the continuum, we find classrooms in which there is a high degree of student success. The learning tasks are frequently mastered by the students. There is strong support for learning in these rooms. When a student does not know how to perform a task, the teacher provides help, or another student is asked to help, until the student performs the task successfully. Mistakes are seen as part of the learning process. Even the teacher makes mistakes. Mistakes are indicators that more work must be done to master the learning task; they are not sources of embarrassment.

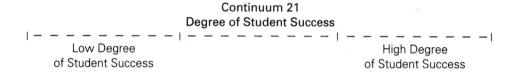

Continuum 21
Degree of Student Success

Low Degree
of Student Success

High Degree
of Student Success

What degree of student success will you foster in your classroom? Low? Moderate? High? Please look at Continuum 21 and place an *x* at the point on the continuum where you believe your personal preference is represented.

Another dimension of the classroom climate is the degree of enjoyment, that is, the extent to which learning experiences are pleasant and interesting, and the degree of enthusiasm and humor that permeates the daily activities. At one end of the continuum, we find classrooms in which there is little enjoyment. Learning is not fun. There is anxiety or boredom. There is no time for laughter. At the other end, we find classrooms where students have fun learning. Enthusiasm is high and anxiety is low. The students and teacher frequently laugh.

Continuum 22
Degree of Learning Enjoyment

Low Enjoyment

High Enjoyment

Which degree of learning enjoyment do you favor? Will you keep your students at a low enjoyment level? Do you want a high enjoyment level in your classroom? Do you favor a moderate level? Please look at Continuum 22 and place an *x* at the point on the continuum where you believe your personal preference is represented.

Another classroom climate dimension is the degree of teacher tolerance for confusion and exploration. Some teachers are comfortable with very structured classroom learning approaches which follow well established learning procedures and leave little opportunity for confusion or exploration on the part of the students. Students know at all times what is expected of them. Other teachers like to have students work in less structured learning environments. There is, at times, a significant amount of exploration going on in these classrooms. While students are able to explore more in these classrooms, there is also more noise and confusion.

Continuum 23
Degree of Confusion and Exploration

| — — — — — — — — | — — — — — — — — | — — — — — — — — |

Low Confusion   High Confusion
and Exploration   and Exploration

Are you more comfortable with a classroom structured to create little student confusion and exploration? Do you prefer a less structured environment where students explore and are at times confused? Do you favor an intermediate position? Please look at Continuum 23 and place an *x* at the point on the continuum where you believe your personal preference is represented.

Approaches to Motivation and Control

Student motivation is the result of several factors. If students are paying attention, spending time on the learning task, putting forth effort with a positive feeling tone, going beyond the required standards, and performing successfully, we can say they are motivated (Stipek, 1988; Hunter, 1982). Motivation problems are not confined to low achievers only. Very successful students, while being able to perform learning tasks, may be bored and lack several dimensions of motivation. "At risk" students (those who eventually may drop out of school) can be found among high and low achievers.

One dimension of motivation is the degree of challenge presented by the learning tasks. On the one hand, learning tasks may be unchallenging to the students. Tasks perceived as too easy are not motivating. On the other hand, tasks may be too challenging to the students. Tasks perceived as too difficult are not motivating. Tasks can be made too easy by providing too much assistance or by allowing too much time for their mastery. Tasks can be made too difficult by not providing enough assistance or by not allowing sufficient time for mastery.

Continuum 24
Degree of Learning Challenge

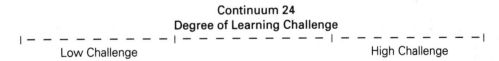

| — — — — — — — — | — — — — — — — — | — — — — — — — — |

Low Challenge   High Challenge

Which degree of challenge do you prefer? Will you present tasks that are less challenging but produce high student success rates? Or will you present very challenging tasks at the risk of lowering the success rates of your students? Will you choose an intermediate position? Look at Continuum 24 and place an *x* at the point on the continuum where you believe your personal preference is represented.

Another dimension of motivation is the type of reward orientation demonstrated by the teacher in the classroom. Teachers may use two major types of rewards when students perform desired tasks. External rewards are at one end of the continuum. External rewards can range from gifts, such as toys or food, to more social rewards such as certificates, grades, or teacher praise. External rewards are given to the learner by the teacher, parents or peers. On the other end of the continuum are internal rewards. Internal rewards are not given by the teacher, parents or peers. Internal rewards are the byproducts of learning. To perceive oneself as competent after mastering a task is an internal reward.

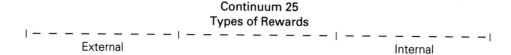

Continuum 25
Types of Rewards

|— — — — — — — — —|— — — — — — — — — —|— — — — — — — — —|
External   Internal

What type of rewards will you emphasize in your classroom? Will you use mostly external rewards? Will you rely upon mostly internal rewards? Will you use a combination of both types of rewards? Please look at Continuum 25 and place an *x* at the point on the continuum where you believe your personal preference is represented.

Teacher expectations are an important dimension of student motivation. At one end of the teacher expectations continuum is the belief that the performance of students follows a bell-shaped curve. According to this belief, some students are very high achievers, some students are low achievers, and the rest are average achievers. According to this line of reasoning, there is little a teacher can do to change this since students come to the classroom with a great diversity of talents. Students will leave school at the end of thirteen years in the same relative position as they entered in kindergarten. At the other end of the teacher expectations continuum is the belief that effort, rather than ability, is the most promising variable in learning. All students are able to give high effort if teachers demonstrate that they believe in their abilities to achieve. When students put high effort into learning, they achieve more.

Continuum 26
Type of Teacher Expectations

|— — — — — — — — —|— — — — — — — — — —|— — — — — — — — —|
Expectations Based   Expectations Based on
on the Student's   the Student's Ability
Achievement Alone   to Achieve

What types of expectations will you have in your classroom? Will you assess your students talents once only and match your expectations to their individual achievements? Or will you have high expectations for all your students? Please look at Continuum 26 and place an *x* at the point on the continuum where you believe your personal preference is represented.

The classroom goal-reward structure is another factor which affects student motivation. On the one hand, competitive classroom goals and reward structures emphasize making comparisons among students and create win-lose situations for them. On the other hand, cooperative goal-reward structures emphasize student interdependence and make cooperation and individual effort, rather than competition and ability, the primary goal in the classroom. Some traditional classrooms foster a competitive orientation. In these classrooms, students tend to work on their own to see who is best. Classrooms where students help each other learn, and are rewarded for it, follow a competitive orientation.

Continuum 27
Classroom Goal-Reward Orientation

|— — — — — — — — —|— — — — — — — — — —|— — — — — — — — —|
Competitive Orientation   Cooperative Orientation

What type of classroom goal-reward orientation do you favor? Will you emphasize a competitive orientation? Will you emphasize a cooperative approach? Or do you prefer a combination of both approaches? Look at Continuum 27 and place an *x* at the point on the continuum where you believe your personal preference is represented.

Student perceptions of control and influence are also related to motivation. Some teachers relinquish very little control over decisions about learning in the classroom. Students of these teachers do not have opportunities to choose among possible tasks and ways of doing things. Other teachers afford students a high degree of influence over classroom procedures and learning. Students, for example, may have a say in the identification of classroom rules and consequences. Or the teacher may seek student input when making decisions about learning tasks.

Continuum 28
Degree of Influence Afforded to Students

| — — — — — — — — | — — — — — — — — | — — — — — — — — |

Low Student Influence   High Student Influence

What degree of student influence will you allow in your classroom? Will students have little say in how your classroom is run? Will students have a lot to say in how your classroom is run? Or do you favor an intermediate position? Please look at Continuum 28 and place an *x* at the point on the continuum where you believe your personal preference is represented.

There are times when the needs of the teacher and the needs of a student, or several students, conflict. Regardless of how well organized a classroom is, how the rules and procedures may have been cooperatively developed by the teacher and students, or how smoothly things may run, conflicts between the needs of the teacher and the needs of the students will occur sooner or later. One conflict resolution approach is when the teacher wins most of the time and the students lose. The opposite approach is when accommodations are made most of the time and both teacher and students find mutually satisfying solutions to the conflict.

Continuum 29
Conflict Resolution Method

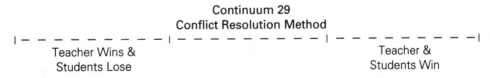

| — — — — — — — — | — — — — — — — — | — — — — — — — — |

Teacher Wins &   Teacher &
Students Lose   Students Win

Which conflict resolution approach do you favor? Will your needs be taken care of at the expense of the students' needs? Will you seek compromises and solutions in which both sides win? Or do you favor an intermediate approach? Please look at Continuum 29 and place an *x* at the point on the continuum where you believe your personal preference is represented.

Approaches to Behavior Management

A very important component of a teaching style is the approach used to manage student behavior. Some teachers have a reactive behavior management approach. Reactive behavior managers intervene only when students are off-task or break rules. They do not intervene while things are going well in the classroom. Other teachers use prevention steps as a way to maintain classroom order and discipline. These teachers are proactive in their interventions. They seek to prevent disruptions by providing quality instruction, a nurturant climate, and by changing circumstances which could lead to off-task student behavior. Proactive behavior managers interact frequently and positively with students while things are going well in the classroom. Over several classroom visits, an observer can determine if a teacher has a reactive approach to behavior management or if the teacher has a preventive style. In one case, the observer will notice that the teacher does not intervene until students go off-task; in another case, the observer will notice a significant amount of positive teacher interventions while students work on task.

Continuum 30
Teacher Behavior Management Approach

| — — — — — — — — — | — — — — — — — — — | — — — — — — — — — |

Reactive Approach   Preventive Approach

Which approach do you prefer? Will you wait until students get off task before you intervene? Will you intervene while students are behaving appropriately? Will you prefer to combine both approaches? Look at Continuum 30 and place an x at the point on the continuum where you believe your personal preference is represented.

Once students get off task and engage in minor disruptions, teachers may intervene by applying consequences or by redirecting student behavior. Some teachers tend to emphasize the use of consequences as a response to minor student disruptions while other teachers choose to use redirection steps. Teachers who use consequences to deal with minor disruptions believe that students will not change behavior unless something happens to them. Teachers who use redirection interventions believe that students will get back on task once their actions are pointed out by the teacher.

Continuum 31
Teacher Response to Minor Disruptions

| — — — — — — — — — | — — — — — — — — — | — — — — — — — — — |

Consequence Steps   Redirection Steps

Which response to students' minor disruptions do you favor? The use of consequence steps? The use of redirection steps? The use of both? Please look at Continuum 31 and place an x at the point on the continuum where you believe your personal preference is represented.

All teachers, sooner or later, have to apply consequences to student misbehaviors. Teachers may choose from one of three types of consequences in the classroom. One type is called penalties. **Penalties** are consequences which are not related to the student infraction. But, because in itself penalties are unpleasant, they function as deterrents (for example, staying after school is a penalty not related to scratching a desk). Another type of consequence is the **logical consequence**. Logical consequences are related to inappropriate student behaviors. Sanding and varnishing the scratched desk is a logical consequence. **Natural consequences** are the natural results of an action. If a student digs a hole in the dirt with a new pen, the pen is ruined. Natural consequences are the best deterrents to inappropriate student behavior because they occur automatically without the intervention of the teacher. When natural consequences do not occur, the teacher has to intervene and choose between penalties or logical consequences. Assertive Discipline uses penalties, while Glasser's method recommends the use of logical consequences. Penalties may be applied quickly to many students misbehaving in different ways at the same time. Logical consequences, because they are individualized, can not be applied as quickly, or to many students misbehaving in different ways at the same time.

Continuum 32
Type of Consequences

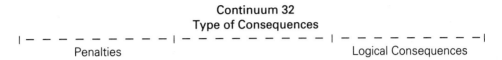

Penalties   Logical Consequences

After considering the advantages and disadvantages of each type of consequence for student misbehavior, which one do you prefer? Do you favor the use of penalties? Do you prefer to use logical consequences? Will you use both? Please look at Continuum 32 and place an *x* at the point on the continuum where you believe your personal preference is represented.

Another dimension of behavior management is the use of assertive language. Assertive language is when teachers describe, to students, how inappropriate behaviors affect them. Low use of assertive language is found when teachers do not communicate how they are being affected by student behavior. Teachers who do not use assertive language are usually polite and considerate persons who believe that students know how their actions affect the teacher and disrupt the classroom. They find it difficult or unnecessary to use assertive language describing their personal teaching needs. High use of assertive language is found when teachers disclose to students how they are affected by inappropriate behaviors, and when they describe their needs as teachers to their students.

Continuum 33
Use of Assertive Language

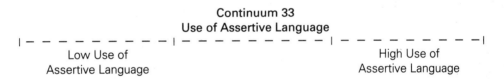

Low Use of   High Use of
Assertive Language   Assertive Language

What degree of assertive language will you use in your classroom? Low? High? Please look at Continuum 33 and place an *x* at the point on the continuum where you believe your personal preference is represented.

Another dimension in the behavior management style of a teacher is the use of outside or team support. On the one hand, teachers may attempt to solve all the classroom behavior management situations by themselves. On the other hand, teachers may seek the assistance of other teachers, parents, and administrators when they experience difficult situations with students.

Continuum 34
Use of Team Support

| – – – – – – – – – | – – – – – – – – – | – – – – – – – – –|

Low Use of Team Support   High Use of Team Support

Which approach to solving difficult classroom behavior situations do you prefer? Will you address the problems by yourself? Will you seek the assistance of other professionals and parents? Please look at Continuum 34 and place an x at the point on the continuum where you believe your personal preference is represented.

How to Interpret Teaching Style Preferences

On Figure 11.2, *Teaching Style Preferences*, the eight areas which contribute to the make-up of a teaching style are listed.

Under each area, the various dimensions on which you placed an x as your read each section of the chapter are also listed. Next to each dimension, there are three spaces indicating the three portions of each continuum from which you chose. Please, enter on this chart the choices you made on each continuum. If you chose the left section of a continuum, you will check the Traditional (T) choice. If you chose the middle section, you will check the Eclectic (E) choice. If you chose the right section, you will check the Open (O) choice.

Once you have entered your choices on Figure 11.2, you may add up the number of T, E, and O choices for each of the eight areas. In general, T choices reflect a traditional orientation to that particular area; while O choices represent a nontraditional orientation. E choices represent an eclectic orientation within that particular area. For example, two Ts in the area of student grouping would suggest a preference toward traditional grouping approaches while two Os would indicate an orientation toward nontraditional grouping practices. Two Es would point to an eclectic approach which you may prefer to group both ways, traditionally, and nontraditionally, depending on the circumstances. Of course there are other possible scoring combinations, such as T, E or E, O, which suggest a traditional to eclectic preference, or an eclectic to nontraditional preference. You may notice that in certain areas your preferences line-up within different sections of the continua. For example, you may have a traditional orientation toward subject matter, and a nontraditional orientation toward classroom climate.

How do you know if your choices coincide with what research in education identifies as sound teaching approaches? Herbert Walbert (1986) presents three research summaries in *The Handbook of Research on Teaching* which were conducted by Horwitz (1979), Peterson (1979), and Hedges, Giaconia, and Gage (1981). These scholars analyzed 398 studies on the effects of traditional versus open education teaching practices. Their results indicate that students in open classrooms do no worse in standardized achievement tests than students in traditional classrooms while they do better in attitudes toward school, creativity, curiosity, independence, and cooperation. Giaconia and Hedges (1982) reanalyzed some of the studies and concluded that unless they are radically extreme, open education classroom practices enhance desirable "nonacademic" outcomes such as attitudes toward school and learning without detracting from academic achievement. From the standpoint of research validation, all teaching style preferences—traditional, eclectic and open—produce similar academic results. The open, nontraditional teaching orientation appears to promote other educational outcomes which are generally valued by our society, such as positive attitudes toward learning and student self-reliance.

Another way of interpreting our scores is to look at two major clusters. One cluster groups the first 20 continua and describes instructional style. The other cluster

Teaching Style Preferences

Choice:

	Traditional	Eclectic	Open
STUDENT GROUPING			
1. Grouping of Students in Elementary Schools	_____	_____	_____
2. Student Grouping Approaches in the Classroom	_____	_____	_____
SUBJECT MATTER			
3. Organization of Subject Matter	_____	_____	_____
4. Selection of Subject Matter	_____	_____	_____
5. Presentation of Subject Matter	_____	_____	_____
INSTRUCTION			
6. Focus of Delivery	_____	_____	_____
7. Types of Learning Experiences	_____	_____	_____
8. Types of Thinking Promoted Among Students	_____	_____	_____
9. Types of Productive Thinking	_____	_____	_____
10. Variety in the Use of Teaching Methods	_____	_____	_____
PLANNING			
11. Sources of Lesson Plans	_____	_____	_____
12. Degree of Detail in Lesson Plans	_____	_____	_____
13. Degree of Compliance with Lesson Plan	_____	_____	_____
14. Types of Objectives	_____	_____	_____
EVALUATION			
15. Degree of Emphasis on Evaluation	_____	_____	_____
16. Grading System	_____	_____	_____
17. Sources of Evaluation	_____	_____	_____
18. Types of Evaluation	_____	_____	_____
19. Type of Test Items	_____	_____	_____
CLASSROOM CLIMATE			
20. Degree of Teacher Affect	_____	_____	_____
21. Degree of Student Success	_____	_____	_____
22. Degree of Learning Enjoyment	_____	_____	_____
23. Degree of Confusion and Exploration	_____	_____	_____
MOTIVATION AND CONTROL			
24. Degree of Learning Challenge	_____	_____	_____
25. Types of Rewards	_____	_____	_____
26. Type of Teacher Expectations	_____	_____	_____
27. Classroom Goal-Reward Orientation	_____	_____	_____
28. Degree of Influence Afforded to Students	_____	_____	_____
29. Conflict Resolution Method	_____	_____	_____
BEHAVIOR MANAGEMENT			
30. Teacher Behavior Management Approach	_____	_____	_____
31. Teacher Response to Minor Disruptions	_____	_____	_____
32. Type of Consequences	_____	_____	_____
33. Use of Assertive Language	_____	_____	_____
34. Use of Team Support	_____	_____	_____

Figure 11.2

groups the last 15 continua and describes management style. Now you may want to add the total number of *T,E* and *O* choices you made in the first 20 continua. A score of 20 *T*s or 15 *T*s and 5 *E*s, could be defined as *very traditional* (see Figure 11.3).

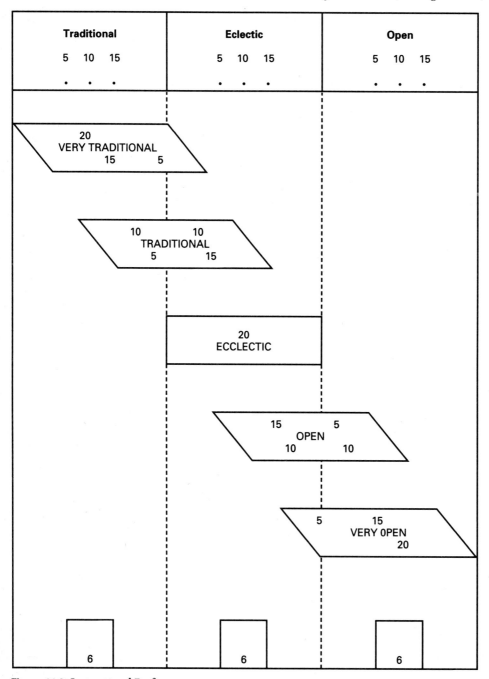

Figure 11.3 Instructional Preferences

A score of 10 *T*s and 10 *E*s could be considered as *traditional*. A score of 20 *E*s or 6 *T*s, 6 *E*s and 6 *O*s could be described as *eclectic*. A score of 15 *E*s and 5 *O*s, or 10 *E*s and 10 *O*s could be defined as *open*. A score of 5 *E*s and 15 *O*s, or 20 *O*s could be identified as *very open*.

What are the implications of these scores? Candidates who score *very traditional* or *traditional* in the instructional style cluster should consider seeking employment in an elementary school which is characterized by a traditional program orientation. These candidates may experience difficulty adjusting to an open, nontraditional school program. Conversely, candidates who score *open* or *very open* in the instructional style cluster may be very unhappy if assigned to a very traditional program. Those candidates scoring with an *eclectic* orientation may look for school programs which are neither very traditional nor very open in order to feel comfortable with the school program. Of course, one can always manage to teach in a traditional setting while making use of many open teaching practices. Likewise, one can manage to teach in an open setting while making use of traditional practices. We feel, however, that teachers should become aware of their beliefs about teaching and should seek school settings which form the best match with their beliefs.

The second cluster, continua 21 through 35, describes classroom management style. You may want to add the total number of *T, E* and *O* choices you made in these last fifteen continua. A score of 15 *T*s or 10 *T*s and 5 *E*s could be defined as *very traditional* (see Figure 11.4).

A score of 7 *T*s and 7 *E*s, or 5 *T*s and 10 *E*s could be considered *traditional*. A score of 15 *E*s, or 5 *T*s, 5 *E*s and 5 *O*s could be described as *eclectic*. A score of 10 *E*s and 5 *O*s, or 7 *E*s and 7 *O*s could be defined as *open*. A score of 5 *E*s and 10 *O*s, or 15 *O*s could be identified as *very open*. What are the implications of scores in the classroom management cluster? Candidates who score *very traditional* or *traditional* in the classroom management cluster may not be suited to teach early childhood or primary students.

All of us, as professional educators, will adopt new teaching practices throughout our careers and will modify our preferred style. Teacher preparation programs and school inservice programs are designed to help us grow as much as possible. For outstanding professionals, life is a succession of efforts to become better at our jobs. The teaching style preferences which you are identifying as part of your teacher preparation will gradually change as you apply yourself to become a better professional. What can you do now? You can reflect on the various profiles which you selected. Are you satisfied with them? Do you have doubts about your style? Are you unhappy with your profile? You may want to discuss this situation with a professor or another educator. Remember that it is important for you to know your style preferences so that you can make intelligent decisions about your teaching. It is also important, however, that you revise your preferences as you learn and grow professionally. Hopefully, as you extend your teaching experience, you will acquire a sense that you have developed your own teaching style, that you know what it is and what it means, and that you are happy to have arrived at it.

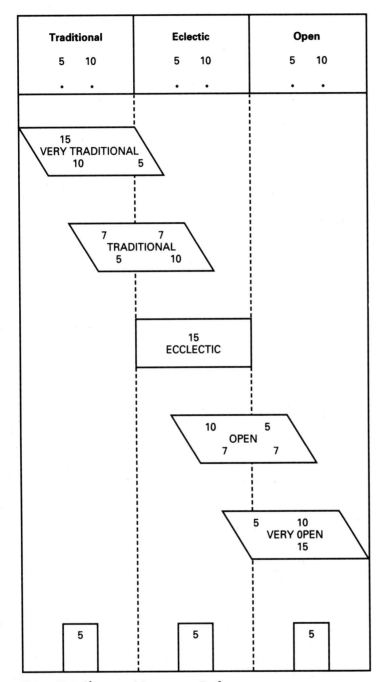

Figure 11.4 Classroom Management Preferences

GLOSSARY

academic tracking The practice of assigning students to ability groups from which they cannot move up or down.

convergent thinking Being led to discover an idea through the guidance of one's teacher.

divergent thinking Similar to productive thinking. Higher-level thinking in which the students go beyond the ideas presented in class and produce their own ideas.

essentialism A view of education which emphasizes the acquisition of basic skills as the major goal of education.

existentialism A view of education which emphasizes the right of a child to choose what he wants to learn in pursuit of personal meaning.

experimentalism A view of education which emphasizes the rediscovery of experience and the learning of problem-solving processes.

perennialism A view of education which emphasizes the exposure of students to the great ideas produced during the history of humankind.

proactive behavior management An approach to behavior management in which the teacher prevents possible problems through positive instructional and managerial interventions. In this approach, the teacher initiates and the students react.

reactive behavior management An approach to behavior management in which the teacher waits for the problems to arise before she intervenes. In this approach, the students initiate and the teacher reacts.

REFERENCES

Airasian, P.W. *Classroom Assessment* (New York: McGraw-Hill, 1991).

Arends, R. I. *Learning to Teach* (New York: Random House, 1988) pp. 88–90.

Aronson, E., et al. *The Jigsaw Classroom* (Beverly Hills, CA: Sage Publications, 1978).

ASCD Issues Analysis, *Public Schools of Choice* (Alexandria, VA: ASCD, 1990).

Bandura, A. *Social Learning Theory* (Englewood Cliffs, NJ: Prentice Hall, 1977).

Beane, J., C. Toepfer, and S. Alessi. *Curriculum Planning and Development* (Boston: Allyn and Bacon, 1986).

Bennett, N., & D. Blundell. "Quantity and quality of work in rows of classroom groups," *Educational Psychology*, 3, (1983) pp. 93-105.

Berman, L. *New Priorities in the Curriculum* (Columbus, Ohio: Merrill, 1968).

Bloom, B. (ed.). *A Taxonomy of Educational Objectives. Handbook I: Cognitive Domain* (New York: David McKay Company, 1956).

————. "Mastery Learning," in J. Block (ed.) *Mastery Learning: Theory and Practice* (New York: Holt, Rinehart and Winston, (1971), pp. 47–63.

————. *Human Characteristics and Student Learning* (New York: McGraw-Hill, 1976).

————, T. Hastings, and G. Madaus. *Handbook of Formative and Summative Evaluation of Student Learning* (New York: McGraw-Hill, 1971).

Boydell, D. *The Primary Teacher in Action* (New St. Wells, Somerset (United Kingdom): Open Books, 1978).

Brookover, W., et al. "Effective Instruction," in E. Erickson and L. Carl (eds.) *Creating Effective Schools: An Inservice Program for Enhancing School Learning Climate and Achievement* (Holmes Beach, FL: Learning Publications, 1982) pp. 128–148.

Brophy, J. E. "Classroom Organization and Management," *Elementary School Journal*, 83, (1982) pp. 265–268.

————. "Teacher Praise: A Functional Analysis," *Review of Educational Research*, 51, (1981) pp. 5-32.

Brophy, J. E., & T. L. Good. *Teacher-Student Relationships: Causes and Consequences* (New York: Holt, Rinehart & Winston, 1974).

————. "Teacher Behavior and Student Achievement," in M.C. Wittrock (ed.), *Handbook of Research on Teaching*, (3rd ed.) (New York: Macmillan, 1986).

Brophy, J. E. & M. Rohrkemper. "The Influence of Problem-Ownership on Teacher Perceptions," *Journal of Educational Psychology*," 73, (1981) pp. 295–311.

Bruner, J. *The Process of Education* (New York: Vintage, 1960).

Bruner, J., J. Goodnow, & G. Austin. *A Study of Thinking* (New York: John Wiley and Sons, 1956).

Bruner, J. *Toward a Theory of Instruction* (Cambridge, MA: Harvard University Press, 1966).

Cangelosi, J. S. *Measurement and Evaluation: An Inductive Approach for Teachers* (Dubuque, IA: Brown, 1982).

Canter, Lee and Marlene Canter. *Assertive Discipline: A Take-Charge Approach for Today's Educator* (Seal Beach, CA: Canter and Associates, 1976).

Carroll, J. B. "Problems of Measurement Related to the Concept of Learning for Mastery," in J. Block (ed.), *Mastery Learning: Theory and Practice* (New York: Holt, Rinehart and Winston, 1971) pp. 29–46.

Clinchy, E., and E. A. Cody. "If Not Public Choice, Then Private Escape," *The Kappan*, Volume 60, Number 4 (December 1978).

Coleman, J., et al. *Equality of Educational Opportunity* (Washington, D.C.: U.S. Office of Health Education and Welfare, 1966).

Combs, A.W. and D. Snygg. *Individual Behavior: A Perceptual Approach to Behavior* (New York: Harper and Row, 1959).

Copeland, R. *How Children Learn Mathematics: Teaching Implications of Piaget's Research*, 2nd edition (New York: Macmillan, 1974).

Cotton, J. & W. Savard. "Student Discipline and Motivation: Research Synthesis," in *Discipline*, Bloomington, IN: Phi Delta Kappa (1984).

Covington, M., M. Spratt, & C. Omelich. "Is Effort Enough or Does Diligence Count Too? Student and Teacher Reactions to Effort Stability in Failure," *Journal of Educational Psychology*, 72, (1980) pp. 717–729.

Covington, M. "The Self-Worth Theory of Achievement Motivation: Findings and Implications," *The Elementary School Journal*, 85, (1984) pp. 5–20.

Dale, E. *Audiovisual Methods in Teaching* (3rd edition) (New York: Dryden (Holt, Rinehart, and Winston), 1969).

Danforth Foundation. *The Danforth's School Administrators Fellowship Program: 1988-89*, (1988), pp. 251–252.

Deci, E. L. & R. M. Ryan. *Intrinsic Motivation and Self-Determination in Human Behavior* (New York: Plenum Press, 1985).

Descamps, J. & R. Lindahl. "A Classroom Management Program for the Middle School," *The Middle School Journal*, 20, 1, (1988) pp. 8–10.

Dewey, John *How We Think* (Lexington: MA: Heath, 1933, renewed 1960).

————. *The Child and the Curriculum* (1902) and *The School and Society* (1900, 1915 revised edition) (Chicago: University of Chicago Press, these two volumes were published together in 1943).

————. *Democracy in education* (New York: Macmillan, 1916).

————. *Logic: The Theory of Inquiry* (New York: Henry Holt, 1938).

Doyle, W. "Classroom Organization and Management," in M. Wittrock, *Handbook of Research on Teaching* (3rd edition) (New York: Macmillan, 1986).

Dreikurs, R., B. Grunwald, & F. Pepper. *Maintaining Sanity in the Classroom: Classroom Management Techniques* (New York: Harper & Row, 1982).

Duckworth, E., "An Interview with Jean Piaget," *Teacher* (October, 1973).

————. "An Introductory Note About Piaget," *Journal of Education*, 161, 1 (Winter, 1979), pp. 5–12.

Duckworth, E., et al. *Science Education: A Minds-On Approach for the Elementary Years* (Hillsdale: Lawrence Erlbaum, 1990).

Dunn, R., K. Dunn, and G. E. Price. *Learning Style Inventory* (Lawrence, KS: Price Systems, 1975).

Edmonds, R., "Effective Schools for the Urban Poor," *Educational Leadership*, 37, (1979) pp. 15–18.

Easley, J., and R. Zwoyer. *Teaching by Listening*, in *Contemporary Education*, 47 (1) (1975) pp. 19–25.

Easley, J., "What I've Learned About Teaching Science and Mathematics: A Memoir," unpublished paper given in honor of his retirement celebration, University of Illinois at Urbana-Champaign, April 9, 1989.

Eisner, E., "Instructional and Educational Objectives: Their Formulation and Use in Curriculum," in *Instructional Objectives*, AERA Monograph Series on Curriculum Evaluation (Chicago: Rand McNally, 1969).

Ellis, A., J. Mackey, and A. Glenn. *The School Curriculum* (Boston: Allyn and Bacon, 1988).

ESS (Elementary Science Study), *Rocks and Charts* (Newton, Massachusetts: Educational Development Corporation, 1967). Distributed by Delta Education, Nashua, New Hampshire.

——————, *Attribute Games and Problems*. (Newton, Massachusetts: Educational Development Corporation, 1967). Distributed by Delta Education, Nashua, New Hampshire.

Erlwanger, S. H., "Case Studies of Children's Conceptions of Mathematics—Part 1," in *Journal of Children's Mathematical Behavior*, 1 (1975) pp. 199–277.

Flavell, J. *The Developmental Psychology of Jean Piaget* (New York: Nostrand, 1963).

Frazier, A. *Values, Curriculum, and the Elementary School* (Boston: Houghton-Mifflin, 1980).

Furth, H. and H. Wachs. *Thinking Goes to School* (New York: Oxford University Press, 1974).

Gagne, E. G. *The Cognitive Psychology of School Learning* (Boston: Little, Brown, 1985).

Gagne, R. M. *The Conditions of Learning* (3rd edition) (New York: Holt, Rinehart and Winston, 1977).

Giaconia, R. M., & L.V. Hedges. *Identifying Features of Open Education* (Stanford, CA: Stanford University, 1982).

Ginsburg, Herbert, and Sylvia Opper. *Piaget's Theory of Intellectual Development* (Englewood Cliffs: Prentice-Hall, 1988).

Glasser, W. *Reality Therapy* (New York: Harper & Row, 1965).

——————. *Schools Without Failure* (New York: Harper & Row, 1969).

Good, T., "Teacher Effectiveness in the Elementary School," *Journal of Teacher Education*, 30, 2, (1979) pp. 52–64.

Goodlad, J., and R. Anderson. *The Nongraded Elementary School*, Revised Edition (New York: Teachers College, Columbia University, 1987).

Gordon, T. *T.E.T.: Teacher Effectiveness Training* (New York: David McKay, 1974).

Gronlund, N. *Measurement and Evaluation in Teaching*, 5th Edition (New York: Macmillan, 1985).

Harris, T.A. *I'm OK—You're OK* (New York: Harper & Row, 1969).

Harter, S., "Pleasure Derived from Challenge and the Effects of Receiving Grades on Children's Difficulty Level Choices," *Child Development*, 49, (1978) pp. 788–789.

Hedges, L.V., R. M. Giaconia & N.L. Gage. *Meta-analysis of the Effects of Open and Traditional Instruction* (Stanford, CA: Stanford University, Program on Teaching Effectiveness, 1981).

Hillson, M., and J. Bongo. *Continuous-Progress Education* (Palo Alto, CA: SRA, 1971).

Hodgkinson, H., "The Right Schools for the Right Kids," *Educational Leadership*, 45, 5 (February, 1988).

Horwitz, R.A., "Psychological Effects of the Open Classroom," *Review of Educational Research*, 49, (1979) pp. 71–86.

Houston, P., "Another Minnesota Miracle?," *Minnesota Monthly*, (September, 1989) pp. 34–38.

Hunter, M.C. *Mastery Teaching* (El Segundo, CA: TIP Publications, 1982).

Hyman, R.T. *Ways of Teaching* (Englewood Cliffs, NJ: Prentice-Hall, 1974).

Jackson, P. *Life In The Classrooms* (New York: Holt, Rinehart & Winston, 1968).

Johnson, D., & R. Johnson. "The Internal Dynamics of Cooperative Learning Groups," in R. Slaving, et al., (eds.), *Learning to Cooperate, Cooperating to Learn* (New York: Plenum Press, 1985).

Jones, F., "The Gentle Art of Classroom Discipline," *National Elementary Principal* 58, (1979) pp. 26–32.

Joyce, B., & M. Weil. *Models of Teaching* (Englewood Cliffs, NJ: Prentice-Hall, 1986).

Kauchak, D., & P. Eggen. *Learning and Teaching: Research Based Methods* (Boston: Allyn and Bacon, 1989).

Kamii, C. *Young Children Reinvent Arithmetic* (New York: Teachers College Press, 1985).

Kelsey, K., "A Perspective on The History of Outcome Based Education in Minnesota," *The ASCD Minnesota Report* (Minnesota Association for Supervision and Curriculum Development), Volume 7, Number 2 (November, 1990), pp. 7–8.

Kohlberg, L., "The Cognitive-Developmental Approach to Moral Education," *Phi Delta Kappan*, 56, (1975) p. 10.

Kounin, J. *Discipline and Group Management* (New York: Van Nostrand Rineholt, 1970).

Louisell, R. *What Teacher Educators Miss: Patterns in the Behaviors of Elementary Teachers* (Ed.D. dissertation, University of Illinois at Urbana-Champaign) (Ann Arbor: University Microfilms International, 1979).

————. "The Key Word Approach to Language Experience," *Twin City Area Reading Council Newsletter* (Minnesota Reading Association), 1, 3 (January, 1983).

Maehr, M., & W. Stallings. "Freedom from External Evaluation," *Child Development*, 43, (1972) pp. 117–185.

Mager, R. *Preparing Instructional Objectives* (Revised 2nd edition) (Belmont, CA: David S. Lake Publishers, 1984) pp. 29–33.

Maslow, A. *Toward a Psychology of Being* (New York: Van Nostrand Rineholt, 1962).

McCarthy, B. *The Hemispheric Mode Indicator* (Barrington, Illinois: Excel, 1986).

A Minnesota Vision for OBE: Outcomes Based Education, The Minnesota Department of Education, Division of Instructional Effectiveness, 1990.

Morgan, M., "Reward-Induced Decrements and Increments in Intrinsic Motivation," *Review of Educational Research*, 54, (1984) pp. 5–30.

Nuffield Foundation, *How to Build a Pond* and *Guide to Math* (Edinburgh, Scotland: Chambers, 1968).

Pearson, P., & J. Dole. *Explicit Comprehension Instruction: The Model, the Research, and the Concerns* (Chicago: AERA, 1985).

Perrone, V. *The Abuses of Standardized Testing* (Bloomington: Phi Delta Kappa, 1977) Fastback Series, Number 92.

Peterson, P.L., "Direct Instruction Reconsidered," in P. L. Peterson & H. J. Walbert (eds.), *Research on Teaching* (Berkeley, CA: McCutchan, 1979).

Piaget, J., "Development and Learning," in *Journal of Research in Science Teaching*, II, 3 (1964), pp. 288–296.

————. *The Growth of Logical Thinking from Childhood to Adolescence*. (Basic, 1958).

————. *Judgment and Reasoning in the Child* (London: Routledge and Kegan Paul, 1928).

————. *The Child's Conception of the World* (London: Routledge and Kegan Paul, 1929).

————. *The Child's Conception of Physical Causality* (London: Routledge and Kegan Paul, 1929).

Piaget, J., and B. Inhelder. *The Psychology of the Child* (New York: Basic Books, 1969).

Purkey, W.W. *Self-Concept and School Achievement* (Englewood Cliffs, NJ: Prentice-Hall, 1970).

Rathbone, C. *Open Education: The Informal Classroom* (New York: Citation, 1971).

Raths, Louis, et al. *Teaching for Thinking: Theory and Application* (Columbus, Ohio: Merrill, 1967).

Raths, L.E., M. Harmin, & S. B. Simon. *Values and Teaching: Working with Values in the Classroom* (Columbus, Ohio: Charles E. Merrill, 1978).

Resnick, L. *Education and Learning to Think* (Washington, D.C.: National Academy Press, 1987).

Rist, R., "Student Social Class and Teacher Expectations: The Self-Fulfilling Prophecy in Ghetto Education," *The Harvard Educational Review*, 40, (1970) pp. 411-451.

Rosenfield, P., N. Lambert, & A. Black, "Desk Arrangement Effects on Pupil Classroom Behavior," *Journal of Educational Psychology*, 77, (1985) pp. 101–108.

Rosenthal, R. *On the Sociological Psychology of the Self-Fulfilling Prophecy: Further Evidence for Pygmalion Effects and Their Mediating Mechanisms* (New York: MSS Modular Publications, 1974).

Ruggiero, V. *Teaching Thinking Across the Curriculum* (New York: Harper and Row, 1988).

Schiller, C. *In His Own Words* (United Kingdom: A&C Black, 1979).

Schmuck, R.A., & P.A. Schmuck. *Group Processes in the Classroom* (Dubuque, IA: William C. Brown Company, 1983).

Sharan, S., "Cooperative Learning in Small Groups," *Review of Educational Research*, 50, (1980) pp. 241–249.

Sharan, S., et al. *Cooperative Learning in the Classroom: Research in Desegregated Schools* (Hillsdale, NJ: Erlbaum, 1984).

Skinner, B. F. *The Technology of Teaching* (New York: Appleton-Century-Crofts, 1968).

Slavin, R. *Cooperative Learning* (New York: Longman, 1983).

Smith, L.M. and W. Geoffrey. *The Complexities of an Urban Classroom* (New York: Holt, Rinehart, and Winston, 1968).

Spalding, R. and W. *The Writing Road to Reading* (New York: Morrow, 1969).

Spodek, B., "Fostering Intellectual Development: Reexamined 22 Years Later," speech presented at the Bicentennial Conference on Early Childhood Education, University of Miami, June 30, 1976.

Stake, R., and J. Easley. *Case Studies in Science Education* (CIRCE, University of Illinois at Urbana-Champaign, 1978).

Stallings, J., & D. Stipek, "Research on Early Childhood and Elementary School Teaching Programs," in M. Wittrock (ed.), *Handbook of Research on Teaching* (New York: Macmillan, 1986).

Stipek, D. *Motivation to Learn: From Theory to Practice*. (Englewood Cliffs, NJ: Prentice-Hall, 1988).

Swyers, B., "How Media Teach," in *Grade Teacher*, 89, 6 (February, 1972).

—————., "Teaching with Technology," in *Grade Teacher*, 89, 6 (February, 1972) pp. 21–26, 90.

Swyers, W.R. *A Human Literacy Curriculum*, Unpublished paper, (1972).

Taba, H. *Teaching Strategies and Cognitive Functioning in Elementary School Children*, Cooperative Research Project 2404 (San Francisco, CA: San Francisco State College, 1966).

—————. *Teachers' Handbook for Elementary Social Studies*. (Reading, MA: Addison-Wesley, 1967).

Valencia, S., "Assessment: A Portfolio Approach to Classroom Reading Assessment: The Whys, Whats, and Hows," *The Reading Teacher*, 43, 4 (January, 1990).

Van Allen, R. & C. Allen. *LEIR, Level II* (Chicago: Encyclopedia Brittanica Press, 1970).

Veatch, J. *Individualizing Your Reading Program*. (New York: Putnam, 1959).

Walbert, H. J., "Synthesis of Research on Teaching," in Merlin C. Whittrock (Ed.), *Handbook of Research on Teaching*, Third Edition (NY: Macmillan Publishing Co., 1986).

Wang, M., "Development and Consequences of Students' Sense of Personal Control," in J. Levine & M. Wang (eds.), *Teacher and Student Perceptions: Implications for Learning* (Hillsdale, NJ: Erlbaum, 1983).

Wasserman, S., and G. Ivany. *Teaching Elementary Science: Who's Afraid of Spiders* (New York: Harper and Row, 1988).

Weber, W., "Teacher Perceptions of Effective Classroom Management Strategies," in *Effective Classroom Management* (Bloomington, IN: Phi Delta Kappa, 1984).

West, C., & T. Anderson, "The Question of Preponderant Causation in Teacher Expectancy Research," *Review of Educational Research*, 46, (1976) pp. 185–213.

The Wisconsin Design for Reading, The Board of Regents of the University of Wisconsin System, 1972.

Zahorik, J., "A Task for Curriculum Research," in *Educational Leadership*, 33, 7 (April, 1976).

—————., "Teachers' Planning Models," in *Educational Leadership*, 33, 2 (November, 1975).

Zimmerman, B., & C. Kleefeld, "Toward a Theory of Teaching: A Social Learning View," *Contemporary Educational Psychology*, 2, (1985) pp. 485–493.

Sample Topic Unit "Remembering Long Ago" by Jay Houck

BRAINSTORM WEB

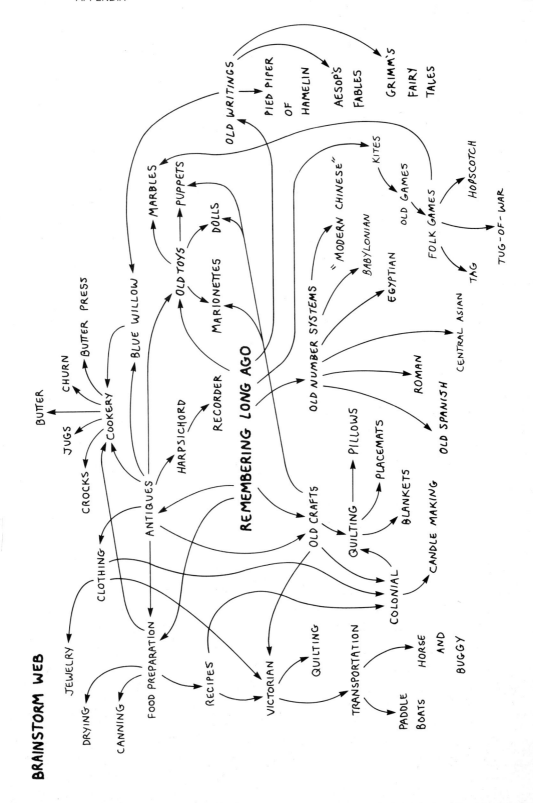

PRUNED WEB OF ACTIVITIES

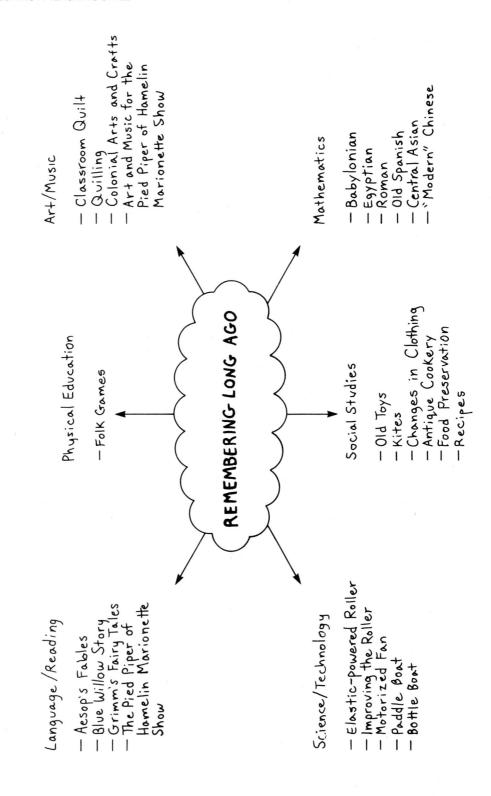

REMEMBERING LONG AGO

Art/Music
— Classroom Quilt
— Quilling
— Colonial Arts and Crafts
— Art and Music for the Pied Piper of Hamelin Marionette Show

Mathematics
— Babylonian
— Egyptian
— Roman
— Old Spanish
— Central Asian
— "Modern" Chinese

Physical Education
— Folk Games

Social Studies
— Old Toys
— Kites
— Changes in Clothing
— Antique Cookery
— Food Preservation
— Recipes

Language/Reading
— Aesop's Fables
— Blue Willow Story
— Grimm's Fairy Tales
— The Pied Piper of Hamelin Marionette Show

Science/Technology
— Elastic-Powered Roller
— Improving the Roller
— Motorized Fan
— Paddle Boat
— Bottle Boat

ACTIVITY PROGRESSION AND KEY SKILLS ANALYSIS

Activity Progression	Key Skills
Aesop's Fables	Language Arts: Listening
Blue Willow Story	Language Arts: Listening and writing
	Art: Pattern design
Grimm's Fairy Tales	Reading and Language Arts: Reading and Storytelling
Pied Piper of Hamelin Marionettes	Language Arts: Listening and writing
	Art: Marionette and scenery design
	Music: Instrumental (Recorder)
Early Systems of Numbers	Mathematics: Number
Elastic Energy	Science: Physical
Old Toys	Social Studies: History
	Art: Doll Design
Kites	Science: Physical
Changes In Clothing	Social Studies: History
Antique Cookery	Social Studies: History
Food Preservation	Social Studies: History
Recipes	Social Studies: History
	Science: Chemistry
Classroom Quilt	Art: Stitchery
Quilling	Art
Colonial Arts and Crafts	Art: Weaving, stitching, making rugs
Folk Games	Physical Education
	Language Arts

Subject Prediction Chart
Language Arts, Weeks One and Two

1. Aesop's Fables
   Read several fables to the children. After reading, discuss applications of these fables to real life.

2. Blue Willow Story
   Using the 1834–48 Blue Willow pattern meat platter made by George Phillips in Longport, England, tell the story behind the pattern. Examine one of the dishes as you read the story. Have students create their own scenes for a platter and write the story depicted by that scene.

3. Grimm's Fairy Tales
   Have each child select a Grimm's fairy tale, study it, design a costume for it, and wear the costume while presenting the tale to the class.

4. Pied Piper of Hamelin Marionettes Show
   Read the story "The Pied Piper of Hamelin" to the children. Have them write their own version to present to class or a school assembly. Have students create scenery and marionettes for the presentation. Integrate recorder tunes.

Statement About Grouping

Some activities will be carried out with the whole class. Others will be completed individually by each student. Still others will be conducted via small groups. Each student will participate in every activity.

RESOURCES

Texts:

Tonson J. and R. and J. Watts. *Fables of Aesop and Others* (London, England: 1754).

The Complete Grimm's Fairy Tales (New York: Pantheon Books, 1944).

Leeming, Joseph. *The Costume Book* (Philadelphia: J.B. Lippincott, 1938).

Browning, Robert. *The Pied Piper of Hamelin*, illustrated by Kate Greenaway. (London, England: Fedrick Warne & Company, 1888).

Dilson, Jesse. *The Abacus* (New York: St Martin's Press, 1968).

Johnsey, Robert. *Problem Solving in School Science* (Great Britain: Macdonald, 1986).

Hoople, Cheryl. *The Heritage Sampler* (New York: The Dial Press, 1975).

Downer, Marion. *Kites* (New York: Lothrop, Lee, and Shepard, 1959).

Walker, Barbara. *The Little House Cookbook* (New York: Harper & Row, 1979).

Penner, Lucille Recht. *The Colonial Cookbook* (New York: Hastings House, 1976).

O'Neill, Molly. *A Feast of Irish Cooking* (Portlaoise, Ireland: Dolmen Press, 1986).

MacGregor, Carol. *The Fairy Tale Cookbook* (New York: Macmillan, 1982).

Tudor, Tasha and Linda Allen. *Tasha Tudor's Old-Fashioned Gifts*. (New York: David Mackay, 1979).

Enthoven, Jacqueline. *Stitchery for Children* (New York, Reinhold,1968).

Parish, Peggy. *Let's Be Early Settler's with Daniel Boone* (New York: Harper & Row, 1967).

Worrell, Estella Ansley. *Be A Puppeteer* (New York: McGraw-Hill, 1969).

Magazines:

Country Living
Colonial Homes
Great Country Kitchens

Stories:

Blue Willow Story.

Songs:

Ease on Up, Cumberland Gap, Ev'ry Time I Feel The Spirit, Merrily We Go Along, Hot Cross Buns, Ice Cream Cone, Skip To My Lou, Rocky Mountain.

Old Toys:

Hansi French doll, Paradise doll set, boudoir doll, English dolls, pincushion dolls, marionette puppets, original GI Joe, dominoes, wooden blocks, old tops, marbles.

Antique Cookery:

mortar and pestle, Blue Willow platter, crock jar, 5 gallon earthenware crock, butter press, paddled butter churn, wooden bowls, pewterware, canning jar, cast iron kettle, coffee grinder, wire egg basket.

Folk Games:

Tag, Tug-of-war, Red Rover, Dodgeball, Hopscotch, Simon Says, Jacks, Statues, Steal the Bacon, Marbles, Ghosts In The Graveyard, Follow The Leader, Lemonade.

MONDAY
8:20 to 10:20 and 10:40 to 11:00 ....Topic Work
* L/R   ....Aesop's Fables (The Crow and The Pitcher)......wh/cl
M   ....Intro 6 Systems......wh/cl
S/T   ....Intro activities......wh/cl
SS   ....Intro activities......wh/cl
A/M   ....Intro activities......wh/cl

10:20 to 10:40......P.E.

P.E.......Intro Tag,
Tug-of-War & Red Rover-wh/cl

TUESDAY
8:20 to 10:20 and 10:40 to 11:00 ....Topic Work
* L/R   ....Aesop's Fables (The Fox and The Stork)......wh/cl
M   ....Babylonian System......in
S/T   ....Elastic-powered Roller......wh/cl
SS   ....Old Toys......wh/cl
A/M   ....Classroom Quilt......wh/cl

10:20 to 10:40......P.E.

P.E.......Intro Tag,
Tug-of-War & Red Rover-wh/cl

WEDNESDAY
8:20 to 10:20 and 10:40 to 11:00 ....Topic Work
* L/R   ....Aesop's Fables (The Wolf and The Crane)......wh/cl
M   ....Babylonian System......in
S/T   ....Elastic-powered Roller......in
SS   ....Old Toys......in
A/M   ....Classroom Quilt......in

10:20 to 10:40......P.E.

P.E.......Intro Tag,
Tug-of-War & Red Rover-wh/cl

THURSDAY
8:20 to 10:20 and 10:40 to 11:00 ....Topic Work
* L/R   ....Aesop's Fables (The Wolf in Sheep's Clothing)......wh/cl
M   ....Babylonian System......in
S/T   ....Elastic-powered Roller......in
SS   ....Old Toys......in
A/M   ....Classroom Quilt......in

10:20 to 10:40......P.E.

P.E.......Intro Tag,
Tug-of-War & Red Rover-wh/cl

FRIDAY
8:20 to 10:20 and 10:40 to 11:00 ....Topic Work
* L/R   ....Aesop's Fables (The Young Man and The Lion)......wh/cl
M   ....Babylonian System......in
S/T   ....Elastic-powered Roller......in
SS   ....Old Toys......in
A/M   ....Classroom Quilt......in

10:20 to 10:40......P.E.

P.E.......Intro Tag,
Tug-of-War & Red Rover-wh/cl

* L/R   Language/Reading
M   Mathematics
S/T   Science/Technology
SS   Social Studies
A/M   Art/Music
P.E.   Physical Education
wh/cl   whole class
in   individual
sm/gr   small group   (Small group make-up will vary depending on the activity,
i.e. random, friendship, mixed, etc.)

Lesson Plan
Blue Willow Story

Activity:

1. Read the Blue Willow Story to the students and explain its significance to the patterns on the Blue Willow Dishes.
2. Display a dish for the students as you read and discuss the story.
3. Have the students create their own scene for a platter.
4. Have students write the story that is depicted in the scenes which they have designed.

Possible Outcomes:

1. Students may develop a deeper appreciation for folk tales.
2. Through their exposure to a folk tale from a foreign land, students may develop a sensitivity to the perspectives of children from different cultures.
3. Children may notice the relationship which frequently exists between literature and art.
4. Children may enhance their own abilities in artistic design.
5. Children may further develop their skills in story writing.

Background Information:

The Blue Willow Story is about the daughter of a wealthy Chinese mandarin who fell in love with her father's secretary (Chang) and met him in secret many times. When her father discovered their secret relationship, he forbade his daughter to return to his home and he matched his daughter in marriage to a wealthy viceroy. On the day of the scheduled wedding, the secretary came for his lover and eloped with her, stealing the jewels which had been brought by the viceroy as a wedding gift. They lived together happily for many years, but eventually the viceroy found them living together on a remote island and killed Chang. In her grief, the daughter set fire to her home and burned to death inside it. This story has many variations, but each of the Blue Willow dishes (produced over a period of 170 years) depicts this story through the art on the dishes.

Materials:

1. Copy of the Blue Willow Story.
2. Art instruments and materials (Brushes and paints, or crayons, paper).
3. Writing instruments and paper.

Index

Abstractions, eliciting, 79–80
Academic tracking, 299
Acceptance, 201–202
Accepting language, 194–195, 214
Accessibility, 224
Accomplishments, feedback on
    group, 80
Achievement group, 31, 40–41, 60
Accommodation, 9, 25
Action, group members deciding
    on, 270
Action words, 129
Active listening, 195, 214, 246, 258
Activity
    lesson plan, 132
    movement, 126
    vs. objective, 129
Adopted curriculum, 125
Adult to adult interaction, 241, 243,
    258
Advisors, 51
Aesthetics, 225
Alternative Heights School, 51–57,
    58, 59, 173
Alternative settings, 51–57
Analysis, 65, 66, 102
    questions, 69, 71, 75–76

Analytic observations approach,
    178–179
Application, 65
Application of principles, 108–109
Application questions, 71
Aronson, E., 96
Assertive discipline, 231, 246–248
Assertive language, 194–196, 214,
    293
Assessing student learning, 95,
    160–190
Assessment, purposes of, 161–162
Assessment-placement procedure, 35
Assimilation, 25
Assistance, 261
Atomistic observation approach, 178
At-risk students, 258
Attend, getting students to, 217–220
Attention, 259
    how teachers divide their,
        219–220
    to disruptive students, 239
Attention getter, 78
Authority in groups, 266–267
Autonomy, 264

Basic reader group, 60

Behavior
    matching teacher actions with,
        234–235
    rewards for, 237–238
    standards of, 232–234
Behavior improvement contract,
    247–248
Behavior management, 291–294
Behavior modification, 229, 236
Belonging, fostering sense of, 202,
    203
Berman, L., 158
Bill of Rights, 20
Bloom, B., 65, 86, 100
Bloom's Taxonomy, 68–69, 74, 102,
    104, 113, 176–177, 213
Body language, 1, 194, 196-197,
    196–197
Boredom, student, 125
Brainstorming, 152–153, 272–273
British education, 46–47, 114, 115,
    117, 171–173
Brophy, J. E., 228, 237
Brunner, J., 64, 105, 107, 108, 125
    modes of learning, 64–65
Business-like classroom climate,
    199-200

Buzz groups, 274

Cangelosi, J. S., 194
Canter, L., 228, 229, 231
Canter, M., 228, 229, 231
Carroll, J. B., 100
Challenge, 289
Child-centered work. *See* Topic work
Children in schools, 1–25
Class discussion, 75–77
Class inclusion, 11, 25
Class rewards, 204–208
Classification, 11,
Classroom
    alternative, 51–57
    climate, 199–201, 287–288
    environment, 229
    family grouped, 44–51, 59
    goal-reward structure, 264
    graded, 26–33
    individualized, 33–44
    informal, 44-51, 59
    management, 191–215, 239–240
        dealing with student behavior,
            228–258
        teaching-learning
            environment, 216–227
    multi-aged, 34, 51–57
    meeting, 274–275
    nongraded, 33–44
    organization of, 26–29
    self-contained, 26–33, 44–51, 59
    team-taught, 33–44, 51–57
    traditional, 26–33
Climate, personalizing, 78
Closure techniques, 79–80
Clusters, 56–57, 59, 60, 279
Coaching, 95
Cognitive structures, 12, 25
Coleman, J., 209
Collection of information, 112
Comfort, 225
Communication roadblock, 195
Communication skills, 158,
    193–197, 271
Community projects, 203
Competence, 18
Competition, 204-205, 264
Competitive learning environments,
    204-205

Complex thinking, 102
Comprehension, 65, 104
    questions, 71
Concept, 67–68, 77, 104-105,
    attainment, 105-107, 113
    demonstration of, 80-81
    formation, 108-109
Concrete operations, period of, 9,
    10–14, 17
Conflict-resolution skills, 197–199,
    245–246, 271
Consensus, 266–267
Consensus group meeting 272–273
Consequence steps, 232–235,
    264–248
Consequences, 207–208, 253, 257
Conservation, 9, 13
Conservers, 6, 25
Control, 217
    approaches to, 289
    focus of, 199
    increasing student perception of,
        264
Convergent thinking, 76, 87,
    282–283, 299
Cooperation, 264
Cooperative learning, 88, 96–99,
    100, 202, 205
Core values, 213, 214
Correct responses, 73
Cotton, J., 229
Cound, A., 134
Criterion referenced evaluation,
    161, 163–165, 166, 169, 177, 189
Critical-creative thinking, 75
Critique of student work, 86–87
Cross-age tutoring, 85
Curiosity, 19–20
Curriculum, 121–126
    role plays and, 83

Daily plans, 150, 157
Deci, E.L., 206
Decision making methods, 266–267
Declarative knowledge, 89, 91, 92,
    120
Democracy in schools, 20
Demonstration techniques, 80–81
Departmentalized instruction, 28,
    56, 60

Descriptive language, 194, 214
Desegregation laws, 31
Dewey, J., 44–46, 105, 158
    model of thinking, 105
Diagnosis, 162
Direct instruction. *See* Mastery
    teaching
Discipline, 20-Step System of,
    231–258
Discussion techniques, 76–77, 91
Divergent information, 96
Divergent thinking, 76, 87,
    282–283, 299
Doyle, W., 217, 219
Drug abuse, 18
Dunn, K., 120
Dunn, R., 120

Effort, 259–264
Eggen, P., 89
Ego states, 230
Egocentric, 25
Enactive learning, 64–65, 87, 95
Encouragement, 237–238
Enjoyment, degree of, 199
Environment
    classroom, 49–51
Essay questions, 182
Essentialism, 299
Establish set, 77–79, 91, 93–94, 97
Evaluation, 65–67, 96–98, 102,
    160–162, 189
    in cooperative learning, 99
    mastery learning and, 102
    for purpose of placement, 161
    presentation-recitation-
        discussion, 92
    questions, 72, 75–76
    of student products, 179–180
    of student's progress in learning
        161–162
Existentialism, 299
Expectations, 192, 238–239,
    262–263, 290
Experiences, providing, 217–220
Experiments, science, 15–16
Experimentalism, 299
Expert, 266–267
Expert groups, 96–98
Explicit skill instruction. *See*

Mastery teaching
Expressive objectives, 131, 159
Extension, 260
Extrinsic motivation, 214
Evaluation
    approaches to, 285–287
    of group performance, 270–271

Facts, 67, 77
Family grouped settings, 44–51, 61
Feedback, 237
    on group accomplishments, 80
    providing, 73–74
    techniques, 86–87
Feeling tone, 259
Field trips, 63
Fish bowl, 272
Flavell, J., 14
Flexibility, 225
Focus of delivery, 280–281
Formal operations, 9, 13–15, 17
Formative evaluation, 161
4MAT System, 120
Frost, P., 44, 114, 145, 155

Gage, N., 294
Gagne, E. G., 89
Gagne, R. M., 67–69
    Gagne's Hierarchy, 68–69
General reports, 172, 189
Generalizations, 68
    eliciting, 79–80
Giaconia, R. M., 294
Glasser, W., 228–231
Glasser conference, 246–248
Goal-reward structure, 264, 290–291
Goals
    nonacademic, 157–158
    of school program, 252
Good, T., 237
Gordon, T., 195, 228–231, 246
Graded setting, 26–29, 59, 162–168
Grades, 162–168
    assignment of, 166–167
    deemphasizing, 261
    discussion with parents, 168
    weight of, 165
Grasping reflex, 9
Grooving, 222
Group decision making methods,
    266–267

Group interaction, prerequisite
    skills for, 271
Group Investigation, 97, 99
Group norms, 258
Grouping, 47–48
Groups
    advantages of small, 265
    forming, 266, 268
    leadership structure of, 269
    process skills, 264–275
    projects, 202
    six types of, 272–275
    task, 268
    work, 268
Growth record of, 11–12
Guided practice, 93, 120

*Handbook of Research on Teaching,
    The,* 294
Harmin, M., 214
Harris, T. A., 229–231
Hedges, L. V., 294
Heterogeneous grouping, 27, 61
Hidden curriculum, 212–214
Hierarchy of Knowledge, 67–68
Higher order thinking, 102, 117, 120
Holistic observation approach, 178
Homogeneous grouping, 27, 61
Horizontal grouping, 46–47, 61
Horwitz, R. A., 294
Human relations, 192–197
Hunter, M., 93, 259
Hunter's Mastery Teaching Format,
    135, 136

I message, 195, 214, 236, 244–245,
    238–239
Iconic learning, 64–65, 87, 95
Ideas
    children's, 2–4
    student analysis of own, 111
If...then proposition, 14-15
Ignoring minor disruptions, 241–242
In-basket group exercise, 273–274
Incomplete responses, 73
Incorrect responses, 74
Independence, 18, 117
Independent practice, 94, 120
Individual importance, fostering
    sense of, 201–202
Individual progress, 172

Individualistic learning
    environments, 205–206
Individualized approaches to
    instruction
    traditional vs., 29–33
Individualized settings, 33–44
Inductive teaching, 107–109, 113
Informal settings, 44–51, 171–173
Input techniques, 77
Instruction
    methods of, 280–283
    planning for, 126–157
    teacher provides effective, 236
    tradition vs. individualized, 29–33
Instructional activities, 63–65
Instructional materials, 37
    role in cooperative learning, 99
    mastery learning and, 101
    presentation-recitation-
        discussion, 92
Instructional objectives, 34–35,
    38–40
Instructional settings, 26–61,
    278–279
    framework for interpreting,
        58–59
Instructional tests, 186–187, 189
Integrated day, 48
Integrated teaching. *See* Topic work
Intermediate grades, 189
Internal reward, 275
Interest, 259–264
Interpretation of data, 108–109
Interruptions, 219
Isolation, 244
Intrinsic motivation, 214
Isolation of variables, 15

JIGSAW, 96–97, 99
Johnson, D. & Johnson, R., 204
Jones, F., 229, 241
Joyce, B., 105
Judgmental language, 195, 214
Just-a-job classroom climate, 199,
    200–201

Kamii, C., 16
Kauchak, D., 89
Keeping track, 218–220
Key concepts, 150
Keysort cards, 38–40

Knowledge, 65, 104
    questions, 70
Kounin, J., 219, 228, 229

Laws, desegregation, 31
Leadership structure of group, 269
Learning
    assessing student, 160–190
    environments, 204–206
    support for, 199
    task, making challenging,
        260–261
Learning activity, 281–282
Learning centers, 48–49, 88
Learning
    lower order, 102
    skills, 102
    teacher's assumptions about,
        21–24
Learning style
    teaching to, 119–120
Learning Style Inventory, 120
Lesson
    how to close, 79–80
    how to open, 77–79
    relation to world of students, 78
    whole class, 220
Lesson plans, 131–139
Listening to student response, 73–74
Literacies, 158
Logical consequences, 207, 214,
    292–293
Long-term planning, 150–157
Louisell, R., 44, 114, 145, 216, 221
Love, 201–202
Lower-order learning, 102–104, 120

Magnet schools, 31
Majority vote, 266–267
Management
    classroom, 191–215
    of records, 226–227
    teaching and, 216–217
Mapping, 147–149
Mastery, 128, 161–162, 236–237, 260
    learning, 57, 87–88, 100–102
    teaching, 88, 92–95, 100, 101
McCarthy, B., 120
Matching items, 180–181

Materials
    appropriate for group work, 269
    for lesson, 132
Medium term planning, 150, 157
Memory questions, 69
Mental
    activity, 127
    reflection, 240
Mentor, teacher as, 241
Method I, 197–198, 214
Method II, 197–198, 214
Method III, 197–199, 215, 245–246
Methods of teaching, 62, 87
Microcomputers, 35
Modeling, 80, 87
Misbehavior, 239–240
Mistakes, 287–288
Modules, 144–145, 159
Moral development, 235
Motivation, 259–264
    approaches to, 289–291
"Motor thought," 1
Multi-aged grouping, 34, 61
Multiple-choice questions, 182–183
Multiple solutions, 102

Natural consequences, 207, 215,
    292–293
Negative classroom climate, 199,
    201
Nonacademic aims, 157–158
Nonalgorithmic thinking, 102
Nonconservers, 6, 25
Nongraded settings, 33–44, 59,
    168–171
Nonlinear approach, 131
Nonverbal messages, 242–243
Norm group, 185, 189
Norm-referenced evaluations,
    163–166, 177, 186
Nuanced judgment, 102

Object permanence, 10
Objective, 129, 159, 126–131
Objective tests, 180, 189
Objectives-based approach to
    instruction, 34–37
Objectives-referenced evaluation,
    169, 189
Observation of student

performance, 112, 178
Off-task behavior, 195, 215
Operations, 12–13, 25
Oral skills, evaluation of, 178–180
Organization
    of information, 112
    of subject matter, 279–280
    of a team, 37–42
Organizers, advance, 79
Outcomes-based education, 57–58,
    61

Pace of instruction, 35
Paper-pencil tests, 177, 180
Paraprofessionals, 227
Parent conferences, 169, 173
Parent to adult interaction, 246, 258
Parent to child interaction, 258
Parent volunteers, 51
Parents
    discussing goals with, 168
    self-concept and, 209
    student behavior and, 249–250
Part-whole relations, 12, 25
Peer expectations, 210–211
Peer tutoring, 84–85
Penalties, 207, 215, 292–293
Perceiving, 158
Perennialism, 299
Performance, 130, 259–264
Personal values, 213, 215
Personalizing climate, 78
Peterson, P. L., 294
Physical environment, 224–226,
    239–240
Physical closeness to prevent
    misbehavior, 240–241
Piaget, J., 1–17, 158
    stages, 15–16
Planning
    approaches to, 283–285
    for instruction, 126–157
    for teaching, 121–159
Portfolios, 169, 172, 189
Positive classroom climate, 199
Positive reinforcement, 87, 258
Praise, 237, 262
Preoperational period, 9, 10, 13–14,
    17
Presentation of subject matter,

88–92, 96–97, 279–280
Pretest, 38
Prevention steps, 232–241, 253, 254–255
Previewing next lesson, 80
Primary grades, 189
Principal, 250–251
Principles, 68
Proactive behavior management, 251, 291, 299
Problem-solving context, 87
Problem-solving role plays, 82–83
Procedural knowledge, 89, 92, 120
Procedural question, 258
Process skills, 117
Productive thinking, 75, 87, 282
Professionals, relations among, 204
Profile, 172, 189
Progress, reporting students, 162–173
Project work. *See* Topic work
Promising attention, 220
Pruned web, 153
Purposes, educational, 126
Psychomotor skills, 178–180

Questions, 69-75
    as means of redirecting behavior, 243
    procedural, 258

Raths, L. E., 103, 214
Rational-linear approach, 131
Reaching scheme, 9
Reactive behavior management, 251, 291, 299
Real life operational situation, 63
Reality therapy, 230
Reciprocal tutoring, 84
Recitation, 75, 91, 104
Recognition of desirable behaviors, 96–98, 241–242
Records, management of, 226–227
Redirection steps, 232–235, 241–246, 253, 255–256
Reflexes, 9
Reinforcement, 229
Relating lesson to world of students, 78
Relations, formation of, 11
Reliability, 186, 189

Removal of student from classroom, 261
Report cards, 162–173
Reporting student progress, 162–173
Representation of absent objects and events, 10
Reproductive thinking, 75, 87, 282
Request for change of behavior, 244
Respect, 117
Results, knowledge of, 263
Research papers, 183
Reverse thinking, 10, 25
Reviews, summary, 79
Rewards, 192, 204–208, 237–238, 261–262, 289–290
Rohrkemper, M., 228
Role playing techniques, 81–83
Routines, importance of, 222–224
Rules, 223–224
Ryan, E. L., 206

Safety, 18
Savard, W., 229
Schemes, 25
Schools
    society's expectations of, 17–19
    what children learn in, 19–21
    without failure, 230
Scope, 121–126, 159
Scope and sequence, 121–126
Segregation, 18
Selection of subject matter, 279–280
Self-appraisal, 240
Self-checking, 139, 159
Self-concept, teacher expectations and, 208–211
Self-contained settings, 26–29, 44–51, 61
Self-instructional lessons, 140–141, 159
Self-regulation, 102
Sensorimotor period, 9–17
Sequence, 121–126, 159
Sharan, S., 97
Shared brainstorm web, 153
Short-answer items, 181
Simon, S. B., 214
Simulation, 87
Skill, demonstration of, 80–81
Skill instruction. *See* Mastery

teaching
Skills, 77
    essential, 121–126
    grouping, 31, 61
    teaching of, 92–93
Skills Record, 156
Skinner, B.F., 228, 229, 231
Slavin, R., 96, 270
Social ills, correction of, 18
Social interactions, role plays, 82–83
Social learning, 80, 87
Socialization, 18, 82–83, 221–222
Society, expectations of schools, 17–19
Socioemotional climate, 191–215, 242
Socioemotional dimension, 215
Software, 35
Space, in informal classrooms, 48–49
Specialists, 27
Special education personnel, 27
Spiral curriculum, 125
STAD. *See* Student Teams Achievement Division
Stage-by-stage progression, 153–155
Stallings, J., 204
Standardized achievement tests, 173, 183–190
Standardized diagnostic tests, 173, 190
Standards of behavior, 232–234
Stipek, D., 204, 206, 210, 263
Stream of activity, 217–220
Student
    role in cooperative learning, 99
    involvement, 259–275
    learning, 160–190
    progress, 162–173
    role in mastery learning, 101
    role in mastery teaching, 95
    role of, 253
    role of in presentation-recitation-discussion, 91
    interaction with teacher for teaching thinking, 109–112
Student-initiated questions, 74–75
Student Teams Achievement Division, 96, 97, 99
Subject matter, 279–280
Subject Prediction Chart, 154

Subjective tests, 180, 190
Success, student experience of, 236–237, 263
Summary reviews, 79
Summative evaluation, 161, 162
Supervision of student work, 86–87
Surveys, 186
Swyers, B., 140–141, 158
Swyers, W. R., 140, 146
Symbolic learning, 65, 87, 95
Synthesis, 65, 67, 102
    questions, 71–72, 75–76

Taba, H., 107
Task Groups, 274
Taxonomy of Educational Objectives, 65
Teacher aides, 51
Teacher
    actions, 234–235
    affect, 287, 199–200
    assumptions about teaching and learning, 21–24
    role in cooperative learning, 98–99
    expectations, 208–211, 290
    as facilitator, 48, 114
    in small group work, 265–266
    mastery learning and, 101
    mastery teaching and, 95
    responses, 232–235
    role of, 18–19, 252
    role of in presentation-recitation-discussion, 91
    time management, 220–224
Teacher Effectiveness Training (T.E.T.), 231–231, 238, 246
Teacher-made tests, 175–183, 190
"Teacher-proof" programs, 125
Teacher-student interaction for teaching thinking, 109–112
Teaching
    departmentalized, 56
    inductive, 107–109
    to learning styles, 119–120
    management and, 216–217
    methods, 88–120

    planning for, 121–159
    style, 276–299
    teacher's assumptions about, 21–24
    techniques, 62–87
    thinking, 102–114
Teaching-learning environment, 216–227
Team
    organization of, 37–42, 52–53
    performance, 270
    support, 232, 249–253, 257, 293
    work skills, 203–204
Team-taught settings, 33–44
Team teaching, 27–28, 61
    organization of one member's classroom, 42–44
Team tutoring, 96–98
Techniques, 87
Terrazas, K., 147–149
Testing, 173–189, 261
Tests, 92
TET. *See* Teacher Effectiveness Training
Text, adopted, 125
Thematic units. *See* Topic work
Theme, 44–46, 61
Thinking
    extension of, 111–112
    higher order, 102
    processes used during, 103
    reproductive, 75
    skills, 102
    teaching activities, 102–114
    types of, 282–283
Thought
    development of stages of, 9–16
    different from actions, 1–4
    egocentric, 4–9, 10
Time
    in informal classrooms, 47
    management, 220–221
    on task, 259
Time out, 244, 249, 258
Topic work, 44–46, 61, 88, 103, 112, 114–118, 159, 279
    units of, 145–157

Traditional vs. individualized approaches to instruction, 29–33
Traditional settings, 26–29
Training model. *See* Mastery teaching
Transactional analysis, 230
Transformation, 10
Trust Elementary School, 33–35, 37
Truthfulness, 21
Tutoring, 83–85
    team, 96–97
20-Step System of Discipline, 231–258
Tyler, Ralph, 126
Types of Instruction chart, 63, 65, 68–69, 77, 81, 91, 92, 95, 281

Uncertainty, 102
Understanding, techniques to check for, 75
Unit
    of learning, 161
    work, 44–46
Units, 144–157

Validity, 186, 190
Values, 192, 212–214, 222
Values clarification, 214
Vertical grouping, 46–47, 61
Visibility, 224

Wait-time, 73, 111
Walbert, H., 294
Wang, M., 264
Warming-up climate, 78
Weber, W., 229
Webs shared brainstorm, 153
Weekly planning, 157
Weil, M., 105
Whole class discussions, 48–49
Win-win manner, 215, 271
Wisconsin Design for Reading Skill Development, 36
Work, reviewing past, 79
Worksheets, 125
Worth, sense of, 208–209
Writing instructional objectives, 126–131